Interpreters of Science

A history of the Association for Science Education

David Layton

D1388630

John Murray
The Association for Science Education

© David Layton 1984

First published 1984
by John Murray (Publishers) Ltd
and the Association for Science Education

Typeset by Inforum Ltd, Portsmouth
Printed and bound in Great Britain at
The Pitman Press, Bath

British Library Cataloguing in Publication Data

Layton, David
   Interpreters of science.
   1. Association for Science Education
   —History
   I. Title
   507'.1041   Q181.A1
   ISBNs 0–7195–4180–8 (JM limp)
          0–7195–4185–9 (JM cased)
          0–86357–014–3 (ASE limp)
          0–86357–015–1 (ASE cased)

BUCKINGHAM PALACE.

All good ideas seem obvious in retrospect but when the four Science Masters at Eton College called a meeting of their colleagues in other schools they could hardly have known how successful their initiative would prove to be. In 1900 the teaching of science was still in its infancy and it was by no means universally welcomed. No one was to know how rapidly the subject was to grow or how important it was to become. Public attitudes towards science teaching may have been one of the worries of science teachers at the turn of the century but these gradually changed as did the problems of science teaching in schools at a time when effects of the scientific revolution made their way into education.

This book traces the remarkable story of a body that from small beginnings and after several name changes has today reached a membership of 17,000 and is one of the oldest bodies of its kind in the world. Through its links with all the major scientific and technological societies and industrial organisations in this country and as a founder member of the International Council of Associations for Science Education, it is able to keep its members in touch with a very wide spectrum of opinion and development and exerts a considerable influence.

The history of such an organisation is interesting in itself but Professor Layton has made it much more than a simple account of events. He recognizes that it is individual personalities and their hopes and ambitions which have contributed so much to the development of the Association. In the final chapter of the book, he quotes from a long serving and distinguished member, Miss Frances Eastwood, who describes the Association as "a group of PEOPLE with common interests, common problems and common aims, pursued in a spirit of friendship sufficiently strong to welcome and survive sharp differences of opinion." With that spirit and with the confidence derived from past achievements the Association can look forward to many years of valuable work.

1984

Foreword

When the History Sub-committee of the Association for Science Education held its first meeting in July 1977, we realised that one of our major tasks would be to find a suitable author for this book. After a good deal of discussion, and canvassing outside opinions, we decided, in April 1978, to recommend to the Council of the Association that Professor David Layton, then Director of the Centre for Studies in Science Education, University of Leeds, be asked to undertake this work, and were delighted when he accepted what was obviously going to be a demanding task. He has fulfilled all our hopes and produced what we consider to be a major contribution to the history of education in this country over the first three-quarters of the twentieth century. On behalf of the Sub-committee I tender to David our sincere thanks for the industry and expertise that he has given to this venture.

I must express also personal thanks to my fellow sub-committee members: Andrew Bishop, Frances Eastwood, Elizabeth McCreath, Kit Swinfen, and the late Bill Tapper, for their unfailing support in what has been a long but rewarding task; and also to Cathy Wilson and Brian Atwood for providing the essential back-up services from ASE Headquarters; and to Kenneth Pinnock, of John Murray (Publishers) Ltd, for giving us the benefit of his long experience of book production and inviting us to hold our meetings at 50 Albemarle Street, London.

Ernest Coulson
Chairman, History Sub-committee

Contents

Illustrations

Abbreviations

AAM	Association of Assistant Mistresses
APSSM	Association of Public School Science Masters
ASE	Association for Science Education
AST	Association of Science Teachers
AWST	Association of Women Science Teachers
COSTA	Council of Subject Teaching Associations
DES	Department of Education and Science
FRS	Fellow of the Royal Society
GPDST	Girls' Public Day School Trust
HMC	Headmasters' Conference
IAAM	Incorporated Association of Assistant Masters
IAHM	Incorporated Association of Head Masters
NUT	National Union of Teachers
SMA	Science Masters' Association
SSR	*The School Science Review*
YNSA	Yorkshire Natural Science Association

Preface

The American historian David B. Tyack once wrote an article which he called 'Ways of Seeing'. In it he presented five different interpretations of the same historical events. He went on to argue that awareness of alternative accounts could assist historians to gain a more complex and accurate perception of the past though he cautioned that clarity of vision required more than simple addition of multiple interpretations. A not unrelated point was made by Lord Briggs in 1972 when, as Professor Asa Briggs, he inaugurated a new journal, *History of Education*, with a paper outlining six approaches for the writing of educational history.

These general considerations apply with particular force to the writing of an institutional biography and undoubtedly several different histories of the Association for Science Education could be constructed. 'Officer' perspectives on events would not always be congruent with those of 'ordinary members', whilst an observer external to the Association and to science teaching might provide an account different again. However, as Tyack points out, each of us as historian is 'likely to adopt a framework of interpretation that matches one's own perception of reality and purpose in writing'.

My own position is that of a member of the ASE and of the SMA before it – I joined in 1949 and have remained in membership since – but one who has never served on the committees of the Association or been elected to office, apart from the Presidency of the Yorkshire Region which I was privileged to hold in 1974–75. At the same time I confess to a longstanding curiosity about the inner workings of the Association (manifestly the most influential of the subject teaching associations), and about the reasons for its durability, impressive growth and increasing influence on the definition of science education policy and practice. When in 1978 I was invited to write a history of the ASE I had no hesitation in accepting, particularly as it was clear that the History Sub-Committee, established by Council to advise on the project, had no inclination towards heroic biography, but wished instead to see a carefully researched analysis of the Association's activities from the time of its origin as the Association of Public School Science Masters at the beginning of this century.

This matched my own perceptions of what a history of the ASE should be. A chronological record of the achievements of the past, on its own, held little appeal. But a critical, interpretative account of the Association as an evolving, voluntary organization, adapting to contextual changes, might be of value in relation to deliberations about the future role and policies of the ASE.

The structure of the book requires a word of explanation. It provides, in effect, three histories of the Association constructed around the triple themes of constitution (Part One), communication (Part Two) and control (Part Three). The first, and longest, deals with the constitutional history of the four Associations from which the ASE grew and of the ASE itself during its first twenty years. The focus here is on the principles according to which the associations were composed and governed. The early years and especially the activities of the APSSM and AST have been examined in particular detail because they provide an essential foundation for the understanding of subsequent developments. In passing, it is of interest to note that the scientists were unique among subject specialists in organizing their subject teaching associations on the basis of sex. In so doing, they created some particular problems for any future historian in connection with the writing of 'women's history'. On a number of occasions I have been conscious that, because source material is relatively less plentiful and because of the general 'invisibility' of women in history, I may not always have done full justice to their story. Biographical details of women science teachers, for example, are much more difficult to acquire than those of their male colleagues.

The second history, which I have called a social history, arises directly from the first. Its subject, the problems and modes of communication, became increasingly important for the effective running of the Associations as they grew in size and influence. It deals with the forms of intercourse – meetings and writings in particular – at local, national and international level, by means of which conceptions of good science teaching were engendered and propagated. Through these social activities members acquired a sense of identity and of belonging to a community with shared standards and concerns. The Associations' achievements in this field of 'increased professionalism' were accomplished without any of the normal apparatus of professional institutes such as qualifying examinations, experience requirements, reward systems and powers of expulsion. Each Association began and remained a voluntary body.

The notion of professionalism leads into the third history, in that a profession can be interpreted as a means of controlling an occupation, in this case of defining what counts as 'teaching science'. Part Three then, is concerned with the political history of the Associations. It attempts to throw light on their activities in the curriculum field, their advocacy of particular versions of school science and of the ways in which they have attempted to ensure adoption of their point of view.

The three histories are not mutually exclusive but grow out of, and complement, each other. Problems of communication, especially between the central committees and the ordinary members of the Association, are intimately related to constitutional issues. Similarly, political considerations arise from the growth of power and influence. Hopefully, together, the accounts progressively enrich, although they do not pretend to exhaust, an understanding of what the Association has been, is, and might become.

One question to which there is no easy answer in writing a history of an existing and flourishing institution is where to close the account. No obvious date or event on which to end suggested itself. Too early a terminus would have meant the exclusion of reference to much recent activity which, in the case of the ASE, is clearly both on an unprecedented scale and of unquestionable importance. At the same time, contemporary history, if not a contradiction in terms, is notoriously difficult to write. The very nearness of events makes problematical any judgement of their significance. The solution adopted has been to use many endings, each theme under consideration being carried through to a point at which it seemed logical to leave it. Instead of a clean cut across the broad cloth with sharp scissors, the individual strands have been broken at what seemed their natural fracture point.

In a work of this sort, which is built largely upon unpublished material, Association minute books and records, as well as oral evidence, the number of people to whom I owe a special debt is unusually great. The members of the ASE History Sub-Committee under the Chairmanship of Professor Ernest Coulson have provided me with help of many sorts, not least with the location of sources and with matters of interpretation, although at the end of the day they have left me free to write according to my own judgement. It is also a pleasure to express my thanks to John L. Lewis for invaluable comment on several aspects of the history and for suggesting the project in the first instance. In 1978 I was awarded a grant from the Social Science Research Council to assist the progress of the work. Two successive research assistants, Miss S.L. Martin and Miss C. Manthorpe, appointed with these funds gave valuable assistance. A list of acknowledgements to those many ASE officers and members who kindly provided record material and gave time to talk about their Associations is printed separately. I should like to mention, however, two men, Sir Graham Savage and Emeritus Professor Joseph Lauwerys, sadly both now dead, who in different ways exerted a significant influence on the development of the Associations and of science education generally in England and Wales. I learnt much from them especially about the events of the inter-war and immediate post-war years. Finally I thank the University of Leeds for a period of study leave in which much of the preliminary research for this book was undertaken.

David Layton
February 1984

'Science teaching in schools . . . has one aim in general – namely, the interpretation of nature to youth'.

Archer Vassall, the first schoolteacher
President of the Science Masters'
Association, in his Address to members,
1921.

The ASE – 'the most important repository of knowledge and experience of teaching science to the pupils in our schools'.

B.G. Atwood, General Secretary,
The Association for Science Education,
1971.

The ASE – 'an example to us all of teachers taking responsibility for their own professional development'.

John Barnes, Chief Education Officer,
Salford, 1983.

1 The Association of Public School Science Masters

The context of public school science teaching at the turn of the century

At the opening of the twentieth century elementary and secondary schools in England and Wales were, in R.H. Tawney's phrase, 'two separate worlds'.[1] Unlinked and functionally different, they provided alternative kinds of education for different social classes.

Within the category of secondary school there was further differentiation, again reflecting social class differences. If by 1900 the simple tripartite grading of such schools employed by the Taunton Commissioners was no longer applicable, sharp distinctions nevertheless existed and the pre-eminence of the great public schools was not seriously challenged. Analyses of the schools attended by distinguished men from many walks of life confirmed the value of an education at a small minority of public schools.[2] Whilst there was disagreement, not least among the schools themselves, as to what was a public school, some guide to status was provided by membership of the Headmasters' Conference, established in 1869, fifty schools being listed by 1871 and double this number by 1900. Even here, however, prestige and influence were hierarchical, membership of the committee of the Conference being dominated for many years by a small group of about ten schools.[3]

The curriculum of the great public schools and, more especially, their teaching of science had been a subject of interest to reforming educationalists and scientists from at least the time of the Public Schools Commission in the early 1860s.[4] Following the Public Schools Act 1868, the special commissioners appointed under the Act were able to give some stimulus to the building of science laboratories and the recruitment of suitably qualified science staff. Governing bodies for schools were reconstituted, and in certain cases distinguished scientists nominated by the Royal Society from amongst its Fellows were appointed to serve. John Tyndall became a governor of Harrow in 1871 and T.H. Huxley a governor of Eton in 1879.[5]

Despite these steps, progress was slow and the Devonshire Commissioners concluded in 1875 from their extensive survey of public and endowed schools that 'Science is as yet very far from receiving the attention to which, in our opinion, it is entitled.'

Although individual schools such as Clifton College subsequently acquired high reputations for the quality of their science teaching, overall, in the judgement of two recent historians of science education, 'no really fundamental progress in the position of science teaching in public schools took place throughout the remainder of the nineteenth century.'[6]

Two basic problems had confronted science teachers in the public school context. First, the schools had to offer an education for which parents were willing to pay, and the attitude of the majority of such fee payers towards the inclusion of science in their sons' curriculum was one of indifference or even hostility. Science was not seen as having any value for their sons' careers. Furthermore, possibly influenced by the association of science education with classes for artisans, there was a tendency to look down on this field of study as 'not quite respectable'. Secondly, and more fundamentally, science appeared to be capable of only a very limited contribution to the traditional goals of a public school education: the development of character and the inculcation of moral virtues. The study of science did not make 'a man more human, but simply more intelligent'.

By the turn of the century, however, new forces were reshaping the social context of public school education. In the 1890s, the Arnoldians, as E.C. Mack has termed them,[7] were striving to make public schools the 'fortresses of high culture', the tyranny of compulsory games and the grind of cramming for success in competitive examinations having, in their view, destroyed true learning. Their re-assertion of the educational primacy of the classics had as a corollary an attack on the multiplicity of modern subjects in the public school curriculum. It was certainly not a fortuitous happening that the proponents of certain 'modern subjects' (Modern Languages 1892, Geography 1893) associated in defence of their subject in the early 1890s,[8] as the classicists were themselves obliged to do a decade later. Though reactionary with respect to the content of the curriculum, the Arnoldians were nevertheless progressive in regard to pedagogy and the need for teachers to be aware of the conditions under which their pupils would most effectively learn.

This emphasis on intellectual outcomes, implicit in the Arnoldian advocacy of improved teaching methods, was central to the arguments of other critics of the public schools as the twentieth century opened. The humiliating events of the Boer War had shown that stout hearts and earnest sentiments were no substitute for intellectual efficiency in the maintenance of an Empire threatened from within by disaffection with British rule, and from without by the growth of industrial and military power in Europe and elsewhere. Reporting in March 1902, the Akers-Douglas Committee on the education of Army officers noted widespread dissatisfaction with the general educational attainments of officers. A few notable exceptions apart, the public schools were failing to educate boys sufficiently well to enable them to pass directly from school to Sandhurst and Woolwich.[9]

In 1897, of the 364 Gentlemen Cadets entering Sandhurst, only 148 came directly from schools, the remaining 216 requiring varying periods from a few months to several years under the tutelage of a 'crammer' before passing the entrance examination.[10]

Later in the same year, Sir Oliver Lodge FRS, reviewing *The Schoolmaster*, a new book by A.C. Benson, a house master at Eton, delivered a vigorous attack on the public schools for sending out year after year 'many boys who hate knowledge . . . who are . . . arrogantly and contemptuously ignorant – not only satisfied to be so, but thinking it ridiculous and almost unmanly that a young man should be anything else.'[11]

At the same time, major changes were taking place in the administrative framework of secondary education. The Board of Education Act 1899, had established a unified central authority for secondary education, to replace the previously uncoordinated activities of the Charity Commission, the Science and Art Department, and the Education Department. Understandably, the association of the leading public schools with the emerging state system of secondary education was seen as very desirable, not least to set high standards for government inspection. In the early months of 1899 Michael Sadler, Director of Special Inquiries and Reports within the Education Department, personally visited the headmasters of many public and endowed secondary schools in order to allay any fears they might have about bureaucratic control if inspection was indeed to be agreed.[12] In the event, inspection was not made obligatory, but was available, on payment of a fee, to those public schools who desired it.

However, the issue which provoked most reaction from public schools was the future internal organization of the new central authority, and, in particular, the creation of separate administrative branches for secondary and technical education, as opposed to a single branch for both.[13] An administrative association with the attitudes and practices of the former Science and Art Department was thought likely to 'degrade and weaken the position of the great public schools'.[14] The Department's policy of 'payment on results' and its support of subjects, especially scientific ones, without regard for the overall balance of the curriculum was seen as indicative of a lack of concern for the quality of education and indeed for any broad educational aims. In July 1899 the Headmasters' Conference resolved in favour of 'separate, equal and independent' technical and secondary divisions within the new administrative arrangements, a view which carried the day when the Bill was enacted in August 1899.[15]

The Eton letter of 14 May 1900

It was against this background of state intervention in the field of secondary education and widespread concern over the proper functions of a public school education that the Association of Public School Science Masters came into being. On 14 May 1900, the following circular letter, over the signature of four science masters from Eton College, was sent to the science staff of 57 schools, a hundred letters in all being despatched.[16]

Dear Sir,

At the Conference of Science Teachers held last January in connection with the Education Exhibition at the Imperial Institute, many points of interest were discussed, and the general feeling was that the meetings were eminently successful.

We think, however, that those who have to teach Science in Public Schools in many cases work under difficulties which do not confront teachers in Primary Schools, and which hence did not receive an adequate share of attention at the meeting referred to. We believe, therefore, that a Conference of Science Masters in Public Schools might lead to the attainment of at least some clearer method in the teaching of Natural Science than exists at present, and at the same time, by taking united action, do something towards emphasising the value of Science as a means of education.

We feel that the present time would be peculiarly appropriate for what we are suggesting, since in the near future educational changes will be brought prominently to the notice of the public generally. As a preliminary step, therefore, we would ask you to be kind enough to inform us on the enclosed slip of paper:
 a) Whether you are in favour of a Conference being held.
 b) Whether, this being the case, you would be prepared to act on a Committee to draw up suggestions as to its organization.

We remain, dear Sir,

Yours faithfully,
T.C. Porter
W.D. Eggar
M.D. Hill
H. de Havilland

N.B. All communications to be addressed to M.D. Hill, Eton College, Windsor.

The reference in the first paragraph of this letter to a previous Conference of Science Teachers was to the second of a series of annual meetings held under the auspices of the Technical Education Board of the London County Council, and organized by Dr C.W. Kimmins, the LCC's science teaching specialist. Some of those most active in the future work of the Association of Public School Science Masters had been amongst the two hundred and more teachers attending on 10 and 11 January 1900, and possibly amongst the smaller gathering at the Chelsea Polytechnic the previous year.[17] The success of that inaugural conference in January 1899 had led the editor of *The School World*, a newly established monthly periodical with a special interest in secondary education, to suggest that a

National Association of Science Teachers, meeting periodically at different centres and publishing detailed reports of its proceedings, would obtain a large and active membership.[18]

At the second LCC conference in January 1900, one of the four sessions was presided over by Sir Henry Roscoe FRS, Vice-Chancellor of the University of London and representative of the Royal Society on the governing body of Eton College. Roscoe took a considerable interest in the general welfare of Eton and in the science teaching in particular. In an appreciation of his work, following his death in 1915, it was recorded that he 'took an active part in the formation of the Association'[19] and it seems likely that he encouraged the Eton science masters, if indeed he did not initiate their activity, in the convening of a conference of public school science masters. Shortly after the despatch of the initial letter of May 1900, Hill had written to Roscoe with a request that he should preside over any conference of science masters that might result.[20] It was Roscoe who provided rooms in the University of London for the first meeting when it was eventually held in January 1901 and who, from the chair, urged on those present the advisability of forming a permanent society.[21]

Before looking in more detail at the results of the Etonian initiative of May 1900, some brief account of the personalities involved may be of interest. In 1900, the Rev. Thomas Cunningham Porter[22] (1860–1933) was Senior Science Master at Eton and at forty, was oldest of the four signatories. A former pupil of Bristol Grammar School, he had gained a scholarship in Natural Science at Exeter College, Oxford in 1878, subsequently taking honours in mathematical moderations and finals, and also in chemistry, but achieving only an indifferent degree. After a short period on the staff of Carlisle Grammar School he took up an appointment in 1885 as a teacher of science and mathematics at Eton, where he remained for the next forty-eight years, becoming Senior Science Master in 1894.

An enthusiastic, if idiosyncratic teacher, he was seen by some as 'an amiable buffoon', 'generally considered as a paid charlatan who was employed to entertain the boys by his absurdities', and by others as a brilliant stimulator of the intellects of specialist pupils. One of those captured by his magic was the young H.J.G. Moseley. Porter is reputed to have preached once in Lower Chapel, but was so amusing that he was never allowed to preach again. Some say that the subject of his sermon was the gases let loose at the Creation; others, the possible utility of asbestos in the fires of Hell. Artist, musician, long-distance cyclist, discoverer of Porter's law,[23] contributor of papers to *Nature* and the *Proceedings of the Royal Society*, he was imbued with the spirit of experimental inquiry and influenced deeply those boys who had a disposition towards science. At the same time he lacked patience with the mundane affairs of the daily round; the administrative problems of a new organization such as the Association of Public School Science Masters held no attraction for him. Of the four Eton science masters, he was the only one never to serve on the committees of the new association.

Next in seniority was William Douglas Eggar[24] (1865–1945), physics master at Eton. A former pupil of Brighton College and scholar of Trinity College, Cambridge, he had taken second class honours in the Natural Science Tripos and graduated as thirteenth Wrangler. Following two years on the staff of his old school, Eggar taught from 1890 to 1894 at Wellington College, moving in 1895 to Eton. Previously he had been an unsuccessful candidate for the post of science inspector with the London County Council. Perhaps his failure here was a blessing in disguise, at least for the LCC if not for Eggar, because there is evidence that he was not the most effective of teachers. Julian Huxley recalled from his schooldays at Eton, that Eggar's experiments 'always seemed to go wrong', and the young Harry Moseley likewise reacted adversely to Eggar. 'I have no respect for the man', the eighteen year-old Moseley complained to his mother, 'because he either cannot or will not explain anything and refers you to books.'[25] In his lighter moments, Eggar wrote topical verse for the *Pall Mall Gazette*; more seriously, he produced school text books and examined for various Boards and the University of London. Until his retirement from Eton in 1920 he was an active committee member of the Association of Public School Science Masters, serving as joint-secretary of the Association in 1919.

Hugh de Beauvoir de Havilland[26] (1867–1952), Eggar's junior by two years, and his contemporary at Cambridge, achieved a first class in Part I of the Natural Science Tripos and a third class in Part II in 1890. After experience as a science master at Bath College and the Leys School, Cambridge, he was appointed to Eton College in 1897. A quietly loyal servant of the Association, and its secretary for two years, de Havilland was a man of wide cultural interests which took him well beyond the boundaries of science. Of the APSSM, he himself stated later, 'The original idea and all the early work was M.D. Hill's and my share was very little.'[27]

Matthew Davenport Hill[28] (1872–1958), the youngest of the signatories, newly appointed to Eton in 1896 and not yet twenty-eight years of age when the original letter was sent out, was nevertheless the mainspring of events that led to the foundation of the Association. He was a member of a distinguished and pioneering educational family. His grandfather, after whom he was named, had written a notable work on *Public Education* in the 1820s. His great-grandfather, Thomas Wright Hill, a friend of Joseph Priestley, had started Hill Top School in Birmingham, from which developed the progressive Hazelwood School in Edgbaston founded by three of Thomas's sons. One of these, Arthur, extended the experiment to Bruce Castle School, Tottenham, and in both institutions a major curriculum innovation was the science teaching. Until the mid-1830s this education experiment was actively assisted by another brother, the future Sir Rowland Hill, originator of the Penny Post.

M.D. Hill, then, had teaching, and science teaching in particular, as a strong component in his background. Educated at Eton himself, he was elected to a Natural Science Scholarship at New College Oxford in 1890, abandoning a proposed career in medicine to take a first class in Animal Morphology in 1894, and coming strongly under the influence of the newly appointed Linacre Professor of Comparative Anatomy, Sir E. Ray Lankester. Subsequently, he considered a career as a university teacher and researcher, being appointed to a post of demonstrator at Owens College, Manchester, in October 1895. Before three months had passed, he received the offer of the post of biology master at Eton and, having doubts about his future as an original researcher, accepted, taking up his duties in January 1896.

Temperamentally, the young Hill and the middle-aged Porter were poles apart; as Hill later recorded, in a not ungenerous assessment of Porter's educational work, 'controversies not unaccompanied by friction have divided us'.[29] But, like Porter, Hill was capable of inspiring boys with a love of science. For Julian Huxley he was 'a genius of a teacher'. Meticulous, methodical and taxonomically orientated, he was the ideal man to interest boys in out-of-door work in natural history; as biology master and also ex-officio Keeper of the Museum, he acquired the help of Wilfred Mark Webb,[30] Secretary of the Selborne Society, in encouraging the boys to work as taxidermists and to undertake projects for prizes such as those offered annually by the British Ornithological Union. Together with Webb, he wrote an introductory text, *The Eton Nature Study*, in which the emphasis was on the making, and detailed recording, of accurate observations. Hill's passion for detail and systematisation played no small part in the successful conversion of the May 1900 proposals into an effective and enduring subject teaching association.

The first conference of January 1901

From the response to the May 1900 letter it was clear that there existed a strong feeling in support of a conference. Accordingly, a meeting of those prepared to serve on the planning committee was held on 17 November in the Great Central Hotel, Marylebone – the first of many Saturday afternoon meetings held by members of the Association. Fifteen men representing ten schools were present.[31] Oswald Latter, the senior science master at Charterhouse was voted to the chair, a date for the conference was fixed and a programme of papers agreed, twenty-nine offers being condensed to five substantive contributions of ten minutes each.[32]

Before the end of November, details of the arrangements had been sent to all schools in *The Public Schools Year Book*. The programme, in two sessions, punctuated by an interval for refreshments consisted of:

(a) The order in which scientific subjects should be taught and the

advisability of beginning practical work early.
(Mr C.E. Ashford, Harrow School)

(b) The desirability of establishing closer relations between the teaching of science and mathematics, and of the inclusion of science in the schedule of the entrance examinations for the Universities.
(Mr W.D. Eggar, Eton College)

(c) Natural history societies and field work in biology and geology.
(Mr A. Vassall, Harrow School)

(d) The limit and scope of the science required for Government and Army examinations.
(Mr C.G. Falkner, Weymouth College)

(e) The teaching of science to forms generally, and also to special divisions.
(Mr O.H. Latter, Charterhouse)

The issue of each paper was to be put to the Conference in the form of a resolution on which votes were invited.

As a final item, it was announced that a proposal would be laid before the meeting by Mr M.D. Hill with regard to the organization of a Society for Science Masters in Public Schools. Hill was also to act as secretary and treasurer for the conference, over which Sir Henry Roscoe FRS would preside.

The names of the twenty-four schools represented, with the number of staff from each, are given in Table 1.1.

Table 1.1   *Numbers of science masters from public school represented at the Conference in January 1901*

Bedford Grammar School	1	Merchant Taylors' School	3
Bromsgrove School	1	Radley College	1
Charterhouse	3	Rugby School	3
Cheltenham College	2	St Olave's School	2
Chigwell School	1	Sherborne School	1
Christ's Hospital	2	Stonyhurst College	1
Clifton College	2	Sutton Valence School	1
Crosby School, Liverpool	1	Wellington College	3
Eton College	4	Westminster School	1
Gresham's School, Holt	1	Weymouth College	1
Harrow School	3	Winchester College	1
Liverpool College	1	Woodbridge School	1

Not all those who came in 1901 returned the following year but, for the most part, those who attended the 1901 meeting were to become the core of the permanent association when this was constituted a year later.

What sort of men were these who voluntarily devoted a Saturday afternoon and evening, in the January pre-term period, often after a substantial journey, to a meeting about science teaching? Thirty-two out of the forty-one masters were Oxbridge graduates, those who had taken the Natural Sciences Tripos predominating. Of the 'others' one was W.A. Shenstone, Senior Science Master at Clifton College and Fellow of the Royal Society.

Table 1.2   *Universities from which science masters attending the 1901 Conference had graduated*

Cambridge graduates	22	London graduates	4
Oxford graduates	12	Others	3

More than a third (fifteen out of the forty-one) had followed a substantial university course in mathematics, either instead of or before taking a science degree. Of these, five had graduated by the examination for the Mathematical Tripos only.[33] It would seem that the views of the Headmaster of Cheltenham College, expressed to the Devonshire Commissioners in 1872, were still widely held. In reply to a question about the problem of obtaining competent science masters, Jex-Blake had stated, 'I believe that a scientific and thorough knowledge of mathematics is the best basis if not the *sine qua non* of a scientific and thorough teaching of physics and the natural sciences.'[34] There was also a point about the flexible deployment of staff. When the amount of science teaching was not great, a mathematically qualified science master could be used to teach mathematics also.

An important consequence of this strong mathematical background of many science teachers was their involvement in the activities of the Mathematical Association. Indeed W.H. Brock, in an interesting study of the work of the Association for the Improvement of Geometrical Teaching, the body from which the Mathematical Association developed, suggests that the Association of Public School Science Masters was modelled on the Mathematical Association.[35] In the sense that the Mathematical Association was open to women teachers as well as to men, and that it placed no restriction on the type of school in which its members worked, the extent of the modelling is open to question. But there is little doubt that, by virtue of common membership and from professional contacts in their schools between teachers of mathematics and science, the Association of

Public School Masters benefited considerably from the experience of the Mathematical Association.[36]

A second characteristic of the masters who attended on 19 January 1901 is revealed by analysis of the science subject which they taught. Whilst it is not always possible to draw a firm inference here, nevertheless by using knowledge of the degree subject, biographical information where obtainable, authorship of textbooks, membership of professional scientific societies and other circumstantial evidence, the picture emerges as in Table 1.3.

Table 1.3   Subject backgrounds of science masters attending the 1901 conference

Biology teachers	Chemistry teachers	Physics teachers	Uncertain
4	13	16	8

There is nothing to suggest that any of those in the 'uncertain' category were predominantly teachers of biology, and a strong and not unexpected impression of the dominance of the physical sciences is obtained, the influence of mathematics tipping the scales towards physics rather than chemistry.

Possibly less expected is the military interest and affiliation of many of those attending. This feature is best brought out by an examination of schools rather than of individuals. First, the institutional composition of the list of schools in Table 1.1 is characterized by some significant absences. Neither Dulwich, where F.W. Sanderson had done pioneering work in the teaching of applied sciences in the 1880s, nor Oundle, where he took over the headship in 1892, was represented.[37] Few of the great 'day schools', such as Manchester Grammar School and Bradford Grammar School in the north; King Edward VI High School, Birmingham in the midlands; and the City of London School and University College School in the metropolis, in all of which there were notable teachers of science, sent representatives. Furthermore, the geographical distribution of schools in the list is biased very much to the southern half of England. In short, the twenty-four schools from which the forty-one science teachers came were far from representative of public schools generally in which science was taught.

Two views might be taken of this. First, it could be argued that the schools were simply ones which happened to be within reasonable travelling distance of London and in which at least one member of staff was prepared to give up a Saturday to attend the conference, either out of interest in the programme, or for some other reason.

No doubt something of this is involved in any explanation of the composition of the list. Alternatively, or in addition, one might look for some common bond of interest across a number of the schools in order to account, however partially, for their presence. In so doing, the concern and connection of many of the schools with military education emerges strongly.

The prevailing view on the education of Army officers in the second half of the nineteenth century was that they should first receive a 'thorough well-grounded education of an English gentleman'[38] in the best schools of the land, and then proceed to professional instruction in a military college. For cavalry and infantry officers there was the Royal Military College, Sandhurst; for officers in the scientific corps, the artillery and engineers, there was the Royal Military Academy at Woolwich. Together with the replacement of patronage by a system of competitive examinations as the means of entry to Sandhurst and Woolwich this vesting in public schools of responsibility for the general education of future Army officers had a significant effect on the organization of studies. As long as the subjects of examination were almost identical with those in the classical curriculum, schools had no need to make special provision for their Army candidates. Particular problems arose, however, from 'the shifting currents of thought in the minds of the War Office'[39] which resulted in the multiplication of subjects for examination. Furthermore, for Woolwich, in particular, the mathematical and scientific requirements had become significant by the end of the century.

Provision for Army candidates varied from school to school. In some, such as Cheltenham College, 'the senior of the great public schools founded in the Victorian era', a Military and Civil Department had been established and the extent to which boys took up a military career is demonstrated in Table 1.4 by figures showing the occupations of college-leavers between 1841 and 1910.[40]

Table 1.4   *Occupations of boys leaving Cheltenham College between 1841 and 1910*

Armed forces – home	2301
Armed forces – India	595
Clergy	449
Law	444
Medicine (including Forces)	178
Civil Engineers (including overseas)	161
Civil Service { 81 to Indian Civil Service / 18 to India, Home and Colonial Service	99

At Bedford Grammar School, another institution with an impressive record of entrants to Sandhurst and Woolwich, a Civil and Military Department had been founded in 1879. This was modelled on the department at Cheltenham and prepared candidates not only for Army entrance, but also for 'the Indian Police, the Forests Department at Cooper's Hill, London Matriculation, Mathematical and Science Scholarships.'[41]

At Clifton College, founded in 1862, the Modern Side was almost as old as the school itself. Its history was one of continuous growth and it catered particularly for those boys who intended 'to enter the Army or Commerce or Engineering, or who are to specialise in Science or Mathematics.'[42] W.A. Shenstone, the Senior Science Master at Clifton, had appeared before Lord Sandhurst's committee of 1893, appointed to enquire into the entrance examinations, in non-military subjects, of candidates for commissions in the Army.

Rugby, Eton and Harrow likewise each had their special provision for Army candidates. At Rugby by 1906 the Modern and Army sides together constituted 40 per cent of the boys in the school.[43] At Eton the Army Class was reconstituted in 1887 under the regime of a new headmaster, Dr Warre, largely to improve the success rate of examinees and to encourage boys to stay for longer periods at school. Previously many boys had sought an early opportunity to leave, going to one of the several 'crammers' with an established reputation for achieving passes in the military entrance examinations.[44]

The Modern Side at Harrow was chosen as the subject of the first in a series of pamphlets describing Modern Sides of public schools which the Board of Education hoped would assist those planning the curricula of newly created secondary schools, following the 1902 Education Act.[45] Mathematics was the staple of the curriculum of the Modern Side, with an Army Class existing as a separate provision. Even so, the young Winston Churchill, after four and a half years at Harrow, three of these in the Army Class, twice failed the entrance examination to Sandhurst. His final and successful bid was under the tutelage of Captain James and his partners in Cromwell Road, a firm which 'had made a scientific study of the mentality of the Civil Service Commissioners' and 'knew with almost Papal infallibility the sort of questions' which would be set.[46] Churchill included chemistry amongst his five examination subjects.

Despite the young Winston's unfortunate experience in the Army Class at Harrow, one general result of the special provisions made by public schools was a marked increase in the percentage of 'gentlemen cadets' gaining direct entry to Woolwich and Sandhurst, without an intervening period with a private tutor (Table 1.5). This process was assisted by a closer alignment of the school curriculum with the scheme of examination, following the recommendations of Lord Sandhurst's committee in 1894.

In 1900, the Board of Visitors appointed for the inspection of Woolwich noted that of two hundred Gentlemen Cadets who had come into residence as direct entrants from some sixty-eight schools, ten schools each had seven or more successful candidates accounting in total for 115 (57.5%) of the entry.

Table 1.5   Percentage of candidates per year gaining direct entry from schools [47]

	1887	1897–1900
Sandhurst	11%	55%
Woolwich	33%	78.7%

Table 1.6   Schools providing seven or more candidates entering Woolwich direct from school [48]

Cheltenham	31	Haileybury	8
Clifton	16	Dulwich	7
Wellington	16	Harrow	7
Bedford	8	Rugby	7
Eton	8	Westward Ho!	7

Seven of these 'top ten' schools were represented at the conference of public school science masters in January 1901, sending eighteen members of staff between them, almost half the gathering. Of the other three schools, Haileybury and Dulwich were represented the following year, whilst Westward Ho! was shortly to move to Windsor, from where, as the United Services College, it also provided members for the Association of Public School Science Masters.

Turning now, briefly, to the military (and naval) affiliations of individuals who attended the 1901 conference, C.E. Ashford, Senior Science Master at Harrow, was soon to be appointed first headmaster of the Royal Naval College, Osborne, from where he moved in 1905 to inaugurate the Royal Naval College, Dartmouth, successor to the Admiralty's training ship HMS *Britannia*.[49] In passing, it is perhaps worth noting that the Britannia's 18-month stormy sojourn in Portland Roads, some forty years earlier, had encouraged the foundation of Weymouth College,[50] from which C.G. Falkner came to deliver his paper on the Army and Navy examinations. Another *Britannia* link involves W.D. Eggar, amongst whose publications was a textbook on *Wave motion, sound and light* contributed to the twelve volume *Britannia Science Series* (Macmillan 1898). Prior to his appointment to Eton in 1895, Eggar had taught for four years at Wellington College, a school founded in 1859 to provide especially for the education of 'orphan children of indigent and meritorious Officers of the Army.'[51]

Ashford's Harrovian colleague, the young John Talbot, with a first in both parts of the Natural Sciences Tripos and a London BSc with Class I Honours in Experimental Physics thrown in for good measure, held the rank of Major in the Officers Training Corps during his headship of the Royal Grammar School, Newcastle-upon-Tyne

(1912–21), moving from there to become Master of Haileybury.[52] Other keen soldiers amongst the science masters included Colonel David Rintoul,[53] commander of the Corps at Clifton, and Percy Simpson, who commanded the School Corps at Chigwell.

Perhaps enough has been said to demonstrate that both an institutional and an individual interest in military education characterized the gathering on 19 January 1901. There is also evidence to suggest that those masters who taught Army Classes, certainly in the field of mathematics, had already established a communication network for consultation on matters of professional concern. Appearing before the Akers-Douglas Committee, W.M. Baker (Cheltenham) spoke of a number of syllabus and examination issues on which he had petitioned the Civil Service Commissioners, having first armed himself with the opinions of 'nearly all the Army class masters in those schools that pass boys to Woolwich and Sandhurst.'[54] The meeting, then, was hardly one of strangers.

Other networks existed besides the professional one. Amongst the biologists, Oswald Latter and Archer Vassall had been newly-appointed master and upper school pupil respectively at Charterhouse in the early 1890s, with Vassall now on the staff of Harrow.[55] Although leaving Oxford two years later than M.D. Hill, Vassall had worked in the same zoology laboratory and the two men were friends from those days. The chemist G.W. Hedley (Cheltenham) graduated from Oxford in 1894, the same year as Hill, and fellow chemists H.P. Fitzgerald (Wellington) and F.R.L. Wilson (Charterhouse), both Keble men, each the previous year. A.E. Field, physics master at Bedford, graduated in the same year as Latter, and R. T. Bodey, chemistry master at Liverpool College, a year earlier. Both Field and Bodey were at Trinity.

Turning to the Cambridge connection, Eccles (Gresham's School), Lempfert (Rugby) and Talbot (Harrow) had all taken firsts in Part II of the Natural Sciences Tripos in 1898, Simpson (Chigwell) a first in Part I in the same year and H.T. Holmes (Merchant Taylors') a first in Part I the year previous. In their mid-twenties at the time of the 1901 meeting they represented the youthful edge of the membership. At the mean age of around thirty-five were the three Trinity physicists, Ashford, Falkner and Eggar, and de Havilland also a Cambridge contemporary.

Extending linkages back into the schools, we find Rintoul, from 1886, and Shenstone, from 1880, as long-serving members of the science staff of Clifton College, where Ashford also had spent a year teaching, between demonstrating in the Cavendish Laboratory and taking up his post at Harrow in 1894. Of the younger men attending the 1901 meeting, H.P. Fitzgerald, J.R. Eccles and G.L. Thomas had all been at Clifton as pupils of Rintoul and Shenstone.

A similar picture emerges in relation to Dulwich College. Although unrepresented at the 1901 meeting of science masters, two of those present, J.E. Legg of Woodbridge Grammar School and C.I.

Gardiner of Cheltenham College, were 'old boys', both of whom had returned to the staff of the College for a year's teaching experience after graduating. A third, F.R.L. Wilson, a near contemporary of Gardiner's, had spent six years on the staff of Dulwich before moving to his present post at Charterhouse.

For many of those attending in January 1901 the occasion clearly provided the opportunity for a reunion with friends and acquaintances. The picture is of a close-knit group of enthusiasts, united by common professional concerns and educational backgrounds, 'a band of brothers' as Archer Vassall was later to describe the early members of the Association of Public School Science Masters.[56]

The formal business of the meeting consisted of the reading and discussion of the advertised papers. In each of these, the special problems of teaching science in public, as opposed to other secondary, schools were central. For boys who were to be landowners, 'employers of gamekeepers', 'pioneers in a new country as civil servants, soldiers or colonists', Archer Vassall contended that field work in biology and geology was important, not only because it trained powers of observation, but also because it helped to develop conservationist attitudes to nature. In so far as most of the field work had to be undertaken as an extra-curricular activity under the auspices of a school Natural History Society, the greatest obstacle to progress was the public school preoccupation with compulsory games. That 'There ought not to be compulsory games on six days of the week at school, since thereby individualism is extinguished' was the single resolution which Vassall submitted for the approval of his colleagues.[57]

Oswald Latter, Vassall's mentor, likewise challenged the institutional structure within which much science teaching had to take place, urging that 'forms' should not be constituted, as was then the practice, in terms of the attainments of boys in classical studies, but that, for science lessons, their composition should reflect proficiency in science. Furthermore, in stressing the importance of science teaching in general education, he advocated the provision of science lectures for those upper school boys, the majority, who had chosen to specialise in subjects other than science.[58]

A further important difference between the public schools and other secondary schools was said to be the extent to which it was possible to coordinate the work of the science and mathematics departments. Fresh from attendance at the LCC Conference of Science Teachers the previous week, W.D. Eggar admitted to envy, not so much of the new laboratories he had seen in the South Western Polytechnic, Chelsea, but of 'the ideal groupings of boys in the Physical and Chemical Laboratories, and the workshop' at Raine's School, and especially at the better coordination of subjects such as mathematics and science which 'the Board School master' seemed able to achieve. At Eton, science and mathematics were 'in separate compartments' and mathematics was taught without reference to its practical applications. As a result, the Eton science masters felt obliged to devote precious time to 'preliminary exercises of measurement and expression in decimals', use of the metric system, and similar matters, all of which could have been part of the ordinary mathematics lesson. Again, in the most elementary measurements in light, electricity and magnetism, there was need to make use of trigonometrical ratios. The science masters could not delay teaching these subjects until pupils had begun trigonometry in their mathematics lessons. Hence a beginning had to be made in the physics course, using the practical and applied approaches advocated by reformers such as Professor John Perry, and frequently used by those, like Eggar, who had to teach Geometrical Drawing to the Army Class. Extending his argument to university level, and underlining the relationship between applied mathematics and physics, Eggar urged that the present requirement of alumni that they possess 'a modicum of unapplied and undigested Algebra' should be modernised to the extent that 'a knowledge of the elements of some branch of Physics be required of all candidates for a University degree'.[59]

The case for physics was also forcefully argued by C.E. Ashford in his paper on the order in which science subjects should be taught. Commenting on a tendency of 'the Classical Head Master' to regard science and chemistry as synonymous, Ashford disputed the value of teaching chemistry early and advocated instead a course on practical mensuration and physics, without much associated theory. Powers of manipulation and habits of accuracy would thereby be cultivated. A logically developed course of physics lectures could follow. As for chemistry, it required that a boy should first be introduced to 'many dry and disconnected details' before general laws could have any meaning. An understanding of molecular changes and the constitution of matter should come later in the sequence of subjects. In Ashford's opinion, it was expedient that some physics should be taught before chemistry was begun; and it was essential that before leaving school, every boy should have followed a course of practical measurement and experiment.[60]

From the papers delivered it was clear that the institutional context in which science was taught in public schools was a major determinant both of the problems to which priority was assigned and of the solutions which were advocated. The mathematical backgrounds of many of the leading members was also an important factor, disposing them to adopt a particular view of the nature of science.

As to teaching methods, although H.E. Armstrong attended the meeting, heurism appeared to have few supporters. Ashford was quite explicit on this point; the practical work which he regarded as essential was 'far from aiming at the rediscovery of say the law of Conservation of Energy or that of Avogadro'. The 'cultivation of accuracy' and of 'powers of manipulation' were the prime objectives; 'the faculties of observation and description' being little used. Subsequently, physics was to be taught by a course of logical lectures.

For the sixth-form specialist something different was required. Each boy would follow a connected course of experimental work 'to make the measurements and verify the laws about which he had learnt in lecture.'[61]

Oswald Latter, also, in speaking about the teaching of science in the main body of the school, saw no need for lectures at this stage to be connected with laboratory work. Indeed the lectures for these 'non-specialising forms' need not form a systematic course, but could be based on a series of topics. 'A couple of object lessons on the geology of the . . . neighbourhood . . . followed by a catechetical lecture on the physical geography of the surrounding country, and then one formal lecture summarising' would for him constitute an adequate handling of the topic. There should also be laboratory work. Indeed, at least half (and with lower forms, more than half), of the time allotted for science ought, in his opinion, to be devoted to 'systematic laboratory work in the elements of physics and chemistry'. However, the purpose of this work was quite distinct from that of the lectures.[62]

The birth of the Association

The 1901 meeting closed with a discussion on the desirability of forming a permanent society of science masters. No decision was reached, but a committee was elected, with Ashford as secretary, to arrange another conference in a year's time. When this body met in the autumn of 1901, plans were laid for a second conference to be held on Saturday, 18 January 1902. Professor A.W. Rücker FRS, Principal of the University of London, was to be asked to preside, and, failing him, Sir Michael Foster, Professor Oliver Lodge or Professor A.W. Tilden, in that order.[63] Details of the conference were to be sent to all science masters in schools listed in the *Public Schools Yearbook* for 1901, with a special letter of invitation going to 'sundry scholarship examiners at Oxford and Cambridge' and all members of the Headmasters' Conference. On this occasion the proceedings were to be limited to three papers:

M.D. Hill (Eton) – On the connection between science scholarships at the universities and science work at schools.
G. Stallard (Rugby) – On the arrangements for specialists at Rugby.
C.I. Gardiner (Cheltenham) – On Army examinations.

Furthermore, Gardiner was instructed to form a sub-committee, with assistance from his colleagues at Cheltenham, to draw up a scheme of definite proposals for the formation of a society. After comments and approval by the main committee, these were to be submitted to the conference at the meeting for private business.[64]

It is not clear how Gardiner interpreted this mandate as no record of the activities of any such sub-committee exists. Amongst his

Cheltenham science colleagues were G.W. Hedley, an Oxford chemistry graduate, and W.G. Borchardt, a Natural Science Tripos graduate, member of the Mathematical Association and writer of elementary mathematical textbooks. Both Hedley and Borchardt were to attend the 1902 conference of public school science masters. It is possible that 'the assistance of his colleagues at Cheltenham' might also have included advice from others such as W.M. Baker, head of the Military and Civil Department, and a prominent member of the Mathematical Association. It would certainly be reasonable, in drawing up the constitution for a new subject teaching association to look carefully at the rules and regulations of existing associations, in particular, those of the Mathematical Association which had the closest affinity to the proposed association for science teachers. Indeed, one of the names suggested for the new association, when its formation had been agreed, was the Natural Science Association by analogy with the Mathematical Association.[65]

Whatever the process of consultation, Gardiner's motion put to the private business meeting at the conference on 18 January 1902 was unequivocal in calling for the formation of 'an association for the promotion of the interests of natural science teaching in secondary schools.' An amendment was moved to add the words 'of Public School Masters' after the word 'association', but this was lost and the original motion carried. So, as the record has it, 'the Association was formed.'[66]

A draft memorandum, setting out the objects of the Association and its name, was then read by Gardiner. On the question of the name there was a great deal of discussion, the following proposals being made:

Natural Science Association
Science Education Association
Association for the Promotion of Natural Science in Secondary Schools
Association of Public School Science Masters.

The origin of the first proposal has already been suggested. As regards the second, with its almost modern ring, no subject teaching association in existence at that time had the word 'Education' in its title, although 'Technical Education' was a term in current use. The third proposal was most probably an adaptation of the name of a major pressure group, the National Association for the Promotion of Technical and Secondary Education, created through the initiatives of Henry Roscoe and others in 1887, and of which Roscoe was still honorary secretary in 1902.

Neither of the first two names contained any hint that membership might be restricted to a particular type of school. The third made specific reference to 'Secondary Schools', but it was the last, even more precise name, proposed by Ashford, which was finally adopted by a large majority.

The objects of the Association, as set out in Gardiner's *Memorandum*, were:

(a) To promote the teaching of natural science in secondary schools.
(b) To afford a means of communication between natural science teachers in secondary schools themselves, and between them and others engaged in teaching natural science elsewhere.
(c) To afford a means of communication between natural science teachers in secondary schools and examining bodies.[67]

It was agreed that these would be adopted provisionally for the year 1902, on the understanding that they would be reviewed. Professor Rücker was elected President, with Ashford as Secretary and Treasurer and the organizing committee for the conference was to become the committee of the new Association. As his first presidential act, Rücker charged the committee to prepare draft rules and regulations for the government of the Association, and to circulate them before the annual meeting of 1903.

Membership

By May 1902, the rules and regulations had been prepared and revised by the committee. Under rule 11, members of the Association were to be 'Teachers of Natural Science in Secondary Schools', or . . . 'others interested in such teaching.' For the teachers, at least, graduate status was assumed. Each application for membership, duly proposed and seconded by two members of the Association, had to come before the committee where it required a majority of two-thirds of the votes for success.

From the start, control over entry to the Association was strict. The reference in the rules to 'Teachers of Natural Science in Secondary Schools' might appear to suggest a degree of liberality which belied the name of the Association. In practice, many men (and all women) who taught science in local authority, and other secondary schools in the early decades of the century were excluded. The extent of exclusiveness is difficult to quantify, but D.S.L. Cardwell has noted that of the 3870 graduate masters listed in *The Schoolmasters' Yearbook and Directory* for 1903, the first year of issue, some 510 were scientists (excluding mathematicians) who had read Natural Sciences at Oxford or Cambridge, or held a BSc, MSc, or DSc degree of one of the newer universities.[68] Indeed, Cardwell estimates that there were probably over 1000 graduate science teachers in secondary schools in 1902, after which date the number increased rapidly up to the time of the war, although not at a rate sufficient to meet the demands for graduate teachers of chemistry and physics from the expanding local authority secondary schools.[69] By 1914, the *Directory* listed some 15,000 biographical entries of those engaged in secondary, university and technical education.[70] If we assume a conservative fraction of one-eighth of this total as the number of those either teaching science in secondary schools or, if not teaching there, directly interested in this work, approximately 2000 men would have been eligible to join under the original membership rule. By that date, however, the rule had been rewritten to specify with greater precision the conditions of eligibility, the prime and explicit concern now being the type of school in which a teacher worked. It was agreed that candidates for election were to be '(a) Teachers of Natural Science in Public Schools, or (b) such other persons as in the opinion of the Committee have contributed to the advancement of Science Teaching in such Schools. . . . For the purpose of this rule, "A Public School" shall be understood as meaning any School which is represented on the Headmasters' Conference, or which, in the opinion of the Committee, is of similar status to the Schools so represented.'[71]

The committee made a brave attempt, over the years, to arbitrate on the state of schools. Thus, the application in 1907 of Mr W.S. Rowntree, from the newly-founded Quaker school, Leighton Park, was successful because, although unrepresented on the Headmasters' Conference, the school was reputed to send 25 per cent of its boys to Oxford and Cambridge. The following year, after a discussion on the standing of Battersea Grammar School, Mr E.M. Eagles was elected, but Mr A. Pickles, King Edward VII School, Lytham, was less fortunate, as it was felt that time was needed to see how his school would develop. The homogeneity of the Association was constantly under mild threat, nevertheless, and the problem of members who had taken up headships of municipal grammar schools moved D.P. Berridge, Secretary of the Association in 1909, to call for a separate listing of members, additional to an alphabetical one, under the heading 'Recognised Schools and their representatives.'[72]

As Table 1.7 shows, members in 'Public Schools represented by the

Table 1.7   The Association of Public School Science Masters: membership

Year	Total number of members	Members teaching in public schools	Number of public schools represented
1902	68	67	44
1903	96	—	—
1909	196	175	94
1910	207	187	94
1912	229	202 (88.2%)	97
1914	286	251 (87.7%)	111
1916	289	256 (88.5%)	113
1918	308	253 (82.1%)	107

Association', as Berridge's supplementary list was entitled, formed a decreasing percentage of the total membership in the second decade of the Association's life.[73]

Influenced possibly by egalitarian tendencies which had been engendered nationally during the First World War, and certainly by the expansion of secondary education outside the public schools sector, the Committee of the Association was obliged to reconsider the basis for membership in May, 1917.[74] A small group of three, consisting of G.H.J. Adlam of City of London School, V.S. Bryant of Wellington and Archer Vassall of Harrow, was instructed to look into the matter.

No doubt the move was also encouraged by the recognition that others besides masters in public schools were expressing views on science teaching and seeking to influence educational events. Although the Association had provided a deputation to give evidence on school science teaching to the Prime Minister's Committee, appointed in August 1916 to enquire into the position of natural science in the educational system, so also had the Incorporated Association of Assistant Masters. Again, following the publication in July 1914 of Circular 849 on 'Examinations in Secondary Schools', the Board of Education had started a wide-ranging process of consultation about the form of the proposed School Certificate Examination. The Association's views on the place of science in the examination for the new leaving certificate had been transmitted to the Board in July 1916, but its voice was merely one amongst several. At the same committee meeting at which this matter was reported,[75] a request was received from the British Association for the Advancement of Science for cooperation in the work of a committee being established to consider 'the Method and Substance of Science Teaching in Secondary Schools, with particular reference to the essential place of Science in General Education'. Berridge and Vassall were nominated to represent the public school science masters. The B.A. committee, however, brought together an altogether wider community of interests, including representatives of the Incorporated Association of Assistant Masters, the Incorporated Association of Head Masters and women science teachers.[76]

When Adlam presented the report of the group to the Committee of the Association in October 1917, it was decided to recommend a change to the membership rule. In the case of an applicant from a school unrepresented on the Headmasters' Conference, the requirement that his school should be 'of similar status' to a public school was to be replaced by one that 'the aims and interests of the science masters should be similar to those of members of the Association.' It was also decided to seek power from the next General Meeting to offer membership to a maximum of twenty science masters from schools 'of a type different from our own.'

These recommendations provoked strenuous opposition when they were put to the Business Meeting at the Annual Conference on

8 January 1918. Some of the longer serving members, notably D.P. Berridge (Malvern) and the Rev. A.L. Cortie (Stonyhurst), argued strongly against any alteration to the constitution 'until the conclusion of the war.' After prolonged discussion, their amendment for 'no change' was narrowly defeated by 17 votes to 16.[77] The alteration was then approved (24 votes to 8) and, with a reduction from twenty to ten members from 'different schools', the Committee was empowered to open the doors, albeit fractionally.

Such a cautious move was clearly little more than a re-affirmation of the status quo and even before the armistice the Committee had returned to the issue, expressing a unanimous view that it was desirable to include within the membership of the Association 'science teachers from universities and schools of types other than our own.'[78] The principal benefit of so doing was that the Association would become more representative of science teaching throughout the United Kingdom. To those who feared the consequences of a reduction in homogeneity of interests which had characterised the APSSM, it was argued that the problems of particular types of school could be dealt with by sectional committees.

In furtherance of their aim, the Committee invited for discussion a number of leading science masters from outside the Association. These included: G.D. Dunkerley, senior science master at Watford Grammar School, an official of the Incorporated Association of Assistant Masters in Secondary Schools, and a member of the British Association's Committee on Science Teaching in Secondary Schools; H.P. Lunn, science master at the County Secondary School, Holloway, a past chairman and secretary of the IAAM and a member of the IAAM deputation which had presented evidence to J.J. Thomson's committee; G.J. Francis, chemistry master at Latymer Upper School and another IAAM member; and S. Skinner, Principal of the South Western Polytechnic Institute, Chelsea. In addition, the Committee enlisted the views of one of the Association's newer members who taught in a 'different type of school', J. Hart-Smith, science master at Battersea Polytechnic Secondary School, another leading figure in the affairs of the IAAM.

At a meeting on 13 July 1918 unanimity was quickly established on the need to extend the Association's membership. Although by this stage another national organization of science teachers had been set up, the Association of Science Teachers, its membership was drawn predominantly from the ranks of women science teachers. There was a clear feeling that the needs of men would be provided for more satisfactorily by their inclusion within a reconstituted APSSM, rather than by any expansion of the AST. Accordingly, it was agreed to recommend a major change in the rules so as to extend eligibility to any science master in a secondary school who had either a university degree or its equivalent, or was registered by the Teachers' Registration Council. At the General Meeting of the Association held at the London Day Training College on 31 December 1918, the new rules governing membership were approved and, as the minutes of the committee meeting held the following day boldly record in red ink at the top of a new page, *The Science Masters' Association* came into being. With a minor amendment in 1924 designed to enable preparatory school masters with the specified qualifications to join, the membership rules of the SMA remained unaltered for over a quarter of a century. Only after the Second World War and a major Education Act was the next step taken in the progressive democratisation of the Association.

Before concluding this examination of the membership of the APSSM, one special category of members deserves brief mention. From the first, the Committee had recognised the value of involving university and 'non-science teaching members' in its work. Such persons were eligible to join the Association provided their number did not exceed 20 per cent of the total membership at the time of election.[79]

Of course the Association had dealings with many university scientists and others influential in the worlds of education and science. The Secretary's Address Book for 1907 lists the names of some 73 non-members with whom the Association had corresponded, their distribution by institution being, perhaps, some indication of priorities accorded to concerns: University of Oxford, 18; University of Cambridge, 17; University of London, 8; other universities, 5; Board of Education, 12; London County Council, 2; others, 11. Furthermore, apart from Past Presidents who, under the constitution, enjoyed permanent association, a number of distinguished scientists and educationalists who were not members, frequently attended annual meetings and contributed to discussions.[80]

In addition, however, there were the 'non-science teaching members' elected by the Committee. In one or two cases, sentiment alone might explain the Committee's action, as with J.D. Cogan of Bath, elected in 1908 at the age of 92, after a lifetime of science teaching dating from 1836. A collection of Cogan's apparatus used in the teaching of physics was included in the Members' Exhibition at the Annual Meeting in January 1910. A more purposeful election was that of Leonard Blaikie, Civil Service Commissioner, a first class honours graduate in physics (Natural Science Tripos, Part 2, 1896) and an examiner in connection with the Army entrance schemes, with which so many of the founder members were involved. C.S. Jackson, Ashford's contemporary at Trinity College, Cambridge,[81] eighth wrangler in 1889 and class 1 in Part 2 of the Law Tripos the following year, an able teacher of mathematics and physics on the staff of the Royal Military Academy, Woolwich, was another valued 'special member.' From the small population of scientifically qualified headmasters, the Association recruited Fred Harrison, previously in charge of the Engineering Side at Dulwich College, and, at the time of his election in 1908, Headmaster of Newcastle High School, Staffordshire. Through him the Association had a voice in the discussions of the Headmasters' Conference and the Incorporated Association of Head Masters, whilst a social link with several prominent members of the Association was strengthened through his membership of the Alpine Club. However, from the standpoint of the future development of the Association, perhaps the most influential 'special member' to be elected by the APSSM was 'H. Hartley (Balliol College)' in 1910. The future Brigadier General, later Sir Harold, Hartley CBE, MC, MA, FRS was to retain a deep interest in the work of the Association throughout his long and distinguished life.

Constitution and Administration

Although the administration of the APSSM throughout the seventeen years of its life was characterised by voluntary action and a high degree of informality, nevertheless a written constitution existed from the time of the 1902 conference.[82] Such changes as were made to this were responses to growth in membership and to increased activity resulting from an authority to pronounce on science education issues which the Association progressively acquired.

C.E. Ashford's initial appointment in 1902 as combined Honorary Secretary and Treasurer rapidly proved unworkable, the burden being excessive for one man. After a year he was provided with an aide, his younger colleague at Harrow, J. Talbot, who was elected to the new post of Assistant Secretary and, in effect, Treasurer.[83] Ashford was, in any case, much occupied with other matters in 1903, moving in May to be the first head of the Royal Naval College, Osborne. His successor as Secretary, W.A. Shenstone (Clifton) produced minutes of a brevity which both underlined the pressures on his time and ultimately provoked concern about the need for a fuller record of the transactions of the general meeting.[84] By October 1905 it had been agreed that two secretaries were needed and the constitution was amended accordingly.

With the election of D.P. Berridge (Malvern) as Honorary Secretary in 1907, the Association acquired an administrator of outstanding dedication and efficiency. Apart from a break in 1911, necessitated by the Association's rules, he held the office of Secretary until 1914, in all giving thirteen years of continuous service to the Committee. Under his régime the minutes of the Committee meeting became more detailed and informative, setting a standard for future secretaries. Rules and regulations were continually under review; and, during a period when the number of members almost doubled, there was no more scrupulous guardian of the conditions of eligibility. His acceptance of a second period of office from 1912, this time as Annual Meeting Secretary, was conditional upon the provision of clerical assistance, the sum of £5 being made available to him for this purpose.[85]

It was Berridge who, at the end of his period as secretary in 1915, proposed what would have been a major change in the Constitution of the Association.[86] One of the problems resulting from increased size was the greater difficulty which the Committee experienced in determining the views of the membership on issues before them. In the early years much use had been made of postal questionnaires. The Annual Meeting also helped, particularly at the stage when most members of the Association knew each other. By 1915 this was no longer so; the location of the meetings in London also made it difficult for some members to attend. Drawing on his experience of the British Association for the Advancement of Science,[87] Berridge proposed that the present Committee should become an Executive Committee and that there should be established, in addition, a General Committee. This latter body was to consist of the Executive Committee together with fifteen additional members; in this way it was hoped that a more representative expression of opinion would be obtained and the more senior members of the Association would have an opportunity, then denied, of meeting and working alongside a wider cross-section of newly-appointed members.

It was agreed by the Committee that the formal proposal for this change should be put to a General Meeting of the Association for its approval. In the circumstances of the war, this was delayed until January 1916, by which time the problems of maintaining the work of the Association had become so acute that any change in the Constitution was seen as likely to aggravate an already difficult situation. Berridge withdrew his proposal and the Association continued to manage its affairs by a General Committee until 1963. The danger of remoteness from the main body of the members was, however, to be a recurring concern.

The composition of the Committee during the life of the Association of Public School Science Masters is of interest in that the contribution and influence of a limited number of schools is clearly demonstrated. Allowing for changes in the Constitution, there were 198 man-years of service to the Committee in the seventeen years of the formal life of the Association. Some thirty-two schools provided committee members over this period, those contributing six man-years or more being listed in Table 1.8.[88]

It is seen from this that two schools, Eton and Harrow, provided between them almost a quarter of the man-years of service to the Committee. Throughout its life, the Association was never without a science master from Eton on its Committee. Hill, Eggar and de Havilland leap-frogged into office and between them provided 23 man-years of service, including chairmanship for five years (Hill) and the secretaryship for two (de Havilland). A similar record of unbroken representation is found in the case of Harrow, with rather more members of staff being involved. Ashford, Talbot, Vassall, the mathematician A.W. Siddons, Middleditch, C.L. Bryant and Calvert all served, sometimes simultaneously, filling the offices of chairman for one year (Vassall), secretary for five years (Ashford one,

Table 1.8   Schools contributing six or more man-years to the APSSM Committee

Man-Years	School
24	Harrow
23	Eton
15	Cheltenham
13	Malvern
11	Charterhouse
8 each	Clifton, Repton, Winchester
7 each	Dulwich, St. Olave's
6 each	Gresham's, Rugby, Tonbridge

C.L. Bryant four) and treasurer for five years (Ashford one, Talbot four). No other schools were comparable, though Cheltenham, represented for all but two years, ran a close third – Gardiner and Hedley each filling the office of chairman on one occasion, and Hedley serving as treasurer for five years. In terms of continuity of influence, Berridge's one-man stint of almost thirteen years' continuous service, including seven as secretary, was unequalled by any other member and brought Malvern into fourth place.

The supreme office of the Association was, of course, the presidency and here full advantage was taken of opportunities to enlist the services of distinguished men of science, and, less frequently, education.[89] Initially the formal duties of the President were confined to that of chairman at the Annual Meeting, but, from 1907, the delivery of a substantial address became the tradition.

An indication of the Association's growing prestige was its ability to secure as President its first choice in all but one instance. Occasionally, difficulties arose from the constitutional requirement that the President should be elected at an Annual Meeting, and his term of office should commence at the following one. In practice this meant that a prospective President must be approached in the autumn two years before that in which he was to hold office. The long interval between consent to serve and assumption of office, especially in the case of busy public figures, led to cases in which unforeseeable circumstances prevented a President-elect from attending the Annual Meeting, a substitute having to be recruited at short notice. Those Presidents who through illness or the unanticipated calls of high office were absent invariably returned in future years to aid the deliberations of the Association. Thus, the elderly Sir Michael Foster, who had agreed to serve during 1905, and was prevented by illness from attending the Annual Meeting, was replaced by Dr Gow, the Head Master of Westminster School.[90] The following year, Sir Oliver Lodge was similarly prevented from fulfilling his duties at the Annual

Meeting and Sir Michael Foster substituted, making good his default of the previous year. Some time later, Sir Ronald Ross, when requisitioned by the War Office for an overseas assignment in 1918, enlisted Sir Harry Johnston in his place, returning himself to preside over the meeting in 1919. Only in 1909 was there failure to secure a President from the short list agreed by the Committee. None of the three prospective candidates, the Rt Hon. R.B. Haldane, Secretary for War,[91] Sir E. Ray Lankester, Hill's former professor of comparative anatomy at Oxford, and Professor J.A. Ewing, Director of Naval Education,[92] was available. In the event, the Association turned to a President whose influence could be exerted in connection with another important issue of concern to members, the scientific education of future medical students, and elected Sir Clifford Allbutt, Regius Professor of Physic in the University of Cambridge.

The names of those who filled the office of President, together with those who were considered but did not serve, are given in Table 1.9.

Clearly the Association bestowed the distinction of its highest office on a person it wished to honour for services to science education. This was perhaps especially the case in 1904 when, during Shenstone's tenure of the secretaryship, Professor W.A. Tilden was elected President. Tilden had been a science master at Clifton College in the 1870s, bringing the young Shenstone with him as demonstrator from the school of the Pharmaceutical Society. Shenstone, whose early education was closely modelled on Tilden's, eventually succeeded to Tilden's post at Clifton. The election in 1910 of Professor H.E. Armstrong, a persistent and vocal attender at the Association's meetings, though by no means the best-loved scientist of his day,[93] had a degree of inevitability about it at a time when 'a chemical president' was due. The septuagenarian Sir Archibald Geikie, President in 1913, had been a Royal Society Governor of Harrow since 1892, whilst his successor as President, Professor H.B. Baker, had been an active committee member of the Association in its earliest days whilst he was still associated with Dulwich College.

There were, however, other motives underlying the choice of President, not least the opportunity to make the Association's views known to, and to enlist the support of, a person of influence. Sir Michael Foster, for example, not only served on the Board of Education's Consultative Committee, but had strong connections with military education, being the representative of science on the Akers-Douglas Committee which reported on the education of Army officers in 1902. The first non-scientist to be elected as President (1907), the Rev. the Hon. E. Lyttelton, was the newly-appointed Head Master of Eton, late Head of Haileybury, member of the Committee of the Headmasters' Conference and past chairman of that body, as well as being on the Board of Education's Consultative Committee. Similarly, Dr James Gow, Head Master of Westminster, who deputised for Sir Michael Foster in 1905, succeeded Lyttelton as chairman of the Headmasters' Conference, served with him on the

Table 1.9 APSSM Presidents

	Biologists	Chemists	Physicists	Medical	Engineers	Other scientists	Educators and others
Formally elected (1903–1919)	Sir M. Foster (1905)	Sir W.A. Tilden (1904)	Sir A.W. Rücker (1903)	Sir C. Allbutt (1909)		Sir H. Miers (Mineralogy) (1908)	Rev. the Hon. E. Lyttelton (Eton) (1907)
	Sir E. Ray Lankester (1911)	Prof. H.E. Armstrong (1910)	Sir O. Lodge (1906)	Sir W. Osler (1915)		Sir A. Geikie (Geology) (1913)	Sir Harry Johnston (1917)
							(Colonial Administration)
		Prof. H.B. Baker (1914)	Sir J.J. Thomson (1912)	Sir R. Ross (1918)		Prof. H.H. Turner (Astronomy) (1916)	W.W. Vaughan (1919) (Wellington)
							[Dr J. Gow (1905) (Westminster)]
Reserve list of those never elected by the APSSM	Sir W. Ramsay (1907)	Sir W. Ramsay (1907)	Prof. J. Perry (1907)		Prof. J.A. Ewing (1908 & 1909)	Prof. W. Somerville (Agric. & Forestry) (1910)	Rt Hon. R.B. Haldane (1909) (Politician, Secretary for War)
					Prof. F. Jenkin (1910)	Dr J.H.H. Teal (Geology) (1913)	C.E. Ashford (H.M., R.N.C., Dartmouth) (1913)
					Dr H.S. Hele-Shaw (1915)		Prof. J. Adams (London Univ.) (1914)

Board's Consultative Committee and also chaired the Council of the Incorporated Association of Head Masters in 1902. Of the three 'medical' Presidents, Sir Clifford Allbutt (1909) and Sir William Osler (1915) represented Cambridge and Oxford respectively, whilst Colonel Sir Ronald Ross (1919) brought both military and medical perspectives to bear in his Presidential Address 'Observations on the results of our system of education'.[94]

Both Allbutt and Osler were of assistance to the Association in its long battle to secure recognition of public schools as institutions approved for the preliminary scientific education of medical students. However, with their involvement and that of Ross we move into another orbit of interest. By 1916 a Neglect of Science campaign, initiated by the Association, was under way and all three men, together with Professor H.H. Turner (President in 1916), Sir E. Ray Lankester (1911) and Sir Harry Johnston (1917) were actively involved. At a packed meeting at Burlington House in May 1916 and to prolonged applause, Johnston moved a resolution urging the Government to encourage the study of natural science by assigning importance to it in the competitive examinations for the Home and Indian Civil Service and by requiring some knowledge of the natural sciences from all candidates for admission to Sandhurst.[95]

The Association's President in the year of change, and the first to address the Science Masters' Association was W.W. Vaughan, Master of Wellington.[96] When it is recognised that Vaughan had been previously head of the Modern Side at Clifton and Head Master of Giggleswick School (both institutions with a strong science tradition); that Wellington was sending by 1919 a higher proportion of boys to Woolwich and Sandhurst than any other school; that Vaughan's cousins included Professor H.A.L. Fisher, President of the Board of Education, and Admiral Sir John Fisher, who, with Professor J.A. Ewing, inspired and implemented many of the reforms in the education of naval officers; that Vaughan himself was a member of the Education Committee of the Conjoint Board of Scientific Societies, a new body formed by the Royal Society in 1916 to express the collective opinion of scientific interest; that he had served on the Prime Minister's Committee under J.J. Thomson to report on the position of natural science in the educational system of Great Britain, and that in 1918 the chairman of the Committee of the APSSM was Major V.S. Bryant, science master and commander of the Officers' Training Corps at Wellington, Vaughan's election is explained. Although a non-scientist himself, his spheres of influence were singularly congruent with the Association's concerns over the first two decades of its existence.

A foundation for the future

It remains to ask why the Association of Public School Science Masters endured, providing a stable foundation for future growth.

Unquestionably, amongst contributory factors, was the sharp focus on a set of limited and well-defined problems associated with the teaching of science. The Association had no ambitious plan for the overall reform of the public school curriculum but, more modestly, set out to serve the practical needs of public school science masters as they themselves perceived them. At one stage the main effort was towards a greater degree of uniformity in the entrance examinations in science set by the various colleges at Oxford and Cambridge; at another, influence was exerted to secure a greater degree of correlation between the teaching of mathematics and science or a place in the preparatory school curriculum for nature study; yet again, during the war years, much attention was directed towards 'military scientific studies' in the school curriculum.

The Association also functioned as a sensitive monitor of the educational environment, alerting members to the implications of changes and continually seeking to extend its influence and control. When the School Certificate Examination was being introduced, a deputation presented views to the Board of Education, where one of their former members, F.B. Stead (Clifton) was Staff Inspector for Science. When the Secondary School Examinations Council was established, the Association sought representation on the new body. Direct representation was denied, but Talbot, by then Master of Haileybury, was soon nominated in his capacity as a member of The Teachers' Registration Council.

Certain concerns recurred throughout the life of the Association. The Sub-Committee on Debatable Questions Set in Examinations, for example, was in constant communication with representatives of the Oxford and Cambridge and other Schools' Examination Boards, on matters arising from the complaints of members. The two central issues that run as unbroken threads through the records of the Association's activities were, however, the entrance examinations for Oxford and Cambridge, and for Sandhurst and Woolwich. A close third was the preparation of students for medical studies. A detailed examination of the Association's work in relation to these issues is provided later, in Part Three of this book.

In all these matters the Association either possessed, or quickly acquired, effective lines of communication to the centres of power and decision-making. In this, the members were greatly assisted by the fact that they shared a similar educational and social background with those they sought to influence. Previous school and university links were exploited to the full. The high intellectual quality of the Association's members was undoubtedly also an important factor, in that they could meet university scientists, headmasters and civil servants on equal terms. Including a Fellow of the Royal Society, several who had taught in university science departments, others who were pursuing original research and publishing in scientific journals, some who were active in British Association circles and involved with 'invisible colleges' of scientists,[97] the membership was impressively qualified. Most importantly, as a study of presidents reveals, the Association was able to enlist the support of some of the most distinguished scientists of the day, almost all of them Fellows of the Royal Society.

At the anniversary meeting of the Royal Society on 1 December 1902, the Presidential Address by Sir William Huggins was devoted in part to the defects of the public schools and in particular their failure to assimilate the principles and methods of science into the curriculum of future leaders of society.[98] This was seen as the root cause of national malaise, the symptom of which was 'the absence . . . of a sufficiently intelligent appreciation on the part of the leaders of the nation . . . of the supreme importance of scientific knowledge and scientific methods.'

As to the cure for the malaise, in Huggins' view it was imperative that 'the living breath of the spirit of research' must enter the dry bones of the present academic system through which 'our public men' and 'the influential classes of society' pass. It was essential that science should become an integral and essential part of the curriculum, not just a subordinate part to be barely tolerated. As to the achievement of these reforms, the first step would have to be taken by the universities. Without some relaxation of university entrance examination requirements, schools would never be free to reshape their curricula.[99]

Once such changes had been made, the benefits to science, in Huggins' view, would be immeasurable. It was obvious, he asserted, that with a fuller knowledge and appreciation of science on the part of the nation, 'public money would be liberally voted by the Government in aid of technical colleges and laboratories', 'competent chemists, electricians and engineers would be forthcoming in sufficient numbers' to satisfy the enlarged demand, and 'institutions for the teaching and advancement of knowledge would be freely founded and liberally endowed'.[100] The attainment of this millenium clearly placed a heavy burden of responsibility on the shoulders of public school science masters!

The Council of the Royal Society followed Huggins' clarion call by appointing a special committee to look more closely into the possibilities for action. In this step they were influenced not least by information that the public schools would welcome advice and assistance in this matter. The membership of the special committee of six included Sir Michael Foster and Professor H.H. Turner, both future Presidents of the APSSM.[101] By January 1904, the results of the Committee's deliberations had been sent to the universities.[102] In a letter, cautiously worded so as not to offend university sensibilities over their autonomy, it was suggested that an expansion and improvement of their tests of preliminary general education, so as to make them correspond with the education, both literary and scientific, which a student matriculating at the age of 19 years should be expected to have acquired, would have a beneficial influence on the schools. Beyond this exhortation, the Royal Society could not act further and responsibility was passed to individual universities. The essence of the committee's report, that a broad general education, comprising both literary and scientific studies, should be required of all university entrants, was a prominent theme of Huggins' final address as President of the Royal Society in November 1905.[103]

It is a matter of record that individual universities did not feel able to move far in the direction advocated. The competition for entrance scholarships to Oxford and Cambridge remained both severe and a dominant influence on the organization of the school curriculum. Additionally, the entrance requirements for work in particular fields of science became increasingly specialised. Laments about too early specialisation in school studies, or, as Huggins expressed it, 'science students careless of literary form, and classical students ignorant of scientific method',[104] were to be a persistent refrain in the years ahead.

The significance of Huggins' remarks, however, representing as they did a widely held view amongst scientists, was that a congruence had been established between the objectives of the APSSM and the most powerful association of scientists in the land. The Royal Society, primarily concerned with the conditions necessary for the advancement of scientific inquiry, saw the necessity for fostering a more hospitable attitude to science amongst the nation's political and industrial leaders. As these persons were drawn predominantly from those educated in public schools, the improvement of science teaching in such schools became a matter of prime importance. Furthermore, the intended outcomes of this science teaching, the training of intellectual faculties – 'the constant control of inferential conclusions by the unbending facts of direct experiment'[105] – leading to 'the habit of reasoning correctly from the observations', were the same for both educationalists and scientists.[106] So defined, the interests of teaching and research were coincident.

At the time of its formation, the APSSM was a limited association of able, and predominantly young, men, closely knit in respect of educational backgrounds and social class, and bonded by affiliation to a frequently disparaged – at best tolerated – school subject. By concentrating on limited educational objectives, avoiding trade union concerns, and assimilating its interests to those of external and powerful groups such as the Royal Society, it was able to achieve over two decades a controlled growth in both membership and occupational authority. Its opinion on science teaching matters was being sought, either through formal or informal channels – by Board of Education officials, Civil Service Commissioners responsible for the Army entrance examinations, Oxford and Cambridge entrance examiners, the Headmasters' Conference Curriculum Committee and Joint Standing Committee with the Association of Preparatory Schools, officials of the Oxford and Cambridge Joint Examinations Board, and other bodies. By 1919, a secure foundation for expansion had been laid.

2 The Association of Science Teachers

Science teaching in girls' secondary schools at the opening of the twentieth century

The struggle to increase the opportunities in higher education available to women in the second half of the nineteenth century, and the rapid growth, during that period and in the early years of the twentieth century, of schools offering secondary education for girls, are well documented themes in the recent history of English education.[1]

Although women were not eligible to receive degrees at the University of Cambridge until 1948, admission as of right to the tripos examinations was granted in 1881. In the thirty-year period which followed this 'act of grace', 309 women were classified in Part 1 of the Natural Sciences Tripos and 86 in Part 2. It has been estimated that more than 400 women read science at Cambridge between 1850 and 1914 and, of those who took the Natural Sciences Tripos, over 54 per cent entered the teaching profession.[2] At Oxford, where from 1884 the final honours schools of Mathematics and Natural Science had been open to women, again without eligibility to proceed to a degree, the numbers studying these subjects were fewer. The *Oxford Historical Register* printed a class list for women from 1893 only; in the seven years to the turn of the century, some 21 women were examined in Natural Science. At London, where from 1880 all degrees had been open to women, 55 had been awarded honours in science and 10 had received the doctorate by 1900. In the newer, provincial universities, chartered in the early years of the twentieth century, women were, from the first, admitted to degrees on the strictest equality with men.

Turning to secondary education, there were in the mid-nineteenth century no schools for girls comparable in tradition and prestige to the great public schools for boys. Subsequently, through the activities of bodies such as the Endowed Schools Commission (1869), the Girls' Public Day School Company (1872) and the Church School Company (1883), considerable progress was made in the establishment of 'high schools'. Girls were admitted to the Oxford Local Examinations in 1870 and to the examinations of the Oxford and Cambridge Joint Board in 1877. By the turn of the century, knowledge was no more 'a fountain sealed' to the daughters of the neglected middle classes. With the passing of the 1902 Education Act, whereby responsibility for the provision of secondary education was vested in the newly created local authorities, a further rapid expansion took place (Table 2.1).

The most appropriate curriculum to be offered in these schools was

Table 2.1   Grant-aided secondary schools for girls (England and Wales)[3]

	1904–5	1907–8	1913–14	1921–2
Number of schools	99	262	349	450
Number of pupils	33,519	63,617	87,650	176,207

the subject of debate throughout the period under review. In so far as the education of girls had general traditions on which to draw, these were characterised by 'inattention to rudiments' and 'undue attention to accomplishments, and those not taught intelligently or in any scientific manner'. So the Endowed Schools Commissioners reported in 1867.[4] It therefore required a major transition to reach the situation described in 1911 by Sara Burstall, Head Mistress of Manchester High School, in which increasing numbers of girls, at low fees were able to receive 'a sound and publicly guaranteed training, leading to business and professional life and the universities.'[5]

The case for this change was made in various terms, but at the pragmatic level 'the enormous number of unmarried women in the middle class who have to earn their own bread, . . . the great drain of the male population of this country for the army, for India, and for the Colonies . . . (and not least) the expensiveness of living here, and consequent lateness of marriage'[6] were all factors which contributed to a revolution in the education of girls from middle-class families. The Endowed Schools Commissioners, at least, were also clear that there was 'weighty evidence to the effect that the essential capacity for learning is the same, or nearly the same, in the two sexes'![7]

The rapid growth of new schools, largely uninhibited by academic traditions, yielded a rich diversity of curricula. Nothing comparable to the dominance of classics in boys' schools constrained innovation; whilst, in the specific field of science teaching, the regulations of the Science and Art Department had never influenced the education of girls to the same extent as that of boys. At one extreme, as J.J. Thomson's Committee on 'The Position of Natural Science in the Educational System' reported in 1918, there were many private schools for girls in which science was altogether omitted from the curriculum.[8] In other schools because of priority assigned to ends such as 'the cultivation of the sense and love of beauty', 'training in the manifold ways of expression' and 'preparation of girls for their duties to home, community and state',[9] natural science occupied a relatively minor place on the timetable compared with languages, literature, the arts and domestic studies. Even amongst those schools in which science had an established and prominent place, there was frequent disagreement about the form it should take. The competing educational claims of nature study, botany, physiology, chemistry, physics and domestic science were familiar topics at conferences of women science teachers and headmistresses. Equally contentious was the question of teaching method. As one progressive female advocate of the heuristic teaching of physics assessed the situation in 1900, 'at present the teaching of science is in a state of healthy chaos'.[10]

It might be thought that in the more closely-supervised grant-aided secondary schools, the situation would be less confused. Not only had the 1904 Regulations, issued by the Board of Education, specified the outlines of an approved course of secondary education, extending over at least four years, but they required also that science should be allotted at least three hours per week and that the teaching should include practical work by the pupils. Nevertheless, even here, girls' schools encountered difficulties. The tendency of many girls to terminate their education by the age of sixteen meant that time had to be found in the general course for those domestic and craft studies which would prepare them for their future role as home builders. Similarly, the relatively undeveloped state of advanced work, preparatory to higher education, in many of the newly-established municipal and county secondary schools, did not encourage a view of the general course up to sixteen as a broad foundation for further studies. This contrasted with the situation in the older high schools where a leaving age of eighteen or nineteen was not uncommon.

After one year's working with the Regulations, the Association of Head Mistresses sent a deputation to the Board of Education to petition against the requirement of three hours of science per week, the prospect of this for four successive years being unacceptable in many girls' schools.[11] Subsequently, the regulations were modified to permit the substitution of an approved course in domestic subjects in place of science for girls over the age of fifteen.[12]

Even so, problems remained in regard to the functions of secondary schools for girls and the most effective curricular organisation. During her term of office (1907–9) as President of the Association of Head Mistresses, Mrs Eliza Woodhouse (Clapham High School) initiated a survey of the curricula of schools in the Association. Detailed information was collected by questionnaire from 23 representative schools. Analysis of the results by the Association's Curriculum Sub-Committee led to the publication in 1911 of a comprehensive report, *Public Schools for Girls*.[13] In an informative chapter on the teaching of natural science, Dr Sophie Bryant, Head Mistress of the North London Collegiate School, concluded that 'schemes of study abound and criticisms of these schemes abound likewise.'[14] As guiding principles of science curriculum design, the practical interests of the girls and the logical development of the subject appeared to conflict. The priorities of school mistresses, immersed in the business of educating 'average girls', were not always congruent with those of university and other teachers concerned with the systematic development of the knowledge of selected pupils.

The possibility of offering different curricula for 'the college girl' and 'the non-college girl' had been explored in her presidential address to the Association by Mrs Woodhouse in 1909. Related to this was the criticism by headmistresses that existing examination sylla-buses in chemistry and physics were too abstract, with no direct relation to the life which most girls would lead. Applied science, indeed domestic science, was what was needed here and a resolution to this effect was passed.[15]

The issues of whether existing science courses should be replaced by courses in domestic science; modified to include more illustrations of scientific principles applied to everyday life; or supplemented, by making practical housecraft a basic subject of general education, were hotly debated throughout the early years of the new century. A Department of Home Science and Economics was opened at King's College for Women, London, in 1908[16] and influential figures from the world of university science, notably Professor Arthur Smithells of Leeds University, lent their support to the development of courses of domestic science at university as well as school level.[17] Others, such as the four women science and mathematics tutors from Girton and Newnham Colleges, Cambridge, concerned that the scientific educa-tion of girls should in no way be inferior to that of boys, argued the case for physics, pure and unshorn of any of its mathematical aspects, as the basis of the school science curriculum for girls.[18] One of this quartet, Ida Freund, was to be a particularly severe critic of the academic standards associated with courses of domestic science.[19]

In June 1909, the Board of Education referred the question of the place of domestic studies in the education of girls in secondary schools to its Consultative Committee. After the examination of 52 witnesses and deliberations over a period of four years, this body returned an inconclusive report on the extent to which the teaching of physics and chemistry should be modified so as to form the basis of a scientific study of housecraft. Whilst acknowledging that the case was by no means closed, the Committee did, however, conclude that the teaching of the domestic arts should be preceded by at least two years' teaching of pure science. It was at this critical stage in the shaping of the curriculum that the need for association was especially felt amongst those mistresses engaged in the teaching of science.

The Association of Science Teachers

The Association of Assistant Mistresses in Public Secondary Schools originated in 1884 at a meeting presided over by Mrs Henry Fawcett, one of the leading spirits in the movement for the education of women at Cambridge[20] Any initial sentiment that gentility forbade an active interest in conditions of service was quickly overcome, and the Association entered the twentieth century as a business-like guardian of the professional and pecuniary status of the assistant mistresses. By 1915 the number of members had risen to 1689[21] and the Association had established branches to facilitate the exchange of ideas and information on a regional basis.

The programmes of the Association's Annual General Meeting, held in January, contain frequent references to the curriculum of secondary schools for girls. At the 1908 meeting, most of the morning was devoted to a discussion on a series of resolutions drawn up by the Executive Committee with a view to formulating policy on the general principles of curriculum design.[22] The following year, two papers dealt with the specific issue of science teaching. The first by Miss C.L. Laurie (Cheltenham Ladies' College) stressed the aim of mental training in scientific method, whilst the second, by Miss M. Wood (Leeds Girls' High School), described an attempt to put into practice the ideas of Professor Arthur Smithells on the correlation of domestic and physical science.[23]

At regional level, the teaching of science was of particular concern to a group of mistresses in the London area, to the extent that a Science Section of the London Branch of the AAM was formed at the autumn meeting in 1909. Membership of the section was open to any teacher who became a member of the London Branch of the AAM.[24]

No records of the activities of the Science Section have been traced, the archives of the Association having suffered extensive damage from bombing during the Second World War. It is clear, however, that the Science Section of the London Branch exerted a considerable influence on the formation of Association policy, particularly in relation to the parity of the curriculum provided in girls' secondary schools with that in boys'. The President of the AAM in 1910 and 1911 was Miss Edith Sarah Lees, science mistress at Clapham High School and a leading figure in the future Association of Science Teachers. In 1910 she represented the AAM on the sub-committee appointed by the London University Extension Board to consider 'the question of domestic science', emphasising that, though a closer connection between school and home life was desirable, the Association was anxious that nothing should interfere with the established and efficient science courses then provided in girls' schools.[25] The following year, in her presidential address, she was quite explicit that science teaching should not be made subsidiary to other subjects. The order, system and continuity of development of the subject, so necessary for mental training, were lost when science was made subservient to housecraft or domestic science. If needed, these studies should be offered separately as practical 'extras' and 'not under the name of education'.[26]

By the autumn of 1911 sufficient interest had been shown in the activities of the Science Section for the members to consider forming a larger Science Teachers' Association, open not just to London members but to any past or present teacher of science in a public secondary school or any science lecturer in a women's college.[27] An inaugural general meeting was publicised for November 1912 with an address by Professor H.E. Armstrong on 'Science befitting girls' as a special attraction. Those wishing to join the new body were requested to send a subscription of five shillings to the Honorary Secretary,

Miss I.H. Jackson, Godolphin and Latymer School, Hammersmith.[28]

The objectives of the new Association, as formulated by the inaugural committee in July 1912, were fivefold:[29]

1   To afford opportunities for intercourse and cooperation among those interested in the teaching of science.
2   To provide an authoritative medium through which the opinions of science teachers may be expressed on educational questions.
3   To discuss methods of teaching science and the correlation of school and university work.
4   To bring science teachers into contact with those who are engaged in research work.
5   To co-operate with other Associations for special correlation of subjects.

Apart from the addition of a sixth objective

6   Generally to improve the teaching of science

and the deletion of 'for special correlation of subjects' in 5, these objectives remained unchanged throughout the life of the AST and its successor from 1922, the Association of Women Science Teachers.[30]

In comparison with the objects of the APSSM, those formulated by the AST were both less assertive in relation to the place of science in the school curriculum, and more expansive in relation to the contacts and cooperation deemed necessary for the effective teaching of science. The public school men taught in establishments in which there was no general recognition of the principle that science should form an essential part of secondary education. Within the 'grant-aided' and 'recognised efficient' sector of secondary education for girls the situation was different in that science had a secure, if limited, place in the core curriculum. The 'promotion' of science teaching, then, was not a prime objective of the women science teachers as it was of the public school masters.

Each association recognised the need for improved means of communication both between individual school teachers of science and between teachers of science in schools and universities. However, the men were severely specific in restricting their named avenues of communication to 'others engaged in teaching Natural Science elsewhere' and 'Examining Bodies'; in contrast the women planned to discourse not only with more groups but with more broadly-defined ones. 'Those interested in the teaching of science', not only those actually teaching it; 'those engaged in research work' – a category to which the men made no direct reference; and 'other Associations' of subject specialists, without limit, all fell within the communication ambit of the women. Apart from cooperation with the Mathematical

Association, the APSSM sought no involvement in the activities of other associations of subject teachers, declining invitations to hold its annual meeting in connection with the Conference of Educational Associations.[31] Eschewing insularity, the women from the outset, and throughout the life of the AST, met under the Conference umbrella. For them, the correlation of subjects embraced not only science and mathematics, but even more urgently, the relation of science and domestic subjects.

Interestingly, there was no reference in the objectives of the AST to the need for communication with examination boards, and the Association's activity in this field did not become significant until proposals for the introduction of the School Certificate Examinations were under discussion some years later. The problem of keeping abreast of new advances in scientific knowledge was, however, a major concern of the women teachers. Indeed, both the initial professional training and the in-service training of science teachers were matters taken more seriously by the women than by the men. One of the earliest sub-committees of the new Association was formed to investigate and report on the facilities for training women science graduates for teaching.

Membership

As the record of the first general meeting of the Association of Science Teachers makes clear, the original impetus for founding a national organization of women science teachers came from a recognition that science teaching in their schools was 'passing through a critical period' and that 'it was well for science teachers to band themselves together as a corporate whole, and not to have their influence weakened by votes of members who are not, and have not been, engaged in science teaching.'[32]

Separation from the parent Association of Assistant Mistresses followed, the nucleus of London women science teachers providing six members for a committee which drafted proposals, circulated these to secondary schools in January 1912 and drew up the first list of members, 103 in all, by March 1912.

Of the six, the most senior was Miss Edith Sarah Lees, science mistress at Clapham High School since 1892. Privately educated before going herself as a pupil to Clapham and then on to University College London, she had not taken a degree. Her reputation as a science teacher was, nevertheless, considerable[33] and her situation at Clapham High School, a Girls' Public Day School Trust foundation (1882), had provided first-hand experience of the problems of relating science and domestic subjects.

During the early years of the century, HMIs inspecting GPDST schools criticised their curricula for lacking courses in housewifery or similar subjects intended to prepare girls for domestic life.[34] Initially, the Council of the Trust had resisted pressure for the inclusion of such courses, yielding eventually to the extent of instituting in a number of their schools 'a one-year post-scholastic course' in domestic economy to be taken by girls aged seventeen and over, after the acquisition of a sound foundation of physics and chemistry. Such was the case at Clapham where, in addition, arising from a strong commitment to the professional training of teachers, an associated training college with a noted domestic science department had been established in 1900. Details of the Clapham High School science syllabus and the scheme leading to the 'Elementary Housewife's Certificate' were included by the Board of Education's Consultative Committee in its report on Practical Work in Secondary Schools and Miss Lees, in her evidence to the Consultative Committee, was at pains to emphasise that pure science, for the mental training it provided – elementary physics first, then chemistry – should be a component in the curriculum of all girls before they embarked on any course of housecraft.[35]

Of the other members of the London sextet, three had taken the Natural Sciences Tripos at Cambridge, Miss I.H. Jackson (Godolphin and Latymer School) and Miss Y.C. Raymond (St Paul's Girls' School) being contemporaries in the class list of 1893, whilst Miss R.F. Shove (County Secondary School, Peckham and shortly to move to the GPDST high school at Notting Hill) was examined in 1899. The two remaining science teachers, Miss K. Jeffries Davis and Miss Rose Stern had graduated at London University. Miss Davis taught at Croydon High School, another GPDST foundation (1874) and Miss Stern, a chemist, at the North London Collegiate School under the headship of Dr Sophie Bryant. All were unmarried and remained so. At the time of the formation of the AST their average age was around 40.[36]

Once the new Association was in existence it became desirable to appoint a more representative committee drawing in schools from the provinces. A new committee, elected in June 1912, retained the services of Miss Lees, Miss Stern and Miss Jackson but brought in three newcomers, all younger and more recently qualified. The first, Miss I.M. Oakden, educated at Cheltenham Ladies' College and, from 1905, on the teaching staff of her old school, was a zoologist who had taken the Natural Sciences Tripos at Cambridge in 1904, and the Cambridge Teaching Certificate the following year. Like a number of women who had passed the examinations qualifying for a degree at Oxford or Cambridge she had taken advantage of the regulations then in force at Trinity College, Dublin, to acquire an *ad eundem* degree of that institution.[37] The second, Miss K.M. Mitchener, an old girl of Dulwich High School (GPDST 1878) and subsequently a student at Royal Holloway College and the University of Oxford, had taken the examinations for Honours Moderation in Mathematics at Oxford, achieving a Class 2 in 1899. A member of the Mathematical Association, she had been on the staff of Christ's Hospital, Hertford since 1905 teaching physics and mathematics. The final (and youngest) member, Miss D.B. Pearson, with a first in both parts of the Natural Sciences Tripos, was a physicist who had joined the staff of Miss Stern's old School, King Edward VI High School, Birmingham.[38]

Like its predecessor, the new committee was characterised by membership from schools which had a strong commitment to the intellectual education of girls. In terms of subject allegiances the physical sciences, through Lees, Mitchener, Pearson and Stern, were at least as strongly represented as the biological ones. At this stage the committee did not include any members from the new municipal or county secondary grammar schools for girls. Acquaintance through previously existing networks, notably the Assistant Mistresses' Association[39] and possibly the women's colleges at Cambridge (Jackson, Oakden and Pearson were all Girtonians), was a significant determinant of the committee's composition.

The conditions of eligibility for membership of the Association were less tightly framed than in the case of the APSSM; indeed the contrast between the exclusiveness of the public school masters' association and the inclusiveness of the women's association was marked. Anyone holding, or who had held, a post of science lecturer or teacher in any college or secondary school was entitled to join the AST on payment of an annual subscription of five shillings.[40] There was no requirement that applicants should be graduates or members of the AAM and no restriction on the type of secondary school in which they served.

The absence of any specific reference to the gender of members, either in the name of the Association, or in the articles governing membership, led to an interesting development early in 1916. At the January committee meeting, it was reported that Mr G.F. Daniell, a member of the APSSM (elected under the provisions for persons who 'had contributed to the advancement of science teaching') and a frequent contributor to *Nature* and other journals on topics connected with the teaching of science, had written to the AST inquiring about the acceptance of male members, and advising that its existence would become more widely known if reports of meetings were published in journals read by scientists and teachers.[41] It was agreed to supply Mr Daniell with an account of the annual meeting then under way, and the February issue of *The Journal of Education* subsequently included a note announcing that the Association was open to men as well as to women.[42]

Whether as a consequence or not is unclear, but at its next meeting the committee had before it a letter from a male teacher of science expressing an interest in joining the Association provided other men joined also. With commendable opportunism, a letter was promptly despatched to Daniell offering him membership, and, on the strength of this, it was agreed to recruit the enquirer and any other members of his sex who might apply.[43] Whilst the number of male members never became large, the APSSM opening its doors in 1918 to any graduate science master in a secondary school, the participation of men in the activities of the AST, especially at branch level, was a notable feature of its work up to 1922.

In at least one other way, the Association demonstrated its openness on the question of membership. An awareness that science was being taught to girls and boys in the 'higher grade' tops of elementary schools and in Central and Polytechnical Schools, particularly in London and Manchester where the Association's membership was strong, led to proposals for the enrolment of science teachers from these schools. Their presence, especially at branch meetings, was thought likely to make discussion of science teaching problems more effective. It was therefore agreed in May 1916, at an extraordinary general meeting convened to revise the Articles of the Association, to delete 'secondary' before 'school', making science teachers in any type of school eligible for ordinary membership.[44] Two years later, motivated by the proposals in H.A.L. Fisher's Education Bill for an extension of full-time education for all up to 14 years of age, with compulsory part-time continuation schooling thereafter, the Association again initiated a drive to recruit teachers of science from elementary schools.

Despite this inclusiveness and heterogeneity, the AST remained a numerically small association, both absolutely and in relative terms, as is seen from the figures for the membership of subject teaching associations.[45]

Table 2.2   *Membership of subject teaching associations*

	AST	APSSM SMA	Mathematical Association	Classical Association	Modern Language Association	Association of Teachers of Domestic Science
1912	120	229	900	1500	1060	1116
1915	130	295	950	1600	1140	1315
1918	200	308	800 (+ associates)	1500	1100	1700
1921	360	600	1100	1800	1300	1870

No mechanism was adopted for the scrutiny of applicants, comparable to that employed by the committee of the APSSM; in general, the AST admitted all who applied. One consequence of this liberality was that the committee was spared those problems arising from the promotion and mobility of members. Another was, that with such diversity, there was an uneven and changing commitment to the objects of the Association, manifested in frequent oversights in the payment of subscriptions.[46] The Association was often in financially straitened circumstances which limited its undertakings and placed an unusually heavy premium on the voluntary efforts of a small coterie of dedicated women members.

As with the APSSM, the Association of Science Teachers sought the involvement in its affairs of distinguished persons who, although not necessarily practising school teachers of science, might assist its work. Dr Sophie Bryant, Head Mistress of the North London Collegiate School, was the first to be elected an honorary member.[47] Protegée of and successor to the celebrated Miss Buss; a gifted teacher of mathematics; the first woman to be awarded the degree of DSc by the University of London; a member of the Senate of that University, of the Technical Education Board and first Education Committee of the London County Council, and of the Board of Education's Consultative Committee; Dr Bryant symbolised what an able woman could achieve in the educational world. A second honorary member was Mrs Hertha Ayrton, wife of the physicist Professor W.E. Ayrton and a distinguished scientific investigator in her own right. Hughes medallist of the Royal Society, Mrs Ayrton was the first woman to read a scientific paper before that body.[48] In the same year, 1913, honorary membership of the AST was conferred on Miss Ethel Sargant FLS, the first woman to serve on the Council of the Linnaean Society and to preside over a section of the British Association for the Advancement of Science.[49] Both Mrs Ayrton and Miss Sargant had been to Girton College, Cambridge, the former taking the Mathematical Tripos in 1881 and the latter the Natural Sciences Tripos in 1884 and 1885.

After the election of this initial triumvirate, the practice of bestowing honorary membership seems to have lapsed until 1920 when Miss C.L. Laurie, the long-serving botany mistress at Cheltenham Ladies' College was elected. The following year, Miss Edith R. Saunders, staff lecturer in botany and director of studies at Newnham College, Cambridge, an ex-President of the AST and one of its most diligent committee members, was similarly honoured. In both cases, election might be seen as a distinction awarded for services rendered to the cause.

In general, the category of 'honorary member' was never as fully utilised by the AST as that of 'non-teaching member' provided for by the rules of the APSSM. Until the early 1920s the AST elections were more in the nature of rewards than functional involvements related to the objects of the Association. To some extent this is a reflection on the Association's inability to formulate its goals as tightly and specifically as the APSSM. On more than one occasion in its early life the AST held inconclusive discussions at general meetings on what its future work should be. There was a certain amount of agreement on the needs of members for vacation courses (which were nevertheless often poorly attended) and for abstracts and reading lists offering guidance to the periodical literature and recently published books on science subjects. But perhaps the most appreciated service to members in these formative years, was the opportunity provided by the Association for friendly intercourse, an exchange of problems and professional experiences, preferably in an agreeable social setting. The summer meeting visits – for which the men had no regular counterpart – were as important as the more business-like January general meetings in London. When in July 1917, 37 members visited the Royal Observatory at Greenwich (the expected 50 did not materialise 'owing to a hostile air raid'), the subsequent report was as fulsome in its praise of tea in the Round Pavilion and the wonderful views of London from the roofs and balconies of the Royal Observatory as of Sir Frank Dyson's astronomical exposition. The spirit is well captured in the minuted account of a journey by members of the London branch, using 'private conveyance', to Charles Darwin's house at Down on a June day some few years later. 'It was a lovely day – we all enjoyed the drive from Charing Cross. We ate lunch in a field and then explored the house and grounds where so many of the famous experiments had been carried out. After tea in the village (1s 3d each) we drove back through the pleasant Kentish lanes.'[50]

Constitution and Officers

Under the Articles of the Association, an Executive Committee was to be elected annually by postal ballot. In addition to the President, Vice-President, Honorary Treasurer and Honorary Secretary, this committee comprised five ordinary members, together with a representative from each branch which had at least twenty science teachers in membership.[51] Ordinary members of the committee could hold office for a period of two years without re-election and could serve for up to four years consecutively.

Throughout the first two years of its existence, the Association was without a President, but Miss Rose Stern, in her capacity as Vice-President, took the chair at the General Meetings held in December 1912 at the London Day Training College and in May 1913 at her old school, King Edward's High School, Birmingham. On this latter occasion, Miss Edith Anne Stoney was elected President for the coming year, in due course delivering her address on 'Some physical problems on Mars' at the London meeting in January 1914. Miss Stoney's father, George Johnstone Stoney FRS, had been Professor of Natural Philosophy at Queen's College, Galway and Secretary of the Queen's University, Dublin until its dissolution; he is perhaps best remembered today as originator of the term 'electron'.[52] A strong advocate of the higher education of women, Stoney had moved to London in 1893 largely to secure improved educational opportunities for his two daughters. He could scarcely have been disappointed by the outcome. Edith Anne, having been placed 17th wrangler in the Mathematical Tripos at Cambridge in 1893, was later appointed Lecturer in Physics at the London School of Medicine for Women. Her sister, Florence Ada, after qualifying as a doctor, practised in London and became head of the electrical department in the New Hospital for Women.[53]

Subsequent Presidents during the remainder of the life of the AST are listed in Table 2.3, with information on the university in which they obtained their higher education, their subject affiliation and institution in which they worked.

Table 2.3   Presidents of the AST

President	Educated at	Subject	Position at time of presidency
1914 Miss E.A. Stoney	Cambridge (Newnham)	Mathematics/Physics	Lecturer in Physics, London School of Medicine for Women
1915 Mrs M.G. Bidder	Cambridge (Girton)	Physiology	Lecturer in Physiology, Girton and Newnham Colleges, Cambridge
1916 Miss I.M. Drummond	Oxford	Zoology	Headmistress, Camden School, London
1917 Miss E.R. Saunders	Cambridge	Physiology	Staff Lecturer in Botany and Director of Studies, Newnham and Girton Colleges, Cambridge
1918 Miss E.R. Saunders	,,	,,	,,
1919 Miss E.S. Lees	London	Physical Science	Science Mistress, Clapham Girls' High School
1920 Dr S. Bryant	London	Mathematics	Headmistress, North London Collegiate School
1921 Miss M.B. Thomas	Cambridge (Newnham)	Chemistry	Director of Studies in Chemistry, Physics and Minerology and Lecturer in Chemistry, Girton College, Cambridge
1922 Miss M.B. Thomas	,,	,,	,,

Mrs Marion Bidder (née Greenwood) and Miss Edith Saunders were for many years in charge of the Balfour laboratory for biological subjects at Cambridge. The former was responsible for physiology and the latter for botany.[54] Both women had read physiology under Sir Michael Foster at Cambridge, Mrs Bidder taking the Natural Sciences Tripos examinations in 1882 and Miss Saunders in 1887 and

Newnham College Staff, 1896

Miss M. Greenwood (as Mrs M. Bidder) was President of the AST in 1915. Miss E.R. Saunders was President of the AST in 1917 and 1918. Miss H.G. Klaassen, Miss Ida Freund and Miss A.B. Collier all wrote about the teaching of science and mathematics for girls. Miss P.G. Fawcett was the first woman to come higher than the senior wrangler in the Mathematical Tripos.

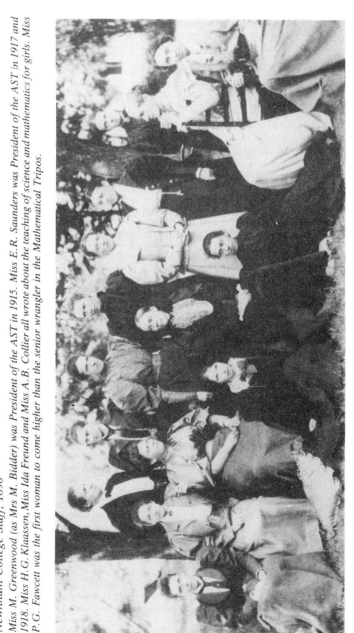

Standing, l to r: E.R. Saunders, H.G. Klaassen, K. Stephen, L. Sheldon, M.E. Rickett, B.A. Clough, A. Gardiner; sitting: A.B. Collier, E.M. Sharpley, I. Freund, M. Greenwood, Mrs Sidgwick, M.J. Tuke, H. Gladstone, P.G. Fawcett.

1888. The other Cambridge President, Miss M. Beatrice Thomas, a former Newnham student of the redoubtable Ida Freund, represented a younger generation and was one of the four Cambridge women science tutors who had argued the case for physics as the fundamental science in the secondary school curriculum for girls.[55]

The Cambridge connection, then, was well established at the level of the Association's highest office, with six out of the nine years of activity being presided over by Cambridge alumni, all but one of whom later became science lecturers in that university.

Of the other three Presidents, the careers of Dr Sophie Bryant and Miss Edith Sarah Lees have already been touched on in a previous section. Miss Isabella M. Drummond, who subsequently achieved a second period of presidential office in 1930 and 1931, was one of the first women to gain first class honours in any science subject at Oxford, where her father was Principal of Manchester College. After a year's research work in zoology, she had taken the Oxford Teaching Diploma in 1902, prior to entering the teaching profession. From 1908 until 1914 she was science mistress under Dr Sophie Bryant at the North London Collegiate School. After three years as headmistress of the related Camden School, another of Miss Buss's foundations, she returned in 1918 to North London Collegiate School, succeeding Dr Bryant as headmistress and remaining there until her retirement in 1940.[56]

In contrast to the APSSM, the AST does not appear to have ever sought for its President a distinguished man from the corridors of scientific power. Perhaps the list of Presidents tells us something of the separate educational worlds of men and women scientists of the day. Awareness of shared problems that had no counterpart in the male–dominated educational and scientific worlds, of a strong bond of sorority arising from participation in a pioneering enterprise, and of a need for the non-patronising encouragement that was derived from exemplars of success, all reinforced a disposition to seek for the highest office of the Association a woman scientist or science educator.

There is also a hint that the Association was not taken too seriously as a body able to influence the course of educational events, despite the credence given to its evidence by the Thomson Committee.[57] Certainly those members of the APSSM who negotiated with the AST committee in 1922 at the time when a possible merger was under discussion had little knowledge of the members with whom they were to deal. In G.H.J. Adlam's assessment of the situation, the AST was 'a weak association that wants to tack itself on to a stronger'. At that stage a combined association was resisted by the men, despite the fact that the meeting did not turn out quite as Adlam had anticipated. 'We expected bluestockings', he wrote. 'What we found was a committee of bright, youngish ladies, quite fashionably dressed'.[58]

Turning now to other offices of the Association, that of Vice-

President was frequently used to retain on the committee a member, usually a Past President, whose services seemed especially valuable. Thus, Miss Edith Saunders, after two years as President, was elected as Vice-President for a similar period.

The honorary treasurer and honorary secretary (secretaries after 1920, when the amount of work necessitated the appointment of an assistant) were almost invariably drawn from schools in the London area (Table 2.4).

Table 2.4   *Honorary Treasurers and Honorary Secretaries of the AST*

Honorary Treasurer	Honorary Secretaries
1912–14 Miss K.M. Mitchener (Christ's Hospital, Hertford)	1912–14 Miss I.H. Jackson (Godolphin and Latymer School)
1915–16 (information not available)	1915–16 Miss R. Stern (North London Collegiate School)
1917 Miss I.H. Jackson (Godolphin and Latymer School)	1917–19 Miss F. Storr (Streatham County Secondary School)
1918–19 Miss F.M. Heaton (Bedford College for Women)	1920 Miss F.M. Heaton (Bedford College for Women) Miss E. Ridley (Kentish Town County Secondary School)
1920 Mrs J.S. Wilson	
1921–22 Miss I.M. Oakden (Notting Hill High School)	1921 Miss E. Ridley (Kentish Town County Secondary School) Miss M. Mortimer (Camden School for Girls) 1922 Miss E. Ridley (Kentish Town County Secondary School) Miss D. Carruthers (Raine's Foundation School)

No doubt ease of attendance at committee meetings was an important consideration in the appointment of Association officers, but what is also evident in the above list is the continued influence on the AST of its parent body, the science section of the London branch of the Association of Assistant Mistresses.

Within the AAM at this period the London branch contributed over 25 per cent of the total membership and the percentage of London members in the AST was even higher. In 1921, out of a total of 360 members, 115 came from schools in the London area. Apart from the representatives of branches of the AST outside London, of 29 women who served on the AST Executive Committee between 1912 and 1922, only nine came from outside London, one each from

Birmingham, King Edward's High School; Brighton, Roedean School; Brighton, Municipal Training College; Cheltenham Ladies' College; Hertford, Christ's Hospital; Northampton School for Girls; and three from Cambridge University.[59] Furthermore, although there was no case of a school providing continuous membership, as did Eton and Harrow on the APSSM committee, a number of schools stand out. Clapham High School, through Miss Lees, was represented on the committee for seven out of the eleven years of its existence. North London Collegiate School through Miss Stern achieved representation for five years: if Miss Drummond and Dr Bryant can be included as North Londoners – though for two of her three years service Miss Drummond was head of the Camden School and Dr Bryant was recently retired at the time of her presidency – the North London Collegiate School representation exceeds that of Clapham High School. Of schools outside London, Cheltenham Ladies' College, through Miss Oakden, was represented for four of the earlier years in the life of the AST. When Miss Oakden returned to the committee as Treasurer in 1921 and 1922 it was in her capacity as a member of staff of Notting Hill High School, an institution she was shortly to head.

One final point about the Association's officers concerns the involvement of lecturers and researchers from institutions of higher education. Each of the three Presidents from the University of Cambridge – Mrs Bidder, Miss Saunders and Miss Thomas – continued their association after the expiry of their term of office by accepting membership of the Executive Committee, contributing in all twelve years of service. From London University, the AST recruited Dr E.M. Delf, lecturer in botany at Westfield College and a former student of Edith Saunders at Cambridge, where she had taken a first class in both parts of the Natural Sciences Tripos.[60] A second London University member was Miss F.M. Heaton, Bedford College for Women, a committee member for five years, including two as Treasurer and one as Secretary. Prior to her appointment to the Training Department at Bedford College in 1910, Miss Heaton had been on the staff of Stockwell Training College. Further indication of the interest which the women science teachers showed in the training of teachers is seen in the election to the Executive Committee (for periods totalling four years) of Miss H.J. Hartle of the Brighton Municipal Training College. Yet another committee member engaged in teacher training was Miss R.F. Shove, one of two science teaching sisters. In 1917, after one year's service, Miss Shove moved from Notting Hill High School to a post of science tutor in the Leeds University Department of Education, resigning her committee membership at the same time, presumably because of the difficulty in attending meetings in London. Some short time later she was to be a crucial link with the committee of the AST when a Yorkshire Association of men and women science teachers was established in an act of independence designed to liberate those north of the Trent from the apparent thraldom of the southern dominated SMA and the AWST.

Branches

Reference to the Yorkshire Natural Science Association leads naturally to a consideration of regional activities. From the first, and unlike the APSSM, the constitution of the AST provided for the formation of branches, the first of which was the science section of the London branch of the AAM, by 1913 formally retitled the London branch of the AST. At the General Meeting of the Association held at London University in January 1914, Mrs A.R.M. Jewel Pearce (Dulwich High School), the Honorary Secretary of the London branch (which then had twenty-two members), presented a report of its year's work.

Constitutionally, the London branch was, in effect, almost identical with the AST. A President and Secretary were elected annually, and the business of the branch was managed by an Executive Committee of the officers together with three elected ordinary members.[61] No Treasurer was deemed necessary at this stage, the expenses of the branch being met by a subvention of one shilling per member from the funds of the parent Association. It was agreed that at least three meetings of the branch should be held each year, including an annual business meeting.

For the first three years of its life, Miss Stern (North London Collegiate School) presided over the activities of the branch, as she had over the early years of the main Association. In 1916, Miss Heaton succeeded her and in 1918 Mrs Jewel Pearce, having the previous year relinquished her duties as Honorary Secretary, was elected President.

By 1920 membership had grown to over a hundred, although a change in the financing of branch activities in 1918 led to some fluctuations in the growth curve. As part of a general revision of the constitution, it was agreed in July 1918 that the payment from central funds to each branch of one shilling per member should be discontinued and that a small branch subscription should be levied, the precise sum to be determined locally. The effect of this on the London branch membership was dramatic as the minutes of the annual business meeting recorded in March 1919 show. When no extra subscription had been required the number of members of the main Association who had expressed a wish to be members of the London branch was 168; following the introduction of a separate branch subscription, only 85 shillings, representing 85 members, had been received in 1918.[62]

This considerable interest, prior to 1919, in the work of the London branch – the total of 168 potential members being almost 85 per cent of the membership (200) of the AST at this stage – can be taken as an indication both of the geographical distribution of the Association's members and of the perceived relevance and attractiveness of the London branch's activities.

On the first point, no full list of AST members at this period appears to have survived, the earliest existing printed list being that for the Association of Women Science Teachers in 1926. However, of the 465 members at that date, almost 200 were in London, or within easy travelling distance of the metropolis. At an earlier period, when the Association's existence and activities were less well known in the provinces, the proportion of metropolitan members could have been even higher. The next most heavily represented region was the north-west, including Manchester, Liverpool and their environs. Approximately one-tenth of the membership came from schools and colleges in that vicinity.

On the second point, the programme of the London branch included regular excursions and visits to places of interest to science teachers, such as the glass works of Baird and Tatlock at Walthamstow in 1916, and the Royal Botanic Society Gardens in the summer of 1918. Such occasions had a distinctly social, as well as an instructional, aspect, as has already been noted in connection with the visit to Charles Darwin's house.

However, papers on more directly educational topics were also a feature of the programme and it is of interest to contrast the issues selected by the women science teachers as being important, with those included in the APSSM programmes. 'Science for backward girls', 'The training of science teachers', 'The correlation of science and geography', 'Experimental psychology', 'Reasons for the present shortage of women science teachers' and 'Hobbies and what they may lead to' were topics which led to lively discussion in the first five years of the London branch's existence. Over the same period, a representative sample of topics from the APSSM programmes included: 'Qualitative analysis', 'The teaching of mechanics', 'Practical examinations in science', 'The relative educational values of physics, chemistry and biology' and 'Science for military purposes'. It is true that on one occasion, in 1912, the public school masters heard a short paper from Archer Vassall on educational psychology and that this was seen by a few of those present as a welcome departure from the usual preoccupations with scientific subject matter and laboratory apparatus. However, this proved to be an isolated occasion; the men were rarely as pupil-orientated and theoretical in their concerns as the women.

The reasons for this difference can only be speculated on, but might include the closer association of the science masters with the community of university and research scientists, on the one hand, and the interest of the women in the training of teachers for both elementary and secondary schools, on the other. Certainly a number of the leading women in the London branch of the AST were involved in teacher training. Miss Heaton (Bedford College) had been a major contributor to the discussion on this topic in 1915, and it was her colleague, Miss Edgell, who delivered a paper on educational psychology the following year. Similarly, it was Miss Rickard of the Maria Grey Training College who opened the discussion on the correlation of science and geography teaching. Miss Wilkins (St Mary's College) and Dr Reaney (Furzedown Training College) were elected members of the branch committee, the latter reading a paper in 1920 on 'The biological significance of play'.

In assessing the influence of teacher training concerns on the selection of topics for discussion by the members of the London branch, it has to be borne in mind that not only was London well supplied with colleges, but many of the leading high schools for girls at this time had secondary training departments or provided schemes of training for university teaching diplomas. Such was the case at Blackheath High School, Clapham High School, Croydon High School, Notting Hill High School, Streatham High School and North London Collegiate School, from all of which officers and active members of the London branch were recruited.

By the end of 1915 a second branch of the AST had been formed in the north-west,[63] followed by a Midlands branch in 1918 and a Welsh branch in 1921. However, attempts to found a branch based on Yorkshire and the North-East did not progress smoothly. As early as the summer of 1915, Miss Stern, as Secretary of the AST Executive Committee, had to report that a proposal to constitute a Northern branch had foundered, although it had resulted in the Association gaining several new members.[64] In December 1917 there was further discussion in the committee of the need for a Northern branch; information had been received from Miss Shove, recently appointed to the staff of Leeds University, that a separate Association was favoured by Yorkshire science teachers, a development which the AST committee members were unanimous in wishing to avoid.[65]

Miss Shove was duly invited to address the business meeting in January 1918 on the problems she had encountered in her attempts to establish a Yorkshire branch and, in doing so, reported that she had found a strongly-held view that a Yorkshire branch would wish to have a greater degree of control over finance than was possible under the present constitution of the AST. In the lengthy discussion which followed, there was general agreement that the financial position of branches was unsatisfactory, and the grant of one shilling per member quite inadequate. On the other hand, it was recognised that unless the bulk of the present membership subscription was retained by the Executive Committee, the publication of valuable reports which went to all members would be impossible.[66] It was also felt that branches should have formal representation on the Executive Committee though whether as voting members or not was an issue on which the meeting was divided. In the end, a sub-committee of five members, comprising Miss Shove (Leeds), Miss McMechan (Liverpool and the North-West branch), Miss Schooley (Northampton and the Midlands branch), Miss Laurie (Cheltenham) and Miss Beard (Bradford), together with the officers of the Association, was appointed to consider the whole question and frame recommendations.[67]

The amendments of the constitution proposed by this group were approved by the General Meeting of the AST in July 1918. In effect, branches were given a greater degree of autonomy in the control of their affairs, and their relationship to the main body of the Association was more precisely defined. In particular, they were permitted to charge a local subscription to cover branch expenses, the grant of one shilling from central funds being discontinued. They were further empowered to elect as 'associates' those who were not eligible for membership of the AST, although these 'associate members' had no voting rights.[68] Finally, each branch with at least 20 members was entitled to elect from its members a representative to serve on the Executive Committee of the Association.

Despite these changes, the AST did not acquire a Yorkshire (or Northern) branch at this time. Plans were already well advanced for the establishment of a separate Yorkshire Natural Science Association, modelled on the lines of the Mathematical and Classical Associations. Whilst catering for the needs of school science teachers, it also brought together members from universities, industry and the general public. The objects of the Yorkshire Natural Science Association, approved at its Annual General Meeting at Leeds University on 23rd November 1918 were:

(i)   To afford opportunities for intercourse and cooperation amongst those interested in natural science (chemistry, physics, botany, zoology, and other natural sciences).

(ii) To discuss the teaching of science in all its bearings.

(iii) To discuss modern developments in science and the applications of science to industry.

(iv) To arrange for visits to places of scientific interest.

(v)   To afford a medium for the formulation of collective opinion upon matters affecting the place of science in the life of the community.[69]

Membership was open to all those interested in the objects of the Association.

For almost a decade the YNSA provided a regional forum for the discussion of science teaching in schools and universities, and, through its lecture programme, contributed to the in-service education of teachers. Its membership of between 100 and 150 men and women overlapped with both the AST and the SMA, Miss Shove of the AST and Fred Fairbrother of the APSSM and SMA being the joint Honorary Secretaries of the new body. Its policy of working towards one national Science Association for men and women teachers of science at all educational levels encouraged the AST in 1920 to explore with the SMA the possibility of union,[70] an opportunity which the SMA felt unable to accept at that stage.

The driving force behind the YNSA was unquestionably Dr Harold

Wager FRS,[71] from 1919 Staff Inspector in the Secondary Branch of the Board of Education and a former member of staff of the Botany Department in the University of Leeds. It was Wager who opened the first discussion of the new Association on the subject of 'The relation between school and university teaching of science' and who served throughout its life as chairman of the Council of the Association. With his death in 1929, the YNSA appears to have come to an end and by the summer of 1930, Miss M.E. Birt, the Secretary of the Association of Women Science Teachers, on the prompting of Miss Shove, was writing to all the women members of the YNSA with an invitation to transfer their allegiance to the AWST.[72]

AST to AWST: relations with the SMA

Three developments which took place in the immediate post-war years brought the Association of Science Teachers into closer relationship with the Science Masters' Association and led, by 1922, to its metamorphosis into the Association of Women Science Teachers.

The first of these has already been touched on, in describing the establishment of the Yorkshire Natural Science Association. At the General Meeting of the AST held in Manchester in the summer of 1920 Miss Heaton [73] and Miss Shove put before the members the suggestion of the YNSA that there should be one National Association representing science teachers in all types of school, and in colleges and universities. The response was sympathetic, the meeting resolving that representatives of the AST, YNSA and SMA should discuss the matter further.

No doubt the case for a concerted voice for science was given point by the recent invitation to the AST to give evidence before the Prime Minister's Committee on the place of Classics in Education.[74] The SMA had been similarly approached and one of their leading members, J.R. Eccles, in his capacity as headmaster of Gresham's School, Holt, and a member of the panel representing the views of the Incorporated Association of Head Masters before the Prime Minister's Committee, had already taken steps to coordinate the evidence of his two organizations.[75] Clearly the danger of self-cancelling opinions was recognised, as was the desirability of a consolidated view representing the interests of science teachers as a whole. Although this did not entail a unified association, it did at least encourage closer cooperation than before.

Whilst a formal meeting of representatives of the three science associations does not appear to have taken place, in the following October, Fairbrother, in his capacity as secretary of the YNSA and member of the SMA, brought before the committee of the SMA a proposal for amalgamation of the three bodies into a single 'National Science Association' on the lines of organizations such as the Classical Association.[76] The general view in the Committee was, however, that the time was not yet ripe. As the minutes record, 'It appeared to be generally felt that much of the success of the SMA (i.e. APSSM) in the past had been due to its having certain well-defined aims and interests, and that it would be unwise to endanger its continued prosperity by extending its interests over so wide and ill-defined a field.' At that stage the Committee was not prepared to support the formation of a national association; clearly its recent step of extending membership to male science graduates in secondary schools other than public schools was regarded as sufficient for the day.

The second development arose from the Board of Education's encouragement, by grant in aid, of advanced coursework in science in the upper forms of secondary schools. The relationship of advanced studies in schools to the work undertaken in the first year of university courses was a matter of concern to both men and women science teachers.

At its inception, the Board of Education's scheme of advanced courses had been strongly criticised, not least because of a fear that 'school universities' would become established; bright pupils from the smaller secondary schools might be creamed off at sixteen to those secondary schools with good facilities for advanced work, which in turn would tend to become 'mere portals to the universities'.[77] Despite these reservations, and related anxieties about the categorising of secondary schools in terms of their ability to offer advanced work, the number of such courses recognised by the Board of Education increased rapidly, especially in science and mathematics (Table 2.5).

Table 2.5   Advanced courses recognised by the Board of Education[78]

	Science and Mathematics	Classics	Modern Studies
1917–1918	76	19	25
1918–1919	140	26	76
1919–1920	171	28	115
1920–1921	193	34	144
1921–1922	206	36	169
1922–1923	205	36	169
1923–1924	207	36	178
1924–1925	212	36	177

It should be added that the subject totals for advanced courses conceal substantial differences in the extent and type of work taking place in boys' schools and girls' schools (Table 2.6).

Both the shortage of women science teachers and the inadequacy of laboratory facilities prevented a more rapid growth of advanced work in science in girls' schools. The situation here underlined the

Table 2.6   *Number of recognised courses: 1924–1925*[79]

	Boys' Schools	Girls' Schools	Mixed Schools
Science & Mathematics	141	37	34
Classics	34	2	—
Modern Studies	50	103	24

need, even more than in boys' schools, for a clear understanding of the relationship between science teaching in the upper forms of secondary schools and in the first year of universities.

One of those in the university world who was known to have expressed views on the need for greater coordination with schools was F.W. Oliver FRS, Professor of Botany at University College London.[80] At a committee meeting of the AST in June 1918 it was agreed that the President, Miss Thomas, should bring the Association to the notice of Oliver and explore with him the possibility of a conference between university and school teachers of science. As a result, the January meeting of the Association in 1919 was largely given over to this topic. Oliver opened the discussion and a supporting point of view was presented by F.E. Weiss FRS, Professor of Botany in the University of Manchester. Both speakers conceded that the failure of universities to recognise the improvements in the teaching of science in schools, where the standard of the Intermediate Examinations was being achieved by many, had led to undesirable repetition of work in universities. Improved opportunities were needed for school and university teachers to exchange views on curricula and teaching methods.[81]

Following discussion, the meeting resolved that a Consultative Council of University and School Teachers be appointed to consider the scope and method of higher work in schools and its relation to the work of universities. The Executive Committee of the AST was empowered to consult with kindred organizations to bring the new Council into being. In fact, an outline proposal for the Council had already been formulated by the Executive Committee of the AST at an 'emergency meeting' in December and this had been put to Oliver for his comment and approval.[82]

On the day following the General Meeting, the committee met again and agreed to invite representatives of the SMA, the Association of Head Mistresses and the Association of Head Masters to a planning meeting in February. On this occasion agreement in principle was reached on the composition of the proposed Consultative Council, the SMA being represented by C.J.L. Wagstaff, Head Master of Haberdasher's School, Hampstead. The following month, when the SMA committee received a report on the developments there was some indication of back-pedalling, at least on the question of who should issue invitations to the various universities. Whilst willing to assist the AST in its endeavours to set up a Consultative Council, the SMA declined to allow its name to be associated with the invitations.[83] Nevertheless, closer links were being forged to the extent that the women resolved to arrange their January meeting on a date as near as possible to that of the SMA, and in answer to their enquiry about the possibility of attendance at the SMA Annual Meeting, the reply came back that they were 'welcome to listen to the discussions'.[84]

The work of the ill-fated Consultative Committee lies outside the present considerations. Never a dynamic body, it lapsed into inactivity after a few years, and was resuscitated in the early 1930s only to expire shortly afterwards from a terminal affliction that had plagued it from the first, namely, a lack of support from the university side.[85]

The third development which helped to forge the link between the AST and the SMA was the decision in July 1918 by the APSSM to publish a journal as a means of keeping its growing membership in touch with recent developments in science teaching. The venture had serious financial implications for the Association and strenuous efforts were made by the editor, G.H.J. Adlam (City of London School) to build up the journal's circulation. To this end 'preferential' terms were offered to AST members, whereby they were supplied with *The School Science Review* at a cost of six shillings per annum, the copies to be supplied in bulk to the secretary of the AST who was to be responsible for distribution, the collection of subscriptions and payment of a lump sum to the treasurer of the SMA. Similar terms were offered to the YNSA.[86]

After a year of this arrangement, Adlam received a request that *The School Science Review* be sent direct to members of the AST rather than to the secretary. His response was to offer a direct distribution to individual subscribers at seven shillings per member per annum, or, alternatively, if all the membership of the AST would subscribe, at five shillings per member per annum.[87] As the latter proposal entailed an increase in the annual subscription of the Association to ten shillings per annum, the matter was brought before the General Meeting of the AST in January 1922. Proposing the adoption of the increased rate of subscription, the President, Miss M.B. Thomas, argued that not only was it desirable that all members should read the journal, but the measure might lead to further cooperation with the SMA.

Not all her audience were as convinced of the merits of the case. It was objected that *The School Science Review* catered entirely for science masters and that most of the articles dealt with chemistry and physics, very few being on biological topics. Despite an assurance that Adlam had expressed his willingness to print articles written by members of the AST, the feeling of the meeting was against the proposal until more information had been obtained about the Association's part in the management of the journal.[88] Further discussions were authorized.

In March 1922, the committee received a report of the meeting with Adlam to which reference has already been made above. A full committee of the women, fashionably fur-clad against the cold, had met a shivering Adlam, accompanied by C.L. Bryant (Harrow School), in a room without a fire and with very defective central heating.[89] The suggestion had been made by the men that the name of the AST should appear alongside that of the SMA on the cover of *The School Science Review*. Furthermore, the AST might have a representative on the advisory committee of the journal, in each issue of which there was to be a full-page advertisement giving details of the AST, the terms of membership and the names of its officers and committee members. Notices would be published of the Association's meetings and publications. The prospect of increased membership, resulting from the wide circulation of *The School Science Review*, was held out.

There were, however, two stipulations. First, no question was to be raised about the appointment of the editor, and similarly, none about the contents of the journal. *The School Science Review* was to remain, in Adlam's phrase, 'SMA property'. Furthermore, the science masters took the opportunity to 'stave off'[90] the idea of a combined association, and, at the same time, eliminate possible competition. The SMA proposals were conditional upon the insertion of the word 'women' into the official title of the AST and the rules governing membership being changed so as to exclude men. As the minutes of the AST committee reported, the science masters 'wished to exclude the possibility of a large mixed Association which might rival themselves.'[91]

At the twentieth General Meeting of the AST in July 1922 these proposals were brought before the membership, Miss Thomas being in the chair and 32 members present. It was formally proposed by Miss Hartle (Brighton Training College) 'That the name of the association be changed to the Association of Women Science Teachers' and that the terms of the SMA be accepted. The clinching argument was that, having no organ of its own the AST was still not well known and the step being contemplated would unquestionably strengthen it. The proposal was carried unanimously.[92]

As a gesture of goodwill and because there had been a strong feeling, especially from the Welsh branch, that men should not be debarred from branch membership, it was proposed, and carried with one dissension, that members of the SMA should be eligible for membership of branches of the new AWST.[93]

There remained one final and mildly embarrassing problem, arising from the debarring of male members. The AST had earlier accorded honorary membership to Sir Richard Gregory and Professor F.E. Weiss;[94] it was not clear from the terms of the settlement with the SMA whether their continued association constituted an infringement. To clarify matters, the secretary of the AWST felt obliged to write to the secretary of the SMA whose committee instructed him to reply that 'the inclusion of a few men as honorary members' would not be taken as a breach of the agreement recently entered into.[95] Fortified by this reassurance, the AWST was able to embark with a clear conscience on its next forty years of collaborative, but separate, existence.

3 The Association of Women Science Teachers

As an exclusively female organization of subject teachers, working alongside a male counterpart throughout its life of forty-one years, the AWST was unique. No other major subject teaching association applied a similar restriction on membership as did the two science associations. At least in terms of written constitutions, membership of each of the other associations of subject teachers – Classics, Mathematics, English, History, Modern Language and Geography – was open to men and women equally.

The dual system in science had both strengths and weaknesses. On the one hand, it enabled a distinct expression to be given to the form of science teaching deemed most appropriate to girls; in so far as there was lack of consensus on this, it also offered a private forum for debate, shielded from direct male influences. As the AWST grew in numbers and reputation, it became a focal point to which the Board of Education's Consultative Committee, the Secondary School Examinations Council and the Examination Boards, amongst many other educational agencies, could turn with confidence for informed professional opinion on the scientific education of girls.

At the same time, the organizational and administrative frameworks within which secondary school curricula and examinations were evolving in the twentieth centry increasingly necessitated collaboration between men and women science teachers. The design and implementation of a common core General Science syllabus for secondary schools and the need for improved provision and training of laboratory assistants were typical concerns which drew the two associations into concerted action and evoked, from time to time, speculation about formal amalgamation. On one such occasion, shortly after the passing of the 1944 Education Act, the prospect that the 'two parallel streams might . . . merge to become a single but more powerful river' was held out before readers of *The School Science Review*.[1] At that stage neither partner showed much enthusiasm for the union. For many of the women teachers, the possible advantages of increased efficiency were outweighed by fears that 'the particular friendly atmosphere' and social intimacy which had come to characterize the meetings of the AWST would be lost on amalgamation. This was especially the case with regard to the cherished summer meeting, for which the science masters had no established counterpart.

Membership

As has already been noted, the rule of the AWST governing eligibility for membership was generously framed, admitting any women who held, or had held, 'the post of Science Lecturer, or Science Teacher in any College or School'. No formal obstacle to membership could arise, therefore, on account of age, experience, non-graduate status, type of educational institution, present occupation or nationality. In contrast to the SMA, such flexibility enabled the Association to recruit science teachers from the different types of secondary school which developed during the first half of the twentieth century without any need for revision of its articles. Thus, in 1928 when applications were received from science teachers in central schools, the Executive Committee readily agreed that any qualified teacher of science in such commercially or industrially biased schools satisfied the eligibility requirement.[2] Again, in 1945, when considering the question of applications from science teachers in the newly designated secondary modern and technical high schools, the Executive Committee confirmed that the existing rule already permitted their acceptance as members of the Association.[3]

Nor was a narrow interpretation placed on 'College or School'. The membership list not infrequently included addresses such as The Royal Infirmary, Leicester; Poplar Hospital, East India Dock Road and even The Realist Film Unit, Great Chapel Street, W.1. The secretary's report of 9 May 1948, typical of the period of rapid growth in membership which followed the Second World War, stated that of 138 new members enrolled over the past seven months, twelve were science teachers in secondary modern schools and nine were Sister Tutors, engaged in the education of nurses.[4]

By this date a distinct international dimension had also begun to characterise the membership. Always interested in the possibility of liaison with science teachers in other countries, the Executive Committee in the foundation year of the Association had encouraged its President, Miss Beatrice Thomas (Girton College, Cambridge) to use her links with the International Federation of University Women to establish contacts overseas.[5] Whilst actual recruitment from abroad was slow, several of those who later emigrated to teaching posts in the colonies retained their membership and helped to publicise the work of the Association. By the mid-century, women science teachers from Australia, Ceylon, Germany, Greece, India, New Zealand, Nigeria, Rhodesia, South Africa and Tasmania had been enrolled.

In terms of overall numbers, the AWST grew from a body of under 400 members in 1922 to one of almost 1800 members by 1962 (Table 3.1).[6]

The difficulty of achieving a precise count of members was a recurrent theme in the reports of the secretary to the Executive Committee, reflecting not only a dependence on voluntary efforts for record keeping, at least until 1946, but also a somewhat lackadaisical approach by a sizeable fraction of the membership to the payment of subscriptions. Reminders to backsliders were sent out in batches six times a year and for a while an annual 'Black List' was published in an

Table 3.1   Membership figures (approximate)

1921 (AST)	360	1942	985
1926 (AWST)	460	1946	1226
1928	579	1950	1437
1934	740	1954	1421
1938	900	1958	1607
		1962	1797

effort to shame defaulters into payment.[7]

Allowing for some inaccuracies in the printed membership figures, the picture which emerges is one of steady growth up to the outbreak of war in 1939; thereafter membership declined slightly, followed by a sharp rise in the immediate post-war period up to 1952. In that year the annual subscription was increased from 15 shillings to £1 in an attempt to rejuvenate the finances of the Association which, for some time, had been in delicate health. An immediate consequence was that a larger number of members than usual failed to renew their subscriptions. Coinciding with an increase in retirements and the deaths of some of the founder members,[8] the net effect over the following two years was a drop in membership for the first time in the peace-time life of the Association. The set-back proved to be a temporary one: by 1956 the position had been more than recovered and a further period of buoyant growth extended to the time of amalgamation in 1963.

By that date the composition of the membership contrasted markedly with that in the 1920s. Some differences were due to changed attitudes in society, for example, towards the employment of married women. In 1926, out of a membership of 465 only 10 women (little more than 2 per cent) were married or widowed. By 1949, 121 out of 1376 members (almost 9 per cent) were in this category, whilst by 1962, 20 per cent of the membership of 1797 comprised women science teachers who were or had been married. Other differences reflected the changing educational employment opportunities for women with a scientific training. Thus in 1926 the Association had no members who worked in technical colleges; by 1949, sixteen members were drawn from these institutions, often from the departments of pharmacy and biology. A decade later the number had fallen to eleven out of an enlarged membership of over 1700. As has already been noted, the Association also recruited teachers engaged in the training of nurses. In 1949, fifteen members were on the staff of pre-nursing schools or hospitals.[9]

On the other hand, the Association's links with university members had been progressively weakened. Increasing specialization of scientific studies and a diminution in the proportion of university science posts held by women were factors contributing to a steady decline in the proportion of university women members engaged in scientific research. Although never a large group numerically, 10 out of 465 members (c.2 per cent) in 1926, the original university women scientists had nevertheless exerted a disproportionate influence on the development of the AWST, serving on its Executive Committee, guiding its activities, and providing a direct link with research frontiers. By 1951 they were seen as having 'largely dropped out'[10] and the divorce of school science teaching from scientific work in universities had become a matter of concern to the Association, especially with regard to the teaching of the most able girls.

In contrast, the connection with teacher training institutions, strong at the beginning of its life, was if anything augmented over the years. By 1949, 49 members of the AWST were on the staff of training colleges, including colleges for domestic science teachers. Furthermore, of the thirteen university women members, over half were in Departments of Education, engaged in the training of secondary school science teachers. In all, at this stage, rather more than 4 per cent of the membership was directly involved in the training of teachers.[11]

The bulk of the membership, however, was drawn from schools, but even here the proportions from schools of different types changed over time. In the early years of the Association, approximately 40 per cent of its membership came from GPDST schools and other leading public schools for girls. By the mid-century, this proportion had been halved.

Again, whereas a mere 13 schools (4.3 per cent) out of 299 represented in the Association in 1926 were coeducational, this figure had increased to 11 per cent by 1949. Indeed, by the early 1950s the membership included a small number of women science teachers in boys' schools. The inclusion of representatives from secondary modern schools and, to a lesser extent, from technical and technical/grammar schools likewise increased throughout the 1950s.

Although, from analysis of membership lists, it is difficult to know with certainty when a member was retired from teaching, the large number of members who gave private, as opposed to institutional, addresses lends support to the view that many retained their connection with the Association on retirement. For the large proportion of unmarried women members, the Association's social functions were as important as, and probably indivisible from, its professional ones. The 'cosy intimacy' of the meetings in the early years, and the 'jolliness and earnestness' of later gatherings were much valued by the predominantly spinster membership. There were many whose sentiments were well expressed by Miss Mary Sutton, in her Presidential address to the AWST in February 1951. A member since 1925, in her view the Association was 'quite the nicest body of women I have ever had any contact with, and I value immensely . . . the many friends I have made among its members.'[12]

Finally, it is of interest to look at the geographical distribution of the Association's members. A high proportion of teachers from

London and its surroundings characterized the AWST in its early years. In 1926 London, Middlesex, the South-East (Sussex, Kent, Essex) and the Home Counties (Surrey, Berkshire, Oxfordshire, Buckinghamshire and Hertfordshire) between them provided over 44 per cent of the membership. By 1949, the same localities were providing little more than a third. Next in order of size of membership came Lancashire and Yorkshire with the aggregated women science teachers from Wales some distance behind (Table 3.2).

Table 3.2   Geographical distribution of AWST members

	1926 (N=465)	1949 (N=1376)
London	118 (25.3%)	177 (12.1%)
Lancashire	38 (8.1%)	131 (9.5%)
Yorkshire	37 (7.9%)	120 (8.7%)
Wales	27 (5.8%)	97 (7.0%)

Whilst the rank order of these major contributing localities remained unchanged between 1926 and 1949, the intervening period saw a steady growth in membership in other areas. Thus Scotland, in 1926, contributed a mere six members; two decades later its membership numbered 71. In the same period, the contribution of the South-West (Cornwall, Devon and Somerset) grew from 9 to 49 members and a similar five-fold increase came from the southern counties of Hampshire, Dorset and Wiltshire (10 to 50). The midland counties, notably Warwickshire, collectively provided a strong group of members, which grew from 70 to 218 between 1926 and 1949. The significant feature here was the increase in the membership from the more sparsely populated counties, Bedfordshire, for example, providing 15 members at the later date, compared with two in 1926. By 1949 recruitment had also begun in Northern Ireland and Eire.

Overall, with a four-fold growth in size over a period of forty years, the AWST achieved a markedly more even geographical distribution of its United Kingdom members than had been the case at the time of its origin. With the extension of its work into less populous areas there arose yet another influence which drew together men and women teachers of science. In such circumstances, it was only by collaboration between all teachers of science that local branch activities could be maintained on an economic and effective basis.

Constitution and Officers

Inevitably growth in numbers brought in its wake the need for organisational change, not least in relation to the administration of the Association. Collection of subscriptions, record-keeping, organization of meetings and communication with an enlarged and diversified membership, together with the greater range of educational activities in which the Association engaged, all placed an increasing burden on the small band of officers and committee members.

By 1933, towards the end of a decade of magisterial service as Honorary Secretary by Miss M.E. Birt (St Paul's Girls' School), it had been found necessary to create the office of Assistant Honorary Secretary. Two years later, however, at the annual Business Meeting of the Association in London, January 1935, the President, Miss Annie Jackson (University College of South Wales, Cardiff) was obliged to draw the attention of members to the problem of secretarial work. It was reported that the experiment of having an Assistant Honorary Secretary had not proved entirely satisfactory; the committee now favoured a clear division of secretarial work into three independent areas, namely, correspondence and committee work; production of the annual Report; and arrangements for annual meetings. The Articles of the AWST were duly amended to allow for the annual election of these officers.[13]

By this stage, Miss P.M. Taylor (High School for Girls, Southend-on-Sea), having served for two years as assistant to Miss Birt and succeeded her as Honorary Secretary in 1935, became Honorary General Secretary in 1937 when the tripartite arrangement was implemented. Miss M.W. Sutton (St Martin's High School, Tulse Hill) was elected Honorary Meetings and Membership Secretary and Miss W. Parkinson (King's Norton Secondary School, Birmingham), Honorary Report Secretary. In 1939 Miss N.M. Whitworth (Grammar School for Girls, Southampton) succeeded Miss Parkinson, and the triumvirate of Taylor, Sutton and Whitworth continued to serve until 1944. A further stage of secretarial fission was then reached, with the creation of a separate, though in the event short-lived, office of Honorary Membership Secretary. Miss E.K. Smeeton (Allerton High School, Leeds) assumed the duties relinquished by Miss Sutton, who continued as Honorary Meetings Secretary.[14]

It was now clear, however, that the secretarial work of the Association could no longer be undertaken satisfactorily on the basis of voluntary help alone. Furthermore, the centrifugal tendency of four independent secretarial roles had perhaps reached an undesirable level. A decision about the future was precipitated by the resignation of Miss Taylor in 1944 on her appointment as woman education officer to the Central Council for Health Education.

Shortly before she took up her new duties, Miss Taylor had made clear to the Executive Committee that the amount of secretarial work, even with the present division of labour and the assistance of some paid clerical help, was becoming impossible to manage.[15] Unlike their male counterparts in the SMA, the women had no spouses who could be enlisted as voluntary helpers behind the scenes. With a membership of over 1000, expanding rapidly, some more permanent solution was necessary. Of possibilities discussed, that most favoured by the Committee was an increase of five shillings in the annual subscription to enable the employment of, optimistically, a full-time secretary at a salary of £250 per annum. Miss Taylor was instructed to write to members, seeking their opinion on this development.

Sufficient agreement was indicated in the replies received to justify taking the step. The remaining honorary secretaries having retired from office in October 1944, Miss A. Lennon was appointed as the Association's first paid official, her duties to include all the routine administration of the Association, including the secretarial duties connected with the work of the treasurer. The position of Honorary Treasurer was however retained as a formal office, associated with the production of the annual balance sheet and the signing of cheques.[16]

Even so, before the year was out, the Committee was obliged to authorize Miss Lennon to seek additional clerical help and members were asked to rack their brains for a solution to her problem of overwork by the time of the next meeting.[17]

On that occasion Miss Lennon tendered her resignation. Whatever stratagems the Committee had devised for the redeployment of Miss Lennon's labours were made redundant at a stroke. The resignation was accepted, with expressions of regret, and a sub-committee was appointed to seek a replacement.[18]

Few applications were received for the vacant post and the Committee's deliberations at this time about the relative weights to attach to experience of science teaching as opposed to administrative competence had a slightly academic flavour.[19] In the end, they were fortunate to appoint Miss L.E. Higson, (St Angela's High School, Forest Gate) who combined both qualities, and into the bargain used her own home in London as the Association's office for the next thirteen years.[20] On her retirement from the post of secretary in 1959, Miss Higson was made an Honorary Member of the AWST. On that occasion a former President, Miss W.M. Casswell, recalled the apprehensions felt by the Committee at the time of her appointment in 1946. In replacing the devoted work of Honorary Secretaries by a permanent official it was feared that friendly informal contacts would be 'lost in efficiency'.[21] In the event, the Association's administration was unaffected by any such tensions.

The replacement of four elected honorary secretaries by one permanent and appointed official obviously carried implications for the Articles of the Association. It was agreed that the number of ordinary or honorary members elected to the Committee by the general membership of the Association should be increased from five to eight, no member to serve for more than four consecutive years. With the officers, and branch representatives – the latter numbering seven by 1946 – such an arrangement maintained an Executive Committee of eighteen members plus the secretary.

There is some evidence that it was not always easy to secure the annual election of eight ordinary members at the General Meeting of the Association. Also between 1946 and 1951 the number of branches sending representatives to serve on the Committee increased from seven to eleven. Accordingly when the Articles were revised in 1950 the opportunity was taken to reduce the number of elected ordinary members from eight to four, the Committee retaining power of co-opt if it deemed a person had special experience of value to its work.[22] The general revision at this stage was described to members at the Annual General Meeting in February 1951 as an attempt to make the Articles 'convenient for modern activities and in some place to fit in with joint SMA work'.[23] The former reference was largely to financial matters, not least the reimbursement of legitimate expenses incurred by committee members, and the latter to collaboration with the men at branch level and at the Christmas vacation general meeting.[24] No other significant changes in the formal constitution of the AWST were to take place during the remainder of its life.

A brief word is required about the Association's survival during the difficult years of the Second World War. Under conditions of evacuation, with travel and communication restricted, it was clearly impossible to maintain the normal programme of annual meetings of members. A policy statement from the Executive Committee in December 1939 in effect suspended the constitution, froze the annual subscription at ten shillings (it being the intention to continue the publication of *The School Science Review*, albeit reduced in size), cancelled all full meetings of members until further notice and resolved to conduct the business of the Association by post, with the publication of an Annual Report, Members List and Balance Sheet maintained as usual. The officers, committee members and branch representatives for 1939 were to remain unchanged for the duration of the war. Such corporate activity as the ordinary members could hope to engage in would be at branch level, at the discretion of branch officers.

Even the Executive Committee was denied a meeting for over two years. An attempt to forgather in May 1940 was frustrated by 'the calling back of people to their school bases and to the sudden evacuation of eastern schools',[25] and it was not unitl June 1942 that the Committee was able to convene. In the meantime, the records and files of the AWST were removed to the comparative safety of the midlands, and the responsibility for continuity of action fell to the President, Dr Marie Dawson, and especially the Honorary General Secretary, Miss P.M. Taylor, supported by the other officers. Following the practice adopted by the General Secretary of the SMA, Miss Taylor contributed a series of notes to *The School Science Review*, giving details of the work of the Executive Committee and other AWST activities.[26]

General meetings were resumed with a one-day conference at Cheltenham Ladies' College in July 1942, when it was decided to

Table 3.3   Members of the Executive Committee of the AWST

	1939		1945
President	Dr M. Dawson	President	Miss M.W. Casswell
Vice-President	Miss D. Bailey	Vice-President	Miss D. Bailey
Hon. Treasurer	Miss M.G. Tomkinson	Hon. Treasurer	Miss E.M. Bull
Hon. General Secretary	Miss P.M. Taylor	Secretary	Miss A. Lennon
Hon. Meetings & Membership Secretary	Miss M.W. Sutton	Committee members	Miss M.E. Birt
			Miss K.M. Cobley
Hon. Report Secretary	Miss N.M. Whitworth		Miss A.V. Crawley
			Miss O.R. Game
Committee members	Miss M.E. Birt		Miss F.R.M. Peecoc⬛
	Miss M.W. Casswell		Miss M.W. Sutton
	Miss A.V. Crawley		Miss P.M. Taylor
	Miss E.E.M. Higgins		Miss N.M. Whitwor⬛
	Miss N.G. Mulligan		
Branch Reps: London	Miss F.S. Cook	Branch Reps: London	Miss E.H. Cherry
North Western	Miss D.M. Scott	North Western	Miss H.M. Bowker
North Eastern	Miss E.W. Mercer	North Eastern	Miss E.J. Du Cane
Midland	Miss C.P. Jones	Midland	Miss C.P. Jones
Welsh	Miss M.E. Chapman	Welsh	Miss M.E. John
Northern	Miss E. Biggs	Northern	Miss E. Biggs
Cambridge & District	Mrs McCullagh	Cambridge & District	Dr W. Gladwell

meet again in two years' time. It was not until January 1946, after an interval of seven years, that it was possible to hold a Christmas vacation meeting in London, in accordance with the Articles of the Association.[27] An approach to constitutional normality had already been made, however, by the time of the two-day Annual General Meeting at Birmingham in April of the previous year. The resignations of Dr Marie Dawson as President, after seven years' service, and of Miss Taylor as Honorary General Secretary, after nine years in that capacity, were coincidental with the restitution of the normal process of postal ballot for the election of committee members and with the appointment of a paid secretary. In contrast to several other teachers associations, the AWST never closed down its activities during the war years, although it was obliged to curtail them substantially. Whilst many of the names remained unchanged from 1939, the Executive Committee for 1945, under the leadership of a new President, Miss M.W. Casswell, was designed to move the Association back into the higher gear which a return to peace-time conditions entailed (Table 3.3).

Several times in the life of the AWST attempts were made to separate the office of President from that of Chairman of the Executive Committee, the duties of the President to include the delivery of an address at the Annual General Meeting, but not direct involvement in the administration of the affairs of the Association.[28] An arrangement on these lines was operated with good effect by the Science Masters' Association. It was the experience of the AWST, however, that eminent women scientists were unwilling to accept the invitation to serve as their President.[29] In consequence, the offices of

President of the Association and Chairman of the Executive Committee were invariably held by the same person, who, with the decline in university representation on the Committee, was typically a headmistress or head of a science department at a well-known girls' school.

Such was the case throughout the 1950s and up to the time of amalgamation of the AWST with the SMA, the only exceptions from the time of the outbreak of the second world war being Dr Marie Dawson (1938–44) and Dr Winifred Gladwell (1947–48). The former, educated at the Roan School and Cardiff University College, had carried out botanical research at Cambridge and been awarded the degree of DSc. From 1905 until 1920 she was science mistress at the Cambridge and County Boys' School, her success there as a teacher of botany and zoology leading to an appointment in His Majesty's Inspectorate. Simultaneously to her school teaching in Cambridge she was in charge of the experimental research in Messrs. Chivers' greenhouses.[30] Though formally retired in 1935, Dr Dawson continued to work for the Board of Education until the outbreak of war, by which time she was in her second year of office as President of the AWST, continuing so until 1944.

Dr Gladwell, of the Cambridge Training College for women, for a number of years represented the Cambridge and District Branch of the AWST on the Executive Committee. Her presidency from 1947 to 1948, at a time of increasing concern about the supply of women science teachers, was characterized by a drive for the recruitment of students into science teaching and encouragement to the Association's members to assist new entrants into the profession.

From 1949 until the time of amalgamation with the SMA, the AWST elected presidents all of whom were, or had been, school teachers of science. Of these Miss P.M. Taylor (President 1951–52) apart from her twelve years of secretarial duty, served for a further twelve years as an elected or coopted member of the Executive Committee, and for two years as a Vice-President, in all a total of twenty-eight years. Miss Mary W. Sutton (President 1949–50) likewise, in a variety of capacities including nine years as Meetings and Membership Secretary, contributed seventeen years of service to the Executive Committee. To this must be added a remarkable thirty years continuous membership of the committee of the London Branch of the AWST. Another London member, Miss E. Lois Buckley, with sixteen years' unbroken service at branch level and in all eight years on the national Executive Committee, presided over the Association's activities during the critical years leading up to amalgamation with the SMA in January 1963. As the Minutes of the AWST's final general meeting record, Miss Buckley 'had not spared herself all the year in working for satisfactory conditions for women' and 'the safeguarding of her members' interests' in the new Association for Science Education. In a valedictory act of appreciation, she and her predecessors as President over the past eight years –

Table 3.4   Presidents of the AWST (with institutions at the time of office)

	University	Other	School
1922	Miss M.B. Thomas (Cambridge)		
1923–24	Miss I.W. Kirkaldy (Oxford)		
1925–26			Miss C.M. Taylor (Headmistress, Redlands H.S., Bristol)
1927			(Mrs Morris) Miss E.M. Ridley (Headmistress, High S. Boston, Lincs)
1928–29	Dr E.M. Delf (Westfield College, London)		
1930–31			Miss I.M. Drummond (Headmistress, N. London Coll. S.)
1932–33			Miss M.G. Tomkinson (Beckenham C.S. for Girls)
1934–35	Miss A. Jackson (Cardiff University College)		
1936–37			Miss D. Bailey (Headmistress, Queen Mary S. Lytham)
1938–44		Dr M. Dawson (HMI)	
1945–46			Miss W.M. Casswell (Headmistress, Edgbaston High S. Birmingham)
1947–48		Dr W. Gladwell (Cambridge T. Coll. for Women)	
1949–50			Miss M.W. Sutton (St. Martin's H.S., Tulse Hill)
1951–52		(Ed. Officer, Central Council for Health Education) Miss P.M. Taylor (Girls' High School, Southend-on-Sea)[31]	

	University	Other	School
1953–54			Miss K.M.H. Chapman (Head-mistress, Woodford County H.S.)
1955–56		✿	Miss J.K. Raeburn (Headmistress, Westcliff H.S.)
1957–58			Miss D.M. Scott (Manchester H.S.)
1959–60			Miss M. Going (Headmistress, Edgbaston Church of England College)
1961–62			Miss E.L. Buckley (The Grey Coat Hospital, Westminster)

Miss Going, Miss Scott, Miss Raeburn and Miss Chapman – were elected, en bloc, honorary members of the AWST, so joining other post-war Presidents as recipients of the Association's highest honour.

In recording the extent of voluntary service to the AWST on the part of some of its leading figures, reference must be made to another honorary member, Miss D. Bailey. President from 1936–37, she had been senior science mistress at Southend-on-Sea Girls' High School to Miss P.M. Taylor, when the latter was commencing her teaching career. Subsequently Headmistress of Hulme Grammar School for Girls, Oldham and then of Queen Mary School, Lytham, she contributed seventeen years of service to the Executive Committee of the Association, including nine as Vice-President to Dr Dawson and, later, Miss Casswell, throughout the years of war and into the period of rebuilding which followed. Frequently called upon to deputise for presidents in times of illness or unavoidable absence, she was also chairman of the Association's Reconstruction Sub-Committee which produced the reports on *Science in Post Primary Education* in the mid-forties.

Of the nine post-war Presidents, three (Misses Sutton, Raeburn and Buckley) were London Branch stalwarts, with Miss P.M. Taylor, though living in Essex, and Miss Chapman (Headmistress, Woodford County High School) in effect London-based. Of the others, Miss D.M. Scott (Manchester High School), like Miss Bailey, reflected the AWST's strength in the North-West whilst Miss Going (Edgbaston Church of England College) and Miss Casswell (Edgbaston High School) were representatives of a long tradition of effective science teaching for girls in the Birmingham area. Viewed from the stand-point of science disciplines, the preponderance of Presidents and officers of the Association with biological qualifications is notable.

Branches

The AWST, in its origins a development from local initiative, and throughout its life a promoter of regional activities, commenced existence in 1922 with four branches inherited from the Association of Science Teachers. In addition to the parent London branch, there were formal associations of women science teachers in the North-West, the Midlands and Wales.

By the time of the amalgamation in 1963, the number of branches had increased to fourteen, half of these having come into being in the post-war years. Each branch was required to operate with a constitu-tion approved by the Executive Committee of the AWST and to present a report of its activities to the Annual General Meeting of the Association. From each branch with at least twenty members, an elected representative was entitled to serve on the Executive Committee.

Members of the Science Masters' Association were, from the first, eligible for membership of the AWST branches on payment of the subscription, though a revision of the Articles in 1951 eventually amended the arrangement to one whereby branches were 'empowered to invite to their meetings members of the SMA and other visitors', a fee for attendance being discretionary.[32]

The powers and responsibilities of the branch representatives on the Executive Committee were the subject of periodic discussion in the Association. A substitute was permitted when a representative was not able to attend a meeting, but, on a proposal from the London branch, it was agreed in 1930 that her power to vote was withdrawn unless she 'were voicing a considered opinion of her branch.'[33] A further limitation was imposed some years later that the substitute must have been elected by the branch.[34]

Branch secretaries had prescribed duties in respect of the work of the main Association, notably the recruitment of new members, collection of subscriptions, provision of up-to-date lists of names and addresses, transmission of information about important local happen-ings, and the preparation of an annual report.[35]

The Branch was therefore an important mechanism for ensuring effective communication between the Executive Committee and the membership. However, as the Association grew in numbers and the geographical distribution of its members became more comprehen-sive, the importance of other means of communication, especially the circulation to members of the Annual Report and the holding of the Annual General Meeting and Summer Conference,[36] was underlined. In its early years, essentially an amalgamation of four regional asso-ciations with over 90 per cent of the membership affiliated to a branch, by the outbreak of the Second World War the Association had become a central organization with less than 60 per cent of its membership involved in branch activities.[37] Despite a doubling of the number of branches in the post-war years, this position remained unchanged throughout the remainder of the life of the AWST.

Although each branch was intended to be financially self-supporting, the Executive Committee of the AWST was empowered to make a 'pump-priming' grant to aid a new branch with less than thirty members with its first year of expenditure. No doubt this was a useful incentive to regional association, though it did not save the Oxford branch, established in the mid-20s, from dissolution after only three years. Thereafter, members from the Oxford region seeking branch activities tended to join their Midland colleagues until 1950 when an unofficial South Midland Branch, covering the counties of Berkshire and Oxford, came into being.[38]

New branches did survive and flourish, however, and their origins were varied and diverse. By 1926, as a counterpoise to the strong North-Western Branch across the Pennines, a Yorkshire branch had been formed, entitled, somewhat incongruously, the North-Eastern Branch centred during its early years in Sheffield. The Yorkshire Natural Science Association still catered at that stage for men and women science teachers in Leeds and North Yorkshire. A Northern Branch was also formed in 1926, based on Newcastle-upon-Tyne where some months earlier the first branch of the Science Masters' Association had been established as the North-Eastern Branch.[39]

No further regional initiatives occurred for a decade after which time, when the AWST was paying close attention to the recruitment of new members and following the establishment of an Eastern Counties Branch of the SMA the previous year, a Cambridge and District Branch of the AWST was inaugurated in 1936.[40] Never strong numerically, its work was curtailed by the war. As the Annual Report for 1944–45 recorded, 'until a petrol allowance makes cross country journeys possible', the Cambridge Branch was unable to re-establish its programme of meetings.[41] Some few years after the resumption of activities in October 1945, the branch was host to the main Association on the occasion of the summer meeting in 1950. Although the formation of a Southern Counties Branch was mooted in March 1938 and initial enquiries had suggested strong local support, the outbreak of war forestalled further development.

The immediate post-war years saw a sharp increase in the membership of the AWST and the creation of several new branches. Following the establishment in January 1947 of a Scottish branch of the SMA, a corresponding branch of the AWST was inaugurated in the following October, with Dr Winifred Gladwell, as President, travelling to Edinburgh to address prospective members.[42] At the same time, the large North-Western Branch of some 130 women drawn from Lancashire, Cheshire and parts of North Wales decided that the high cost of railway fares and the time which members were obliged to spend in travel to meetings made necessary its division into two new branches. The smaller fission product, a Liverpool Area Branch, held its first meeting on 4 December 1948, whilst the larger Manchester Area Branch began its activities on 22 January 1949 with a discussion about its constitution and organization.[43]

Stemming from an initiative outside the AWST and reflecting the genesis of its parent association, a Sussex Branch was established in 1949. The seed for this development came from a local panel meeting of the Association of Assistant Mistresses in September 1946. After a lengthy period of gestation, a constitution was drafted in September 1948 and branch meetings commenced the following spring. Though it was called the 'Sussex Branch', the intention was to serve also those in adjoining counties for whom a journey to meetings of the London Branch would be difficult.[44]

There is little evidence that the membership of the London Branch was affected by this development or indeed by one leading to the formation of an Essex Branch in 1954, although a slight and temporary drop in the number of its members was recorded in the early 1950s.

The evolution of the Essex Branch provides an interesting example of a local association arising in response to the changing context of educational activity. A Government White Paper on *Educational Reconstruction*, published in 1943, had recommended the development of secondary education on tripartite lines, a view which was supported by the Norwood Report, published in the same year. Such a position was unacceptable to those who advocated the multilateral or comprehensive school and, in fact, the Education Act of 1944 made no attempt to prescribe the pattern of organization of secondary education, leaving education authorities free to develop secondary schools according to local preferences.

The implications of such organizational changes for the teaching of science were a frequent subject of debate by AWST members. At the Annual General Meeting in April 1944, following a discussion on the science section of the Norwood Report, a resolution was passed to the effect that 'this Association would welcome experiments in combining different types of education in one school'.[45] Related to this, methods of improving liaison with science teachers in elementary, central, secondary modern and technical schools were examined. On one such occasion in October 1943 approving reference was made in the Executive Committee to a newly founded Essex Science Teachers' Association open to teachers from all types of school, both men and women.[46] Again, in January 1946 at the Annual General Meeting, in the course of a discussion on 'Cooperation of science teachers in different types of schools', the example of the Essex Association was commended.

One of the first tasks undertaken by the Essex STA was the publication of a report on *The Content of the Science Curriculum in Post Primary Schools*, largely with the aim of facilitating transfer between different types of secondary school.[47] After some years of activity, the Association died out, leaving a hiatus which was filled in 1954 by the creation of a new local association linked to the two national bodies. With leading officials of both the AWST and the SMA coming from schools in Essex at this time, the opportunity was taken to establish a joint branch of the two Associations, in effect the first formal act of union.[48]

Informally, concerted action had been a characteristic of the activity of most AWST branches throughout, and even before, the post-war period. This was the case not merely in the less populated and more geographically isolated regions. Mutual exchange of invitations to meetings between the large London Branch of the AWST and the London and Home Counties Branch of the SMA was common. Similarly, joint meetings were a feature of the programmes of most branches. However, Essex led the way in formally constituting a joint branch, a step in which it was followed by the West of England Joint Branch (1959) based on Bristol.[49]

The Northern Ireland Branch of the AWST began as a result of the science syllabus changes introduced by the Ministry of Education in 1950.[50] At that stage the membership list of the AWST included the names of only eight members from Northern Ireland. However, women science teachers attending an in-service summer school on the new syllabuses recognised the need for 'a permanent source of contact and mutual help'. As a result, and following the example of their male colleagues who had established a branch of the SMA the previous year, a new branch was constituted, its membership including almost every woman science teacher in the province. Working closely with their male colleagues, the Northern Ireland branch members established a tradition of one or two 'ladies only' meetings each year, these being 'of a more intimate type, discussion groups around the tea pot'.[51] On the first such occasion in November 1950, they welcomed Dr Winifred Gladwell, attending in her capacity as Vice-President of the parent Association and informant about activities and possibilities.

Unfortunately in the long term 'tea and home-made biscuits' proved an insufficient attraction for many of the members; towards the end of the decade the Committee was complaining of lack of support and the need to give 'serious consideration to closing the Branch'.[52] Combined meetings with the men were better attended, the Joint Biennial Weekend Conference especially so; as the Branch Secretary somewhat tartly observed after the Conference in February 1961, 'it is interesting to see the large number of members who never appear at any other meeting![53]

The establishment of new branches, especially those in regions distant from London, had, of course, financial implications for the AWST. Early in 1949 when the possibility of a Northern Ireland Branch was first discussed in the Executive Committee, the question of the expenses of the branch representative had loomed large, a decision being taken that funds would only permit reimbursement for attendance at one meeting each year.[54] In presenting her Secretary's Report for 1950, Miss Higson warned of the inevitability of an increase in the annual subscription.[55] This rose in September 1952 from 15 shillings to £1, and again in October 1961 from £1 to £2, the fares and accommodation expenses of members of the Executive Committee being a significant contributory factor. By the time of amalgamation, the Executive Committee was twenty-five strong, its fourteen Branch Representatives coming from as far afield as Liverpool, Newcastle-upon-Tyne, Edinburgh, Bridgend and Belfast. Essential to the democratic functioning of the Association, the multiplication of branches was not, however, achieved without financial cost.

That twelve of the fourteen branches of the AWST were centred on university towns and cities is significant, the promotion of understanding between teachers of science in schools and universities being seen as an important outcome of regional activity.[56] Thus, the establishment of the Welsh Branch in 1921 followed quickly upon the opening of the University College of Swansea whose Principal, Professor T.F. Sibley, in his inaugural address to the women teachers, emphasized the need for closer relations between school and college science.[57] Even so, it was the more usual practice to have as Branch President a serving science teacher or a local headmistress rather than a leader from the world of university science. In other ways, too, branch constitutions and programmes of activities replicated those of their parent Association, not least in relation to a summer excursion to a place of scientific interest.

Participation by the membership in the Association's decision-making was probably most effectively achieved by branch representation on the Executive Committee. Attendance at the Annual General Meeting in London, despite the feature for several years of a Presidential Address as part of the business meeting, rarely exceeded 10 per cent of the total membership, this figure normally including a strong contingent from the metropolitan region. At branch level, higher participation rates were usual, with the active London Branch achieving up to 50 per cent attendances at its Annual General Meetings in the 1920s and 30s, though this figure dropped to 25 per cent and below in the post-war period. Occasionally a questionnaire was used by the Executive Committee to obtain the views of members on an issue of importance, such as the extent of the shortage of science teachers in girls' schools in the early 1950s.[58] As the Association grew in size, intercommunication in this way became increasingly expensive and unwieldy. At an informal level links were fostered between the Executive Committee and members by holding the Summer Meeting at a different provincial centre each year, local branches being responsible in turn for the arrangements.[59]

It is difficult to avoid the conclusion, nevertheless, that as the Association gained in size and stature, there was an accompanying shift of decision-making powers from the membership to the Executive Committee. For some years the offices of secretary and treasurer were filled by annual election following a postal ballot involving all members. From 1945 the secretary, thereafter a full-time permanent official, was appointed by the Executive Committee. Simultaneously the term of office of the treasurer was increased to two years and from 1951 her election also was by the Executive Committee. Suggestions were invited from the membership, but a postal ballot or a vote at the Annual General Meeting was no longer held.

The important office of Branch Representative was filled by election, normally by the local committee from amongst its membership, often the Branch Secretary serving.[60] The Articles of the Association did not limit the term of a Branch Representative on the Executive Committee, as was the case with elected ordinary members. Some branches changed their representative regularly, the Northern Branch sending nine different women in the nineteen years from 1944 to 1962. Others allowed their representatives a longer run, Miss Ford (Sussex) serving for thirteen years without break from the foundation of her Branch, and Miss F.M. Eastwood (Secretary of the London Branch) serving for eleven years from 1951 until 1961, continuing as a coopted member in 1962. The Midland Branch, however, with nineteen years of unbroken post-war representation by Miss C.P. Jones provided the outstanding example of continuity of representation. More by accident than design, therefore, the Executive Committee was able to balance the contributions of short-term ordinary members, bringing fresh ideas and varied school experiences, with the accumulated knowledge of the Committee's practices and activities which the longer-serving Regional members provided.

As to initiatives in the work of the Executive Committee, and the question of whether these were centrally or regionally inspired, it was the case that especially after the appointment of a full-time secretary in 1944, the officers of the Association took a clear lead, though proposals for changes in the Articles came occasionally from Branch Representatives. Thus in 1951 the Welsh Branch proposed a new category of membership, to allow students in their teacher-training year to benefit from the activities of the AWST.[61] Whilst the formal adoption of this measure was delayed for a decade, by 1955 students were being invited to attend the Association's Annual Conferences.

The scrutiny of new science syllabuses prepared by the Examinations Board was another activity in which the Branches played an important part, the North-West and Midlands being especially active. In relation to this and the formation of Association policy on matters such as the introduction of General Science, the exemption value of Higher School Certificate subjects and the employment of laboratory technicians, cross-membership of the AWST, the Association of Assistant Mistresses, and the Incorporated Association of Head Mistresses, at both national and branch level, was an important contributory factor.

The most significant proposal to come from a branch, however, was that brought before the Executive Committee at its meeting in the Science Museum Lecture Theatre on 28 January 1961. On that occasion the North-Western (Manchester Area) Branch formally proposed 'that there should be an amalgamation of the AWST with the SMA'. As the Branch representative explained their resolution about union had not been unanimous, 'but there was a strong feeling that it would be desirable and advantageous'.[62] A similar lack of unanimity informed the discussion which followed; nevertheless, it was agreed that general opinion should be sounded, with a view to further consideration of the matter in the autumn. Thus began the process of consultation which led to the creation of the Association for Science Education two years later.

4 The Science Masters' Association

Objects

Numerically and financially the Science Masters' Association differed markedly from the AWST. With more than double the membership of the women's Association throughout most of the inter-war and immediate post-war years, the SMA was accelerating towards a four-fold difference in numbers by the time of amalgamation in 1963.

Similarly, its financial position was impressively secure. As early as 1925 the General Committee was obliged to give attention to the investment of part of 'a large annual balance'.[1] By 1960 the investment 'nest egg' of the SMA had grown to close on £9000 (at cost),[2] compared with an unchanging £450 on the AWST Annual Balance Sheet. Honoraria were paid from 1927 to the Editor of *The School Science Review* and subsequently to other officers of the Association, by 1951 the Editor's honorarium being £250,[3] precisely the annual salary then received by Miss Higson as full-time Secretary of the AWST.

The effect on policy of economic security and numerical strength is difficult to gauge, but they are perhaps not factors conducive to constitutional innovation and change. Certainly the SMA, inheriting as it did a specific and limited programme of objectives from the APSSM, was slower than the AWST to open its doors to non-graduate science teachers in new categories of schools, and to extend the range of its interests.

In formal terms its objects differed little from those of its parent body, other than by the substitution of 'secondary' for 'public' with regard to schools, and of 'other' for 'Examining' with regard to agencies with whom it would seek to communicate. The Memorandum of the new Association also included a clause by which its activities were restricted to 'purposes *specially* connected with the teaching of Natural Science'.[4] In so doing, the SMA explicitly rejected the wider aims of the Yorkshire Natural Science Association, established two months previously, whose members would discuss 'the applications of science to industry' and would attempt to formulate 'a collective opinion upon matters effecting the place of science in the life of the community'.[5] Some time later, the SMA objects were amended to include reference to the issue of 'a journal and other publications dealing with the teaching of Natural Science in Schools'. No further change occurred until the act of union.

Membership

In 1919 membership of the newly founded Science Masters' Association was open to any graduate master in a public secondary school or in a private school approved by the Committee, and to other persons who, in the opinion of the Committee, had contributed to the advancement of science teaching in secondary schools.[6] This latter category was not to exceed 10 per cent of the total membership at the time of election and by 'persons' the Committee meant 'men', no woman, however distinguished, even being elected in the lifetime of the SMA.

'Hard cases' arose almost immediately. The Committee had no difficulty in recognising the Nautical College, Pangbourne, as an 'eligible school', but categorization of the Army Education Corps posed more of a problem. A Diocesan Training College was deemed 'not a school within the meaning of the rule' and despite strong protests from his headmaster, the application of a teacher from the RAF No. 1 School of Technical Training was turned down in 1923, though three years later both he and a previously rejected lecturer on the staff of the Cambridge University Training College were listed as members.[7]

The negotiation of the concord of 1922 whereby the Association of Science Teachers undertook to yield up its male members, notably those from Wales who had sought to join the AST in preference to the SMA because the former offered branch activities, raised for a brief moment the prospect of a mixed association. It was not to be. As the SMA Annual Report for 1922 explained, 'The admission of women to the SMA has been suggested but never pressed'. If this question 'were put to a full meeting of the Association it might be carried, but only in the face of strong opposition. Such an occurrence would be most undesirable. It is the considered view of the committee that two separate associations, working amicably together, are better than one.'[8]

By 1926, then well on the way to doubling its original membership, the Association was obliged to set up a sub-committee to look into the conditions of eligibility. Repeated applications were being received from science masters in central and junior technical schools, in the best of which, it was acknowledged, there were teachers doing work similar to that of many present members of the SMA. After deliberation the Committee concluded that 'the time was not ripe for throwing membership open' to all graduate science masters from such schools, but by the simple expedient of deleting 'private' before 'school' in the membership rule, acquired discretion to meet special cases.[9]

The Committee would appear to have used its new powers sparingly. In October 1934 the question again surfaced and after considerable discussion it was proposed to create a new class of member termed Associate. A final decision was deferred to another meeting when, after further prolonged debate and a volte-face, the *status quo* was re-affirmed; however, it was agreed that the freedom provided by the existing rules should be exploited more fully with a view to bringing forward two or three applications from science masters in central schools to each committee meeting.[10]

Staff from the junior technical schools fared less well, one acceptance being recorded in 1926. That same year, another applicant, pointing to the lack of an organization corresponding to the SMA for such teachers, ingenuously enquired whether the formation of a parallel association would be welcomed.[11] Part of the difficulty which the Committee experienced in dealing with such cases was due to its limited knowledge of the work done in technical schools. Applications were repeatedly referred back with requests for additional information. Whilst the possibility of a special category of membership was apparently in mind, no action resulted and the policy of considering each case on its merits continued.

Apart from a brief skirmish with the idea of special provision for laboratory assistants, prompted by an application from Charterhouse (the applicant eventually solving the problem by moving to different employment),[12] and some unsuccessful pressure for reciprocal branch membership of AWST and SMA members,[13] the conditions of eligibility remained inviolate until after the war. The publication in 1938 of the Spens Report, with its tripartite scheme involving parity between grammar, modern and technical high schools, did, however, foreshadow the changes ahead. In discussing its implications for the membership of the SMA, shortly after its publication, the Committee considered the possibility of inviting a number of selected junior technical schools to provide one member each, but no decision was reached.[14]

Behind the Committee's cautious approach was the fear that the concerns of present members would be swamped if there was an influx of science teachers from schools of a markedly different type. In some junior technical schools a broad educational foundation was provided, prior to industrial employment at about the age of sixteen. In others, a two-year course from the age of thirteen prepared pupils for direct entry into a specific industrial occupation. Such 'trade schools', though designated junior technical schools, with their highly vocational curriculum, were largely confined to the London area and might have been familiar to several Committee members.

Homogeneity of interests, a prime reason for the success of the APSSM, was a guiding principle of eligibility for membership, from which the Committee departed only with reluctance. As late as January 1945 when a reprint of the Rules was authorized, it was emphasized that membership was 'at least at present, limited to masters at schools defined as "secondary" *before* the passing of the 1944 Education Act.'[15]

Change was inevitable, however, and at the first Annual Meeting held after the war, the implications of the extension of meaning of the term 'secondary school' by the Education Act were faced, at least partially. It was recommended again that a new Associate class of member, should be created. Those eligible had to be science masters teaching in approved secondary schools, but it was not essential that they possessed a university degree in a science. The influence of Associate members on the work of the SMA was to be limited by denial of voting rights, and of eligibility for election to the General Committee, as well as by exclusion from the Annual Business Meeting. Furthermore, their number was never to exceed 50 per cent of the number of graduate members. After a period of five years, an Associate member could apply to the Committee for election as an ordinary member, success bringing an increase in his annual subscription from ten shillings to twelve shillings and sixpence.[16]

The main recommendations concerning Associate membership were approved at a Business Meeting in April 1946, though the provision for up-grading after five years disappeared at this stage on a vote. In the event the Committee's fears proved groundless. By September 1951, at a time when the Association's Revenue Account was showing, for the second year in succession, an excess of expenditure over income, and the annual subscription was about to be raised from twelve shillings and sixpence to £1, the number of Associate members had grown to a mere 246 as against 4130 other members.[17] The logical and modestly remunerative step of abolishing the class of Associate member was therefore taken. As the Committee's Report for 1952 reassuringly summarized, 'The admission of non-graduates to full membership since 1 October, 1952 has not produced any increase in the number of applications coming from non-graduates. The great majority of our members hold university degrees.'[18]

Not all found the situation equally satisfactory. For the first time in its peace-time existence, the SMA was about to experience a drop in numbers, 5 per cent of its membership falling away over the following year. The decline was short-lived, however; by 1955 the position had been recovered and a further period of growth inaugurated.

The immediate post-war years brought other pressures for change as the benefits of SMA membership became more widely appreciated amongst science teachers. In February 1948 the South Wales Branch raised the issue of student membership: at that stage the Committee was not prepared to go beyond an invitation to students to attend as guests at branch meetings, plus a reduced subscription for an extra copy of *The School Science Review* to those training college lecturers who were members of the Association.[19] The following year, when members of the Committee met with branch representatives, A.G. Joselin of the Leeds University Department of Education argued strongly for a specific category of student membership, and found sufficient support to oblige the Committee to look again at the conditions of eligibility.[20]

As a result of a comprehensive review, students in full-time attendance at teacher training institutions were admitted to membership on payment of a reduced subscription of five shillings; the class of Associate member was re-defined so as to make it an exclusively non-graduate category; and the incorporation of a block membership scheme for an institution was approved by the Committee. The first to take advantage of this last provision was the Admiralty with a block membership of 20 officers in the Naval Education Service. At a later date, the Director of Army Education took up similar block membership for his science teaching staff.[21] Perhaps the most intriguing response to the block scheme came from local science teacher associations formed by secondary modern school teachers who nevertheless wished to establish a link with the national association of science masters. Their request in 1960 led the Committee to prepare a register of such associations, several of which were subsequently incorporated into the SMA.[22]

Throughout its life, the SMA maintained, in effect if not always in name, a category of honorary membership. Never large, and comprising in the main those distinguished scientists and educationists who had served as Presidents of the Association, the list was extended, especially in the years following the Second World War, by the election of a select number of long-serving officers and others. Amongst the latter were members of His Majesty's Inspectorate; thus, F.B. Stead who had been secretary to J.J. Thomson's Committee on The Position of Natural Science in the Educational System of Great Britain (1918) was elected in 1936, and C.J.R. Whitmore MC, who had served as adviser to the SMA's important sub-committee on General Science in the 1930s, was elected in 1948.[23]

An indication of the growth in membership of the SMA and of the balance between the various categories of membership in the post-war years up to the time of amalgamation is provided by the figures in Table 4.1 and 4.2 respectively.

Table 4.1   Membership of the SMA

1919	364								
1920	494	1930	1578	1940	2637	1950	4080	1960	6697
1921	600	1931	1651	1941	2615	1951	4376	1961	[7024]
1922	729	1932	1745	1942	2613	1952	4540	1962	[7078]
1923	805	1933	1812	1943	2621	1953	4317		
1924	951	1934	1921	1944	2695	1954	4419		
1925	1035	1935	2081	1945	2719	1955	4558		
1926	1166	1936	2294	1946	2870	1956	4773		
1927	1298	1937	2429	1947	3308	1957	5086		
1928	1408	1938	2548	1948	3668	1958	5445		
1929	1468	1939	2664	1949	4015	1959	6188		

Table 4.2   Membership of the SMA at 30 September

	1950	*1951*	*1952*	*1953*	*1954*	*1955*	*1956*	*1957*	*1958*	*1959*	*1960*	*1961* *(4 Mar)*	*1962* *(1 Mar)*
Honorary members	30	33	34	38	38	38	38	43	42	45	42	45	45
Full members	4008	3938	4305	4175	4274	4391	4611	4918	5252	5958	6455	6763	6809*
Associate members		246		—	—	—	—	—	—	—	—	—	—
Student members	42	159	161	64	67	89	84	85	111	145	160	176	204
Block members	—	—	40	40	40	40	40	40	40	40	40	40	20
Total	4080	4376	4540	4317	4419	4558	4773	5086	5445	6188	6697	7024	7078*

*including defaulters[24] (effective 5510)   **effective 528

Membership counts were inescapably subject to error, the returns at different times of the year fluctuating by several hundred and the problems of maintaining an up-to-date list by unpaid, part-time officials became particularly acute as the Association grew in size.[25] Even so, it is clear that the dominating category throughout was that of the secondary school graduate science master and it is of interest to explore how the composition of this varied over time.

At its origin in 1919, the Association's membership was drawn predominantly from schools represented on the Headmasters' Conference, this being a requirement for election to the parent APSSM. Ten years later, the number of schools represented on the SMA had grown almost five-fold to 681, though the HMC schools now accounted for a mere 15 per cent of this total. By the outbreak of war in 1939, the proportion of HMC schools represented on the Association had fallen to 12 per cent.[26]

On their own, such figures convey a misleading impression of the extent to which the public schools dominated the work of the SMA at this stage. Although there had been a rapid growth in the number of grant-aided secondary schools outside the HMC sector, many of these were small, providing a single science master for membership of the Association. Thus, of the 53 Welsh schools listed in 1928, 34 (almost two-thirds) provided only one member. Indeed, the SMA made a significant contribution to professional well-being in the inter-war years by reducing the sense of isolation felt by lone science masters. Many masters from that period commented on the keen anticipation with which they looked forward to the arrival of *The School Science Review* and to news of branch activities and the annual meeting.[27]

At the other end of the scale, an examination of schools with multiple membership demonstrates the potential for influence through the expression of collective opinion which the HMC schools retained, despite their overall numerical inferiority (Table 4.3).

Table 4.3   Schools with multiple membership of the SMA

Number of members per school	1927 (605 schools: 1298 members) ie. av. 2.14 members/school	1938 (886 schools: 2548 members) ie. av. 2.87 members/school
14	—	Oundle
13	Harrow	—
12	—	—
11	—	Dulwich, Harrow, Manchester G.S.
10	Oundle	—
9	Cheltenham, Eton, Marlborough	Ampleforth, Charterhouse, Eton, Haileybury, Leeds G.S., Newcastle R.G.S., Stowe
8	Newcastle R.G.S., Repton	City of London, Marlborough, Repton, Rugby, Taunton
7	Charterhouse, Dartmouth R.N.C., Rugby	Bedford, Bedford Modern, Colfe's, Lancaster R.G.S., Latymer Upper, N. Manchester High
6	King Edward VI Birmingham, Christ's Hospital, Clifton, Merchant Taylors', Tonbridge	Cambridge & County High, Cheltenham, Clifton, Dover County, Dauntsey's, Epsom, Heckmondwike G.S., Hookergate Secondary, Ilford County High, K.C.S., Wimbledon, Lancing, Latymer, Liverpool Collegiate, Liverpool Institute, Portsmouth G.S., Portsmouth Southern, St Cuthberts G.S.; Shrewsbury, Tonbridge, U.C.S., Watford G.S., Winchester

HMC schools provided rather more than a quarter of the SMA's membership in the late 1920s, a fraction which had dropped to just below a fifth by the outbreak of war. More important than relative numbers, however, was the strength of their network relationship. In direct line from Archer Vassall's 'band of brothers', their concentration in a limited number of prestigious schools enabled them to retain a distinct identity and to perpetuate many of the dispositions and concerns of the APSSM. As will become clear when considering

SMA Annual Meeting group, Oxford 1926

the backgrounds of those who served as officers of the SMA and as members of its main committees, the HMC schools were the source of much of the Association's leadership during the inter-war years.

Geographically, the distribution of the membership did not alter in any significant way between the wars. The percentage of secondary schools in England and Wales represented on the Association increased steadily from 25 per cent to 50 per cent between 1921 and 1938, whilst in the same period, the percentage of secondary schools offering advanced courses and represented on the Association rose to over 90 per cent.[28] As with the women science teachers, London, Lancashire and Yorkshire were the regions which individually provided the greatest numbers of members. Their collective contribution accounted for more than a quarter of the science masters in England, a fraction which did not alter significantly in the twenty years up to the outbreak of war. Indeed, even growth was a characteristic of the membership throughout the counties of England, Scotland and Wales at this stage. In Northern Ireland the rate of increase was greater, though the number of schools involved remained small, rising from one in the late 1920s to eleven by 1938. By this later date, also, the number of members from schools abroad had grown to 161 (compared with 26 in 1927) representing 71 schools and colleges in 21 countries. Whilst the majority of these overseas members taught in countries within the British Empire, others came from China, Sweden and the USA.

The printed lists of SMA members in the inter-war years included an indication of the subjects which individuals taught, though the information was not quantitative. Not unexpectedly, the figures confirm the dominance of physics and chemistry in the secondary school science curriculum throughout this period, half of the SMA members being involved to some extent in the teaching of each subject. The small extent to which both general science and biology were taught is also underlined, a greater percentage of the membership being involved in the teaching of mathematics than either of these subjects.

Table 4.4   Percentage of members teaching particular science subjects

	1927	1938
physics	47%	50%
chemistry	44%	46%
biology	7%	15%
mathematics	12%	19%
general science	8%	8%

Finally, in relation to the inter-war years it is of interest to note that many who were appointed to headships retained their membership of the SMA, though the percentage of members in this category fell slightly from 6.5 per cent (84 headmasters) in 1927 to 5 per cent (129 headmasters) in 1938.

Unfortunately it is impossible to extend the analysis of membership on subject lines into the post-war period. Information was no longer systematically recorded about the subjects which members taught. Even the task of eliciting the type of school in which members worked proved difficult for the SMA. Returns around 1950 showed a modest growth in the number of members from secondary modern and other non-grammar secondary schools (Table 4.5), but an attempt in 1958 to obtain reliable figures failed because only half of the 2000 schools to which a circular was sent responded with useful information.[29]

Table 4.5 Numbers of SMA members in different types of school and college

	British Isles				Overseas	
	Secondary Grammar	*Secondary Modern*	*Secondary Technical*	*Training Colleges*	*All Schools*	*Total*
1949	1144 (75%)	144 (9.4%)	81 (5.3%)	29 (1.9%)	130 (8.5%)	1528
1950	1239 (69%)	216 (12%)	122 (6.8%)	51 (2.8%)	164 (9.1%)	1792
1951	1176 (62.5%)	363 (19.3%)	128 (6.8%)	41 (2.2%)	174 (9.2%)	1882

An incomplete list of members arranged according to schools was drawn up in 1960, when an alphabetical list of members was printed. However, the frequent use of home, as opposed to institutional, addresses makes it impossible to infer with any quantitative precision the extent to which the membership had diversified. Certainly it would appear that by 1960 the university and training college membership, negligible in the inter-war years, had risen, those from universities being largely associated with departments of education. Whilst secondary modern and technical school teachers remained in a small minority, the influence and reputation of the Association had grown to such an extent that representatives of publishing houses, scientific apparatus manufacturers, the Science Museum, and major industrial concerns such as Shell Refining Co., Ltd, had sought and been granted membership.[30]

Even so, the SMA was still some way, in composition if not in time, from being an association for all involved or interested in science teaching. In January 1962, only a year before amalgamation with the AWST, revision of the Rules re-affirmed that the SMA was principally an association for science masters in approved secondary schools,[31] the question of the membership of those teaching in primary schools having been raised in November 1959 when it was decided to admit one such member, though the number of applications in this category was to be kept under review.[32]

Constitution and Officers

Initially, the Rules of the SMA provided for a General Committee of eleven members, in addition to two secretaries and a treasurer.[33] The Committee elected its chairman from amongst its membership, all other elections being conducted at the Association's Annual Business Meeting. Committee members served for a term of three years, a further interval of three years having to lapse before they became eligible for re-election other than as officers. The secretaries and treasurer were elected annually up to a maximum of four consecutive years, though they could then be returned as ordinary members of the committee. Such arrangements, devised at a time when the membership was less than 600, representing approximately 300 schools, underwent considerable modification as the Association increased ten-fold over the next four decades, membership by 1960 numbering over 6000 from some 1900 schools.

One early amendment was necessitated by a change in the management of the Association's finances. Following the resignation of M.D. Hill and A. Vassall, who had served as Trustees since 1915, and acting on legal advice, provision was made in the Rules for the appointment of Trustees in whose names the surplus funds of the Association would be vested.[34] At this stage Trustees who were not already members of the Committee were invited to attend meetings when financial business was being discussed. Later, the office of Trustee, along with those of Librarian and Editor of *The School Science Review*, was incorporated into the constitution of the General Committee.

Growth in the scope of the Association's activities and in the amount of business to be transacted also necessitated change. By the time of a revision of the Rules, after the Second World War, the SMA required the administrative services of four honorary secretaries for annual meetings, membership, examinations and general matters respectively, all being members of the General Committee then eighteen strong.[35]

Another factor was increased regional activity by members which led in 1926 to provision in the Rules for the formation of provincial branches of the Association, the first being the North-Eastern Branch for members teaching in schools in Durham, Northumberland and North Yorkshire.[36] South Wales (1928) and North-Western (1930) branches followed. Within a year of its founding, the large North-Western branch had forwarded a resolution to the General Committee urging direct representation of branches on the Committee. At that stage it was the view of the Committee that such a development was not warranted by the strength of the branches, but the need for closer contact was acknowledged. Thenceforth, information about General Committee meetings was sent to the branches with an invitation to submit their views, problems of communication between branches and the Committee being discussed with branch secretaries at the General Meeting in December 1931.[37]

The relationship between the central executive committee and the ordinary members of the SMA, especially those active in the branches, was a recurrent topic throughout the life of the Association. The Rules provided for branch members to attend meetings of the General Committee to take part in discussion of subjects raised by, or of interest to, their branches, but they were not allowed to vote. By 1940, when the number of branches had grown to eight, the suggestion that branch secretaries should be ex officio members of the General Committee was made at the Annual Meeting by E.J. Atkinson (Headmaster, Newport Secondary School). The exceptional circumstances of war, with many members on military service, did not make it a propitious time for a major amendment to the Rules and the General Committee agreed not to recommend change at that stage.[38]

When normal conditions returned, closer links between the Committee and the branches were forged, but not to the extent of representation on the General Committee. It was agreed, however, to publicize the names of branch secretaries in *The School Science Review* and from January 1947 a meeting between the General Committee and branch representatives was to be held each Annual Meeting. Also the minutes of General Committee meetings were to be sent to all branch secretaries.

Behind this reluctance to formalise branch involvement in the policy formation and decision-making of the Association there was an understandable concern not to over-bureaucratize tried and tested modes of operating. Branches were proliferating, twelve having been approved by 1950. The addition to the General Committee of a representative from each would have transformed it into a markedly different body. There were also considerations of expense. The cost of bringing representatives from all branches, including Scotland and Northern Ireland, to meetings in London three or four times a year would have been considerable. An exchange of views at the Annual Meeting, which many members would attend in any case, was seen as a workable compromise. Even so, expense was a limiting factor on developments. When in 1955, at the joint meeting, branch representatives urged that the General Committee should hold more than one meeting with them, the suggestion was turned down because the additional cost was not deemed justifiable unless 'special business' arose.[39]

By the end of the decade, however, continued expansion had made a major restructuring of activities inevitable. At a meeting of the officers of the SMA in October 1959 it was agreed to recommend to the General Committee that officers should be empowered 'to spend reasonable legitimate expenses on secretarial and other assistance'. The burden of routine work by now considerably exceeded what could be undertaken on a voluntary and part-time basis by serving science masters, even with clerical assistance from their wives.

E.W. Tapper of the SMA and ASE

Further fragmentation of officers' work was not the solution; rather, the urgent need was for a central office under a full-time administrator.

This judgement was endorsed by the General Committee.[40] By March 1960 it had been agreed to lease 52 Bateman Street, Cambridge, a large Victorian house, as the SMA's headquarters. On 1 January 1962 E.W. Tapper (Dulwich College) took up appointment as full-time General Secretary of the Association at an annual salary of £1800.

The constitutional repercussions of these changes included abolition of the post of Membership Secretary, his work to be undertaken in future by the Treasurer aided by a newly-appointed Assistant Secretary, Miss E.M. Taylor. A new office of Minuting Secretary was at the same time created. More significantly, the offices of honorary General Secretary and Librarian disappeared, the associated duties now being the responsibility of the full-time General Secretary.[41] A revision of the Rules in January 1962 provided for a General Committee of the SMA's officers (President, Chairman, Treasurer, Annual Meeting Secretary, Examinations Secretary, Minuting Secretary, Editor of *The School Science Review*, two Trustees) and ten other elected members, a total of nineteen. The business of the Association was to be supervised by the full-time, salaried General Secretary, appointed by the General Committee.

Summarising, then, and leaving aside the President who changed from year to year and who rarely played an active part in the work of the General Committee, the alterations in the composition of that body were as shown in Table 4.6.

Despite a substantial growth in membership of the SMA and in the number of its branches, the structure of the General Committee in 1962 was little different from that of the late 1920s. In deciding its

Table 4.6   Composition of the SMA General Committee

| | Honorary Officers | | | | | | | | |
Date	Chair-man	Sec.	Treas.	Trus-tees	Editor	Libr-arian	Other Elected	Total Committee (— Pres.)	Total SMA mem-bership	No. of branches
1921	1	2	1	—	—	—	10	14	600	—
1928	1	2	1	2	1	1	10	18	1408	2
1939	1	3	1	2	1	1	10	19	2664	8
1946	1	4	1	2	1	1	8	18	2870	8
1956	1	4	1	2	1	1	10	20	4773	12
1962	1	3	1	2	1	—	10	18	7078	17

most effective size and composition a number of conflicting considerations had to be borne in mind. As the SMA's executive body, clearly
it could not be too large. At the same time it was essential not to lose
touch with what the grass-root membership was thinking and doing.
Similarly, a balance had to be struck between continuity and experience, on the one hand, and new blood and fresh ideas, on the other.
Representation of the interests of schools of very different types was
a further determinant of composition, especially as the Association
extended its constituency in the years after the Second World War. It
is of some interest, then, to look at the composition of the General
Committee with these points in mind.

Between 1919 and 1939, eighty members of the SMA served on
the General Committee as elected members and officers.[42] No doubt
practical considerations such as the geographical location of their
schools, the quality of the railway service and the compliance of their
headmasters were powerful influences on the ability of members to
participate effectively in the administration of the Association.
Proximity to the metropolis was certainly an important factor, seven-
eights of the committee members being drawn from schools within a
100 miles radius of London, despite the fact that these schools
accounted for only half of the Association's total membership. Some
hint of conservative dispositions towards the composition of the
committee is provided by reference in 1935 to 'the custom of having
. . . some member in close touch with the older universities', this
at a moment when the net was being cast more widely to include
committee members from Stretford, Barnsley and Newcastle-upon-
Tyne.[43] At the same time, as those attending the Annual Business
Meeting were periodically reminded, in order to ensure continuity
and experience in the administration of the Association's affairs, it
was important that new members should include at least some willing
in due course to become officers.[44] In fact many did serve considerably longer than the minimum period of three years, as the information in Table 4.7 shows.

Analysis in terms of the type of school from which committee

Table 4.7   Members with 10 or more years of service on the General Committee between 1919 and 1939

Years of service	
19	C.E. Sladden (Eton): Chairman, General Secretary, Trustee, elected member.
18	G.H.J. Adam (City of London School): Treasurer, elected member, Editor
17	J.K King (George Green School, Poplar): Chairman, Treasurer, Trustee, elected member.
12	Rev. T.J. Kirkland (King's School, Ely): elected member, Librarian.
11	F. Fairbrother (Cedars School, Leighton Buzzard): Chairman, elected member, Membership Secretary.
10	S.V. Brown (Liverpool Institute): Chairman, General Secretary, elected member.

members came during the inter-war years shows that the representation of independent and HMC schools exceeded that of local education authority maintained schools by a factor of approximately two. This is due partly to the continuity of interests and influence from the former APSSM, but it is reflective also of other factors. The small maintained grammar school with one or two science masters was much less likely to generate a nomination, especially one which could command a strong vote at the Annual Business Meeting, than the larger, possibly better known, school with several science staff. Of course, the growth and coordination of branch activity, as well as the extension of secondary education, brought about change in this situation. Even so, it was probably easier at this stage to engage in the work of a national organization, and perhaps a greater social expectation existed that one would, when located in a large independent school than elsewhere.

With regard to the Association's principal executive office in the inter-war years, of the twenty-one chairmen eight were headmasters providing valuable cross-membership with the HMC and the IAHM.[45] As for the schools represented, the overall balance between HMC schools and others, mainly local education authority maintained, was tipped slightly in favour of the former, twelve chairmen coming from public schools with Harrow (4) and Eton (2) the only instances of multiple representation. If comparison is restricted to those who had not previously been members of the APSSM (i.e. had joined the Association in 1919 or after) the chairmanship was divided almost equally between those serving in HMC schools (5) and those from other secondary schools (6). In terms of university backgrounds, Oxford (5) and Cambridge (10) predominated. Other universities represented were Cardiff, Leipzig, London, Manchester and St

Andrews. The level of academic qualification was impressive, three chairmen having science research doctorates; others, such as E.J. Holmyard (1925, Clifton) had acquired scholarly reputations by way of publications in fields such as the history of science. One chairman, T. Hartley (1932, Headmaster, Swindon Secondary School) was also a member of the Historical Association, whilst W.J. Gale (1929, senior science master, Bec School) was for a time music critic for the *Daily Telegraph*.[46] Preparation for the senior executive office entailed, as a minimum, two years' prior service as an elected committee member. Often, too, a period as treasurer or secretary was part of the apprenticeship. In most cases, the year as chairman was the final act of service as an officer of the SMA, although occasionally membership of the General Committee was retained by virtue of some other duty e.g. Trustee, as in the cases of C.E. Sladden (Eton) and J.K. King (George Green's School, Poplar).

With a maximum term of four consecutive years (eventually extended to five) the office of Treasurer was held by six men between 1919 and 1939 (see Table 4.8). Two (J.K. King and T. Hartley) were headmasters, and one, P.W. Oscroft (Uppingham) appears to have been recruited specifically for the task as a senior and respected member, close to retirement. His successor, B.M. Neville (William Ellis School). despite a severe physical disability, made an outstanding contribution to the financial affairs of the SMA, successfully negotiating the Association's claim for relief from Income Tax in 1934, and assuming the office of Advertisement Editor to *The School Science Review* on completion of his term as Treasurer.[47]

Table 4.8   SMA Treasurers, 1919–1939

	Treasurer	Number of years in office
1919–1921	G.H.J Adlam (City of London School)	3
1922–1925	J.K. King (George Green's School, Poplar)	4
1926–1929	T. Hartley (Swindon Secondary School)	4
1930–1933	P.W. Oscroft (Uppingham School)	4
1934–1938	B.M. Neville (William Ellis School)	5
1939(–1945)	A.W. Wellings (Leamington College)	(7)

Although the SMA had two secretaries from the beginning, and a *de facto* division of labour operated, the secretaries were not formally designated 'General' and 'Annual Meeting' until after the creation of a third secretaryship, with responsibility for membership, in December 1931.[48] The first holder of this new office, F. Fairbrother (Headmaster, Cedars School, Leighton Buzzard), initially coopted to the committee and later a constitutional member, remained in post until 1946. Holders of the other secretaryships are given in Table 4.9.

Table 4.9   SMA Secretaries, 1919–1939

	Secretary (later General Secretary)	No. of years in office		Secretary (later Annual Meeting Secretary)	No. of years in office
1919	W.D. Eggar (Eton)	1	1919–1920	W.J.R. Calvert (Harrow)	2
1920	E.R. Thomas (Rugby)	1	1921–1922	V.S. Bryant (St Piran's)	2
1921–1924	C.E. Sladden (Eton)	4	1923–1926	W.J. Gale (Bec School)	4
1925–1928	W.H. Barrett (Harrow)	4	1927–1928	I.M. Bankes-Williams (Harrow)	2
1929–1930	I.M. Bankes-Williams (Harrow)	2	1929–1931	E. Nightingale (St Albans School)	3
1931–1932	C. Mayes (Eton)	2	1931–1934	H.G. Lambert (Moseley Secondary School)	3
1933–1934	A.E. Foot (Eton)	2	1935–1937	R.E. Williams (Repton School)	3
1935–1938	S.V. Brown (Liverpool Institute)	4	1938(–1944)	W. Ashhurst (Stretford Grammar School)	(7)
1939(–1945)	H.P. Ramage (Gresham's School)	(7)			

It will be seen that between 1919 and 1939, the General Secretary came from one of two schools (Eton and Harrow) for 15 of the 21 years. Furthermore, with the exception of a single year, 1920, when in any case the other secretary came from Harrow, there was an unbroken representation of these schools up to 1935. This remarkable contribution to the administration of the affairs of the SMA can be interpreted in various ways, but there is little evidence to suggest that the monopoly was in any serious way resented by the membership. The task of the General Secretary was onerous and time-consuming, and one for which there were few contenders. Certainly there are no indications of the recommendation for appointment made by the Committee being contested at the Annual Business Meeting, though membership of the Committee itself was frequently the outcome of a ballot. At the same time, the ability to determine agendas and a tendency to perpetuate specific concerns, such as the nature or relations with the older universities, contributed to a somewhat conservative stance on the part of the SMA throughout the 1920s and into the 'thirties.

The outbreak of war in 1939 disrupted the administrative practices of the SMA in predictable ways. The geography of membership was transformed by evacuation; travel facilities were restricted; whilst general conscription and the demands of technical training reduced the number of school science teachers. Nevertheless the Committee continued to meet, occasionally seeking an alternative venue to London because of the blitz. No Annual Business Meetings were possible in 1941, 1943 and 1944, and members were asked through the pages of *The School Science Review* to signal dissent in writing if they objected to the Committee remaining unchanged.[49] Throughout this difficult period in the Association's history its officers were:

Chairman: G. Fowles (Latymer Upper School)	5 years, 1940–44
Treasurer: A.W. Wellings (Leamington College)	7 years, 1939–45
General Secretary: H.P. Ramage (Gresham's School, Holt)	7 years, 1939–45
Ann. Meeting Secretary: W. Ashhurst (Stretford Grammar School)	7 years, 1938–44
Membership Secretary: F. Fairbrother (Cedars School, Leighton Buzzard)	15 years, 1932–46

By 1942 the burden of work on the General Secretary had increased to an extent that the Committee established a new office of Examinations Secretary, the first holder being A.E.E. McKenzie (Repton School).[50] As for the elected members, five nominations were obtained for the five vacancies at the Annual Business Meeting at Rugby in 1942. Amongst the new members were two recruits, Dr H.F. Boulind (Cambridge and County High School) and E.H. Coulson (Braintree County High School) who were to make signal contributions to the work of the SMA in the post-war years ahead.[51]

From a constitutional standpoint, the seventeen years leading up to the formation of the ASE in 1963 was a period in which the Committee of the SMA steadily adjusted to an enlarging and increasingly diversified membership. Of the 65 members who served on the Committee between 1946 and 1962, those from schools within a 100 miles of London continued to predominate (approximately 40), though now, for the first time, there were also representatives of schools in Scotland (6) and Northern Ireland (3). Other members came from Yorkshire (8), Lancashire (5), Devon (1) and Durham (1). Local education authority maintained schools were more strongly represented than in the pre-war period, to an extent that they slightly outnumbered HMC schools. The institutions from which committee members came also included a technical college, a teacher training college, a university department of education, and the Royal Naval College, Dartmouth.

In accordance with pre-war practice, after 1946 the chairmanship of the Committee changed annually, though it is noteworthy that C.E. Sladden (Eton) was elected for a second time, in 1947, after an interval of twenty years, one of only three members to hold this position in the SMA for more than one year. It would perhaps be an exaggeration to describe the administration of the Association in this period in terms of a London–Cambridge (or East Anglian) axis, but many of the principal offices were held by men from schools in that vicinity. At the opening of the period, the General Secretary was R.H. Dyball (City of London School) who served from 1946 until 1950, to be followed by H.F. Boulind (Cambridge and County High School and, later, Department of Education, University of Cambridge), 1951–1955 and 1957. Dyball who had been Librarian, 1941–46, remained as an elected member of the Committee after relinquishing the post of General Secretary and, following a year as Chairman, 1954, became editor of *The School Science Review*. Boulind had previously served for five years as Examinations Secretary, being succeeded by R.P. Ayres (The Leys School, Cambridge), this secretaryship being for a decade in Cambridge hands. Boulind's work in connection with the SMA Policy Statement of 1957 and his chairmanship in 1959 are considered later.[52] His successor as General Secretary in 1958 was H.F. Broad, Membership Secretary since 1946, an office previously held by only one other member, F. Fairbrother, Broad's predecessor as headmaster of The Cedars School, Leighton Buzzard.

Other long-serving members of the Committee were C.E. Sladden, a Trustee for 34 years from 1926 until 1960, and H.P. Ramage (Gresham's School, Holt) who, after seeing the SMA through the war years as General Secretary, was appointed a Trustee in 1946, an office he held for the remainder of the life of the SMA. Ramage also served as Chairman in 1950. As for the Treasurership, E.H. Coulson (Braintree County High School), 1946 to 1949, was succeeded by Charles Holt (Harrow Weald County Grammar School), 1950 to 1954, and S.W. Read (The Henry Thornton School, London), 1955 to 1959. After that date the Cambridge link was made with the appointment of F.C. Brown (Perse School) as Treasurer. It was within the seven years of Brown's term of office that the move to a permanent headquarters was achieved.

This picture of a network of officers centred largely around London and Cambridge needs overlaying with other contributions of importance from further afield. Thus, W.G. Rhodes (Firth Park Grammar School, Sheffield) and E.W. Moore (Thorne Grammar School, Doncaster and, later, King's Norton Grammar School, Birmingham) each served on the Committee in various capacities, including Annual Meeting Secretary and Chairman (Rhodes) and Librarian and Chairman (Moore), for twelve years continuously. W.H. Dowland (West Hartlepool Grammar School) likewise, as elected member, Annual Meeting Secretary and Chairman, served continuously for eleven years, whilst R. Thurlow (Leigh Grammar School) after nine years as elected member and Examinations Secretary on the SMA Committee had the distinction of being the first chairman of the ASE in 1963. Slowly, but inevitably, the leadership became more reflective of the broad provincial membership which the Association had acquired in the post-war years of rapid growth.

A final point about the SMA's officers concerns the Presidency. Here the APSSM practice of annual appointments from the world of science and higher learning was continued with little break. In exceptional circumstances such as wartime a distinguished headmaster (P.H.B. Lyon, Rugby, 1942) and even one of its own elder statesmen (e.g. G.H.J. Adlam, 1941; C.L. Bryant, 1945) might be invited to serve. In 1952, Sir Graham Savage CB, recently retired as Education Officer to the LCC and about to embark on an extended retirement considerably more active than many working lives, became President. The normal appointment, however, was that of a Vice-Chancellor or distinguished science professor from the university which was to accommodate the next annual meeting. It was a reflection of the SMA's considerable reputation that it could aim high and rarely fail to secure the active support of the most eminent men proposed for its supreme office. The crowning achievement in this field, shortly before amalgamation, was the acceptance by the Duke of Edinburgh of an invitation to become the Association's first Patron.[53] Initially, given the Duke's expressed interest in science and engineering, it had been hoped he might serve as President. The requirement for a Presidential Address to be delivered at the Annual Meeting in January, when the Royal Family would normally be away on holiday, proved an obstacle to progress on this front. Instead the more permanent relation of Patron was suggested, and accepted, with consequences of significance for the direction of the Association's efforts in curriculum development in the years ahead.[54]

Branches

Provision was not made in the Rules of the SMA in 1919 for the development of branches, the risk of fragmentation being deemed to outweigh possible local benefits. Only with the first excursion to the North of England, when the Annual Meeting was held in the University of Leeds in 1925, was the case for formalised regional activity accorded due weight.

The issue which induced change was how best to represent the views of science masters to the Examining Boards conducting the still new School Certificate Examination, and to provincial university science departments. It was argued that a board of examiners, for example, did not want to deal with a distant central committee in London; instead, it needed direct communication with representatives from the schools which it examined.[55] In its Annual Report for 1925, the SMA Committee acknowledged that the present organization of the Association was inadequate in this respect and that the establishment of branches would provide the machinery for dealing with these problems more effectively. The necessary changes in the rules were proposed and adopted, with six dissentient votes, at the Business Meeting in 1926.[56]

An immediate response came from the north-east where, at a

meeting on 10 February 1926, it was agreed, subject to approval of the General Committee, to form a branch to serve teachers in Durham, Northumberland and North Yorkshire. Travel difficulties caused by the General Strike delayed the inaugural meeting until the autumn, when Brigadier Harold Hartley, President of the SMA, addressed the assembled members at the Royal Grammar School, Newcastle-upon-Tyne.[57]

Other developments followed quickly. In December 1928 it was decided to form a South Wales Branch, the inaugural meeting being held the following March, at the Physiology Institute, University College Cardiff.[58] A North Western Branch, serving the counties of Cheshire, Cumberland, Lancashire, Westmorland and Flintshire, was established in 1930 when 50 members met at Manchester Grammar School.[59] In another area heavily populated with SMA members, the void created by the demise of the Yorkshire Natural Science Association was filled by the inauguration of a Yorkshire Branch in November 1934.[60] In all, by the outbreak of war, the existence of eight branches had been approved by the SMA Committee.

Table 4.10   Branches of the SMA to 1939

North Eastern	1926
South Wales	1928
North Western	1930
Yorkshire	1934
Eastern Counties	1935
Midland	1936
Southern Counties	1937
London and Home Counties	1938

Centred for the most part on a university town or city, the branches were intended to

(a) Afford means of maintaining touch with provincial universities, examining boards, and the local education authorities, in matters relating to the teaching of natural science in secondary schools.
(b) Promote closer contact between the General Committee and members of the Association.
(c) Provide members with more opportunities of meeting one another.[61]

At a later date the objects were amended by the deletion of 'provincial' in (a) and by a reformulation of other objectives to read:

(b) Promote closer contact between science masters in independent schools, grammar schools, technical high schools, and modern schools.

(c)   Provide activities additional to the Annual Meeting.[62]

Any member of the SMA was eligible to belong to any branch, and non-members could attend meetings by invitation. Indeed, regional activities were seen as an effective means of attracting science masters to the Association, the number of new members so recruited being mentioned in the annual reports which branches were required to submit to the General Committee.

A further aspect of branch activity was collaboration with women science teachers. As the pioneering North Eastern Branch recorded in its first report, 'Members of the Association of Women Science Teachers have been invited to all meetings, and their cooperation has been greatly appreciated'.[63]

Control over the creation of branches, the geographical area which a branch would serve and the nature of its activities was exercised firmly by the General Committee. Branch rules had to be submitted for approval, and a branch could not take action with respect to any outside body, nor publish any material in the press, except after approval by the General Committee.

On the important matter of finance, expenses arising from the initial meeting at which the establishment of a branch was discussed were met from SMA central funds. Beyond this, branches could collect an annual subscription from their members, initially not to exceed two shillings and sixpence, though this maximum had risen to five shillings by the 1950s. All branch expenditure had to be met from this source, the Branch Treasurer being required to provide an annual statement of accounts for the General Committee.

The financial independence of branches was an issue which recurred at intervals throughout the life of the SMA. Eventually a proposal from the Midland Branch that branch subscriptions be abolished and branch activities financed from central funds was accepted, despite strong opposition from the Yorkshire Branch, always a staunch advocate of branch autonomy.[64] From October 1961 each branch was credited with a sum of four shillings for every declared branch member, the possibility existing for a supplementary grant if reasonable expenditure exceeded the capitation allowance. It was emphasized, however, that the financial liabilities of the Association extended only to SMA members and not to members of the AWST in the case of branches where there was collaborative activity.[65]

War put an end to branch activity for four years. By the autumn of 1944, however, despite 'V' bombs and the continued evacuation of many schools, the London and Home Counties branch had resumed its meetings on a regular basis.[66] The North Eastern Branch followed, and in its Report for 1946, the General Committee was able to include accounts of the activities of each of the pre-war branches except the Southern Counties.[67] Furthermore, new branches began to proliferate again, initially North Wales (1946) and Scottish (1946), and subsequently South Midlands (1948) and Northern Ireland (1949), making a total of twelve active branches by the Association's Jubilee Year. The Scottish branch, in particular, was successful in enrolling many new members, within a year its list included some 300 names. At the same time its territory was considerably greater than any other branch. A pattern of meetings resulted which included a three-day General Meeting, the first at the University of Glasgow and the second at St Andrews, whilst 'fellowship and interest' in the different regions was maintained by smaller group meetings open to any member of the branch.[68] Appropriately, the Annual Meeting of the SMA was held in Edinburgh in January 1950, the first time it had crossed the border.

Not all branch developments prospered so well. An initial inquiry about the formation of a branch in Dublin was received by the General Committee in 1948,[69] but it was not until twelve years later that a Republic of Ireland Branch of the SMA came into being.[70] Its life was short. The business meeting at the first (and last) Annual Meeting, held in the Science Buildings of University College Dublin in January 1961, was given over almost completely to the formation or the Irish Science Teachers' Association.[71] This act of secession, not unrelated to requirements for financial support from the Irish Department of Education, was achieved amicably and with an advantageous offer of purchase of *The School Science Review* to members of the new Association.[72]

The South Midlands Branch also failed to prosper, fading into inactivity in the late 1950s. But this was exceptional. Elsewhere vigorous development continued, by the time of amalgamation the number of active branches being seventeen.

Table 4.11   Branches of the SMA since 1945

North Wales	1946
Scottish	1946
South Midland	1948
Northern Ireland	1949
Essex	1954
West of England	1959
Republic of Ireland	1960–61
South West	1960
Lakeland	1961
East Midland	1962
Reading	1962

Of the more recently formed branches, that established in Essex in March 1954 was a herald of constitutional change. Whilst informal collaboration between members of the SMA and AWST characterized the activity of many branches, the Essex Branch was from the first formally constituted as a Joint Branch of the men's and women's Associations.[73] It was from the Essex Branch that the General Committee of the SMA received a resolution in 1961. 'The members of the Essex Joint Branch of the AWST and the SMA, after six years of work at this Branch, would like to recommend as the result of their experience, the fusion of both Parent Associations, and would therefore ask the Committee of the Parent Associations to put this proposal before the next Annual General Meeting of both Associations, to start steps towards fusion of both Associations.'[74]

5 The Association for Science Education

Amalgamation

Contextual influences of several kinds made amalgamation of the SMA and AWST inevitable. At national level the need to speak with one voice on science education issues led to increased collaboration between the Executive Committee of the AWST and the General Committee of the SMA. The revised Policy Statement of 1961, *Science and Education*, was but one product of alliance: the provision of school science laboratories and the training of science teachers were other subjects on which a joint opinion was expressed.[1]

Within the schools the classroom context of science education was changing. An increase in the number of coeducational secondary schools brought together men and women science teachers as colleagues on the same staff, teaching the same children. Furthermore, in a period of severe shortage of graduate women science teachers, it was not unusual to find a man employed in a girls' secondary school. Similarly, social attitudes no longer prevented a married woman from pursuing her career as a science teacher, although the combination of domestic and professional responsibilities made it less likely that she would be active in the administrative affairs of the AWST.[2] As has already been noted, at branch level there was often *de facto* federation, if not fusion, a state of affairs deemed both necessary and desirable for the efficient management of local programmes.

From the standpoint of the AWST there were many considerations to be borne in mind in contemplating a closer constitutional relationship with the SMA. Miss E. Lois Buckley, President of the Association, identified three possible courses of action in a letter to her members early in the year 1962.[3] First, the AWST might remain as a separate organization, in which case it would face a 'heavy load of work and responsibility' as well as increasing expenditure. Secondly, a federated arrangement, retaining separate executive committees for the two Associations, might be sought, thus enabling something of the present identity of the AWST to be retained. Thirdly, the AWST might be merged with the SMA in a new joint Association. The overwhelming preference of those members who replied was for complete fusion into a new Association, though it was recognised that a price might have to be paid. A major fear was that the 'intimacy and friendliness' of meetings would disappear though the possibility of a greater number of 'smaller and more concentrated' branches might compensate here. Indeed, in regions such as Oxford and the South

Midlands, where the viability of a branch had proved difficult to sustain, the new arrangement could bring relief. Others were concerned that 'girls' problems' would no longer be given the consideration they deserved and that the experience of leadership which a separate Association had given to women would be lost. Members of the AWST were divided on these issues, some arguing that 'the problems of girls and boys seemed to be becoming more unified' and that 'science should come first and women afterwards'.[4]

Only a small minority of AWST members (2 out of 241 who responded) wished to keep a separate identity, the benefits of union being judged by most to outweigh costs. The Association was growing in membership, with the prospect of new commitments of premises and staff ahead, and a consequential increase in subscription. The sharing of administrative and accommodation charges with the SMA, already in occupation of its new headquarters in Cambridge, had a strong appeal. Also, the efficiency and speed with which decisions could be taken in one Association, compared with the two separate Associations, each with its own executive committee, was an important potential gain.

From the SMA side, there was widespread support for the resolution of the Essex Branch in favour of a single Association. However, under the existing Rules, the resolution could only be carried at the Annual Business Meeting if 10 per cent of the members cast their votes. The prospect of some 700 members attending and voting was unrealistic and so the General Committee formulated and gave due notice of its own resolution, that from the Essex Branch being withdrawn by agreement.[5]

When the Annual Business Meeting was held on 4 January 1962 in Imperial College, London, H.F. Broad, as retiring honorary General Secretary, proposed that:

In view of the close and harmonious way in which Branches and members of the AWST and SMA are working together for the improvement of science teaching the Committee desires from this meeting a Mandate to draw up, in collaboration with representatives of the AWST, detailed proposals for the formation of a single association open to all teachers of science.

An amendment that the words 'in secondary schools' be added was overwhelmingly defeated, with only eight votes in support, the resolution itself being carried by the same large majority. W.H. Dowland (chairman-elect), D.W. Harlow (annual meeting secretary), F.C. Brown (treasurer) and E.W. Tapper (the newly appointed full-time secretary) were then named as representatives of the SMA to conduct negotiations and undertake discussions leading to amalgamation. The name of the chairman, J.S.G. McGeachin, was later added to this team.[6]

In the meeting of the Joint Steering Committee which followed, the

AWST was represented by Miss E.L. Buckley (president), Miss F.M. Eastwood (executive committee), Miss M. Going (vice-president), Miss E. O'Shaughnessy (Essex branch representative) and Miss K.E. Parks (executive committee).[7] The simplest way of achieving the merger seemed to be for the numerically stronger SMA to amend its title and admit women members, with the AWST being wound up and its assets transferred to the SMA. Women members could then join the new body either individually or collectively. At an early stage, however, it became apparent that the constitutional position was more complicated than had at first been thought. Thus, there was no provision in the constitution of the AWST for winding up the Association and transferring or distributing its assets. It was possible that some women members would not wish to join the new joint Association and provision for them to retain their share of the assets had to be considered. There was also the fact that the SMA was registered as a charity under the Ministry of Education, whereas the AWST was not.[8] Clearly, legal advice was necessary.

One option which the Associations' solicitor described was for the new body to be constituted as a company limited by guarantee, in this way protecting the committee and officers from the personal liability which might arise from acts they carried out on behalf of the Association. In such a case the need for Trustees to hold the Associations' property would disappear. An alternative, favoured by the Ministry of Education and adopted by the AWST and SMA, involved the constitution of Trustees under a Trust Deed which stated the objects of the Association and contained all its rules.[9] With the advice of counsel, and in consultation with the Ministry of Education and the Charity Commissioners, much of 1962 was given over to formulating the necessary Trust Deed in preparation for a proposed inaugural business meeting of the new Association during the Annual Meeting at Manchester in January 1963.

Various possibilities were considered for a name. 'Association for the Advancement of Science Teaching' commanded some early support, but was rejected as too cumbersome. 'Science Teaching Association' likewise fell by the way, being judged 'not correct' because 'an association can only be of persons'. By September 1962 opinion had crystallized around 'The British Science Teachers' Association' which indicated that the Association spoke nationally for science teachers, gave a clear signal to overseas correspondents at a time when international contacts were being extended, and rolled 'off the tongue very nicely'.[10] Whilst the Joint Steering Committee agreed on this title without any votes against, there were nevertheless two abstentions. When members of the SMA General Committee met branch representatives on 22 September 1962 it was clear that the matter of title could by no means be regarded as settled, and it was left that further discussion would take place at the Annual Meeting in January.[11]

The Charities Act of 1960 might, in any case, have necessitated a revision of the constitution and rules of the Association though perhaps not as fundamental a reformulation as entailed by the merger. In contrast to the SMA, which even by January 1962 managed to accommodate its rules under a mere sixteen headings, and to the AWST for whom administrative formalities had never been a strong point, plans for the launching of The British Science Teachers' Association incorporated no less than 77 rules in the first draft, annexed to a lengthy Trust Deed. Within the latter provision was made for the appointment of 'Transitional Trustees' who would convene the inaugural business meeting of the new Association and in whom all the assets of the SMA and AWST would be vested for the limited period between formal termination of the life of the old Associations and the birth of the new.[12]

At the Annual Meeting at Manchester the five days commencing Tuesday, 1 January 1963 were ones of continuous constitutional activity. On the Tuesday evening, the SMA General Committee met with Branch Officers to secure agreement on the nominations for officers for the new Association. There followed the Annual Business Meeting at which it was resolved to wind up activities and transfer 'all property . . . after satisfaction of all debts and liabilities' to The British Science Teachers' Association. On Friday, the final General Committee Meeting of the SMA was held, as well as the Annual General Meeting and final Executive Committee meeting of the AWST, leading in each case to the decision that 'no further business be undertaken . . . after 12 noon on 5 January 1963'. Finally, on Saturday morning, at its inaugural business meeting under the chairmanship of Dr B.V. Bowden, the retiring President of the SMA, the Trust Deed and Rules of the new Association were approved.[13]

Its name was contested to the end. First, two senior officers of the SMA (H.F. Broad, honorary General Secretary until 1961, and F.C. Brown, honorary Treasurer) proposed 'The Association of Science Teachers' as an alternative, but, fittingly, the last word went to an ordinary member. From the floor of the meeting, D. Tomes (Loughborough Grammar School) moved as a further amendment that the name be 'The Association for Science Education'. His seconder was W.H. Dowland (retiring SMA Chairman). Both propositions were put to the assembled members, the second being carried. By 12 05 on the 5 January 1963 the formal business of the meeting had been completed and, a mere five minutes late, the Association for Science Education was commissioned and officered for the work that lay ahead, a united Association for all teachers of science.[14]

The Trust Deed and Rules

The statement of objects included in the Trust Deed was to a considerable extent a reformulation, in more general terms, of the particular objects of the AWST and SMA. Thus, instead of according primacy to promoting 'the teaching of science in secondary schools', the Trust Deed now referred to promoting education

(a)   by improving the teaching of science; and
(b)   by providing an authoritative medium through which opinions of teachers of science may be expressed on educational matters; and
(c)   by affording means of communication among all persons and bodies of persons concerned with the teaching of science in particular and with education in general.[15]

Compared with the SMA objects, the significant changes were, first, the omission of any mention of type of school or sector of the educational system with which the Association was concerned; and, secondly, the explicit allocation to science of an instrumental role in relation to general education. In addition, reference to the issuing of publications dealing with the teaching of science disappeared as an object, being transferred to a section of the Deed dealing with the activities by means of which the ASE would promote its objects. There was also a detailed statement of what the Association would not do. Under the heading 'Not a Trade Union', the ASE bound itself to eschew activities connected with

(i)   the regulation of the relations between employers and employees or between employees and employees or employers and employers; or
(ii)   the imposing of restrictive conditions on the conduct of any trade, business or profession; or
(iii)   the provision of pecuniary benefits for members.[16]

From the earliest meetings of the Joint Steering Committee there had been recognition that a new constitution would need to incorporate safeguards for the position of women, at least initially. It was a cardinal principle that men and women would have equal status in the Association, and in their eligibility for election to any office. Beyond this, however, there needed to be some guarantee that women could not be totally excluded from the honorary offices of the ASE.

It was decided that the honorary officers of the Association should be 'the President, the Chairman, three vice-chairmen, the honorary Treasurer, not more than four honorary Secretaries, the honorary Editor and the Trustees'. The inclusion of three vice-chairmen was an innovation designed in part to provide continuity, the maximum term of office being three years. There was also the possibility that a retiring Chairman could become one of the vice-chairmen, so that the services of an experienced honorary officer would not necessarily be lost on termination of his year. The Rules required that at least one of the Trustees, the vice-chairmen and the honorary secretaries should be a man, and one a woman.[17]

As for the conduct of the Association's affairs, a governing Council was established, its membership to consist of the honorary officers, six elected members and one representative from each branch of the Association, together with those Trustees who were not, by virtue of office, election or branch representation, already members. This policy-forming body was to meet not less than three times per year. Two elected members changed each year, and of the six elected members at any given time at least one had to be a man and one a woman.[18]

Management of the Association's business was the responsibility of a smaller body, an Executive Committee of seven members appointed by Council, to include the Chairman (or one of the vice-chairmen acting as deputy), the honorary Treasurer, two of the honorary Secretaries and one Trustee. The Rules made no reference to a minimum presence of men or women on the Executive Committee.[19] For special purposes Council was empowered to appoint other committees, the most important of which was the Education Committee, successor to the Science and Education Committee of the SMA and to the Joint Education Committee of the AWST and SMA.[20]

Accommodation

Statements of purpose and of administrative structure would have been of little avail without an operational focus. Their translation into effective action, given the scale of the ASE's activities with nearly 10,000 members, required something more than peripatetic existence, with meetings in hired rooms, records kept in the homes of members, and postal addresses changing with those of office holders.

The need for a permanent headquarters had been recognised by the SMA as far back as the autumn of 1959. In the course of a review of the work of the Association, consequent upon its enlarging membership and increasing influence, H.P. Ramage, one of the Trustees, presented a paper in which he argued the case for a Science Education Centre to coordinate the activities of the numerous agencies then becoming involved in curriculum reform. It was envisaged that such a Centre would also provide the SMA with headquarters. Until a more appropriate location could be found, and to expedite the establishment of the Centre, Ramage offered his own home, Thatched House, Holt, in Norfolk as a base. The General Committee approved in principle the proposal to set up a Science Education Centre, in the first place in Ramage's home. At the same meeting the Chairman and General Secretary were asked to make enquiries about office accommodation in London and Cambridge.[21]

London property was prohibitively expensive, but F.C. Brown (Perse School), the newly-appointed honorary treasurer, drew the attention of his fellow officers to a three-storey Victorian house at 52 Bateman Street, Cambridge, recently vacated by the Perse Girls' School Preparatory Department. The ground landlord was Trinity Hall and an 11 year lease was available from the Perse Trust at a rent

Bateman Street – the SMA's first permanent headquarters

of £450 per annum. Some income might be earned by letting part of the house as flatted accommodation to a resident warden, an administrative officer and a caretaker; office space might also be rented by the AWST. For an estimated capital outlay of £1350 and a net annual expenditure of some £350 it seemed possible to establish a permanent home for the SMA.[22]

At a General Committee meeting on 5 March 1960, after a discussion minuted as 'lengthy and detailed', it was decided to proceed with the renting of 52 Bateman Street on the maximum lease. The effect of this on the SMA annual subscription was taken into account, a substantial increase from the current rate of £1 11s 6d to £2, or over, being anticipated.[23] Nevertheless, the urgent need for a headquarters, if the Association was to fulfil its plans for growth, left no acceptable alternative.

A House Committee responsible for negotiating the renting, decorating and furnishing of the Headquarters was appointed, consisting of R.P. Ayres, F.C. Brown, H.F. Boulind, E.H. Coulson, and H.P. Ramage. In practice, though three members were Cambridge-based, it did not prove easy for the Committee to meet and act with the speed necessary to secure the property. Of necessity, many decisions had to be taken by F.C. Brown, as Treasurer, trusting that the General Committee would support him when he reported. In the event, the Committee approved and the SMA was in possession of the property by 16 May 1960, though not before the County Council had invoked the Town and Country Planning Act of 1947 in refusing permission to convert the house to offices. Only some 'strenuous back-stage work' by Brown, and support from Trinity Hall, achieved a reversal of the decision, the application for use of 52 Bateman Street as 'residential flats, office, a library/conference room' being deemed not to constitute development within the meaning of the Act.[24]

At this point, if not before, some conflict of interest became apparent. Ramage's conception of the house as a Science Education Centre, with himself as Resident Warden, and part of the premises being used by the SMA for its Headquarters, was at odds with that of some other officers. Their alternative view was that the house should be 'run' by the SMA, with the Science Education Centre being accommodated to the extent that proved convenient. Ramage had recently retired from his post of science master at Gresham's School and he and his wife were intending to move from Holt to Cambridge. Resolution of any difference in opinion about the use of 52 Bateman Street was not assisted by his appointment as Warden for 5 years from 1 July 1960. At the same meeting of the General Committee, it was agreed that 'as a way of commemorating its Diamond Jubilee' the SMA should sponsor the Science Education Centre by giving it hospitality in the house, Ramage 'being recognised as its Director'. Neither the Wardenship nor the Directorship carried a salary, but Mr and Mrs Ramage were to reside in the first floor flat, free of rent. The Committee also appointed, at a salary of £600 per annum, Miss E.M. Taylor as Assistant Secretary to be resident in the Headquarters house.[25]

Over the summer months work proceeded on the preparation of the accommodation. When Ramage, as Warden, reported to the General Committee in the autumn, the Chairman's expression of appreciation to F.C. Brown and to Mr and Mrs Ramage for all they had done to secure and prepare Headquarters was received with acclamation.[26] Whilst it was clear that some estimates of expenditure would be exceeded, Ramage indicated his preparedness to help personally to defray certain costs. His suggestion that a Headquarters Management Committee be set up was acted upon, though this committee was short-lived, being dissolved in March 1961. Amongst its decisions was a decree that the Assistant Secretary should be fully employed on SMA work 'which had priority, but at slack times Science Education Centre work may be arranged for her by the Warden'.[27] It was also agreed that there should be an official opening of the building in June 1961.[28]

At a meeting of officers in London on the day appointed for the official opening at Cambridge it was explained that matters had been postponed because 'the Warden had felt he could not undertake the responsibility of supervising the arrangements'. Reviewing the situation, J.S.G. McGeachin, Chairman of the General Committee, urged the need for the appointment of a full-time, salaried General Secretary to administer the SMA's affairs. In the same context it was reported that the present Assistant Secretary had intimated that 'she was feeling the strain of the present arrangements and there was the possibility of her resigning'. Further office accommodation at Headquarters would be needed by a General Secretary and any additional assistant staff. It was therefore proposed 'that the present interim arrangements should be terminated' and the Warden should vacate the Headquarters flat.[29] Ramage's letter of resignation as Warden was received shortly afterwards[30] and he and his wife moved to a house in Cambridge. No further development of the Science Education Centre took place.

52 Bateman Street was declared open as the headquarters of the SMA on 30 September 1961 by Sir Patrick Linstead FRS, President in that year.[31] At the same occasion it was announced that His Royal Highness The Duke of Edinburgh had agreed to become Patron of the Association.[32] A short time later, a newly constituted Headquarters Committee appointed E.W. Tapper, a member of the General Committee by virtue of his office as Librarian, as 'full-time Secretary of the Association'.[33] The ASE therefore inherited Headquarters accommodation sufficient for its purpose in the short term, but under a lease which expired in 1971. With an eye to the future, a Building and Development Fund was started in 1963, in preparation for the day when new premises would be needed. Growth in membership and in the scope of its activities brought this nearer than many had thought. By December 1965 the Headquarters Committee was considering the specification of new accommodation and had begun the processes of searching for sites and gauging costs.[34] Though London seemed out of the question on grounds of expense, easy access to it was important, the General Secretary having to make frequent visits for meetings at the Royal Society, the professional scientific institutes and the Schools Council. Some support was found for Birmingham as a base and a property in Cheltenham came under close consideration,[35] but a fortuitous set of circumstances led the Association in a different direction. S.T. Broad, county Education Officer for Hertfordshire, a local authority with a high reputation for its building programme, was the brother of H.F. Broad, Chairman of the ASE in 1966. Hertfordshire County Council administered an Educational Trust which owned the 100-acre site which was the campus of Hatfield Technical College. An offer was made to lease land on this site to the ASE, under appropriate conditions, 'for a peppercorn rent', so that the Association might design and build its own Headquarters. Following a visit to Hatfield in February 1966,

Hatfield – the opening of the HQ in 1969
The Chairman, Miss Helen Ward, with Professor Eric Laithwaite, Mr John Rose, Mr E.W. Tapper and Mr John Onslow

the Headquarters Site Committee made a firm recommendation to the Executive Committee of the ASE to pursue negotiations with this end in mind.[36] By the turn of the year it had been agreed that Mr J. Onslow, an Architect for Hertfordshire County Council would take on the work of designing the new Headquarters. Considerable assistance was also given by Mr D. Erskine, Assistant Education Officer, especially in obtaining DES permission for the college to allow the ASE to build on the site, and Board of Trade permission to have office accommodation in Hatfield. A schedule for developments, drawn up in the Spring of 1967, indicated a possibility that the Association could be in possession of new, purpose-built premises by September 1969.[37] To the credit of all concerned, there was little departure from this projection, staff and machinery moving in during October 1969.

The removal from 52 Bateman Street was clouded by disputes over 'dilapidation claims' requiring unanticipated payments by the ASE, but the major financial hurdle, £40,000 for the new Headquarters, was cleared by prudent financial management and by an Appeal. By 1968, the Building and Development Fund stood at around £7000. An increase in the annual subscription paid by members, from £2 to £3 in 1967, yielded a surplus of income over expenditure for 1967/68 of £5000. Estimated surpluses for 1968/69 and 1969/70 added a further £7000. A decision was taken to realise 50 per cent of the Association's investments, the £9000 so available making a grand total of £28,000 from existing resources. The balance of £12,000 was sought from members, on current membership figures requiring £1 per member, and from industry.[38] Despite exhortations from the President, J.D. Rose of Imperial Chemical Industries Ltd, the Chairman, E.H. Coulson, and the Honorary Treasurer, E.G. Breeze, by the end of the Association's financial year in July 1969, the Hatfield Appeal Fund stood at only £8957 of which 1308 members had contributed £1607.[39] A further appeal to the 90 per cent of the membership who had not responded had some effect and a year later the fund stood at £15,681. With satisfaction, Breeze could report that 'The new building is our own property and we have paid for it'.[40]

Both functional and attractive, the Headquarters building proved a major asset to the Association in the development of services for its members. By 1977, however, expanding activities had exhausted the building's capacity and Council decided that an extension of 220 square metres was needed.[41] An appeal fund was again opened, yielding more than £20,000, a sum covering nearly one-third of the cost, the balance being met from the Association's own accumulated reserves. This time the approach was directed more towards industry and commerce, including publishers and scientific apparatus manufacturers, than to members. It was a reflection of the ASE's reputation and national standing that it could attract financial support on this scale.[42]

Membership

Numerically, the membership of the ASE grew steadily over the years, though not without occasional falterings, notably at times when the annual subscription was increased. Commencing in 1963 at £2 per annum for the ordinary member, an adjustment to £3 was necessitated in September 1967 by the cost of the move to Hatfield. After five years at this level it was increased to £5 in October 1973 and then continued to rise with inflation of costs until, by October 1983, ordinary membership was costing £16 per annum.[43]

The Rules of 1963 provided for several categories of membership, as well as for Student Associates who were required to be in full-time attendance in institutions of teacher training. Student Associates were elected for one year only, with renewal possible, and had no voting rights as well as being ineligible for election to any office of the ASE, to Council or the Executive Committee. The principal category of voting member was designated Ordinary and was open to any science teacher in a school, university or college of further or higher education. There was also provision for the election to this category of other persons who, in the opinion of the Executive Committee were specially interested in, or had contributed notably to, the advancement of science teaching. An ordinary member who had ceased to be employed as a science teacher other than through retirement, or who could demonstrate special need, formed a category of Special Members, paying a reduced subscription rate. Provision was also made for those retired to retain membership as Exempted Members.[44] Both the SMA and the AWST had employed a category of Honorary Member, and their respective lists under this heading were consolidated at the inaugural business meeting of the ASE to yield a further category of membership for the new Association.[45] Similarly, the block membership which the SMA had offered to the Royal Navy was continued after the merger.

Though the broad structure of the membership categories stood the test of time, inevitably as the Association grew, the need for new categories arose whilst others were merged. Thus, enquiries were received from firms in the UK about the possibility of corporate subscription, access to membership lists and the support of the Association in connection with conferences and exhibitions being amongst benefits which could accrue. At the same time a new grade of corporate subscriber was seen as a means by which the Association could express its appreciation to friends who had provided material and financial help with its activities. By the end of the 1960s a number of organizations had been enlisted including English Electric, Philip Harris, The Royal Society, The Nuffield Foundation, John Murray (Publishers) Ltd, and Longmans, Green and Co. Ltd.[46] Later, at a time when links with industry were being strongly developed, and with the support of Sir Denis Rooke (chairman, British Gas Corporation and ASE President, 1981) a grade of Corporate Membership for industrial and commercial organizations was instituted, in the hope that such organizations would become involved in the work of the ASE and give constructive support to activities at national and regional level. Within a year, 44 organizations had joined.[47]

A different type of corporate membership was offered to overseas schools. Its origins were inadvertent, arising from the movement of teachers from one school to another, the head of the initial school continuing to pay the subscription. The amount of correspondence needed to put right this matter was deemed 'not worth it' by the General Secretary and so the overseas schools' group membership had come to exist. Another form of overseas corporate membership was by affiliation of a local science teachers' association. In these cases, one copy of each journal published by the ASE was provided and 'honorary' membership offered for a year when a member visited the UK.[48]

Finally, a small but interesting category of membership appropriately introduced at the time of the 'marriage' of the Associations in 1963, was that termed Joint. Intended for science teachers who were husband and wife, it provided one copy only of ASE journals at an advantageous joint subscription rate. The numbers under this heading grew to over 250 couples by the early 1980s.

An indication of the extent of the growth of membership in various categories is provided by the figures in Table 5.1.

Some indication of the extent of diversification in the institutional affiliations of members is provided by the appearance of special

Table 5.1   Growth of membership

Numbers at 31.07	Ordinary UK	Ordinary Overseas	Exempted	Joint	Honorary	Total
1963	8238	538	336	8	63	9183
1982	14090	1045	702	261	61	16159

Numbers at 31.07	Students	Corporate	Industrial & Commercial Corporate
1963	364	—	—
1982	690	101	44

interest groups with concerns different from the traditional secondary grammar school ones of the SMA and AWST. As early as January 1963 the Science and Education Committee had recommended an extension of its work to include the teaching of science in schools of all types and a primary school sub-committee was established under the chairmanship of D.H.J. Marchant (Kesteven Training College).[49] Before the year was out a Policy Statement on *Primary School Science*, commending discovery methods and 'finding out activities', had been published.[50] This was supported by a series of books prepared by the ASE's primary school sub-committee.[51] When the Association's general policy statement on *School Science and General Education* was issued in 1965 it contained for the first time a section on Primary Stage Science Education.

Recruitment of primary school teachers was limited, however, few being prepared to subscribe to ordinary membership when relatively little of the Association's programme of activities and services was seen to have direct relevance to their work. In 1967 the problem was referred to a Working Party instructed 'to look into the matter of publicity for the ASE in primary schools'.[52] Some time later the old sub-committee was discharged and a new one, under the chairmanship of Dr Margaret M. Collis (Kent Education Committee), was established to consider what further action was needed in the field of primary education.[53] The appearance of middle schools in certain parts of the country, and questions about the place of science in the middle school curriculum, brought into being around the same time a Middle School Working Party under the chairmanship of E.H. Coulson.[54] When in 1975 the Association announced the establishment of an Award Scheme, intended to encourage science teachers to communicate their ideas for the benefit of others, the chosen theme for the first award was Science in the Middle Years of Schooling, covering work with pupils aged 8 to 13 years.[55] Another initiative designed to stimulate and support science teaching in first and middle schools was the publication and distribution in 1980 of *ASE Primary Science*, a termly news-sheet. By 1982, over 23,000 copies were being sold in bulk to local education authorities.[56] Encouraged by this venture the ASE Council sought to encourage primary school teachers into individual membership by instituting a special Primary Teacher Subscription (in 1983–84 this was £5 compared with the ordinary member's subscription of £16), which provided a personal copy of *Education in Science*, and *ASE Primary Science* as well as access to regional and national meetings.[57]

A second group of science teachers, unrepresented in any collective way in the membership of the SMA and AWST and, indeed, in the ASE in its early years, came from institutions of Further Education. By the early 1970s, however, their presence was sufficient to oblige the Association to consider its policy on science education in Further Education. The Education (Coordinating) Committee established a small group to prepare a draft statement on Science in Further Education and this document was the subject of a one-day Conference at Wolverhampton Polytechnic in November 1972. The response was such that a Further Education sub-committee was formally constituted with instructions to prepare a Policy Statement.[58]

The Association's progress towards this goal was delayed by important changes then taking place in the organization of examinations in Colleges of Further Education. The Haslegrave Report on *Technician Courses and Examinations* (1969) had envisaged the formation of a Technician Education Council (TEC) as had the Hudson Report on *Technician Courses and Examinations in Scotland* (1971) in its proposals for SCOTEC, but considerable delays were associated with the establishment of these bodies. It was not until March 1973 that the Technician Education Council was in being. In November of that year, the ASE's sub-committee published an Interim Report in *Education in Science* with a request for members' views.[59] In the light of these a further statement for discussion was printed, urging the Association to use its resources to spread greater awareness of opportunities for students offered by further education and to encourage staff development, including liaison between scientists in all sectors of education and industry.[60]

The value of this statement was acknowledged by F.G. Hanrott, Chief Officer of the Technician Education Council, at the second ASE Conference on Science in Further Education at Wolverhampton Polytechnic in October 1974.[61] Taking into account comments made at the Conference, and also further developments in TEC and SCOTEC, a final revised statement from the sub-committee was prepared, and approved at the spring meeting of the ASE Council in 1975, the sub-committee then being disbanded.[62]

The years ahead were to see an increasing convergence of interests, especially with respect to the 16 to 19 age group, between schools

The Duke of Edinburgh presenting Prize Scheme Awards, 1977

and institutions of Further Education. The Statement of 1975 was merely the beginning of the Association's involvement in this field. In 1977 the phasing-in had begun of the TEC science education programmes designed to replace Ordinary and Higher National Certificate and Diploma courses, on the one hand, and technician courses offered by the City and Guilds of London Institute, on the other. In the same year the Further Education Curriculum Review and Development Unit was established by the Department of Education and Science. It was clear that not only did the ASE have an important future role to play in relation to the work of science teachers in institutions of Further Education, but also that such teachers, especially those with qualifications in technologies, could make a significant contribution to ASE activities in the field of school science teaching and its relations to industry.[63] A new sub-committee was convened in 1978 under the chairmanship of D. Hardaker (Stevenson College of FE, Edinburgh) together with Ursula Bowen (Oxford Polytechnic), H.R. Jones (HMI for Industrial Sciences), R. Marks (Technician Education Council), W.A. Tovell (Loughton College of FE) and R. Whitcutt (CEGB).[64] Through the pages of *Education in Science* the sub-committee provided information and comment on science education developments in the field of Further Education for the benefit of the ASE's membership.[65]

Another group which came into existence earlier in the life of the ASE was composed of local education authority science advisers and others with a similar responsibility. Their first meeting was held at Nottingham during the Annual Meeting on 29 December 1966. On the proposal of the Chairman, R. Thurlow (Leeds LEA and ex-Chairman of the ASE, 1963) it was agreed that a group be formed of 'members of the ASE engaged in educational administration'.[66] By 1973 the membership had grown to 115, representing 94 local education authorities, and an annual programme had become established including a day conference, a meeting at the ASE annual meeting, and a three-day residential conference in the summer.[67]

The practice of holding a meeting within the programme of the Annual Meeting was adopted by other special interest groups such as university science education tutors. The Association was increasingly being seen as manifesting Broad Church tendencies which readily accommodated diverse professional interests. An illustration of the comprehensiveness with which the conditions of eligibility for members were being interpreted was provided in 1978. In reporting on the Technical Advisory Service for laboratory technicians inaugurated two years previously by the Laboratory Technicians Sub-Committee of the Education (Coordinating) Committee, the General Secretary was able to state that 'the Association welcomes applications for membership from laboratory technicians', a pronouncement which contrasted markedly with the prevarication following an enquiry from a laboratory technician, albeit from Charterhouse, in the 1930s.[68]

Constitution and Officers

The Executive Committee of the ASE met on no less than eleven occasions in 1963, such was the flow of business in the first year of merged existence. However, a few weeks only of operation of the new constitution were sufficient to expose ambiguities and at least one omission resulting in proposals to change the Rules as early as the second meeting. Thus, an attempt had been made to take advantage of the provision for block membership, the rate of subscription for block members being lower than that for ordinary members, when the complete science staff of a London school made a joint application. This was turned down and, in reviewing the rule in question, Student Associates were likewise excluded from its provisions. Similarly, the conditions of eligibility for membership were tested by applications from Fife County Council and the Southern Universities Joint Examinations Board, both refused. The most significant change, however, was that necessary to enable continuation of the patronage which the Duke of Edinburgh had extended to the SMA, no provision for this being included in the original ASE Rules.[69]

It also became clear, at an early date, that decision-taking within the Association was hindered because the chairman of the important Education Committee, at the time the only Standing Committee of

Council apart from the Executive Committee, was not a member of Council. Accordingly he was invited to attend Council meetings from March 1964 until his position could be regularised at the following Annual Business Meeting.[70] At a later date, when the work of the Education Committee was divided between two committees, designated Education (Coordinating) and Education (Research), the chairman of each became a member of Council, and, from 1977, of the Executive Committee also.[71]

The ASE began life with its full complement of four honorary secretaries, one of whom, Miss B.G. Ashton, was designated Secretary for Girls' Schools, the others being responsible for Minuting (I.G. Jones), Annual Meetings (D.W. Harlow) and Examinations (H. Tunley) respectively. Also, in accordance with Rule 21(b) one of the three Vice-Chairmen was a woman (Miss F.M. Eastwood) as was one of the three Trustees (Miss E.L. Buckley).[72] The office of Secretary for Girls' Schools had been established to ensure that any problems of science education in girls' schools with which the Association might have to deal, would be handled by someone with first-hand experience of the education of girls. In fact little specific business for the Executive Committee and Council arose under this heading and, although after three years, on her appointment as Vice-Chairman of the ASE, Miss Ashton was replaced in her secretaryship by Miss J.D. Ling, by 1968 the post of Secretary for Girls' schools had disappeared. In passing, it is noteworthy that as a member of the first Executive Committee, Miss Ashton explored the possibility of holding a Summer Meeting for women members of the ASE in 1964, only to find that since the union, and despite eulogistic accounts of the last AWST Summer Meeting at Brighton in 1962, demand had evaporated.[73] Not only did the specific interests in the scientific education of girls and the specific organizational practices which had characterised the AWST appear to fade away at this stage, but also, with the changing social climate which led to the Sex Discrimination Act of 1975, it was thought appropriate to remove from the Rules any references to women. At the Annual Business Meeting at Leicester in January 1977 all clauses which indicated the necessity of at least one of the Officers or Elected Members being a male and at least one a female were amended and it was indicated, as in the Trust Deed, that throughout the Rules the masculine included the feminine.[74]

The Executive Committee began its work in 1963 as a compact team of seven, with the General Secretary in attendance. In practice its composition proved too limited for its work. With a membership of the Chairman (R. Thurlow, in 1963), three of the Honorary Secretaries (Minuting, I.G. Jones; Annual Meeting, D.W. Harlow; Girls' Schools, Miss B.G. Ashton), the honorary Treasurer (F.C. Brown) and two Trustees (Miss E.L. Buckley and E.H. Coulson), the absence of the honorary Editor of *The School Science Review* (R.H. Dyball) proved an early disadvantage, overcome initially by invitation to attend meetings and, from 1964, by constitutional change. Another problem related to the Chairman-elect who clearly needed experience of the work of the Executive Committee before assuming office. Like many subsequent chairmen, Miss F.M. Eastwood, Thurlow's successor in 1964, attended meetings by invitation following election by Council in the previous year. As for the retiring Chairman, experience acquired during the year of office was inevitably retained for the Committee by election as a vice-chairman, the arrangement being formalised after 1975 when specific reference was made to the immediate past Chairman and the number of vice-chairmen was reduced to two.

From a committee of seven, the Executive increased to ten in 1964 by the inclusion of the honorary Editor, all four honorary secretaries and two vice-chairmen, the number of Trustees being reduced by one. With the reorganization of the Education Committee and the abolition of the offices of Examinations Secretary and Secretary for Girls Schools, there was an effective reduction to nine members in 1968, a third Vice-Chairman having by then been added. The affairs of the ASE were managed by an Executive Committee of this composition (Chairman, three vice-chairmen, honorary Treasurer, honorary Editor, honorary Minuting Secretary, honorary Annual Meeting Secretary and one Trustee) for almost a decade.[75] Eventually, by 1977, further change was necessitated.

First, after prolonged negotiations, approval was given for the ASE to nominate a representative for membership of the Science Committee of the Schools Council. A new office of Secretary for Schools Council Liaison was instituted, its holder, Dr R.W. West (University of Sussex), becoming a member of the Executive Committee.[76] Secondly, by that date, the Association's authority in the field of science education had grown to an extent that it was receiving an increasing number of approaches from other bodies, including the House of Commons Expenditure Committee, the Science Group of H.M. Inspectorate and the Department of Education and Science, for opinion and advice.[77] The preparation of appropriate responses in a limited space of time required a more effective disposition of available expertise. Accordingly, the two chairmen of the Education Committees, Coordinating and Research, were recruited to the Executive Committee which, by 1977, had grown to twelve members. The following year, as a result of a major review of the structure and function of the Association's Council which revealed a pressing need for improved communication between members and their elected officers and committees, a Standing Committee on Publications was established. Its chairman, Miss E.W. McCreath (Education Section, Unilever Ltd) was likewise immediately appointed to the Executive Committee.[78] Increase in the number and diversity of the ASE's members, as well as in the influence which the Association could exert, had brought about a near doubling in the size of the committee in fifteen years.

An account of the Education Committee (which was also a Standing Committee of Council until January 1968), is provided in Part Three of this book where detailed consideration is given to its role in curriculum review and development.[79] From a constitutional point of view it is sufficient to note that by 1966 the committee itself was aware that it had extended itself to a point where fission was inevitable. Its membership had enlarged with each of the many sub-committees it established, and its concerns ranged over both policy issues and routine practical matters (Table 5.2). Apart from examinations, apparatus, teaching aids and teacher training, to mention only some of the subjects with which its sub-committees were involved, the Education Committee supervised the representation of the ASE on external bodies such as the education committees of the professional scientific institutes and the Consortium of Local Education Authorities for the Provision of Science Equipment (CLEAPSE).[80] In 1968, the transfer of sub-committees and groups to the new Education Committees (Coordinating and Research)[81] revealed that life was infused unevenly through the bewildering array of activities involved, to an extent that obliged the ASE Chairman in 1970, Miss Helen Ward, to publish an appeal to convenors to report to the Chairman of the Education (Coordinating) Committee by a specified date.[82] If no communication was received, it would be assumed the sub-committee was defunct.

A long process involving much detailed correspondence followed before the initial instalment of active ASE committees, with names and institutions of members, appeared in 1973.[83] In many ways this was a landmark; it consolidated in a single statement the multifarious involvements of the Association in science education nationally and, equally, testified to the impressive voluntary contributions of members. At the same time, it was a significant contribution to 'openness' in the administration of the Association. For the first time members had ready access to information about who was representing them below the level of elected honorary officers, and whom they might approach on specific issues. At this stage the sub-committees and working groups of the Education (Coordinating) Committee numbered ten, namely: Apparatus; Science 13–16; Teaching of Electricity; Laboratory Technicians; SI Units; Chemical Nomenclature; Laboratory Safeguards; Science Advisers' Group; Primary Schools Science; and Science in Further Education. Further, updated lists were published at regular intervals thereafter.[84] As an indication of growth in activity and changes in concerns the comparable list a decade later included sixteen sub-committees and groups: Chemical Labels; Chemical Nomenclature; Examinations; Girls and Physical Science; Health and Safety at Work; Joint Sub-Committee with the Association of Teachers of Geology; Laboratory Safeguards; Safety in Science; Laboratory Technicians; Microelectronics and Science Education; Primary Schools Science; SI Units; Science Advisers' Group; Science, Industry and Technology; Science in Further

Table 5.2   ASE Committee structure, 1967 (taken from Education in Science, February 1967)

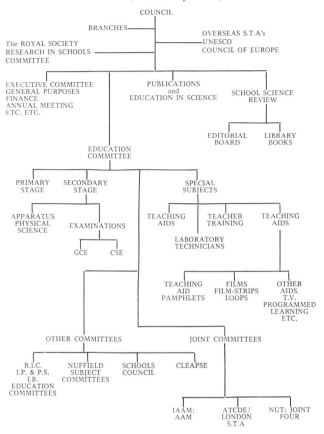

Education; and Science Teacher Education.[85]

The Education (Coordinating) Committee was responsible for 'the month-by-month coordination of and comment on matters arising in the science teaching field'. In contrast the Education (Research) Committee was designed for policy and pioneering, with a longer-term perspective. Just as the work of the Science and Education Committee of the SMA was said to have led to the Nuffield Projects, so, it was argued, the new Committee would initiate projects of a research character by establishing working parties with precise terms of reference. Though one of the members of the Committee might act as chairman or convenor of a working party, the Committee itself would not carry out research.[86] Its role was more that of the Association's 'Research Council', though, in contrast to national bodies like the Science Research Council and the recently established Social Science Research Council it had no significant funds at its disposal.

This was a novel and difficult concept for the Association to realize and clearly the qualifications, experience and interests of the members of the Committee were crucial to its success. Yet, in common with other ASE committees, the Research Committee was elected by the Council of the Association where regional interests were strongly represented. Writing in 1974, it was the opinion of Dr R.W. West, a member of the Committee from 1970 and its chairman from 1972 until 1977, that 'regional and political criteria have been as important in determining membership as any considerations of research expertise.'[87]

Within the period 1968 to 1971 under two successive chairmen, R. Schofield (Brunel University) and I.D.S. Robertson (Jordanhill College of Education, Glasgow), the committee initiated and collaborated in a variety of projects. Significantly, progress of working parties investigating matters such as systems of standard units and chemical nomenclature was notably better than those concerned with, for example, children's attitudes to science. As a report on one such enquiry into attitudes, involving over 2000 children in nine schools in the West Midlands region, disarmingly concluded, 'It is not felt that one year's results should be taken too seriously as there is no doubt that the problem of attitudes to science is a very complex one'.[88] In his annual report for 1969–70, the chairman, I.D.S. Robertson, acknowledged that the committee had become 'increasingly aware of the need for sophistication in research' and that fundamental research in science education was 'normally beyond the capacity of a school-based working party'.[89] A general review of the committee's policy followed in 1971.

Premised on the assumption that curriculum renewal and development were central to the ASE's concerns, a different role for the Education (Research) Committee was expounded with considerable effect by the chairman-elect, R.W. West. In his view the transfer of prevailing models of educational research to the work of the committee was fruitless. Rather than analyse and evaluate existing practice as a prerequisite for curriculum development, the committee would be better employed in first identifying, and then assisting, worthwhile innovations in science education, especially at the school level. The committee's role would be three-fold: first, as a collector and disseminator of information about successful curriculum and examination innovations; second, as a 'link agency' putting teachers in touch with available support systems; and third, in connection with future curriculum development, the exploration of models alternative to the research, design and development approach used by the Nuffield teams in the 1960s. 'If the ASE is to continue to play a *central* part in defining science education policy and practice', West contended, involvement in the development role was crucial. In essence the change in role for the committee which he proposed, and which was in large measure adopted under his chairmanship, was from 'a think-tank creative ideas Committee' to 'an agency for supporting the innovations found in our better schools and amongst our professional colleagues who concern themselves with defining science education'.[90]

Writing at a later date, mid-term during his chairmanship, he described the three activities of the committee as:

(i) developing methods for increasing the flow of information on current practice in the teaching of science to pupils of all abilities in the 11–16 age range;

(ii) extending the discussion on the aims and objectives for science in general education within the same age and ability range; and

(iii) increasing the overall level of research and development skills of the committee itself.[91]

Within this revised policy orientation were the seeds of the Secondary Science Curriculum Review, the joint ASE/Schools Council project initiated exactly a decade later. In the intervening years the Education (Research) Committee led the ASE into school-based curriculum development through the successful LAMP (Science for the Less Academically Motivated Pupils) project,[92] and into externally-funded research activity, seeking and securing for the ASE in Spring 1978 a grant of £41,000 over two years from the Schools Council to finance Studies in Decision Making in Science Education.[93] When the constitutional link with the Schools Council's Science Committee was established in 1976 West became the ASE's Honorary Secretary for Schools Council Liaison, the chairmanship of the Education (Research) Committee passing in 1977 to M.J. Savory.

Following the Macmillan Education Lecture by Mrs Shirley Williams, Secretary of State for Education and Science, at the Annual Meeting of the ASE at Liverpool in January 1978, and her call for a balanced and effective science curriculum for all pupils in secondary schools, a small working party of representatives of DES, the Schools Council's Science Committee and the ASE began to meet under the chairmanship of Dr John Spice to consider what action was needed.[94] Their eventual proposal for a national review of the secondary school science curriculum was incorporated and funded as part of the Schools Council's programme for 'Developing the Curriculum for a Changing World'. Additional financial support was provided by the ASE and the Northern Ireland Council for Educational Development, yielding a total of some £850,000 over a five-year period. In the summer of 1981, Dr West was appointed Director of the Review,[95] with another leading officer of the ASE, Professor J.J. Thompson (University of Bath and Chairman of the ASE in 1981), as Chairman of the Review's Steering Committee. Also on the Steering Committee as ASE representatives were J.C. Heaney, who in 1982 succeeded Savory as chairman of the Education (Research) Committee; J. Nellist, another member of the same committee and a Vice-Chairman of the ASE in 1981); and Mrs C. Edwards, Head of Science at High Cross Girls' School, London.[96] The Schools Council's representatives included E.O. James, for some years chairman of the Examinations Sub-Committee of the ASE's Education (Coordinating) Committee and in 1983 Chairman of the parent committee itself; and J.L. Lewis, who had been Chariman of the ASE in 1977. Amongst other Steering Committee members, and representing the Examinations Boards, was W.F. Archenhold (University of Leeds), another ex-Chairman of the ASE (1973) and a Trustee of the Association from 1976 to 1981.

The route which the Association had travelled since 1968 may have been very different from that in the minds of those who established the Education (Research) Committee, but the relationship of the ASE to the Review, constitutionally, financially, and in terms of the involvement of individual officers, was a remarkable realization of the original hope, expressed by H.F. Boulind, that the Research Committee would act as 'a spear-head of advance'.[97] Regional involvement of the ASE's membership in the work of the Review was endorsed by Council in February 1983, the coordination of this and the task of liaison with the Review's Central Team becoming the responsibility of Mrs C.M. Wilson, the ASE's Deputy General Secretary, and a former honorary secretary to the Education (Research) Committee.[98] The direction of constitutional change was clear. Principles of partnership and self-determination, openness and participation, had steadily come to assume a greater importance in the activities of the Association and mechanisms for the determination of policy by decisions in small groups were under transformation.

Further evidence of the process of democratization at work is provided by an examination of the honorary officers of the Association over the period 1963 to 1983. Under the Rules and given the strong regional representation on Council it became less likely that any individual would serve for an extended period as had been possible with the SMA and AWST. The sole exception was the special case of the honorary Editor of *The School Science Review*, A.A. Bishop (Harrow), who succeeded to the editorship in 1966 and served as Chairman and immediate past Chairman in 1975 and 1976 respectively, being a member of the Executive Committee for seventeen of the twenty-one years under review. As for the Trustees, their term of office, initially without limit, was soon reduced to nine years. The maximum term for the Chairman was one year, for a vice-chairman three, and for the honorary Treasurer and honorary Secretaries, five consecutive years. Two officers, J.J. Bryant (Quarry Bank High School, Liverpool) and Miss F.M. Eastwood (Godolphin and Latymer School London) achieved eleven years of continuous service, each as Chairman, vice–chairman and Trustee. F.W. Archenhold (University of Leeds), Professor E.H. Coulson (University of London), Mrs J. Glover (Godolphin and Latymer School), Miss Helen Ward (North Manchester High School for Girls) and Dr R.W. West (University of Sussex) each contributed nine years of service, their offices including Chairman and vice-chairman. Those who served as honorary Treasurer or as one of the honorary secretaries are listed in Table 5.3.

No doubt the member whose letter was published in *Education in Science* in 1978 had a point when he maintained that 'teachers in state non-selective schools are not well represented either on the Executive or on Committees of the ASE'.[99] In reviewing the schools and institutions from which officers came with this criticism in mind, it has to be recalled that it was not until 1965 that the DES issued its circular requiring local education authorities to implement schemes of non-selective secondary education. Reaction to this was in any case not always immediate. Also, there is inescapable inertia in any voluntary organisation – loyal servants cannot be dropped overnight, terms of office have to be run – which inhibits rapid response to change; and many factors other than institutional affiliation need to be taken into account in the election of officers. Their geographical distribution suggests that proximity to London (or Hatfield) still remained an important consideration. Over the twenty-one year period, at least 60 per cent of the ASE's honorary officers came from institutions within a 100 miles of London. Beyond this there was strong representation from the Yorkshire Region and the North-West. Only one officer came from Scotland and one from Northern Ireland; none from Wales.

As for the public schools they still provided some officers, but the continuity of influence from a small number of such schools had disappeared and the special problems of science education in public schools now tended to be addressed outside the circles of the ASE. What was evident was the emergence of other groups, including local education authority science advisers and university science education tutors, as important contributors to decision-making in the Association. Of those serving on the various committees of the ASE in 1983, although school teachers of science predominated, roughly a third held administrative or university appointments.[100] Depending on the point of view, this might be interpreted as a regrettable dilution of teacher control or an encouraging manifestation of partnership in a joint exercise.

Servicing all the varied activities of the Association was the permanent salaried staff of Headquarters. In its appointments to the non-clerical grades in what was, in effect, a new type of career, the administration of a subject teaching association, the tendency of the ASE was increasingly to draw upon its own ranks. The first General Secretary, E.W. Tapper, had been a member of the General Committee of the SMA. On his retirement after supervision of a decade of growth and consolidation, including the move to Hatfield, he was succeeded in January 1972 by B.G. Atwood (Great Barr Comprehensive School, Birmingham) Chairman of the Association in the previous year, as well as Chairman of the important Branches Committee which planned the reorganization of the Association's local

Table 5.3

Honorary Treasurer		Honorary Minuting Secretary	
1963–1966	F.C. Brown (Perse S.)	1963–1967	I.G. Jones (Doncaster Grammar School)
1967–1971	E.G. Breeze (Grammar S., Welwyn Garden City)	1968–1972	R.M. Lee (St Bede's College Manchester)
		1973–1977	Rev. M.D. Phillips (Ampleforth College)
1972–1976	A.M. Kavanagh (St Thomas Aquinas Grammar S., Leeds)	1978–1982	Miss F.L.R. Barlow (Finham Park S., Coventry)
1977–1981	Dr J.A. Darby (Wolverhampton Grammar School)	1983–	Mrs N. Broadbridge (Convent of the Holy Child Jesus, Birmingham)
1982–	E.N. Bonsall (Hucknall National S., Nottingham)		

Honorary Annual Meeting Secretary	
1963–1967	D.W. Harlow (Testwood Sec. S., Totton)
1968–1972	Dr C. Briske (King's Norton Grammar S., Birmingham)
1973–1974	B. Nicholl (Newman College, Birmingham)
1975	Dr J.J. Thompson (Dept. of Education, Univ. of Oxford)
1976–1980	M.J. Wilkinson (Magdalen College School, Oxford)
1981	G.E. Siddle (Hull College of Education)
1982–	Dr D.S. Moore (Caludon Castle S., Coventry)

Table 5.3 (contd.)

Honorary Examinations Secretary		Honorary Secretary for Girls' Schools	
1963–1967	H. Tunley (Merchant Taylors' S., Crosby, Liverpool)	1963–1965	Miss B.G. Ashton (Edgbaston High S. for Girls, Birmingham)
		1966–1967	Miss J.D. Ling (The Technical Secondary School, Grismby)
(Office abolished)		(Office abolished)	

activities in 1967.[101] In September 1973, the rapidly expanding and financially important publications section at Headquarters became the responsibility of a new Assistant Secretary, Mrs C.M. Wilson, who as Miss C.M. Meredith (Clitheroe Girls' Grammar School) had previously been active on the Education (Research) Committee. In 1983 Mrs Wilson was promoted to Deputy General Secretary of the ASE[102] and her previous post of Assistant Secretary filled by Mr C.B. Hodge. The production of *The School Science Review* and *Education in Science* similarly had reached a point by July 1969 when assistance to the editors was an urgent requirement. R.L. Brown, who was appointed for this task, served for a decade, and was succeeded by Mrs C.A. Abbott as Assistant Secretary on 1st January 1980.[103]

A further appointment of Assistant Secretary occurred in June 1975 when R.G. Turner joined the Headquarters' Staff with particular responsibilities for the Annual Meeting, servicing of the Education (Research) Committee and the increasing work on all aspects of safety in school science laboratories.[104] Supported by a considerable secretariat and clerical staff, the 'permanent officials' gave the ASE a stability and administrative efficiency without which the further development of its services and influence would have been impossible.

Branches to Regions

Within broad guidelines, the constitutional problems of establishing branches of the ASE were left to members in the localities. By the end of 1962 the SMA had approved the existence of seventeen branches, including three with joint AWST membership (Essex, Eastern Counties and West of England) and three in their infancy (East Midlands, Oxford and Reading), formalities having only just been completed by the date of amalgamation.[105] The ASWT ran ten branches, most of which were geographically close to existing SMA branches. The practical problems of merging branch activities did not, therefore, pose serious problems. Indeed, the London and Wales branches of the AWST had already amalgamated with their local SMA branches by the time that Branch Officers met SMA Committee members at the Annual Meeting in January 1963.[106] On that occasion, in anticipation of the new constitution, the branch representatives to serve on the Council of the ASE were named. Apart from Miss E. O'Shaughnessy, nominated by the joint Essex Branch, all the other sixteen representatives were male.

Branch representation on the new Council raised several issues which were to recur in subsequent deliberations of the ASE. Not all branches were of equal numerical size; thus, by 1967 the London Branch had over 1600 members, with the North-Western, Yorkshire and Midland Branches only slightly smaller, each having at least 1100 members. In contrast, the Lakeland Branch could muster a mere 120, other small branches being Oxford (200) and South Wales (270).[107] Yet each was entitled to the same representation on Council. Understandably, some members of larger branches were led to consider the advantages of binary fission in the hope of improved representation of their points of view. The attractions of this were not lessened by the fact that the areas covered by these branches were frequently extensive and a member could be involved in considerable travel in order to attend meetings. For instance, the Midland Branch in 1965 covered the counties of Hereford, Stafford, Warwick, Worcester, and parts of Leicester, Derby, Northampton and Nottingham.

There was also the question of multiplication of branches by colonization of fresh parts of the country in which ASE activity had hitherto been relatively undeveloped. A new branch for Kent was approved in 1964, and one for Wrexham in 1965, whilst the possibility of a local committee for North Bedfordshire and North Buckinghamshire was being actively explored in 1966.[108] This growth of regional activity by its members could only be applauded by the ASE officers. At the same time, each new branch meant one more representative on Council. The uncontrolled proliferation of branches would clearly lead to an unwieldy and unbalanced policy-forming body.

A preliminary skirmish with these and related issues, including the relationship of the ASE to the numerous local Associations of Science Teachers then springing up, took place in the Executive Committee as early as July 1963 when it was agreed to recommend to Council that a group be established, its members to include one from the London Branch (because of its experience of running a branch with large numbers), one from the North-Eastern Branch (which had established 'centres' as a measure to overcome the geographical dispersion of its members), one from the active and independently-minded Yorkshire Branch, and one from the Reading Branch, a small newcomer, but one keen to retain its identity. A report based on the results of a questionnaire was produced and discussed by Council. At that point, however, it seemed that branches needed more time to accumulate experience of the new arrangements and it was agreed to keep the problem under review during the next two years.[109]

A proposal to establish yet another branch, this time in Derbyshire, brought the matter into prominence again in 1966, when Council agreed to a moratorium on the formation of branches whilst a sub-committee gave consideration to the whole question of the future of branches and their position in the constitution of the Association. The members of this sub-committee were B.G. Atwood (Chairman, Midland), E.J. Vernon (London), D.M. Chillingworth (Eastern Counties), S.J. Browning (Yorkshire) and D.F. Wright (East Midlands).[110] Their important recommendation that the Association should be organized geographically on a three-tier basis – national regional, and sectional – was implemented on 1 August 1968. England, Scotland, Wales and Northern Ireland were divided into 17 Regions, each of which, under revised Rules, had the right to elect annually a representative to serve on Council. That body would then consist of the Honorary Officers of the ASE, including the Chairmen of the two Education committees, six elected members, and the 17 Region Representatives (See Table 5.4).

Compared with the previous composition (13 officers and 24 members, i.e. 6 elected and 18 branch representatives, making a total of 37) the new Council was slightly bigger (39) and the balance between officers and members had shifted in favour of the former (16 officers and 23 members i.e. 6 elected and 17 Region Representatives). At the same time the recommendations that each Region should establish territorial sub-divisions to be known as Sections, each with its own officers and committees, and that Sections should be financed by and be responsible to the appropriate Region committee on which they had membership, provided, hopefully, an improved mechanism for the organization and representation of the opinion of members.[111]

The difficulty facing the ASE in attempting to constitute a policy-shaping body such as Council was expressed by its Chairman, J.J. Bryant, in discussion of the report of the Branches sub-committee. 'In the past', Bryant argued, 'policy often sprang directly from decisions taken in small groups. Fruitful ideas are still likely to arise in such groups but the size of the Association makes central control a necessity and it is essential that central authority shall not become divorced from the initiative of individual members'.[112] On the new Council, members were still in a majority: the territorial boundary lines for Regions had reduced some of the grosser inequalities in size of the previous branches; the proposal for Sections offered the prospect of a more representative expression of opinion within Regions; and the overall size of Council had been kept under control, a point not only important for the efficiency with which it would conduct its business, but also relevant to the increasing cost of holding Council meetings.

In fact, it was clear that any decision on the constitution of Council could be *pro tempore* only, given the rate at which the ASE's membership and activities were expanding and diversifying. The

Table 5.4   ASE Council and Committees, January 1977

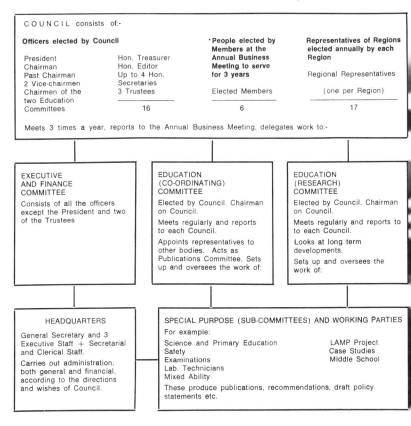

COUNCIL consists of:-

Officers elected by Council		*People elected by Members at the Annual Business Meeting to serve for 3 years	Representatives of Regions elected annually by each Region
President	Hon. Treasurer		
Chairman	Hon. Editor		Regional Representatives
Past Chairman	Up to 4 Hon.		
2 Vice-chairmen	Secretaries		(one per Region)
Chairmen of the	3 Trustees	Elected Members	
two Education			
Committees	16	6	17

Meets 3 times a year, reports to the Annual Business Meeting, delegates work to:-

EXECUTIVE AND FINANCE COMMITTEE

Consists of all the officers except the President and two of the Trustees

EDUCATION (CO-ORDINATING) COMMITTEE

Elected by Council. Chairman on Council.

Meets regularly and reports to each Council.

Appoints representatives to other bodies. Acts as Publications Committee. Sets up and oversees the work of:

EDUCATION (RESEARCH) COMMITTEE

Elected by Council. Chairman on Council.

Meets regularly and reports to each Council.

Looks at long term developments.

Sets up and oversees the work of:

HEADQUARTERS

General Secretary and 3 Executive Staff + Secretarial and Clerical Staff.

Carries out administration, both general and financial, according to the directions and wishes of Council.

SPECIAL PURPOSE (SUB-COMMITTEES) AND WORKING PARTIES

For example:

Science and Primary Education
Safety
Examinations
Lab. Technicians
Mixed Ability

LAMP Project
Case Studies
Middle School

These produce publications, recommendations, draft policy statements etc.

structure and function of Council had to be kept under review as the Association evolved. By the Autumn of 1976 a new working party of the six elected members of Council (D.P. Bennett, Mrs M.C. Casebourne, D.V. Clish, C.P. Elliott, Mrs E.A. Leonard, and A.F. Price) had been established, its recommendations leading to further changes.[113]

Growth led to Region boundary changes also. By 1980 the London Region had acquired over 1900 members, whilst the territorially extensive Eastern Counties and South-East Regions had memberships of 1020 and 938 respectively. A recommendation from the Regions Sub-committee for the creation of two additional Regions (North-East London and Essex; Surrey and Sussex) was accepted by Council, a redistribution of members from the original three Regions following.[114]

Behind the transformation of Branches to Regions and central to the concerns identified by the Working Party of elected members in 1977, was the problem of communication, both within Regions and Sections between members, and between the Regions and the central

administration. The supreme importance of this had been acknowledged by the ASE Council when B.G. Atwood was asked to convene
a Working Party to consider 'communication with and within
Regions', shortly after the completion of Region reorganization in
1968.[115] The problem, however, was an enduring one for any association, the ways in which the science teachers attempted to solve it
being an aspect of Part Two of this book.

6 Communications (i) Conference and Communion

By the opening of the twentieth century it could no longer be said, as it had been some thirty years previously, that 'science teaching is scarcely ever followed as a profession, but only as an addition to some more profitable employment'.[1] Increasing numbers of men and women worked in full-time, salaried posts as school teachers of science, a situation reflected in the rising membership figures of the APSSM, AST, SMA and AWST.

Though established, the occupation was nevertheless poorly defined. There was little in the way of tradition, or even opportunity to observe successful practice, from which a beginner could derive guidance and inspiration. An advocate of heurism such as H.E. Armstrong, despite – or perhaps because of – the vehemence with which he stated his case, found few disciples in the APSSM. Elsewhere, in the maintained secondary schools, institutional and other constraints depressed performance. A shortage of science teachers handicapped the work in many schools, especially those for girls; time for rehearsal of experimental work was limited; laboratory assistance was frequently lacking; and opportunities for the pursuit of independent research or curriculum development were uncommon. Professional training for teaching, in so far as it existed, was rarely undertaken by men and as the Thomson Report stressed in 1918, there was a need for pioneering 'educational research' to improve the methods of teaching science.[2] In his evidence to the Thomson Committee, the Chief Inspector of Secondary Schools, W.C. Fletcher, made a related point: what the schools lacked were 'science teachers with a wider outlook and a more developed skill in handling their subject' than was customarily acquired by taking a university degree in science.[3] Indeed, developing this argument a stage further in his Presidential Address to the SMA in January 1924, Professor Arthur Smithells (University of Leeds) saw 'the greatest difficulty for a science master in entering upon his duties in school' as that of divesting himself of what the universities had constructed and now transmitted, 'a kind of canonical version of physics, chemistry, botany'.[4]

Smithells was speaking at the end of his distinguished career as a university scientist, in the course of which he had observed much of the work of schools as well as providing regular in-service courses for science teachers. Nothing gave him greater hope that science would become an established component 'in the general education of the multitude' than the activities of the SMA. 'You are associated in a way that, if not unique, is rarely to be found today among any class of workers, namely, for the simple and direct purpose of helping one another to do better work,' he told his audience.[5]

Mutual assistance was certainly one of the major benefits of membership for the ordinary members of the Associations. Dispersed as they were, often in small schools, the Annual Meetings and later – as regional activity became more developed – the branch meetings, were occasions when they could meet colleagues wrestling with similar problems, exchange and evaluate new ideas, and strengthen their sense of identity and of belonging to an established, purposeful community.

For both the men's and women's Associations, however, the Annual Meeting had other purposes and its structure and function changed as the Associations grew in size and influence. The contribution of the Annual and other Meetings to the clarification and definition of what the occupation of science teacher might entail is examined below.

Annual Meetings

The earliest APSSM Annual Meetings, often held in school premises in London, were little more than Saturday afternoon gatherings at which a number of members read papers for discussion and a business meeting was held. The model was very much that of the learned society. Although the President frequently took the chair, it was not the practice initially that he should deliver a formal address. When in 1906 plans were laid for Sir Oliver Lodge to perform this duty he was unfortunately absent on the day of the Annual Meeting and it was not until the following year that the Head Master of Eton, Rev. the Honourable Edward Lyttelton, as President of the APSSM, inaugurated the tradition. The 1906 meeting did successfully introduce another innovation, however, the programme being extended into the evening to include an exhibition of scientific apparatus by various firms, as well as exhibits by members of the Association.[6]

The manufacturers' exhibition of apparatus was to become an important feature of Annual Meetings as well as an influence on their pattern. At an early date, a complaint from firms about the short time given to the exhibition induced the committee to plan a full day's programme for 1908, the exhibition then being open from 10 a.m. until 7 p.m.[7] Furthermore a substantial catalogue containing advertisements, in addition to the Annual Meeting Programme, was printed and sold. A fee for bench space was charged to firms wishing to exhibit, in 1907–8 the receipts from this (£34 2s 0d) amounting to 22 per cent of the total revenue of the APSSM, although the Association was at pains to stress that it made no profit from the exhibition,

An intent SMA group of the 1960s

The Annual Meetings – the Members' Exhibition

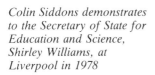

Colin Siddons demonstrates to the Secretary of State for Education and Science, Shirley Williams, at Liverpool in 1978

merely covering its expenses.[8] One firm, Philip Harris & Co. Ltd, paid £10 for its advertisement to appear on the back outer cover of the catalogue and an additional £2 to have its catalogue of exhibits next to that of the members' exhibits. It was also agreed by the committee of the APSSM that the exhibition should be open to non-members such as science teachers in technical schools as the willingness of firms to exhibit depended on the number of orders they received.[9]

By 1910, on the occasion of a joint meeting with the Mathematical Association to discuss a report on the correlation of the teaching of mathematics and science, the duration of the Annual Meeting had been extended to one and a half days, now mid-week, the exhibitions being open throughout. A further lengthening to two full days took place before the outbreak of war and this pattern of events was carried through into the inter-war years when the duration was increased yet again, first to three days and then to four, an arrangement continued by the ASE.

In passing it is of interest to note the strong emphasis on British workmanship in the advertisements of apparatus manufacturers, especially as the First World War drew near. Watson's telescopes were described as 'British made by British workmen at a British factory', where 'Everything that British Genius, allied with Science, can suggest is put into the Watson "Century" telescope'. With the outbreak of hostilities, firms such as F.E. Becker and Co. included, along with their exhortation to 'Buy British Balances. Why buy Foreign Balances?', a War Notice 'Issued by an all-British Firm employing all-British Labour whose capital is and *always* has been *entirely* held by Englishmen, and who has never employed a single German or Austrian, naturalised or otherwise'.[10] By 1917 the title of the catalogue had been amended to *Catalogue of Exhibition of Scientific and Military Apparatus and Books*, the members' exhibition now including items on 'The teaching of military subjects in schools' as a contribution to the war effort.[11]

From modest beginnings with a mere nine firms exhibiting in 1910, the manufacturers' exhibition became a major, established event in the programme of all Annual Meetings, some forty to fifty firms regularly displaying their wares at ASE Annual Meetings in the 1980s. The exhibition provided the Association with an important source of revenue which helped to balance the books for the Annual Meeting. It offered manufacturers access to existing and potential customers in a way that no other occasion did, and it enabled science teachers to inspect apparatus and equipment in the company of colleagues, as well as to express their requirements directly to a manufacturer. Ideas for new apparatus were frequently broached. Over the years there were numerous instances of collaboration between inventive teachers of science and manufacturing firms leading to improved designs and new items of equipment.

Similar developments occurred in connection with publishers of school science textbooks. Four publishers accepted the invitation of the APSSM to exhibit books at the Annual Meeting in 1910; more than forty exhibited in 1983.[12] Again, the exhibition provided revenue for the Association, enabled publishers to hear reactions from a wide cross-section of science teachers and, from time to time, led to encouragement to potential authors to submit their manuscripts. Initially the APSSM had a separate exhibition of works written by members, but this was later merged into the general exhibition of books organized by the publishers.

In contrast, the members' exhibition of apparatus and teaching materials went from strength to strength as a distinct feature of the

W.H. Dowland (right) with W.B. Nicolson

The Annual Meetings – Manufacturers and Publishers

Publishers' Exhibition at the University of Kent at Canterbury, 1982

Annual Meeting. Science teachers displayed apparatus they had constructed, new ways of performing familiar experiments, novel uses for
old and new materials, models, charts, lesson notes, indeed anything
likely to be of professional interest to others engaged in the common
task. At the APSSM meeting in 1910, the twenty-eight exhibits in this
category included: an aim tester for teaching shooting; the Tan-
gentometer (a device marketed by Philip Harris); a simple form of
Hare's apparatus; a new lightweight form of carbon dioxide apparatus; models for illustrating valency; apparatus to show the dissocia-
tion of ammonium chloride; and a device for drawing connecting
tubing on a blackboard.[13] In its emphasis on physics and chemistry
the exhibition was typical of most subsequent occasions. For many
APSSM and SMA members this exhibition became the focal point of
the Annual Meeting. Over the years, it was here that gifted experi-
menters such as F.A. Meier, J.W. Cottingham, W. Llowarch, J.P.
Stephenson, R. Thurlow and J.C. Siddons (to mention only some of
the most prolific exhibitors) informed and delighted colleagues with
their skill and inventiveness. Such displays of science teaching
virtuosity, especially in relation to apparatus design and experimental
work, set impressive standards of performance for which others could
strive. Until 1937 it was considered possible to mount a Members'
Exhibition only when the Annual Meeting was held in London.
In that year the success of incorporating it into the programme
of a provincial meeting at Manchester, established the event as an
obligatory part of future Annual Meetings. On two evenings in
Manchester, long after the other buildings were in darkness, the
lights still burned in the room housing the Members' Exhibition and
eventually visitors had to be requested to leave.[14]

By the officers of the Association, at least, the Presidential Address
was seen as a main attraction of the Annual Meeting which would
encourage members to attend. For most of the life of the SMA and
not infrequently with the ASE the President was a Vice-Chancellor
or a distinguished science professor from the University which was
host to the Annual Meeting. As a speaker remarked at the SMA's
Jubilee Dinner in 1951, to read the list of Presidents was 'to contem-
plate an epitome of the development of science in that period'.[15]
Equally impressive was the interest in the work of the Associations
demonstrated by many Presidents. Whilst some were content to serve
as a figurehead whose major contribution was the delivery of an
address, others such as Sir Harold Hartley, Sir Graham Savage, Lord
Todd, Sir Patrick Linstead and Sir Ronald Nyholm became keenly
involved in the affairs of the Association. Often the President was
able to link the Association with agencies outside the field of school
science which could assist the attainment of its goals. Wider perspectives than the committee members were able to command were also
brought to bear upon the Association's problems. And if the Association made use of its President to further its ends, the reverse process
was not unknown, the address being a means of persuading the

Tuesday, 4 January

4.30 to 5.30	Tea will be provided for early arrivals.
7.0	Dinner in Balliol College Hall.
8.30	President's Address, " Some Aspects of Science and Education," by A. Vassall, Esq., followed by an informal concert.

Wednesday, 5 January

8.30	Breakfast.
10.0	Lecture on " Indicators and the Law of Mass Action," by Brigadier-General H. Hartley, to be followed, if the weather is wet, by the Business Meeting.
1.0	Lunch.
2.0 to 4.0	Demonstrations in the various University laboratories.
4.15	Tea.
5.0 to 6.30	Simultaneous Lectures and Demonstrations : " The Study of Crystals," by T. V. Barker, Esq. " Glass Blowing," by B. Lambert, Esq.
7.0	Dinner.
8.30	Lecture on " Recent Advances in Genetics," by J. S. Huxley, Esq., followed by an informal Concert.

Thursday, 6 January

8.30	Breakfast.
10.0	Lecture on " Spectroscopy," by Professor T. R. Merton, F.R.S.
11.15	Business Meeting (unless held on the previous day).
1.0	Lunch.
2.0 to 4.0	Demonstrations in the various University laboratories.
4.15	Tea.
5.0 to 6.30	Simultaneous Lectures and Demonstrations as on Wednesday.
7.0	Dinner.
8.30	Lecture, " The Hedjaz," by D. G. Hogarth, Esq., D.Litt., followed by an informal Concert.

Friday, 7 January

8.0 to 9.0	Breakfast.

Table 6.1   Programme, SMA Annual Meeting, Oxford 1921

science teachers to a point of view, such as the need for more biology in the curriculum of boys' grammar schools and the form that the teaching of this biology should take.[16]

The Presidential Address was supplemented by a lecture programme which became more densely packed as the years went by. The Annual Meeting was an occasion when science teachers could bring up to date their knowledge of developments in the subjects they taught. At the same time it offered an opportunity for the host university to display its wares and parade its academic stars before those whose students might one day be applying for admission. Tours of science and engineering departments were a feature of many early programmes though as the pressure of events on available time became greater, and as the scale of the Annual Meeting increased in size, formal provision of these became less practicable. The transformation from the leisurely deliberations at the Oxford meeting in 1921, the first occasion on which the SMA left London, to the varied and competing activities on a single day in the Warwick meeting sixty years later is well illustrated by the detail in Tables 6.1 and 6.2.

Discussion rather than lectures had been the staple of the APSSM Annual Meetings. Apart from the Presidential Address it was rare for the public school masters to involve an outside speaker. One of their own number would introduce a topic; 'Symbols in physics', 'Teaching of oxidation and reduction', 'Education of medical students' were typical subjects. Thereafter, members contributed from their own experience. Possibly their existing university contacts made the need for up-dating of scientific knowledge less urgent; possibly the pace of scientific advance was less rapid. More likely, the opportunity for a formal programme of scientific lectures did not clearly present itself until the SMA embarked on its arrangements for peripatetic Annual Meetings. With one exception, in 1917 when it met at Eton College, all the meetings of the APSSM were held in London in premises such as Westminster School and the London Day Training College and were non-residential. For the SMA, during the forty-five years of its existence, and bearing in mind that for three war-time years no meeting was possible, London provided the venue for the Annual Meeting on twenty-one occasions, although now a university base such as King's College for Women and, later, Imperial College of Science and Technology was used with residence available. Meetings at Oxford (1921) and Cambridge (1923) were early innovations in the programme of the SMA, each of the older universities entertaining the science masters on four occasions in all. Not until 1925 did the Association venture on its first truly provincial excursion, to the University of Leeds. Meetings in Birmingham (1931), Bristol (1933) and Manchester (1937) followed. The SMA returned to Leeds in 1958 and to Manchester in 1963, these being the only provincial universities to receive the Association twice. Two meetings of the SMA were also held in Scotland; Edinburgh in 1950 and Glasgow in 1961. After the end of the Second World War and until the time of amalgamation there was little departure from the pattern of a London meeting alternating with a provincial one, Sheffield (1948), Liverpool (1952), Newcastle-upon-Tyne (1955) and Southampton (1960) all receiving the SMA for the first time.

In part a consequence of the increased numbers attending Annual Meetings, this adoption of a university venue and the development of an associated lecture programme brought about a reduction in the time available for contributions from members themselves. As early as 1924 a complainant was writing to *The School Science Review* that genuine discussion on 'The introduction of chemical theory' had been stifled by an over-formal structure to a session at the Cambridge Annual Meeting earlier that year. Prepared statements had been

MONDAY MORNING 5 JANUARY

Breakfast in Rootes Social Building 0730—0855

Exhibitions open 0915

Visits
6.   British Gas Research Station, Solihull 0900—1300
7.   Warwickshire College of Agriculture 0900—1300

Lectures 0930—1030
13.   'Interferon: an active agent against viruses and cancer':
      Professor D. C. Burke
14.   'Perfumes and the chemistry of smells': Dr. G. H. Dodd
15.   'Wave energy: Britannia rules the waves': Dr. L. J. Duckers

Symposia 0930—1230
6.   'A common core in science-academic pipedream or
      educational necessity?'
7.   'Resource and responsibility — the developing role of
      ITV's schools service in the field of teaching'

Talks and Discussions 0930—1030
The making of 'Search for Solutions'
'Pupil-centred learning in A-level science'
'The DES Microelectronics Development Programme'

Coffee 1030—1115

Talks and Discussions 1115—1215
'The Nuffield O-level Physics revision'
'The revolution peters out here'

Annual Business Meeting 1115—1230

Lunch in Rootes Social Building 1200—1400

*Table 6.2   Programme for one day, ASE Annual Meeting, Warwick
1981*

MONDAY AFTERNOON 5 JANUARY

Visits
8.   Albright and Wilson, Oldbury 1230–1730
9.   British Industrial Plastics, Oldbury 1230–1730
10. Motor Industries Research Association (MIRA), Nuneaton 1245–1700
11. Rolls-Royce, Ansty 1245–1630
12. National Vegetable Research Station, Wellesbourne 1300–1700
13. Police Force Control Unit, Birmingham 1315–1700
14. Courtaulds, Coventry 1330–1630
15. Severn Trent Water Laboratories 1330–1630

Poster Session 1330–1630

Lectures 1400–1500
16. 'Teaching modern microbiology in the VI form':
     Dr. E. C. Hill
17. 'Engineering systems for the blind': Professor J. L. Douce
18. 'Catastrophe theory and its scientific application':
     Professor E. C. Zeeman, FRS

Symposia 1400–1615
8.   'Safeguards in the school laboratory'
9.   'Strategies for science education of pupils in the
     14-16 age range'

Films programme 3 (Chemistry) 1400–1530

Talks and Discussions 1400–1500
Manufacturer's Lecture: Griffin & George Ltd.
'Microprocessors serving science'

Tea 1500–1545

Lectures
19. 'Life in extreme environments': Professor D. P. Kelly
20. 'How does your fluid flow? Aspects of medical
     instrumentation': Dr. M. J. A. Smith
21. 'Lasers and computers in modern metrology':
     Professor D. J. Whitehouse

Presidential Address
'Science: fundamental to the school curriculum and the
nation's future'
Sir Denis Rooke, FRS, Chairman, British Gas

Exhibitions close 1745

Dinner in Rootes Social Building

Association Dinner 1930 for 2000: Jaguar-Daimler-Climax
Social Club, Coventry
Buses leave the University at 1915 and return at 2230

Films Programme 4 (General) 2000–2130

Discotheque 2100–2400 Rootes Social Building

delivered by several speakers whereas these might have been circulated beforehand, so leaving time for debate. G.H.J. Adlam's editorial response was that in the past members had tended to compare experiences in groups of two or three round the fire at night, although there was no reason why provision for discussion should remain at that informal level. [17] Time for discussion sessions on topics such as 'Relations between science teaching in school and universities' and 'Laboratory assistants' was incorporated in many future SMA programmes, although with almost 400 members present when the first of these was considered, the opportunity for individual contributions was limited. [18]

In the 1960s a prime concern of a sequence of Annual Meetings was the promulgation of messages about the national importance of applied science and technology. This interest was reflected in the content of the lecture programmes and the provision of special exhibitions. [19] Important though these were they did not altogether match the grass-root concerns of teachers faced with an array of new science curriculum projects, reorganization of secondary education and, just ahead, the raising of the school leaving age. At the Bristol meeting in January 1969 the provision during the afternoon sessions of opportunities to examine these and related matters clearly met a need. Many discussions 'were crammed to capacity'; as a report on the Annual Meeting indicated, more attention to 'pedagogical matters' appeared to be what members wanted. [20] A memorandum on the Bristol meeting from the West of England Region to the ASE Council, however, produced a contrary view. The Education (Coordinating) Committee responded to the comments in the memorandum with the assertion that 'It should be faced, and it *is* true to say, that members at the Annual Meeting do not want education. This is borne out by the poor attendance at "education" discussions over a dozen years'. [21] This may well have been true of 'education' in the abstract, but subsequent meetings were to prove that examination of 'science education' issues was of very direct concern to the membership. A turning point in the balance between science and science education components in the programme of the Annual Meeting came at Leeds in 1974.

On that occasion the Honorary Annual Meeting Secretary, Brian Nicholl, was successful in incorporating in the programme a range of workshops, symposia and discussion sessions on the 'problems of specific age groups, ability groups or methods of organizing teaching and the curriculum'. These included a symposium on 'Science in the middle years'; discussions on 'Mixed ability teaching in science' and 'Independent learning in science'; a workshop entitled 'ROSLA and after'; and a further symposium on 'The teaching of technology through school science'. This 'larger than usual number of sessions devoted to aspects of science education, as distinct from developments in pure and applied science' induced the Education (Research) Committee to monitor the innovation, a report being produced from which it was hoped points would emerge of interest to those planning future Annual Meetings. The value of the change was acknowledged and subsequent meetings continued the practice of regarding serving teachers as 'valuable resources in initiating and developing discussions in areas of the curriculum where no single pattern of content, organization or method is universally acceptable or desirable'.[22]

In many ways this was no more than a reversion to the original practice of the APSSM. In the context of the 1970s, however, it required interpretation in other ways. It represented an adaptation of the Annual Meeting programme to the constitutional changes in the direction of participation and self-determination which had accompanied the work of the Education (Research) Committee.[23] It was an exemplification of what, at the 1975 Annual Meeting in an Overseas Science Education Symposium, were identified as 'important criteria in assessing the professionalism of a particular activity', namely 'demand for in-service growth' and 'independence or autonomy restrained through a sense of responsibility for standards'.[24] It foreshadowed feelings on the part of some members that the ASE should not merely respond to events, but should take a lead in defining what school science ought to be. Following informal discussions at the Leicester Annual Meeting in 1977 one member wrote, 'I gathered . . . a strong feeling that the time is ripe for the Association to assume much more the role of a "professional" body than it has in the past . . . I am not alone in feeling that an organization offering strong professional support to the teacher and speaking in an authoritative capacity on matters of concern to all teachers of science is needed'.[25]

The professional development of science teachers was the theme of the Education Conference at Nottingham in 1981. Summarising at the close, Professor J.J. Thompson addressed the question of what it meant 'to be professional', arguing that 'professionalism was likely to be involved with mutual support of each others interests through discussion, dialectic and information'. It could also entail the production of 'a programme for professional development which was different in kind' from anything which the ASE had attempted before, a reference to the Association's impending entry into the field of validation of science teacher qualifications. The way forward, for Thompson, required the activities of the ASE to be designed to 'increase the confidence of science teachers in themselves' and for the occupation of science teacher to give teachers more autonomy and personal responsibility in relation to curriculum decisions.[26] To both of these objectives the restructured programme of the Annual Meetings had an important contribution to make.

The 1974 Annual Meeting was the occasion of innovations other than those concerned with programme content. In its response to the memorandum from the West of England Region the Education (Coordinating) Committee had stressed that the Annual Meeting was a 'closed' event, not open to the public apart from lectures organized and financed through the Science and Citizenship Fund. In connection with the 1974 Meeting it was agreed by the ASE Council that a Visitors' Day should be introduced when non-members could 'see the Association in action' and, hopefully, be persuaded that it truly was an Association for all science teachers. Over 200 non-members took advantage of the arrangement.[27] Further testimony to the value of the meeting as a form of in-service education was provided in 1977 when it was agreed that parties of teachers under the sponsorship of local education authority science advisers might be 'bused' to the Annual Meeting for a one-day visit.[28]

The rich programme of lectures of many kinds, symposia, talks, discussions, workshops, members' poster sessions and exhibitions which had come to characterize the Annual Meeting in the 1980s was augmented by traditional ingredients of industrial visits and films which had been a feature for many years. There was also, as from the very first Annual Meeting, a distinct social dimension to the gathering. Always an occasion when old friendships were renewed and new links of acquaintanceship formed, now ASE membership receptions, university receptions and, from 1948 when Sheffield broke new ground,[29] civic receptions contributed to the furtherance of these ends. Informal concerts with members singing at the piano may have been replaced by a late night at a Discotheque 'for those who still have some energy left or think they have'.[30] Nevertheless, for many members the sense of community and comradeship, engendered as much by extra-curricular activities as by any pre-arranged programme, remained one of the most valued outcomes of attendance.

It is difficult to arrive at a precise figure for the proportion of ASE members who have attended an Annual Meeting over, say, a five-year period. It was the estimate of the Education (Coordinating) Committee in 1969 that compared with other associations the ASE attendance was 'above average' and that over a five-year period at least half of the membership who could, did attend a meeting.[31] Comparing published attendance figures with membership figures, this would seem a slightly generous interpretation. What is not in dispute is the vitality and energy which characterises present-day meetings. A formidable burden of preparation is borne by a local *ad hoc* committee, although, as the Education (Coordinating) Committee stressed, the responsibility for the meeting lies with the ASE Council which delegates the broad plans to the Executive Committee and to the Honorary Annual Meeting Secretary. Regional initiative in relation to what the meeting might be is, therefore, always subject to the approval of Council. It is the Association's Annual Meeting and not a Regional Meeting open to all. As for the Annual Meeting Secretary, the problem of continuity especially in relation to the building up of contacts with manufacturers and publishers was difficult to solve when one secretary was regularly replaced by another at the end of each term of office. Eventually, in 1975, an Assistant Secretary was appointed as a salaried officer at Headquarters to provide this continuity as well as to assist with other administrative apects of the Annual Meeting.[32]

Local enterprise

If the Annual Meeting was the high point in the Association's calendar, the solid foundation of its work and reputation was laid in the branches and regions. Many members could summon the effort to attend an Annual Meeting and by the 1980s well over 2000 men and women were doing so each year. To turn out regularly for meetings at the end of a busy school day, or at the weekend, was quite another matter. Yet, as has been indicated, branches of the AWST and SMA proliferated from the early years[33] and, once established, almost all prospered, building up membership figures and developing ambitious regional programmes.

The establishment of a branch often depended on the enthusiasm and energy of a few committed members. Once the benefits of association had been experienced and appreciated, such individuals when translated to posts elsewhere were often instrumental in 'seeding' new areas. The pioneering North-Eastern Branch of the SMA was brought into existence largely at the instigation of E.R. Thomas, headmaster of the Royal Grammar School, Newcastle-upon-Tyne, a former science master at Rugby and Honorary Secretary of the SMA in 1920. Thomas presided at the inaugural meeting which was attended by staff from the university of Durham, as well as by members of the AWST and of the Society of Chemical Industry.[34] When F.W. Turner, another SMA Committee member moved from Thames Valley County School to take up the headship of Morley Grammar School he played a leading part in stimulating the inauguration of a Yorkshire Branch of the SMA.[35] The establishment of the North-Western Branch of the SMA in 1930 owed much to the presence in the region at that time of E.G. Savage HMI who chaired the initial meeting and was Branch President in 1932–3, a predecessor in that office being Professor W.L. Bragg.[36] The active involvement with branch activity of 'authority figures' such as headmasters and members of HM Inspectorate may have been an inducement for science masters to participate. At a later date a Chief Education Officer was occasionally associated with the establishment of a branch. Thus, in 1961, when D.H.J. Marchant, a former chairman of the SMA and at that time a science lecturer at Kesteven Training College, with two colleagues convened a meeting of science teachers in their area, so starting the train of events which led to the East Midlands Branch of the SMA, the chairman for the occasion was the Director of Education for Kesteven.[37]

Whatever strategy was employed to achieve the energy of activation, to sustain the interest of members over a prolonged period required a nucleus of men and women who would be prepared to apply themselves steadily and purposefully to the construction of attractive programmes of meetings (Table 6.3). This is not to say that branches organized their events all to a pattern. Apart from anything else, geographical differences prevented this. London, with its condensed urban situation and large numbers of science teachers, found it necessary to offer two programmes, north and south of the river. It could also draw on unique resources unavilable elsewhere. Thus, from its inception the London Branch of the ASE was able to include as a member of its committee the Education Officer of the Royal Institute of Chemistry, D.G. Chisman. The London Branch of the AWST likewise availed itself fully of the opportunities of the metropolis, often, in the 1950s, holding its Annual Meetings in the Science Museum. Joint Meetings with the SMA also took place in the Royal Institution.[38] This contrasted with the North-Eastern Branch of the SMA and the Northern Branch of the AWST whose regional activities became centred on sub-groups along the Tyne, Wear and Tees well before branch reorganization by the ASE in 1968 established sections, and where cooperation between the men and women was essential from the start to sustain local meetings.[39]

In Scotland and Northern Ireland the situation was different again, each branch finding the need to establish residential meetings of two or three days. Half-day meetings proved unpopular with those who had a long journey to make, as it was not thought to be worth all the travel for such a short time. Whole day meetings likewise posed problems; those from a distance tended to be excluded because they could not arrive in time. Early in its existence the Scottish branch organized a three-day meeting at the University of Glasgow, attended by about 250 members, and the tradition of an Annual General Meeting of similar duration, based on one of the Scottish universities was continued thereafter.[40] Northern Ireland, likewise, with an educational system administratively distinct from England and Wales, and with a dispersed membership, had by 1955 discovered the advantages of a week-end meeting. After the second experiment in 1957 it was agreed that the occasion had been 'again excellent' and decidedly something to repeat on a regular basis.[41]

Proximity to a sympathetic and cooperative university was also an important determinant of the type of programme a branch could develop. The Midland Branch, later the West Midland Region, had long established links with the University of Birmingham, an annual conference between the University and all the secondary schools in the seven midland counties going back to 1921.[42] At a later date the university was active in the provision of courses for the up-dating of the scientific knowledge of teachers. In fact most branches of the SMA and AWST were centred on or near a university town though not all universities were equally responsive to the needs of science teachers in their vicinity. Many, however, provided Presidents for SMA and AWST branches, and it was often the case that university science departments would arrange tours of their laboratories and demonstrations of research in progress.

In the same way, the industrial context of Branches and Regions influenced the programmes, visits to see science in action being popular local activities. Within a year of its inaugural meeting, the

1969 – Winter Term

BRITISH IRON & STEEL FEDERATION LECTURE.
Thursday 25th September   7.30 p.m (A).
Speaker :
Redborne School, Flitwick Rd, Ampthill, Beds.
Reply slips to : Miss A.S. Jones (at Redborne)

"SCIENCE IN THE SECONDARY SCHOOL".
Thursday 2nd October   4.30 p.m. (C).
Speaker : J. Forrest Esq.
Burnham Co. Sec. Sch, Stomp Rd, Burnham, Bucks.
Reply slips to : Hon. Sec. Bucks South.

"SCIENCE IN THE PRIMARY SCHOOL".
Thursday 2nd October   7.30 p.m. (B).
Speaker : Mr. Stockdale.
Water Eaton Primary School (Bletchley).
Reply slips to : Hon. Sec. Bucks North.

"PRODUCTION TECHNOLOGY".   (D/A).
Saturday 18th October
Joint meeting with H.S.T.A. in Hertfordshire.
Speaker : Professor Heginbotham.
Reply slips to : Hon. Sec. H.S.T.A.

"FORENSIC SCIENCE".
Friday 21st November   7.30 p.m. (A).
Speaker : Dr. Holden.
Kingsbury School, Meadway, Dunstable, Beds.
Reply slips to : Hon. Sec. Beds. Section.

"EXPLOSIONS".
Friday 28th November   7.30 p.m. (B).
Speaker : Dr. Shaw of Nottingham University.
Denbigh School, Cornwall Grove, Bletchley.
TICKET HOLDERS ONLY. Applications for tickets
to Hon. Sec. Bucks North Section.

"HOW I TEACH . . . . .".
Monday 1st December   4.30 p.m. (C).
Local teachers lectures/demonstrations.
Venue : to be arranged.

1970 – Spring Term

"EDUCATION IN SCHOOL & INDUSTRY".
Monday 19th January   7.30 p.m. (A).
Speaker : G.C.C. Gell Esq.
Bedford School, Bedford.
Reply slips to : Hon. Sec. Beds Section.

"NUFFIELD 'A' LEVEL BIOLOGY".
Monday 2nd February   7.30 p.m. (B).
Speaker : P. Kelly Esq.
Fletchley Grammar School, Bletchley.
Reply slips to : T.G. Page (at the school).

"EXAMINATIONS IN SCIENCE".
Tuesday 17th February   7.30 p.m. (A/D).
Joint meeting with H.S.T.A. in Bedfordshire.
Speaker : J.F. Eggleston Esq.
Luton area. Reply slips to Hon. Sec. Beds. Section.

A.G.M. and FILM EVENING.
Thursday 5th March   7.30 p.m. (B).
Buckinghamshire North Section.
Denbigh School, Cornwall Grove, Bletchley.
Reply slips to : Hon. Sec. Bucks North.

A.G.M. and FILM EVENING.
Wednesday 11th March   4.30 p.m. (C).
Buckinghamshire South Section.
Slough Boys Grammar School, Lascelles Road.
Reply slips to : Hon. Sec. Bucks South.

A.G.M and FILM EVENING.
Wednesday 11th March   7.30 p.m. (A).
Bedfordshire Section.
Redborne School, Flitwick Rd. Ampthill. Beds.
Reply slips to : Hon. Sec. Beds Section.

1970 – Summer Term

VISIT to a SEWAGE FARM.
Tuesday 12th May   4.30 p.m. (C).

"DOPE".
Wednesday 13th May   7.30 p.m. (A).
Speaker : Professor A.H. Beckett.
Redborne School. Flitwick Rd. Ampthill. Beds.
Reply slips to : Miss A.S. Jones (at Redborne).

"PROJECT ELECTRONICS".
Thursday 9th July   7.30 p.m. (A).
A schools competition/exhibition.
Mander College, Cauldwell Street, Bedford.
Details will be sent to all Secondary Schools.

OTHER INFORMATION

VISITS

It is hoped to arrange visits by each Section during
the currency of this 1969/70 programme. Details will
be published seperately as they become available.

REPLY SLIPS for the year are being sent out with
this 'fixture card'. Please assist the Sections by
returning slips at the very latest ONE WEEK in
advance of the date of the meeting you are hoping
to attend.

TICKETS

Where it is anticipated that large numbers may
wish to attend a meeting, admission will be for ticket
holders only, and tickets will be limited to the
capacity of the Hall.

Table 6.3   Programme of meetings, Home Counties Region, 1969–70

South Wales Branch of the SMA, in collaboration with the AWST, had visited the National Oil Refineries at Neath and the Powell Duffryn Bye-Product Works at Bargoed.[43] Elsewhere sewage farms were investigated, the manufacture of glassware observed, and occasionally the depths of coal mines plumbed. Links were sometimes established between the Association's branches and the local committees of the professional scientific institutes, notably the Royal Institute of Chemistry and the Institute of Physics. From 1977, after prompting by the then chairman of the ASE, J.L. Lewis, similar links were established with local secretaries of the Council of Engineering Institutions.[44]

If the Branches benefited from local resources they contributed to developments as well. Sometimes independently of the AWST and SMA, sometimes in collaboration with them, local Science Teachers' Associations of men and women ineligible or unwilling to enter into full membership of the national Associations had sprung up. One of them, the Hertfordshire STA held its first meeting in 1948 following a course for teachers of science in secondary modern schools arranged by A.W. Wellings HMI, a former Honorary Treasurer of the SMA. For a number of years F.W. Kaye, SMA General Committee member from 1953 to 1956, was secretary-treasurer of the Hertfordshire STA, his successor being E.G. Breeze, another SMA committee man and a future Honorary Treasurer of the ASE. The first President of the STA was E. Nightingale, Honorary Annual Meeting Secretary of the SMA back in the 1930s, who in retirement edited *Hartshorn*, the Bulletin of the Hertfordshire Science Teachers Association.[45]

Another local development, the London Association of Science Teachers collaborated with the SMA when in 1949 a sub-committee under H.F. Boulind's chairmanship was established to consider what help could be given to science teachers in secondary modern schools. W.F.J. Hamblin, Secretary of the London AST, E.G. Breeze at that stage Secretary of the West of England STA, and R.J. Bartle, chairman of the East Kent STA, were also members of the sub-committee.[46] At a later date, the London AST entered into agreement with the London Region of the ASE to circulate notices of its meetings to ASE members, continuing on this basis until it was replaced in 1974 by the School Natural Science Society.[47]

The Leeds STA was formed in 1960, largely at the instigation of R. Thurlow, Science Adviser to the Leeds City Education Department and first Chairman of the ASE in 1963. It published a journal, arranged meetings, organized visits to local industries, and generally provided a practical stimulus to science teachers working in secondary modern schools.[48] Like many such STAs it benefited from local ASE resources and experience. In some cases, local STAs were constitutionally absorbed into the ASE Region and Section structures. In others, although there was interest in amalgamation, separate financial arrangements with local education authorities disposed STA members to prefer a looser affiliation. Thus in 1976 the Sandwell STA, having explored the implication of reorganisation as a Section of the Midland Branch, concluded that continued separate existence was in its own best interests.[49] Similarly, the Hertfordshire STA did not become a Branch of the SMA because its officers 'did not want any member to feel he could not afford the subscription of the larger association'.[50]

The emergence of separate associations of science teachers, when coupled with the appearance of biology, chemistry and physics centres sponsored by the professional scientific institutes, and with teachers' centres financed and administered by local education authorities, posed a threat to ASE regional activity by the early 1970s. The North-East Region Committee, for example, was complaining in 1971 that 'attendance at meetings had fallen drastically during the last few years . . . the annual meeting was poorly attended in September, outings have been cancelled, and embarrassing situations involving colleagues and outside lecturers have occurred'. 'What', it was asked, 'is the future role of the ASE in a Region where, within a distance of 40 miles, there are seven subject centres all offering a programme of activities for science teachers?'[51]

In the short term, it appeared that the answer was coordination of the diverse offerings and an improved information service to members about what was available. In the longer term, a clearer division of labour needed to be negotiated between the providing agencies. Additionally, and more significantly, the role of the Regions as a source and test bed for the ASE's policy on science education was to increase in importance.

The relationship between the Regions and the central committees of the ASE has already received some consideration in Chapter 5.[52] The three-tier structure of national, regional and sectional activity was introduced in 1968 to improve the organization and representation of the opinion of members for the guidance of Council and Executive. The subsequent review of the structure and function of Council likewise arose from concerns that in essence were ones about effective communication between the Regions and Council.[53] In considering the relationship, one point to be recalled is that many who served on the ASE's central committees, as well as the Association's principal officials, had substantial experience of committee work at regional level. Indeed, involvement as an officer or committee member in a Region was a valuable training for service at national level. To give just one illustration, the committee of the Midland Branch of the ASE in 1966 included a future General Secretary of the ASE (B.G. Atwood), three future Honorary Annual Meeting Secretaries (Dr C. Briske, B. Nicholl and G.E. Siddle) and a future Honorary Treasurer (Dr J.A. Darby).[54] For the most part, personnel at national level had considerable past experience of regional problems and needs.

Even so, there persisted a strong feeling that the interaction between the centre and the Regions was too limited in kind. At the practical level of administration of the affairs of the Association, Regions were certainly vocal when Headquarters displayed symptoms of overload in connection with the distribution of Region notices, and improvements followed.[55] Likewise, the policy of holding the Annual Meeting in different locations brought increased local involvement in the planning of a major event, reflective of Association concerns at all levels, whereas previously London members had been required to shoulder the responsibility every other year. The downward flow of policy matters requiring a regional response also moved Regions and Sections in the direction of greater professional responsibility for the definition of science education. But there was little evidence that critical issues were being systematically identified in the Regions for transmission to Council. From time to time local resolutions were passed and sent forward; the London Branch, for example, in 1964 registered distress 'at the lack of interest in the technological side of science in our schools' and urged Council 'to take suitable action, especially at the January Annual Meeting'.[56] There were also recurrent comments on the contents of *The School Science Review* and on the efficiency of the *Bulletin* as a means of keeping members informed of central deliberations and decisions.[57] But the articulation of opinion at different levels needed more effective procedures. The role of the Education Conference, to be considered now, was important in this respect.

The Education Conference

What was to become known as the Education Conference of the ASE was first held at Cambridge in May 1965. On that occasion members of the Education Committee together with the Association's officers gathered to take stock of recent science curriculum changes and of issues likely to arise in the years ahead. Their deliberations brought home sharply the need for branch opinion to be available in such discussions and a request to branches followed, seeking their diagnosis of problems facing science teachers at that time. 'The really serious problem', the Education Committee's report for that year stated, 'is how to involve the individual member in new ideas and problems, and to provide a means whereby he can express his views . . . A solution must be found'.[58]

Matters were taken forward with the assistance of a grant from the Royal Society which enabled the ASE to bring together some thirty of its younger members to express their views in December 1966. Many present on that occasion joined branch representatives, Council and Education Committee members the following March at the University of Nottingham for a further conference, again aided by a Royal Society grant. One important development which followed this meeting was the restructuring of the Education Committee into two bodies, one for research and policy, the Education (Research)

Committee, and the other for more routine and ongoing matters, the Education (Coordinating) Committee.

From 1967, Education Conferences were held annually at the University of Nottingham in the Easter vacation, the agenda being determined largely by the two Education Committees. With about equal numbers of representatives from the Regions and of members from Council and the Education Committees, the purpose of the conferences was, in the words of Helen Ward, Chairman of the ASE in 1970, 'to share views and ideas on current situations and to look into the future. In order to express the views of the Association in official quarters, Council and the Education Committees require to hear from the Regions'.[59]

Opinion was not restricted to sources from within the Association however. The net was cast wide and experts from other areas were frequently invited. Members of HM Inspectorate attended regularly and contributed papers on a number of occasions. When the subject of examinations came up for discussion in 1969 and again in 1972 the Secretary of the Joint Matriculation Board, R. Christopher, addressed the Conference. Directors of Schools Council Projects, R. Irvine Smith of the General Studies Project in 1972 and P. McPhail of the Moral Education Project in 1973, described their work. In response to interest in the relations of science and society and the problems of teaching in this area Dr J. Ravetz, University of Leeds, and Dr W.F. Williams, Coordinator of the SISCON Project, spoke at the Conference in 1975. When science education for the 16 to 19 age group came under discussion in 1978, representatives of the Technician Education Council and of the National Association of Teachers in Further and Higher Education were amongst the one hundred delegates present. More recently, the chairman of the Royal Society's Education Committee, Sir Harry Pitt, attended the Conferences in 1981 and 1982. The 1981 Conference was addressed by Mr Neil Macfarlane, Under-Secretary of State for Education, the second time within a few weeks that he had taken part in a major Association activity. Also present was Sir Denis Rooke, Chairman of British Gas Corporation, and ASE President. The principal speaker at the 1983 Education Conference was Sir James Hamilton, Permanent Secretary at the Department of Education and Science.[60]

Although the staple of the Conference programme remained the contributions of the ASE members, this recent involvement of a wider community of interests in science education can be seen, in part, as a response to an address at the 1977 Education Conference by Norman Booth, HMI. Entitling his talk 'Forward the ASE!', Booth argued that education was moving into an era when teachers needed 'to be accountable to politicians, to parents, to industrialists, and to "customers of education" at all levels'. It followed that the performance and claims of science teachers had to be able to stand up to public scrutiny. In this connection, Booth continued, the ASE was the organization 'to speak for science teachers . . . and to specify the requirements for the future'. Its perspective was wider than anything that could be achieved by other agencies.[61]

The role outlined was by no means an unattractive one for the ASE, being in close accord with the thinking of the Education (Research) Committee. However, a corollary of a shift from communication directed internally to the profession to communication directed to a wider, external public was that claims had to be both authoritatively attested and made in terms that would be convincing to others. As well as being an occasion when the opinion of members was consulted, the Education Conference had come to serve as an incubator and testing ground for the ASE's policy pronouncements.

International relations

Writing in 1982 about 'courses for international development', it was the opinion of Professor P.J. Black and John May of the Chelsea College Centre for Science and Mathematics Education that 'science and mathematics education has come of age as an international movement'.[62] The coherence of this movement is perhaps debatable, given the diverse cultural contexts in which science teaching takes place and the often sad recent history of uncritical international transfer of science curriculum materials. The extent of international communication about issues and developments in science education is not, however, in question.

In 1956 at the instigation of the International Relations Committee of the National Science Teachers Association in the USA an enquiry from UNESCO was directed to the SMA about the existence of science teacher associations in other countries and the value of a projected international newsletter.[63] Cooperation between organizations concerned with the teaching of science remained informal at this stage until a Committee on the Teaching of Science was established by the International Council of Scientific Unions at its 12th General Assembly at Paris in 1968. The first secretary of this Committee was Dennis Chisman, a London Region member of the ASE. At a conference organized by the Committee at the University of Maryland in 1973, when the theme was 'The Training of Teachers for Integrated Science', it was proposed to establish an international association linking together associations for science education world wide. This led to the foundation of the International Council of Associations for Science Education (ICASE), affiliated to the Committee on the Teaching of Science and supported by representatives of 25 organisations from 19 countries. From the first, the ASE was a member association of ICASE, its General Secretary being elected to the Executive Committee and D. Chisman becoming Executive Secretary. ICASE grew rapidly, by the early 1980s having over 40 member associations. In late 1975 its first General Assembly was held at Oxford immediately preceding the ASE's Annual Meeting, many of those attending the Assembly staying on to participate in the ASE's activities. In 1977 the ASE's General Secretary was elected a Vice-President of ICASE, becoming President in 1982. The Committee on Science Teaching likewise developed its educational activities energetically, J.L. Lewis (ASE Chairman in 1977) succeeding Chisman as Secretary on the completion of the latter's term of office.[64]

Beneath these international organizations, the ASE established working links with specific science teaching associations overseas, and notably with the National Science Teachers Association in the USA. The first NSTA delegates, aided by grant from the National Science Foundation, attended the Annual Meeting of the SMA at Glasgow in 1961, contacts made then leading eventually to regular visits by delegations from each Association to the annual convention of the other.[65] A successful appeal to industry for funds for overseas travel by officers of the ASE assisted considerably in making such exchanges possible in the early stages. The Chairman of the ASE also frequently represented the Association at annual meetings of the German Association for the Advancement of the teaching of Mathematics and Science, and, nearer to home, the Irish Science Teachers Association. Sessions on Overseas Science Education became incorporated as a regular feature in Annual Meetings, that, for example, at Durham in 1975 involving a one-day Symposium on Science Teacher Associations and Educational Development. Coordinated by D. Chisman, by now Deputy Director (Science Education), Education Project Department, British Council, contributors from several overseas countries as well as from UNESCO, addressed a packed lecture theatre containing 'a wider range of national representatives than ever before'.[66]

By 1982 the ASE had well over 1000 overseas members. The forging of its international links and its part as a leader in the activities of ICASE had moved the Association out of a limited national framework to membership of a world-wide community it had itself helped to create.

7 Communications (ii) Publications and Pronouncements

Like conferences, publications can serve many purposes. Whilst the printed word may lack the immediacy and personal quality associated with conversations and meetings, it nevertheless can reach a wider audience.

From the first the APSSM printed a record of its annual meetings, including details of papers read, for circulation to all members irrespective of attendance. Those unable to be present were thereby kept in touch. For the propagation of information and opinion of professional interest, and provided cost did not prove a barrier, publication was a surer way of reaching an audience than verbal report at a meeting. It also yielded a permanent record which served to make more widely known the aims and activities of the Association, so assisting recruitment.

There were, however, other functions which publications could serve. The joint report of the Mathematical Association and the APSSM on the correlation of the teaching of mathematics and science[1] provided a case in point. Issued as a pamphlet in 1910 it recommended changes designed to achieve a better coordination of teaching effort, especially in public schools, and was clearly intended to influence practice. Although not formally designated a policy statement, and in any case limited in scope to 'certain debatable ground' between the two subjects, the report was nevertheless a forerunner of the policy pronouncements which the Associations were later to make about the purposes, methods and content of science education in schools.

Consideration of the publications which an Association issues, their range, purposes, contents and intended audiences, clearly can reveal much about the Association's perception of its role. These and related matters are the concern of the present chapter. And just as the functions of annual and regional meetings changed over the years as the Associations grew in size and influence, so the characteristics of the Associations' publications also altered, with developments of particular significance taking place as we approach recent times.

The School Science Review

The suggestion that there was need for a national journal devoted to the teaching of science was made by the Thomson Committee in its report in 1918.[2] For some years previously articles on particular aspects of science education had appeared intermittently in general educational magazines such as *The School World*. There was, however, no recognised outlet for the publication of ideas and comment on science teaching, nor any systematic communication of good practice, and of the results of experiments in science teaching, to interested practitioners.

One of the public school science masters who, as a representative of the IAAM, appeared as a witness before the Thomson Committee was G.H.J. Adlam (City of London School) and it is possible that the idea of a science teaching journal was broached on that occasion. Certainly it was Adlam who first suggested the idea of publishing a journal to the Committee of the APSSM, arguing that the Association had grown to a point when it should have a regular publication for the benefit of its members, much as the Mathematical Association already had. As a result of Adlam's initiative a sub-committee of V.S. Bryant (Wellington), D.R. Pye (Winchester), W.J.R. Calvert (Harrow), F.A. Beesley (St Olave's) and Adlam was appointed in May 1918 'to consider ways and means of keeping members in touch with recent developments in the teaching of science by means of periodical publications by the Association'.[3] Its report later in the summer led to a decision to publish a journal entitled *Natural Science in Education* (the same title as that of the Thomson Report) provided members would agree to an increase in the annual subscription from five to ten shillings a year.[4]

Looking back on the origins of the venture, Adlam recalled how warily he and C.L. Bryant, secretary to the Committee in 1918, had to tread in presenting the idea to 'extremely conservative' fellow members. The financial implication of a doubling of the annual subscription was not a major sticking point, but the innovation did entail a change in the constitution of the APSSM, always a matter calculated to arouse strong feelings. Adlam and Bryant together worked out the constitutional position of the editor. Bryant's concern was that a satisfactory editor should not be subjected to the rule about retirement that applied to other officers. Adlam was anxious to ensure that an incompetent editor could be got rid of, quickly and quietly. In the end, the election was made annual and placed in the hands of the General Committee, a situation which remained virtually unchanged thereafter.[5]

The proposed title of the journal provoked second thoughts, eventually, at the end of 'a long and barren sitting' J.R. Eccles's (Gresham's School) suggestion of *The School Science Review* commanding support. Another committee member, J.R. Durrant (Marlborough) wanted a pictorial cover, 'something allegorical with the sun just coming over the horizon', but this 'dangerous corner' was turned safely, others alleging 'fearful expense'.[6] Not surprisingly the duties of editor fell upon the initiator of the idea, Adlam, who remained in office for a remarkable twenty-eight years.

The production of a journal clearly entailed the APSSM entering into an agreement with a firm of publishers. Additionally, war-time conditions still prevailing, the sanction of the Director of Paper Economy was needed. Armed with this, and the promises of Board of Education support for 'a Priority Certificate', Adlam approached the publishing firm of John Murray in Albemarle Street, London.[7] In so doing he was acting on advice given by the President of the APSSM in 1918, Sir Ronald Ross FRS, who sent a supporting letter to Mr Murray. 'The Association has come to stay', Ross wrote, 'and is very well managed by a number of capable young men. . . . I think its Quarterly Journal is likely to do well'.[8] Agreement was quickly reached on the production details, a copy of the first number of *The School Science Review* reaching Adlam in June 1919, eight months after the date of his initial letter of enquiry. Thus was initiated a long-standing relationship between the Associations and the publishing firm of John Murray.

On his own acknowledgement Adlam knew little about editorial work when he embarked upon his duties. He received some advice from R.A. Gregory, Editor of *Nature*, who later, as Sir Richard Gregory, was President of the SMA in 1928. On the production side, Murray's Educational Editor, R.B. Lattimer, ensured the establishment of a house style and handled all matters relating to illustrations and block-making.[9] *The School Science Review* was the property of the Association, but was published by John Murray. Under this arrangement, the Association was responsible for all aspects of distribution, including keeping an up-to-date list of members' names and addresses, addressing wrappers for despatch of copies, and dealing with all complaints about non-receipt. In these and other editorial matters, help for Adlam was essential. Throughout the early years and up to the outbreak of war in 1939 his first wife typed all his letters, read all proofs and kept a register of books sent for review, a not untypical example of domestic, 'behind the scenes' support which many SMA officers received.[10] More formally, the Journal Sub-Committee which had been established to oversee the publication of the early issues of *The School Science Review* was disbanded in 1921, to be replaced by an Editorial Sub-Committee of members whose task was to assist the Editor in his work and whose names were to appear on the title page of the journal. Of those on the first Editorial Sub-Committee F.A. Beesley had special responsibility for advertisements by publishers and apparatus manufacturers, an important source of revenue for the Association.[11] In turn, Beesley was succeeded by B.M. Neville (William Ellis School) who also edited all the physical apparatus and experiments notes in *The School Science Review* until his death in 1942. At this point, at Adlam's suggestion, it was agreed that Mrs Olive Farquharson should take over the responsibilities of Advertisement Editor. For a number of years previously Mrs Farquharson had looked after the distribution of the journal from John Murray's office, receiving a modest payment from the Association for these duties. Her involvement extended into the 1970s when an increasing share of the work of the Advertisement Editor was undertaken by Mr Robin Brown, a member of the permanent full-time staff at the ASE headquarters, Hatfield.[12]

Although B.M. Neville's contribution to *The School Science Review* was in effect that of an Assistant Editor he was never so designated. By the time of his death there was growing concern in the SMA General Committee about the question of Adlam's successor and two Assistant Editors, A.E.E. McKenzie (Repton School) and A.W. Wellings (Leamington College) were formally appointed in 1942.[13] In fact Adlam continued in office for another four years until his own death in 1946 at the age of seventy. By this time the SMA Committee had established a team of eight Assistant Editors, one of whom, S.R. Humby (Winchester), was appointed as the second Editor of *The School Science Review*,[14] serving until 1955 when ill-health obliged him to relinquish the office. His successor, R.H. Dyball (City of London School), presented the Association with a novel situation when, after eight years as Editor, he announced his intention to resign from the office on his retirement from active teaching at the age of sixty-five in July 1964. This was the first time in the life of *The School Science Review* that the Association had received such notice. In view of the importance which the journal had come to assume in the affairs of the Association, Dyball drew upon his experience as Editor to outline various possibilities for the future, including the appointment at Headquarters of a Publications Officer who could relieve the Honorary Editor of much of the considerable burden of work now associated with the office. An alternative suggestion, that he himself should continue as Editor for a further short period, with office accommodation at headquarters and with part-time secretarial assistance, was eventually adopted. Such an arrangement gave the ASE more time to assess the situation and to seek an appropriate replacement.[15]

The eventual recommendation from a joint meeting of *The School Science Review* and Publications Committees in July 1965 was firmly against the appointment of any full-time Editor to be responsible for all the Association's publications and journals. Instead, the preference was for an Honorary Editor to succeed Dyball, the new officer to come from a school and to be provided with adequate secretarial assistance and 'a suitable fee' of £500 per annum. At the same meeting it was agreed to recommend to Council that A.A. Bishop (Harrow), an Assistant Editor of *The School Science Review*, should be asked to accept the office of Editor on Dyball's retirement the following year.[16] Bishop assumed the editorship in 1966, continuing in that office throughout the period covered by this history.

The School Science Review, then, has the remarkable record of being published continuously since June 1919 under only four Editors, the last of whom was still serving in 1984. It appeared as a quarterly journal until 1941 when the loss in the blitz of the Association's paper stocks and the general rationing of paper obliged Adlam

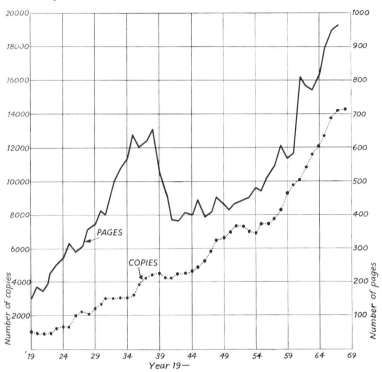

Table 7.1   *The unbroken line shows the number of pages in the volume of SSR which started in the year indicated; the broken line shows the average number of copies of each issue printed in a given year. (From The School Science Review, 50, No.173, June 1969, p.713)*

to reduce the issues to three per year. At one stage it seemed that the *Review* would be classified as a school magazine and made subject to a war-time order that all such publications should be reduced to six pages. However, a War Office request that sixth-form science masters should give prescribed courses to engineering cadets was turned to good purpose. For such courses the latest and best scientific information was clearly essential. Both *Discovery* and *Science Progress* had ceased publication. The only appropriate journals for science teachers were *Nature* and *The School Science Review*. 'Can't we be classed as a technical journal?' G. Fowles, Chairman of the SMA Committee, asked E.G. Savage when discussing the matter at the Annual Meeting at Rugby in 1942. Until 1940 Senior Chief Inspector in the Board of Education, and subsequently Chief Education Officer, London County Council, Savage was in a position to exert influence and *The School Science Review* continued to appear without dramatic reduction in its number of pages.[17] Even so, as Table

7.1[18] shows, it took over twenty years from the outbreak of war before the number of pages per volume of *The School Science Review* reached again the pre-war level.

Adlam's editorial policy was, in his own words, to 'let the journal shape itself'.[19] He meant by this that the membership, by its own contributions, should largely determine the contents of the *Review*. This is not to say that on occasions he did not actively seek contributions on various topics. In this matter members of the Editorial Committee, and especially Archer Vassall who 'seemed to know everybody', were helpful in putting him in touch with likely authors. But to a great extent the commanding position which the journal achieved under his editorship was due to his ability to encourage and elicit contributions from members. Few if any members of the SMA and AWST received payment for their articles, although 'professors and the like' were usually paid, especially if they had been asked to write.[20] It should be added that Adlam and his successors in the office of Editor were much less successful in finding women authors than men. Whilst members of the AWST served on the Editorial Committee and later as Assistant Editors, relatively few women contributed articles to the journal.

It is interesting to look at the results of this *laissez-faire* editorial policy over the years up to the time of amalgamation of the AWST and the SMA. Between 1919 and 1962 there is little evidence of dissatisfaction with the contents of *The School Science Review* expressed either in the deliberations of the committees of the Associations or in the records of regional activity. Indeed, the member who stated that he 'picked out the *SSR* from the post with a genuine thrill of pleasurable anticipation which has so far never deceived me' was typical of many of his colleagues.[21] Even the initial reservation of some women science teachers that the *Review* catered largely for science masters appears to have disappeared by the 1940s. At the AWST Annual General Meeting in 1945 it was agreed that the journal was 'one of the best of its kind' and a congratulatory message was despatched to Adlam on the publication of the centenary issue.[22] By that date the early tendency towards a preponderance of physics and chemistry articles had been substantially modified; indeed, during the 1930s the number of articles on biological topics exceeded those on physics. Another interesting feature of the journal during the same period was the increased number of articles dealing with aspects of applied science, especially industrial chemistry and extractive metallurgy. Thus, the issue of *The School Science Review* published in December 1934 contained fifteen articles, of which six were on applied science topics such as the alkali industry, the metallurgy and uses of zinc, neon tubes in advertising, models of early steam engines, storage batteries, and the synchronous motor electric clock. Up to the outbreak of war university and industrial scientists, and others based in institutions such as the National Physical Laboratory, Rothamsted Experimental Station, Plymouth Marine

Laboratory, the Meteorological Office and the Royal Botanical Gardens, Kew, were frequent contributors to the pages of *The School Science Review.*

It would appear that the composition of the journal at this stage accurately reflected the perceived needs of many members of the SMA and AWST. Adlam certainly sought ideas for suitable topics for articles, inserting a circular letter inviting suggestions in some issues of *The School Science Review* and making full use of the many industrial and research contacts established by the Associations through visits and meetings. A prime function of the journal was to keep members up-to-date in relation to scientific subject matter, interpreted broadly, though here some members sought even more than the *Review* offered. 'I crave . . . something . . . that will tell me if anything really vital, affecting my teaching, has occurred', one correspondent wrote to the Editor in 1929, urging that the journal should include an annotated list of references to scientific papers of major importance.[23] He was not alone in seeking such an abstracting service, members of the Yorkshire Branch incorporating one in their regional publication, *The Periodical*, in the late 1930s.

Supplementing the articles other sections of the *Review* concerned with new scientific information were developed in the inter-war years. From December 1929 a special section on Apparatus and Experiments was introduced, this becoming Physical Apparatus and Experiments from 1933 following the successful trial the previous year of 'a new and entirely "unsensational" feature' called Chemical Notes. In turn, the latter was expanded into Chemistry and Biology Notes. In 1936 a University Section appeared, its subsequent title, Scholarship and University Section, conveying more accurately its focus on advanced science teaching for sixth formers seeking State Scholarships and university awards. It was in these sections, and in the popular Notes and Correspondence, that the membership came into its own, most contributions being from serving teachers. The quality was often impressively high with references to recently published scientific research, a reflection in part of the strong academic qualifications of those who, in a period of economic recession and chronic over-supply of teachers, had been able to secure teaching posts in independent and grammar schools.

Despite the difficulties of war-time, most of the established features of the journal were maintained between 1939 and 1945, only the Scholarship and University Section disappearing in this period. Indeed, meetings for the most part being impossible to hold, the importance of *The School Science Review* as a means of communication between the Committee and the membership increased markedly. In consequence the reports of numerous SMA subcommittees were printed in the journal. Another notable innovation was the appearance of AWST Notes designed to keep women members informed of developments, although this feature did not survive beyond the end of the war.

S.R. Humby's period as Editor, coinciding with the first decade of peace-time conditions, was one of consolidation of the journal structure which Adlam had so conscientiously built. In this period and up to the time of amalgamation of the Associations, the proportion of articles on applied and industrial science was distinctly less than in the 1930s. At the same time the proportion of articles written by authors from universities and research establishments increased, as did the number of contributions from overseas countries, the latter reflecting, amongst other factors, the extension of membership of the Associations.[24] From 1953 an additional section on Elementary Science Notes was introduced, coinciding with increased attention being directed to the teaching of science in secondary modern schools.

Book reviews had been an important component of the journal from its inception. One innovation which Humby attempted to introduce was the signing of such reviews, but the decision of the General Committee went against him.[25] The policy was later adopted under A.A. Bishop's editorship. Additional to the book reviews, and reflecting the development of audio-visual aids for science teaching purposes, from 1949 reviews of films became an established section of the journal.

The attitude of different Editors to letters from members was interestingly varied. Adlam welcomed correspondence, rarely rejecting anything provided it was signed.[26] In contrast, Humby disliked letters and tended to avoid publication of them if he could. It was, however, Hugh Dyball, more than either of his predecessors, who succeeded in encouraging the membership to express itself in print on a wide range of science teaching issues. Under his editorship Notes and Correspondence became 'a veritable journal within a journal' and the first section to which many readers turned on receipt of a new issue of *The School Science Review*.[27]

Even in correspondence, however, the main emphasis at this stage, in keeping with the rest of the journal, was on scientific subject matter. Letters tended to deal with topics such as the solution of problems not covered in textbooks, the need for hitherto unrecognised safety precautions in particular experiments, and the most effective way of presenting specific scientific ideas. Relatively little space in the journal was devoted to general educational issues. Occasionally the implications for science teaching of some external event might be examined, as when consideration was given to the Spens Report in 1939.[28] Again, in the prolonged debate about General Science in the 1930s, psychological evidence on transfer of training was invoked.[29] Presidential Addresses from Annual Meetings from time to time offered a broader view of science education as did occasional comparative accounts of science teaching in other countries. But the general picture over the first forty years of the journal's existence is one in which the context of science teaching for the homogeneous membership was relatively stable and the definition of what was problematic was principally in terms of the transmission of scientific knowledge. In so far as the journal contributed to the setting of professional standards of performance to which science teachers might strive, these were in terms of competence in subject matter and mastery of experimental detail.

Representing the public face of the Associations, *The School Science Review*, through the academic quality of its contents, undoubtedly helped to maintain for the SMA and AWST the reputation within the community of professional science which the APSSM had earlier acquired. At the same time it delivered a clear message to science teachers in schools other than secondary grammar and independent that their concerns were not those of the Associations. As the SMA in particular broadened the base of its membership it was inevitable that change should take place. It was also the case that by the end of the 1950s the SMA had grown to a point where more effective communication between the General Committee and membership was essential than that available through the medium of *The School Science Review*. Consequential developments in the publications of the Association are considered in the following section.

A second journal

At a meeting of the SMA General Committee in June 1961, the Chairman, J.S.G. McGeachin, expressed the view the 'the time was ripe for a change in the method of running the Association'.[30] Numerically, the SMA had more than doubled in size in the post-war years. It had become deeply involved in science curriculum reform activities following the publication of its *Policy Statement* in 1957. From May 1960 it had been in possession of a permanent Headquarters building in Cambridge and amalgamation with the AWST was a mere eighteen months away. In short, the scale of its activities had been transformed without any significant alteration in the internal mechanisms of communication between the General Committee and the members. With the appointment in November 1961 of a salaried, full-time General Secretary, E.W. Tapper, it became feasible for the SMA to think of a publication different from *The School Science Review* where accounts of SMA committee activities, reported briefly under Notes and Correspondence, were often months out of date. A less substantial periodical than the *SSR* was proposed, in effect a quick-to-produce news bulletin, the first issue being distributed in April 1962.

The advice to members from E.W. Tapper, Editor of the *Bulletin*, was that they should detach the centre pages containing the Association's Annual Report and Balance Sheet for filing, then throw away the remainder which was not intended to have permanent value.[31] This modest assessment of the contents of the *Bulletin* was belied by subsequent issues. It continued to include news and information of

contemporary interest, but in addition it quickly became an important medium for dissemination of information about Branch activities, as well as containing from time to time reports of important
lectures and addresses, such as that by the ASE's Patron, the Duke
of Edinburgh, on the Challenge of Modern Engineering, in March
1965.[32]

The respective functions of the *Bulletin* and *The School Science
Review* were the subject of discussion in the ASE Council in 1965,
the context being broadened to include considerations of ways in
which membership might be increased. The matter was referred to
Branches from which came confirmation of the view that many
teachers did not join the ASE because they felt that *The School
Science Review*, and the meetings, were too much orientated towards
sixth-form work and did not give enough practical help in teaching the
younger or less able pupils.[33] The London Branch, for example,
viewed with dismay the reversal of the original policy regarding the
use of the *Bulletin*, favouring a consolidation of everything apart from
notices and announcements in a modified *SSR*, increased in scope to
incorporate articles relevant to middle and junior school science
teaching. Better coordination with recently published journals such
as *Education in Chemistry* was also urged.[34] The Midland Branch
took a similar line in relation to the contents of the journals, recommending that the Association should reconsider the composition of
the Editorial Board of the *SSR* 'with a view to making the publications more relevant to the needs of the present day'.[35] Apart from the
need to cater for newer categories of membership, however, the
general picture which emerged from the Branch replies at this stage
was one of substantial satisfaction with the publications. As the
newly-appointed Editor, A.A. Bishop, was able to point out to
members, *The School Science Review* had from November 1965 been
sub-titled The Journal of the ASE, implying that it was intended to
address the interests of the whole Association and not just a section
of it.[36] At the same time the title and format of the *Bulletin* were
changed, it becoming *Education in Science*, The Bulletin of the ASE,
and clearly a distinct second journal of permanent value.

In the years which followed, further changes occurred in the contents and organisation of *The School Science Review*. From June
1967 a section was devoted to Nuffield Science, this becoming later
the Curriculum Development Section, itself replaced in turn by
Science Education Notes. In 1968 it became possible to re-establish
the practice of issuing the journal four times per year. The amount of
work which the editorship entailed, estimated as equivalent to two-
thirds of a full-time job,[37] was the subject of discussion in 1969
which resulted in the appointment at Headquarters of R.L. Brown as
Assistant to the Editors of the ASE's two journals. Following his
retirement ten years later, Mrs C.A. Abbott joined the Headquarters'
staff as Third Assistant Secretary with responsibility for the journals,
acting as Assistant to the Editors and as Advertisement Manager.[38] A

change of major significance was the decision in January 1976 that the ASE itself should publish *The School Science Review*, so ending an agreement with the firm of John Murray (Publishers) Ltd which went back to the first issue in 1919. By 1976, however, the Association's own publishing activities had grown to a point such that, in an extensive range of publications, the only one for which the ASE was not directly responsible was its principal journal. There was also a case for working with a printer close enough to Hatfield for easy communication. The break was achieved amicably, John Murray providing a typically generous reception at Albemarle Street to mark the publication of the 200th issue of the *SSR* in March 1976. Indeed the special relationship between the Association and John Murray remains as close as ever; in particular, the help and support of Murray's Educational Director, Kenneth Pinnock, who for many years had a special responsibility for the *SSR*, has been continuously extended to the Association.[39]

For some members, however, the basic problems remained unaddressed. In a strongly worded article, a London teacher, Brian Matthews, informed readers of *Education in Science* in 1977 that he had become 'increasingly disenchanted with *The School Science Review* and the type of article it contains'. For Matthews the emphasis was still too heavily on 'the content of science', whereas teachers involved in comprehensive reorganization would be more helped by discussion of

(a) Teaching topics to the average pupil.
(b) Mixed ability, the pros and cons and the practical implications.
(c) Linguistic and social deprivation and the classroom.

It was time for a movement to balance the 'Science' and the 'Education', Matthews concluded.[40]

Responding, the Editor, Andrew Bishop, did not dissent from the case for articles of the type indicated by Matthews but pointed out, first, that previous appeals for them had met with limited success and, second, that when 'educational' material had been received it was frequently written 'in a special sort of jargon' unacceptable to practising science teachers.[41] Regional comment was elicited on the subject and the Editorial Committee spent most of a day in formulating a list of suggestions which it was within their power to implement. Apart from reference to specific topics such as the need for more articles on 'science and industry' and 'relating science to life in general' two central points emerged. The first was that the Editor could print only what he received: if no one wrote on the teaching of science to mixed-ability classes, and if encouragement to those with relevant experience brought no result, it was difficult to go further. The principle of paying a fee for articles was rejected as impractical although some incentive might be offered by a prize in the ASE Award Scheme. The second point concerned the relationship of the Association's journals, *The School Science Review* in particular, to the, by now, considerable range of other publications which the ASE sold. The journals came to members without charge, as part of the services to members on payment of their annual subscription. Other publications had to be purchased separately, on an individual basis, and the question arose as to the distribution of material between them and the journals. A greater degree of coordination was clearly needed and in recognition of this a new Publications Committee, as a standing committee of Council, was established.[42] Before considering further the response of the Association's journals to the changing needs of members it is appropriate, therefore, at this point to turn to a brief examination of other publications for which the Association was responsible.

The growth of occasional publications

The practice of the APSSM to issue occasional publications was continued by the SMA and to a lesser extent by the AWST. An early production by the SMA was a series of educational pamphlets, inaugurated in 1931 with the report of an Association committee on *Science in Senior Schools*. There followed other pamphlets on the science papers set in the School Certificate Examination throughout the 1930s; these provided an annual distillation of members' critical comments on the suitability of individual questions, and of question papers, in all the science subjects offered by the several examination boards.[43] At this stage the SMA also published a number of tracts on the teaching of general science, including a major statement of the aims of the movement, together with a detailed syllabus, in 1936.[44] In response to requests from members the APSSM and the AWST separately had each compiled a list of science books suitable for school libraries. In 1930 a joint committee of the SMA and AWST produced a revised list, one of the earliest collaborative ventures. A new list in 1940 was published under the name of the SMA alone, as were subsequent revisions and annual supplements. A pamphlet of considerable practical significance, drawn up by the AWST in response to a request from the Association of Head Mistresses, was *Safeguards in the Laboratory* (1933),[45] a guide for inexperienced teachers and 'non-scientific headmistresses'.

The most substantial publications from the SMA in the pre-war period were, however, derivative, being composed of material which had previously appeared in *The School Science Review*. At the Annual Meeting at Oxford in 1927 it had been suggested that the Association should publish monographs on scientific topics of special interest to members and a series of *Modern Science Memoirs* was inaugurated soon afterwards by the publication in paper covers of Harold Hartley's two articles, 'The study of indicators and the law of mass action' and 'The ionic theory of electrolytic solutions', the latter being his Presidential Address; G.R. de Beer's 'Introduction to the study of genetics'; and N.V. Sidgwick's 'Atomic structure and the periodic table'.[46] Other memoirs were quickly added to this quartet, including classics such as E.G. Savage's 'The teaching of "Colour" in elementary courses of science' and one paper by a woman scientist, Dr E.M. Delf, on 'The distribution and movement of water in plants'. By 1950 thirty titles had been accumulated in the series of *Modern Science Memoirs*, published for the SMA by John Murray.

Shortly after the *Memoirs* were launched, the SMA General Committee agreed to publish a book made up of accounts of experiments drawn from the pages of *The School Science Review*.[47] This was called *The Science Master's Book*, a title which accurately reflected the authorship of the accounts whilst somewhat ignoring the stake which the AWST had in the editorial management of the *SSR*. The first volume, edited and arranged by Adlam, appeared in 1931 being reprinted in 1939 and 1948. It was devoted entirely to physics, over half its contents being concerned with sixth-form experiments. There followed a companion volume of experiments in chemistry and biology. The formula was successful, over 2000 copies of each volume being sold by 1936[48] when it was decided to publish a second series. Despite Adlam's reservation that 'I don't think very highly of what I have in chemistry'[49] a third series, including separate books for chemistry and biology plus an additional volume of *Experiments for Modern Schools*, was published in the 1950s, another volume of physics experiments, as Series 4 Part 1, appearing in 1961.

Also published by John Murray in the 1950s as a result of collaboration between the AWST, the SMA, the London Association of Science Teachers and the Association of Tutors in Colleges and Departments of Education, was a series of books on *Science Teaching Techniques*. These were directed more at the non-graduate teacher of science in a secondary modern school and included topics such as use of small mammals; safe chemistry; use of scientific toys; pre-nursing courses; and bird watching. Another joint enterprise, this time between the SMA and the IAAM and again under the Murray imprint, was *The Teaching of Science in Secondary Schools*, a comprehensive *vade-mecum* on all aspects of science teaching. Completed in draft form before the outbreak of war, the book was eventually published in 1947 after a new joint committee had revised the original manuscript. A second edition appeared in 1958. With its broadening membership in mind the SMA also produced *Secondary Modern Science Teaching*, the work of a sub-committee, in 1953.[50]

Up to the late 1950s the publications which the SMA produced were designed primarily to serve the needs of members, interpreted almost exclusively in terms of the up-dating of scientific knowledge and the extension of skills in experimentation. To a lesser extent, because it was responsible for fewer publications, the same was true of the AWST, although here the largely ignored but farsighted Interim Report on *Science in Post-Primary Education* (1944) constituted an exception. The significant turning point, however, came in

1957 with the publication of the SMA's *Policy Statement*, a pronouncement on the aims, content and methods of science teaching clearly intended to influence opinion outside the Association. Around the same time there appeared other publications whose purpose was to stimulate action by local education authorities and government in relation to matters such as the improved provision of laboratory technicians.[51] A highly critical survey of conditions and staffing for *Science Teaching in Secondary Modern Schools* was issued in 1959 whilst the following year, in collaboration with the NUT and the Joint Four Secondary Associations, the SMA and AWST published a report on *Provision and Maintenance of Laboratories in Grammar Schools*. We have here the beginnings of the movement detected in the earlier examination of the Association's conference activities in which communications directed internally to the membership became increasingly supplemented by communications directed outside the Association in its quest for authority to pronounce on the definition of school science.

The progressive reshaping and reinterpretation of policy since 1957 can be traced through the ASE's subsequent publications under this heading. The preliminary SMA document of 1957 was followed by a separate statement from the AWST in 1959, the two Associations collaborating in the production of a joint *Policy Statement* in 1961. This served as the introduction to the important series of *Science and Education* reports which developed in greater detail the syllabuses and teaching approaches being advocated, as well as making recommendations on the training of graduate science teachers. In 1963 a *Policy Statement* was prepared by the ASE's Primary Schools Science Committee, a new section on the Primary Stage being incorporated when the 1961 document was revised and published in a second edition as *School Science and General Education* in 1965.[52] Before the end of the decade, however, the ASE's Council had come to the view that the pace of events in the educational world necessitated a reformulation of policy. A statement intended to serve as a basis for regional discussions was printed in *Education in Science*[53] although this was, uncharacteristically, so badly constructed that much of the critical comment on it was concerned with clarification of meaning. Eventually a new publication, *Science and General Education – 1971*, appeared, followed by supporting statements on *Science for the Under-Thirteens* and *Science for the 13–16 Age Range*.

When in 1977 the Association was requested by the Education, Arts and Home Office Sub-Committee of the House of Commons Expenditure Committee to give evidence on the attainments of school leavers, it became clear that yet a further revision of policy was needed, the previous documents no longer providing an adequate mandate for officers. A small working party under the auspices of the Education (Research) Committee and chaired by Dr J.J. Thompson was established to prepare a new statement.[54] In the event the controversial report of this group emerged as a consultative document, *Alternatives for Science Education* (1979), which evoked a considerable debate both within the Association and outside. In the light of comments from members and others, guidelines for the construction of a new Policy Statement were laid down at the 1980 Education Conference and a Special Policy Group was brought into being by the ASE's Council to prepare a definitive statement. Under the title *Education through Science* this was published in 1981 not, it was emphasised, as 'the culmination of the policy-making process but rather as the beginning of a further stage of development'.[55] One feature of this further stage, as has been noted earlier, was the Secondary Science Curriculum Review. The words of the ASE's Chairman in 1978 had been heeded. 'We are a force in the land', Dr R.W. West informed members in his annual report, 'but need nevertheless to find more and better ways of making our voice heard. This is our future . . .'[56]

Parallel to this shift in emphasis from communications directed internally to members to communications intended for a wider audience, the ASE extended the range of its publication services to members. Under the auspices of the Education (Co-ordinating) Committee an increased number of professionally useful pamphlets and books on subjects of immediate relevance to the everyday work of science teachers was produced. Thus, the implications of the Health and Safety at Work Act, which came into force in 1975, were examined by a sub-committee which worked closely with the Laboratory Safeguards sub-committee on a revision of *Safeguards in the School Laboratory*, published in 1976. Outstanding among members who over many years had contributed to the knowledge of science teachers on hazards in laboratories and their prevention was H.G. Andrew (Lower School of John Lyon, Harrow), Chairman of the Laboratory Safeguards sub-committee until 1976.[57] A Laboratory Technicians sub-committee reviewed the duties of science laboratory technicians, made proposals for an establishment of such staff for schools, and prepared a series of practical guides, published from 1981, on topics such as *Microscope Care and Maintenance, Laboratory Photography* and *Records and Paperwork*. From other sub-committees came publications on *Chemical Nomemclature* and *SI Units* whilst a series of *Science and Primary Education Papers* was inaugurated in 1974.[58]

In the same year the Education (Research) committee sponsored the first of a *Study Series* of publications aimed to provide information for teachers about current science education issues and to serve as the basis for discussion in science departments and teachers' centres. Resulting from meetings of the Environmental Science group of the London Region of the ASE. *The Place of Science in Environmental Education* (1974) was followed by other booklets on topics as diverse as *Non-streamed science: a teacher's guide* (1976), *The Head of Science and the task of management* (1978), *Resource-based*

Learning (1978), *What is Science?* (1979) and *Language in Science* (1980). Following the review in 1971 of the role of the Education (Research) Committee a number of new research initiatives were taken. One of these, started in 1972, yielded an interim publication *Case Studies in Science Education in a Changing Context* (1976) whilst it also provided the basis for a successful application for grant to the Schools Council for a project, Studies in Decision Making in Science Education, which commenced in 1978. A subsequent report, *Decisions in the Science Department*, was published jointly by the ASE and Schools Council in 1981. Following this, the ASE President in that year, Sir Denis Rooke, began discussions between the British Gas Management Centre and the ASE on the relation between educational and industrial management which led to the production by a joint ASE/British Gas Project of four training modules for use in in-service courses with science teachers.[59]

The LAMP (Science for the Less Academically Motivated Pupils) Project, organised as a network of local groups working on different aspects of a common problem and coordinated initially by Dr Rosalind Driver, published its first three Topic Briefs (*Fuels, Pollution* and *Photography*) at the Annual Meeting at Leicester in January 1977. Twelve other Briefs and two Teachers Handbooks were produced by this successful and innovative project. In 1976 a Science and Society Project, organized by John L. Lewis, commenced its activities, its publications (ASE/Heinemann Educational Books, 1981) including a *Teachers' Guide, Student Readers* and *Decision Making Simulation Exercises*. Somewhat later the materials of the Science in a Social Context project, organized by Joan Solomon, were published (ASE/Blackwell) as an additional resource for post-16 courses in this new field. A subsequent report, *Rethinking Science?* (1984), was the outcome of deliberations by a committee of the ASE established to investigate how consideration of the interactions of science and society might be incorporated into courses for pupils in the 11 to 16 age range.[60]

The range of publications available to members from the ASE's Headquarters at Hatfield was further extended by agreements negotiated with other agencies. From March 1975 all titles published by the School Natural Science Society were marketed by the ASE. Safety information was supplemented by the CLEAPSE Hazcards (Chemistry) and a *Technician's Handbook* was published on behalf of the Institute of Science Technology. Collaboration with industry yielded *The GASS Book* (Gas Applications for School Science) and *Physics at Work*, joint publications with British Gas and British Petroleum respectively. *Help for New Heads of Science Departments*, a document produced by Gloucestershire Education Committee, was printed and distributed by the ASE which also produced *APU Science Reports for Teachers*. In addition the science textbooks of many commercial publishers were made available with a 10 per cent discount to members. The impact of new technologies on publishing activites and in particular the marketing of computer software, is a potential development for the future.

In the face of this impressive range of publications, both scientific and educational, which the ASE made available to its members especially from the mid-seventies onwards, the suggestion that the Association might publish a third journal, in effect an annual yearbook of science education, met with a cool reception when the newly-formed Publications Committee held its first meeting in March 1978. The opinion from the Education (Coordinating) Committee was that the roles of the existing two journals should instead be reviewed. It was also urged that *The School Science Review* in future should publish more articles on 'key educational issues' such as Core Science, the work of the Assessment of Performance Unit and the implications of falling school populations, a view that the Editor accepted readily. Good examples of industry liaison work in schools were also suggested as appropriate for inclusion in the *SSR*.[61] As for *Education in Science* it became increasingly 'the official means of communication with members of the ASE', a phrase which replaced its description as 'The Bulletin of the ASE' when a new format was adopted in 1981. As well as current news and information, reports from active sub-committees were printed regularly.

Some indication of the extraordinary extent to which the Association's printing, publishing and bookselling activities had grown since the appointment of Mrs C.M. Wilson as Publications Officer in September 1973 is provided by repeated references in subsequent Annual Reports to large percentage increases in the turnover of the Publications Department. In the year ended 31 July 1978 over 30,000 volumes of the ASE's in-house publications were produced with a record sales income of £227,837 compared with £170,000 for the previous year. By June 1983, the annual Income and Expenditure Account showed a surplus arising on sale and production of publications of almost £44,000 compared with approximately £6500 in 1975–76.[62]

As we have seen, however, increase in scale was accompanied by increase in purpose. The service to members in terms of their everyday occupational needs had been augmented. Resources necessary to enable science teachers to define better their educational problems and to contribute themselves more effectively to the solution of these problems had been developed. Publications provided an opportunity for greater involvement of teachers in corporate thinking about science education issues and for the fostering of stronger feelings of corporate membership. But perhaps of most significance, publications had become important instruments in the ASE's pursuit of occupational autonomy and self-determination. Documents such as *Education through Science* were considered pronouncements about the nature of science teaching in school, contesting other opinion, making public the ASE's position in recognition of the need for accountability, and bidding to become the authoritative influence on the shaping of the future curriculum.

The extent to which the collective pronouncements of science teachers are regarded as authoritative contributions to the definition of school science might be taken as an index of the degree of control which such teachers have established over their occupational affairs.[63] Unlike medicine and law, which by the nineteenth century had acquired occupational authority to a degree which permitted un-fettered determination of recruitment and training policies and a monopoly on practice in the field, science teaching as an occupation through most of the twentieth century remained auxiliary to the interest of other groups including professional scientists and those who provided and managed educational resources. The endeavours of the Associations to increase their control over the science curri-culum, and hence the professionalism of the science teacher, is the subject of Part Three which follows.

8 Science Education for an Elite

Science differentiated

As educationally organized knowledge, science entered the twentieth century in a highly differentiated and variable condition. Under the provisions of the Science and Art Department, over twenty-five distinct branches of theoretical and applied science had been constituted for examination purposes. Thus, separate components of Science and Art Department physics included 'mechanics', 'sound, light and heat' and 'magnetism and electricity'. 'Human physiology', 'zoology', 'biology' and 'elementary botany' were the constituents of natural history. 'Hygiene', 'nautical astronomy' and 'steam' were representative of applied variants, whilst, by 1900, T.H. Huxley's synthetic 'physiography' had become the Department's most popular subject, after mathematics.[1]

In similar manner, though less finely divided, the Oxford and Cambridge Schools Examination Board offered its Higher Certificate science in five divisions – mechanical, physical, chemical, physical geography and geology, and biology.[2] As for the Qualifying Examination for Sandhurst and Woolwich, the shifting boundaries of an amorphous 'science', alternative to Greek or Latin, were set by whatever combination of experimental or natural sciences the Advisory Board on Military Education might deem to be appropriate.[3]

Such diversity did little to assist rational approaches to the construction of school science courses. For those teachers in grant-aided secondary schools, the Board of Education's *Regulations* for 1904 had framed the broad possibilities with some precision, laying down a requirement for a coherent four-year course of instruction up to the age of sixteen, including at least three hours per week of practical and theoretical work in science. Within this allocation, the general tendency was to divide the time equally between chemistry and physics; though in the fourth year one subject only might be studied in preparation for an external examination. Thus, physics might start in year one with mensuration; the second and third years would cover easy experimental work in hydrostatics, statics, dynamics and heat – exceptionally, some light might be included; and in the fourth year, pupils would be prepared for a Matriculation examination. Here the university examination boards had tended to divide physics into a number of 'subjects', a candidate being required to offer only one for examination purposes: a common division was into 'Heat, Light and Sound' and 'Electricity and Magnetism'. Often a boy or girl would leave school without taking the fourth year. Those who stayed to sit the Matriculation examination in 'Heat, Light and Sound' would leave largely ignorant of the science of electricity.[4] It appeared that secondary school courses in physics as with most other sciences, had been planned as mere preliminaries to a fuller study of the subject by the minority of pupils who continued after Matriculation.

For those teaching in public schools, there were other complications. They received their pupils from preparatory schools at a later age than that at which most pupils entered grant-aided secondary schools. Few preparatory schools included science in their curriculum so that no foundation of earlier work could be assumed; also, the later starting age meant that less time was available for subsequent science studies. In any case, science was not usually seen as a subject of general education to be taken by all boys. It tended to be confined to special divisions, rather than being a form subject. Even in science classes the mathematical skills necessary for physics and chemistry were not available in any coordinated way, the prestige of mathematics in the curriculum ruling out any question of its subservience to the newly-arrived and lower status science. For those pupils who resisted the blandishments of classics and mathematics, and elected to specialise in science in the upper forms of public schools, the demands of university scholarship and army entrance examinations were diverse, unrelated, changing and severe.[5] It was in terms of these institutional constraints on the development of science education in public schools, that the programme of the APSSM, as an interest group concerned to improve curricular provision in the schools of its members, was shaped in the early years of the century.

Strengthening the foundations: science in preparatory schools

Even before the Association came into being, individual science teachers had pressed the case for the inclusion of science in the curriculum of preparatory schools. In 1897 and 1898 W.A. Shenstone (Clifton) and Archer Vassall (Harrow) had contributed articles to *The Preparatory School Review*,[6] urging the desirability of engaging the natural inquisitiveness of boys and outlining possibilities for observational studies which would not necessitate expensive laboratory provisions. 'The cricket ground, the sky and the kitchen will afford ample material for five years' work', Vassall wrote. Nothing elaborate was intended; two periods of half an hour each week would suffice as the basis for later work in the public schools. At the same time, the importance of fostering powers of observation and of arousing an intelligent interest in natural phenomena could not be over-emphasized. In state-aided elementary schools such matters were being taken more seriously than in the independent sector, the

London School Board's recent decision to buy microscopes and lay out beds of plants suitable for the study of nature being cited by Vassall.[7]

These efforts had only limited success. When, in 1904, a common examination for entrance into public schools was inaugurated, science was included, but merely as an alternative to Latin verse and as an extra, seventh paper.[8] Even so, the joint control of this examination by a board of five managers, three representing the Headmasters' Conference and two the Association of Headmasters of Preparatory Schools, provided the APSSM with a focus for its influence. A sub-committee was appointed in May 1904 to confer with preparatory school masters on the subject of Nature Study and to formulate a syllabus.[9] The report of this group was published, with sample lessons, in *The Preparatory School Review*, one of its members, O.H. Latter (Charterhouse) attending the annual conference of the Association of Headmasters of Preparatory Schools to speak on the teaching of science.[10]

As Latter himself acknowledged some years later, it was inevitable that such attempts to press science into the curriculum of preparatory schools would fail because of the dominance of classics and mathematics in public schools and their ability to specify well-defined standards of attainment for the common entrance examination.[11] No such agreed standards were possible in the case of science. Moreover, science had no place in the examinations for the valuable Entrance and Junior Scholarships awarded by public schools. In classics and mathematics, the preparatory school masters knew with precision what was required, felt confident to provide it and saw clearly what rewards ensued. In contrast, few masters had any training in science where the requirements were in any case less clear and where excellence, if achieved, remained unrewarded in material terms. Not surprisingly there was a lack of enthusiasm for the alternative paper in Nature Study which was dropped from the common entrance examination in 1915.

There was ample evidence that few assumptions could be made about the previous education in science of boys entering public schools. The results of a survey of science teaching in schools represented by the APSSM showed that, in 1908, most of the elementary work deemed appropriate for preparatory schools was having to be undertaken in the junior forms of public schools.[12]

This position remained unchanged throughout the life of the APSSM, and beyond. Indeed, far from gaining ground, the Association had at times to fight hard to hold it. In 1910, a report of the Curriculum Committee of the Headmasters' Conference provoked an extraordinary meeting of the APSSM Committee when it appeared that the headmasters were recommending that the teaching of science in their schools should be postponed until pupils had reached the age of sixteen.[13] The offending passage in the report included a reference to Geography, which 'as interpreted in this syllabus includes as much science as it is desirable to teach at this stage'. L.I. Garbutt (Winchester), currently chairman of the APSSM, was re-assured by his headmaster, Dr Burge, chairman of the HMC Curriculum Committee, that the passage was intended to refer to the preparatory school stage only. This was less than convincing to other members who, after a prolonged discussion, appointed a sub-committee which was instructed to seek a meeting with the HMC Curriculum Committee. On 3 March 1910, the headmasters of Eton, Winchester, Merchant Taylors', Marlborough and Tonbridge met de Havilland (Eton), Siddons (Harrow), Hedley (Cheltenham), Seargent (Tonbridge) and Berridge (Malvern). Amongst other matters, consideration was given to an amended recommendation that 'geography as interpreted in this syllabus, together with elementary notions of Nature Study and practical measurement . . . includes as much science as it is desirable to teach at a Preparatory School'. The outcome, as recorded in the minutes of the APSSM committee, was that 'the Head Masters promised to adopt in their revised report all the proposals of the Association'.[15]

The following year, the Association decided to republish the 1905 report on Nature Study which had appeared in *The Preparatory School Review*,[15] but no progress was achieved towards changes in the common entrance and scholarship examinations. During the war years, when the Neglect of Science Campaign was under way, Latter took the opportunity to raise again the question of the teaching of science in preparatory schools and was asked to bring 'a plan of action' to the next meeting of the APSSM committee.[16] On that occasion he was able to report that some members of the Joint Standing Committee of the Headmasters' Conference and the Association of Preparatory School Headmasters supported the view that there should be a compulsory Nature Study paper in scholarship examinations and that boys taking the Common Entrance examination should be required to produce evidence of work done in Nature Study. Sympathy did not lead to action, however. In 1918, the Prime Minister's Committee, under the chairmanship of Sir J.J. Thomson, appointed to report on the position of natural science in the educational system of Great Britain, found that few of the 307 preparatory schools replying to its questionnaire made any provision for the teaching of science. The views of the Committee coincided with those of the APSSM in recommending strongly that 'the elements of Natural Science', defined as 'physiography and an elementary study of animal and plant life together with practical exercises' involving measurement, manipulation and calculation should be a necessary subject in the entrance examinations of public schools.[17] Following consideration of the Thomson Report, the APSSM Committee instructed its secretary to write a letter to *The Preparatory School Review* on the importance of science, whilst Latter, who had by now made the issue a personal crusade, offered to provide in-service courses for preparatory school masters during their Easter and summer vacations.[18]

Five years later, at the annual Conference of the Association of Preparatory Schools, Latter was again addressing an audience on the teaching of elementary science. On this occasion he was supported by William Stradling of the Dragon School, Oxford, who gave an impressive account of what he had been able to achieve in this field with preparatory school boys.[19] Nevertheless, the common examination for entrance to public schools still consisted of two Latin papers, three mathematical papers, two French, and one each in Scripture, Geography, History and English. Though Winchester still preferred to set its own examination, the majority of public schools had by now accepted the common examination. As for the candidates, they had grown in number from just over 1000 in 1914 to almost 5000 by 1924; such limited knowledge of science as they possessed, however, if displayed at all in their scripts, was available only under the guise of geography.[20]

Interest in the preparatory school curriculum continued unabated for some years after the widening of the Association's membership in 1919 and was not restricted merely to science. Early in the life of the SMA a sub-committee met representatives of the Council of the English Association to discuss the inability of boys 'to describe simple concrete objects adequately and to write a clear and complete account of a simple experiment'.[21] This resulted in a deputation to the Joint Standing Committee of the Headmasters' Conference and the Association of Preparatory School Headmasters, urging that English should be given greater prominence in scholarship and entrance examinations. Membership of the Science Masters' Association was extended in 1924 to include preparatory schoolmasters with appropriate qualifications, though few took advantage of the opportunity.

Perhaps the most remarkable development of this period was the decision by one of the Association's leading figures, Major V.S. Bryant (Chairman of the SMA Committee in 1918) to relinquish his post at Wellington College in order to start a preparatory school at St Piran's, Maidenhead. Much was hoped of this venture, described by Archer Vassall in his Presidential address to the SMA in January 1921 as 'one of the most pregnant experiments in preparatory-school education for many years past in this country'.[22] Such an outpost, sympathetic to science, would hopefully stimulate much-needed reforms in the preparatory school world. At the Annual Meeting in London in January 1920, Bryant gave an account of his views on science in the preparatory school curriculum. Acknowledging the importance of the previous efforts by the APSSM, and especially by Latter, with the emphasis on nature study, Bryant nevertheless identified and commended an alternative approach through mechanics, elementary engineering and practical mathematics. Examples of this had been provided by F.W. Sanderson, Headmaster of Oundle School, in an address at the Annual Conference of the Association of Preparatory Schools some years previously.[23] Although no more than two or three periods per week could be devoted to science, much could be done outside the classroom: for Bryant, 'the biological side of Nature Study' ought to be relegated to 'the leisure side of school life', though not as an alternative to games. The teacher of English and of Geography had a contribution to make also, the former through an appreciation of the beauty and poetry of Nature, the latter through a more scientific treatment of certain topics.[24]

Unhappily this bold and ambitious venture never fulfilled the hopes associated with it. The innovative curriculum of St Piran's understandably commended itself to H.G. Wells whose son, Anthony West, was sent there in 1921 as a young boy of seven. As West later recorded, it soon became clear that Bryant 'was no longer in full control of himself or his school' and his régime came to a sudden end some few years later.[25]

Concern over preparatory school science had a diminishing priority on the curriculum agendas of the SMA until interest rekindled at the time of the Nuffield projects. When in 1959 the aims of preparatory school education were reconsidered by the Council of the Incorporated Association of Preparatory Schools, it was reported that 'overwhelming support' existed for the teaching of 'some science, formal or informal', additional to 'the usual Nature Study'.[26] However, the practical obstacles, not least the availability of competent staff, remained formidable. Membership of the SMA was commended, but the main initiatives to support science work in preparatory schools, though involving SMA members, tended to come from outside the Association. Thus, J.L. Lewis, senior science master at Malvern College, was adviser to the Esso Junior Loan Service of Scientific Apparatus, introduced in the autumn of 1959.[27] Contributors to the IAPS Science Refresher Conference at Oxford in 1961 included Sir Graham Savage and W.H. Dowdeswell, as well as Lewis.[28] With support from the Nuffield Foundation, Lewis and his science colleagues at Malvern developed an abbreviated version of the introductory two-year programme of the Nuffield O level schemes, suitable for use in preparatory schools and this was the basis for a recommended course approved by a science panel appointed by the Joint Working Party of the Headmasters' Conference and the Incorporated Association of Preparatory Schools on the Common Entrance Examination.[29] A revised version was later printed and distributed by the ASE.[30]

The major achievement, however, was a return to the position prior to 1915 when science was included in the Common Entrance examination. Initially accepted as an optional paper, it became 'compulsory supporting' in June 1971, with a view to becoming 'compulsory qualifying', though not before 1975. This latter restrictive clause was an unnecessary safeguard. Past history, if nothing else, suggested that a move from curriculum marginality to mainstream would not be achieved speedily. By the opening of the 1980s, science still remained in its supporting role as far as marks in the Common Entrance examination were concerned.

Adjusting the goals: the university interface

Unfavourable comparison with state-aided secondary schools was frequently used as a stimulus to the growth of science teaching in independent schools in the early years of the twentieth century. The availability of 'whisky money' under the administrations of Technical Instruction Committees in the 1890s had enabled many maintained secondary schools to develop their science work to an extent which eventually provoked concerns about their neglect of literary studies.[31] By the turn of the century there was general agreement with the judgement of Gilbert Bourne, science tutor at New College, Oxford, that the second grade schools were leading the way in science teaching.[32]

For Bourne, given the strong connection between public schools and the universities (by which he meant Oxford and Cambridge), it was essential for the latter to change their requirements so that science assumed a place of greater importance in their entrance and scholarship examinations. Once taken, this step would oblige public schools to follow.

Certainly, the unsatisfactory nature of scholarship examinations set by the Oxford and Cambridge colleges was a matter to which the APSSM immediately directed its attention.[33] So far as the science work was concerned, the requirements at Oxford were very different from those at Cambridge, the choice of subjects being more limited and the standard uncertain. Although college tutors at Oxford were informed by candidates of the ground they had covered at school, the papers set did not always reflect this knowledge. Often boys were given an honours paper and told to do what they could of it. The educational consequences included a tendency to 'cramming' and 'tip' giving. No account was taken of laboratory work done at school, the scholarship being awarded on the results of a written examination only.

As for the Cambridge colleges, they offered a wider choice of science subjects in which a boy might specialize. Whilst the standard of their tests was more predictable than at Oxford, the lack of common ground in the syllabuses for the scholarship examinations at the two universities made life very difficult for science masters responsible for preparing candidates. The weight given by both universities to performance in the special science papers was a strong encouragement to premature specialization.

As for the test of general education in the scholarship examinations, it was usually based on classical and modern languages, and mathematics, together with an English essay or general paper. In the early years of the APSSM the inclusion of science in this component of the scholarship examination was seen by many members as an important objective. Not only would it make science an essential ingredient of general education, but it would ensure that every boy in a public school would study science for some four or five years, up to the time when he decided on his field of specialization. The possibility of specializing in science would thus be opened up to the ablest boys, in contrast to the prevailing situation in which, outside the Army Class, it was only 'the intellectual refuse'[34] from classics who were allowed to devote their energies to science. The contrast between the conceptions of a liberal education embodied in the university and the Army entrance examinations was marked, science being a compulsory subject in the latter. Comparing these, it was Bourne's opinion that 'superiority seems to lie with the Army'.[35]

Papers on the deficiencies of scholarship examinations were read at both the first and second conferences of the public school science masters, Falkner (Weymouth) in 1901 stressing the need for dialogue with the college examiners; with Hill (Eton), the following year, urging the inclusion of science as a general requirement, as well as the need for a more uniform standard in the special papers. From the comments of those university science tutors present in 1902 it was clear that the unsatisfactory nature of the present system was conceded and a small committee was established to negotiate on behalf of the APSSM with the university examiners.

This sub-committee, the first in the life of the APSSM and consisting of Baker (Dulwich), Hill (Eton), Shenstone (Clifton) and Slater (Charterhouse),[36] was one of impressive intellectual strength. Shenstone was already a Fellow of the Royal Society and Baker was soon to be elected, following his appointment as Lee's Reader in Chemistry at Oxford. Their initial step was to clarify the views of members of the Association on desired changes both in the scholarship examinations and in the Previous Examination (Cambridge) and Responsions (Oxford). Proposals based on the answers to a questionnaire sent to all members were considered by the main committee of the APSSM in November 1902, amended and then supplemented by the views of science masters in some major public schools, such as St Paul's, not yet represented in the Association. At the Annual Meeting in January 1903 a revised version of the sub-committee's report was approved, the objectives being the inclusion in the university scholarship examinations of, first, a paper in elementary physics and chemistry for all candidates, and second, papers and practical work in not more than four subjects (physics, chemistry, botany and zoology, and geology), a candidate to offer not more than two of these.[37]

A meeting with Cambridge science tutors, the Vice-Chancellor presiding, followed on Saturday 7 February. On the university side, academic territoriality increased the range of science subjects to six (physics, chemistry, geology, natural history of plants, zoology, and elements of botany and zoology). It was accepted that a candidate should not offer more than two, and no candidate could offer the elements of botany and zoology if he took either of the other biological subjects. The proposal for an elementary examination in physics and chemistry to be taken by all candidates was not well received; whilst deemed appropriate for those specializing in geology and biological subjects, an elementary paper in mathematics had higher priority for those offering physics and chemistry.[38]

A similar meeting was held at Oxford the following weekend, when the proposals agreed at the Cambridge meeting were presented by Baker for consideration. Apart from disagreement amongst the university science tutors as to whether botany and zoology should form one subject or two, there was general concurrence.[39] Important gains had been achieved by the APSSM on the issue of uniformity of requirements in the science scholarship examinations, but the desired goal of science as a compulsory subject for all scholarship candidates, irrespective of field of specialization, was as remote as ever. Perhaps of greater significance than specific changes in regulations was the recognition accorded the APSSM as a respected source of opinion and influence, and the establishment of lines of communication with science tutors at Oxford and Cambridge. It was also clear that a fundamental curriculum problem had been identified. For the public schoolmasters the most effective strategy in their attempt to incorporate science in general education was to reduce differentiation of knowledge as much as possible; the fewer the school subjects into which scientific knowledge could be organized, the more manageable their task. For the university science tutors, specialization encouraged differentiation with an attendant concern for the inclusion of their subject in entrance examinations. Nowhere was this tendency more pronounced than in the biological sciences. Until 1884 a single section D within the British Association for the Advancement of Science embraced zoology, botany, anthropology, anatomy and physiology. By 1895 independent sections for zoology (D), anthropology (H), physiology (I) and botany (K), had been established.

Of course, the APSSM was not alone in its endeavours to improve the university entrance examinations. The Royal Society's letter, urging universities to encourage the study of science in schools,[40] had contributed to a proposed revision of the Previous Examination at Cambridge. In their report, the Syndicate had recommended the inclusion of two papers, one on experimental mechanics and elementary physics, the other on elementary inorganic chemistry, as options within a revised scheme of examination.[41] They had also proposed that Greek should no longer be an obligatory subject and it was largely on this issue that the proposal foundered, the Headmasters' Conference insisting on the retention of compulsory Greek, and the University Senate, in an unusually heavy poll, voting decisively against change.[42]

Interestingly, the drudgery of grinding through compulsory Greek became so widely recognized that opinion swung away from the desirability of compulsory science. Following a paper by Talbot (Harrow) on 'The Tyranny of Greek' at the annual meeting of the APSSM in January 1903, Sir Arthur Rücker had warned members against making the same mistake as their classical colleagues by attempting to force science on all students.[43] When, in 1916, the Oxford Hebdomadal Council recommended that a knowledge of science should become a necessary preliminary to an Oxford degree, there was vigorous opposition from the APSSM. Major V.S. Bryant, representing the APSSM Committee, met members of the Hebdomadal Council in January 1917, urging that it was not in the true interests of science teaching in schools that science masters should be required to spend their time 'forcing unwelcome knowledge down unwilling throats'. Whilst the Council rejected the possibility of alternatives to a written examination, such as certification by science masters on inspection of science work, it was willing for the syllabus to be prepared in consultation with the APSSM and to be based on the Association's own proposals for school science up to the age of sixteen.[44]

At Cambridge, the problem was different. A proposed revision in the Previous Examination on the lines of the newly-established School Certificate had placed science together with mathematics in one of three Groups of subjects, a pass in each Group being essential for certification. As V.S. Bryant and O.H. Latter, representing the APSSM Committee, pointed out in an interview with the Syndicate in November, 1917, able boys could pass in the science–mathematics Group by studying mathematics alone. Hence, science masters would be faced with classes of 'duller boys' sent to them in order to 'cram' sufficient science for a bare pass in the Group. Their subject would be used as a prop for those weak in mathematics. As the Syndicate's scheme was in accordance with the newly-agreed structure for the School Certificate examination, the APSSM proposal that science should become a separate Group met with no response other than that it should be directed elsewhere, namely the Secondary School Examinations Council, the advisory body set up by the Board of Education to coordinate and supervise the new examination arrangement. A more hospitable reception was accorded to recommendations from the APSSM about the nature of the science papers which might be offered.[45]

In terms of influence on large structural reforms in university entrance requirements, the APSSM was inevitably eclipsed by more general and senior bodies such as the Headmasters' Conference, the Incorporated Association of Head Masters, the Royal Society and, ultimately in the general rationalization of the uncoordinated examination provisions that prevailed in the early twentieth century, the Board of Education.

Within the agreed examination structures, however, there were important decisions to be taken about the selection and organization of scientific knowledge and the means of assessing its attainment by students. It was in this domain that the APSSM was most successful in imposing its views. Its sub-committee on Debatable Questions set in Public Examinations, established in 1908,[46] was in frequent communication with examiners to ensure the reasonableness of their demands and the propriety of individual questions. Changes in the time allowed for practical examinations was achieved after protest to the Oxford and Cambridge Joint Board.[47] The separation of mechanics and hydrostatics from the rest of physics in the Oxford and Cambridge Higher Certificate Examination was criticized on the grounds that it was difficult for a boy to take both papers and hence his view of physics was partial.[48] Changes in the regulations were promised, though their implementation was overtaken by the structural changes accompanying the establishment of the new School Certificate. A meeting with representatives of the Joint Board in December 1914 led to further changes in the general character of the science papers set. The following year the Joint Board was scolded for including 'an impossible question' in the Practical Chemistry Paper of the Higher Certificate Examination and an apologetic letter was received, with a promise to do better in future.[49] It was a mark of the standing achieved by the APSSM that it was invited by F.B. Stead HMI in 1915 for discussions at the Board of Education on the proposed new leaving certificate. Having overcome some initial caution about this involvement, the Association gave its views on the position and conduct of science examinations.[50]

Change in the examination context was one important influence which obliged the APSSM to crystallize a view on the nature of the school science curriculum. Before considering this in detail, however, there is a further strand of activity to explore, that connected with the education of public school boys destined for the Army.

Science Education for Officers

If, as O.H. Latter contended in his review of science teaching in public schools, external examinations conducted by the universities were the most potent long-term determinant of the position of science in the curriculum, the Army entrance examinations had been unquestionably the outstanding short-term influence. The number of boys learning science in the Army classes of public schools had increased greatly in the 1890s; as a result, additional science staff had been recruited, new laboratories had been built and improved scientific equipment purchased. 'There is no doubt', Latter concluded, 'that the action of the War Office has had a most beneficial effect on the teaching of science throughout Public Schools.'[51]

This association of the Army with science education was longstanding. When Henry Cole had needed inspectors for the supervision of the complex programme of examinations arranged by the Science and Art Department, the Corps of Royal Engineers was his main source. By 1880, some fifty officers of the R.E. were engaged in the inspection of science schools and a similar number in the supervision of examinations. As Cole acknowledged, 'You could hardly find a numerous corps of scientific inspectors at present, except in the Royal Engineers.'[52]

Engineering officers, along with artillery officers, were educated at the Royal Military Academy, Woolwich, whilst infantry and cavalry men went to the Royal Military College, Sandhurst. As for theories about the education of officers, there were three which had exercised opinion in Victorian times. The first, uncompromisingly, discounted the influence of formal education: officers were not made, but born; aristocratic lineage and natural ability were the significant factors. The second, exemplified *par excellence* by naval tradition and commended by the Admiralty well into the twentieth century, was that officers were best moulded by vigorous training, both physical and intellectual, from early youth. The third, which became the favoured view in the Army, was that officers should be recruited from the liberally-educated sector of society and then trained for service by practical instruction in specialized professional institutions.[53] With the extension of the principle of competitive examinations to the selection of entrants to Sandhurst and Woolwich, it became possible to put this third theory into effect.

Reference has been made earlier to the establishment by public schools of Military and Civil Departments where boys were prepared to sit the entrance examinations for the R.M.A. Woolwich, R.M.C. Sandhurst, the Royal Indian Engineering College at Cooper's Hill, the Indian Forest Service and similar organizations. In many instances these departments were of considerable size and vital to the economy of the school.[54] The existence of such provisions enabled the foundation curriculum of the military colleges to be transferred to the schools and the age of entry to the college to be raised. Through their specific examination requirements a degree of control was exerted by the military colleges over what the schools taught. From the school side there was pressure for the subjects of examination to approximate closely to those which constituted a general education. In this way, those who prepared for entry to Woolwich and Sandhurst, but failed would not suffer a disadvantage through over-specialization when attempting to enter alternative professions. This tension between the special requirements of professional training and the general requirements for a liberal education was particularly marked in the teaching of science and mathematics.

The army entrance examination in non-military subjects had been revised in 1894 by a departmental committee chaired by Lord Sandhurst, Parliamentary Under-Secretary of State for War, and including Sir Henry Roscoe FRS as spokesman for science. Amongst witnesses who gave evidence before the committee were public school masters who taught the Army classes, and notably W.A. Shenstone (Clifton College), a future secretary of the APSSM.[55]

The recommendations of the Sandhurst Committee made inorganic chemistry and heat obligatory subjects for examination of candidates for Woolwich, the intention being to permit the R.M.A. lecturers to dispense with the teaching of these subjects and concentrate their efforts on electricity, deemed a more difficult science because of its greater mathematical requirements.[56] Elementary electricity, magnetism and light together constituted an optional subject in the entrance examination, as did geography and geology, and biology. Not all the Sandhurst Committee's recommendations were adopted but, without question, the selection of inorganic chemistry and heat for special attention, as well as the requirement that the examination would be 'partly practical', had a major influence on the content and conduct of science teaching in public schools in the 1890s. As the syllabus for the R.M.A. entrance examinations in natural science subjects explained, 'the standard of examination . . . will be such as may be reasonably expected from the education given at schools possessing appliances for practical instruction, such as a laboratory'.[57]

Even so, those preparing candidates for the examination clearly found some difficulty in interpreting the syllabus. At the second meeting of public school science masters in January 1902, C.I. Gardiner (Cheltenham College) elaborated on this theme in his paper on 'Science in the Army Examinations'. The present syllabus was 'as vague as it possibly can be'; the amount of inorganic chemistry, both metallic and non-metallic, disposed teachers to neglect large sections of work. A candidate's understanding of heat was tested by, at most, a few questions tacked on to the end of the chemistry paper. 'Is a boy to go through a proper course of Elementary Heat on the chance of one question on thermometers?', Gardiner asked. The practical examination was limited to chemistry, and, within that subject, to qualitative analysis. As for the conduct of the practical examination, invigilators had been known to forbid candidates to make notes of their observations as they carried out their testing of an unknown substance, a complete account to be written only at the end of the analysis.[58]

In an effort to achieve improvements, Gardiner proposed a number of resolutions which were carried and subsequently transmitted to the Civil Service Commissioners responsible for the army entrance examinations. First, it was urged that the marks for the written and practical parts of the examination should be published separately, as long as that distinction was maintained. Secondly, the examination was regarded as laying insufficient stress on the practical side of science education, where quantitative operations, especially volumetric analysis, should be included. Thirdly, more physics should be introduced to provide a better balanced account of the subject, though more important than a knowledge of the facts of natural science were the habits of mind and ways of looking at problems engendered by a course of practical instruction in chemistry and physics. 'This practical habit of mind, this practical attacking of problems, this reliance on oneself, this release from the cramping effects of formulae and books, can be produced in a natural science laboratory, and in no other room in our schools', Gardiner maintained.[59] The importance of these qualities for an Army officer was self-evident.

Even as the public school masters debated the weaknesses of the Army entrance examination, others were engaged in the same task. Following the humiliating defeats in the South African (Boer) War, the Akers-Douglas Committee had been appointed in April 1901 to consider the education of Army officers. Again, a representative of science, Sir Michael Foster, FRS, was a member of the committee, his inclusion eliciting expressions of satisfaction from the scientific journal *Nature*, with a reminder to its readers that the emphasis on science in the present scheme owed much to the previous exertions of Sir Henry Roscoe. As that scheme had not taken practical effect until the late 1890s, it was clear to *Nature* that present defects in the education of officers, as revealed in the recent war, were due to recruitment under older regulations.[60]

Unfortunately this argument failed to safeguard the position of science in the scheme of examination. Despite the presence of Foster on the committee, and the evidence of witnesses like Shenstone, who argued strenuously against any reduction in the importance of science, the Akers-Douglas Committee made 'Experimental Science' an alternative to Latin in their proposals for a preliminary qualifying examination. Their point of departure was agreement on five school subjects as the basis of a sound general education: English, Mathematics, a Modern Language, Latin, and Science. But, bearing in mind many complaints from schools that a large number of examination subjects prevented a sound training of the mind, they took the view that to make all five compulsory would be to overburden a candidate. Of four required examination subjects, candidates had to include English, Mathematics and a Modern Language. The choice left was, therefore, between Latin and Science.[61]

This apparently regressive and, in the words of *Nature*, 'so astonishing' proposal, seemed designed to make science a negligible quantity in the education of most officers. Given a known performance in Latin at age fourteen, few boys would abandon that subject to embark instead on the study of an unknown science. The gains which science had achieved in the public school curriculum, notably through the efforts of Roscoe and others, were now seriously threatened. 'Who amongst our leaders in science will come forward in this fresh emergency?' *Nature* implored.[62]

Within the APSSM the announcement of the scheme of examination provoked a deputation to the newly-established Advisory Board on Military Education which, from April 1903, had been responsible for the education of Army officers. The attitude of the science masters towards the new proposals was one of ambivalence, however. Though the new arrangements clearly posed some threat to their subject, there were potential benefits also. The congruence between the subjects in the Army entrance examination and those required for the school leaving certificates of examinations boards and for the London University Matriculation meant that it would no longer be necessary to separate army boys from the rest at the age of fourteen in public schools. The general move away from a multiplicity of examinations and early specialization was one which they could only welcome. Provided their subject survived the change, it would become more integrated into the main stream of the public school curriculum and subjected to less conflicting and severe external pressures.

Minor adjustments to the proposed examination and, perhaps, more importantly, recognition that the educational case for science teaching was becoming more generally accepted by public school headmasters, brought reassurances to members of the APSSM. Thus, at the fifth annual conference in January 1905, in his Presidential Address, Dr James Gow, headmaster of Westminster School where the meeting was held, advocated the teaching of science to *all* boys.[63] When, the following year, the Association again met in Westminster School, the discussion which followed a paper by J. Talbot (Harrow) on the present state of the Army Entrance Examination focused largely on the unsatisfactory conduct of the practical examinations. In curriculum matters of this sort, the APSSM had very effective lines of communication for making known its views. One of the Civil Service Commissioners responsible for setting the examinations was a member of the Association[64] and through Sir Michael Foster, there was direct access to Mr R.B. Haldane, Secretary of State for War. Possibly encouraged by helpful replies from Haldane's private secretary to matters raised by the APSSM in connection with the Army examination, Haldane's name was first choice out of three considered for President of the Association when this matter was discussed in 1907.[65]

The assimiliation of the Army qualifying examination to the examination for leaving certificates of Examination Boards was a major contextual change which greatly assisted the development of science in public schools at this stage. Here 'science' in the leaving certificate was defined as 'such combination of experimental or natural sciences as the Advisory Board (on Military Education) may approve'. The focus of concern of the APSSM was directed therefore to the science syllabuses in leaving certificates, to ensure they would exempt candidates from the Army qualifying examinations. At the third annual conference in January 1903, Dr T.J. Baker (King Edward's School, Birmingham) delivered a paper on the London Matriculation Examination, criticizing the separation of chemistry from physics in the scheme of examination, and the division of physics into two independent papers, each counting as one subject, in heat, light and sound, and electricity and magnetism. This was regarded as encouraging early specialization to an undesirable extent.[66] A review of the experiences of members teaching science subjects in the Senior Certificate Examination of the Oxford and Cambridge Schools Examination Board was carried out by Hill, Gardiner and Shenstone in 1904 on behalf of the General Committee of the APSSM. Subsequently this sub-committee was empowered to negotiate with the Board to secure changes helpful to the schools.[67] Thus, they wished the syllabus in Experimental Science in the Army qualifying examination to be regarded as an acceptable alternative to the combined subject, Chemistry and Physics, in the Oxford and Cambridge Board's regulations. Imperceptibly, consideration was moving from the specifics of science education for officers to the general issue of science education for gentlemen.

It was in this context that the General Committee agreed to include in the programme for the 1907 annual meeting a paper on 'The internal economy of school science' from R.E. Thwaites of Wyggeston School, Leicester.[68] Thwaites had previously read a paper on the possibility of combining mathematics and science teaching in public schools,[69] but his concern now was solely with 'the conditions of science work', drawing on information about staffing, laboratories, equipment, technical assistance, curriculum arrangements and finance from a survey of thirty-six schools. Similar information was later obtained from the same number of maintained secondary schools, and comparative data provided Thwaites with material for a further paper to the Education Section of the British Association at Leicester later that year.[70] On the basis of his sample, it appeared that the provisions in the two types of school were remarkably similar, apart from a marked inferiority on the part of the day schools in the matter of annual expenditure per boy on science equipment and materials. The following year the General Committee of the APSSM adopted Thwaites' suggestion that a more extensive survey of the science work in public schools should be undertaken; this was subsequently published by the Board of Education, in a pamphlet, edited by O.H. Latter.[71] This review confirmed the 'very satisfactory and encouraging' position with regard to finance and material resources for science teaching in public schools. It was apparent that a number of schools were now operating without any formal division into classical and modern sides, or other differentiation into Army, engineering or special science classes. In such schools 'it was possible to employ science as a medium of general education more easily and efficiently than when utilitarian demands and semi-technical training of a special Modern Side' made themselves felt.[72]

Having stimulated the growth of science in public schools and especially the building of laboratories and provision of curriculum resources, the influence of the Army examinations had now become muted; correspondence with the curriculum of general education encouraged the development of science courses which served this end, rather than the pre-professional needs of Woolwich. In Latter's words, a scientific net was now being stretched wide across the middle of the great majority of public schools.[73]

By 1912 the Army qualifying examination had been abolished, as serving no further useful purpose. In the new scheme for competitive entry to the R.M.A. Woolwich, science (interpreted as physics and chemistry) became one of six obligatory subjects, each carrying the same allocation of marks. The APSSM's interest now centred on the balanced coverage of content in the new examination and especially on the conduct of practical examinations. Disillusioning experience over a number of years eventually led the APSSM to press for the abandonment of practical tests in the chemistry and physics examinations; in the opinion of most members it was sufficient that 'the questions in the papers should be framed so as to penalize severely boys who had not had satisfactory laboratory training'.[74]

The outbreak of war in 1914 and the commissioning of young men direct from public schools brought other influences to bear on the school science curriculum. At the annual meeting in January 1916 the teaching of military subjects to boys in the upper forms of public schools was strongly urged by the Honorary Secretary of the Association, C.L. Bryant (Harrow).[75] The War Office supported the idea and technical information on explosives, field telephones, signalling devices, range finders and the combating of poisonous gases was provided by a member of the APSSM on the staff of the R.M.A., Woolwich. Much of this was incorporated into an outline syllabus, including experimental work and information about teaching resources, which Bryant published,[76] and the exhibitions of members' apparatus at the Association's annual meetings in 1917 and 1918 included extensive sections on 'Military Science'.[77] The great importance of instruction in these matters was stressed by members who had served in France where, it was stated, 'countless lives had been needlessly lost through lack of information which should be in the possession of every officer'.[78] This adaptation of science curricula to the changed values of wartime, with its stress on useful knowledge, was of finite extent and duration, however. Concurrently there were developments of more lasting significance associated with a clearer role for science in the general curriculum of secondary schools as these had developed in the early years of the century.

Science education for gentlemen

En route to its goal of science for all boys in public schools, the APSSM fought numerous campaigns to secure its curriculum territory from threat and to increase its influence over the definition of school science. One such episode involved the General Medical Council whose recent refusal to recognize public schools as institutions where preliminary science subjects might be taught was brought to the notice of the APSSM's General Committee by C.I. Gardiner in 1902.[79] Little was done at that stage, but opposition to the GMC's attitude grew and five years later a sub-committee was appointed to enquire into the matter. For some schools the GMC's decision was having adverse financial and education consequences; boys were being withdrawn from public schools at sixteen to go to recognized institutions, such as the London Polytechnics, where their science studies would earn for them exemption from more expensive courses in medical schools. As a result public schools were losing not only fee income, but also some of their more promising science students. Consultation with the Deans of London medical schools brought a partial solution when it was revealed that some important medical schools, including Oxford, Cambridge and London, refused to recognize the GMC's registration procedures. A continued struggle for public school recognition by the GMC would be of benefit therefore only to those boys going to a provincial university and for a while it looked as if the matter could be laid to rest.[80] However, two years later the APSSM had returned to the campaign with a memorial to the GMC which led to general recognition for public schools as 'approved institutions in which medical studies may be commenced'.[81] Approval entailed inspection, not least in relation to the provisions for the teaching of biology; given the pre-eminence of physics and chemistry in the public school science curriculum, the medical connection was an important counter-balance which safe-guarded biological resources, at least in the upper forms of the school.

Returning, however, to Latter's 'scientific net' across the middle part of the schools, there was an increasing inclination in the APSSM to a more general approach than that provided by the formal study of physics and chemistry. At the annual meeting in 1906, the Rev. Walter Madeley, Headmaster of Woodbridge School, and a classics graduate, delivered a paper on the possibility of introducing a comprehensive science syllabus into the classical curriculum.[82] In essence, his contention was that the classical boys needed scientific knowledge as a cultural resource; a single branch of science thoroughly studied would not yield sufficient 'gentlemanly information concerning natural phenomena'. A broad course was needed. Others took a different view: G.H. Martin (Bradford Grammar School), in an effort to overcome marked resistance to science on the classical side, had experimented with the teaching of geology, a subject which had transformed the attitudes of his students.[83]

At the tenth annual conference, an elder statesman of the APSSM, Linnaeus Cumming, who had been teaching, first at Cheltenham then at Rugby, since the 1860s, made a special plea for the study of geology and biology by the classical boys. Reaction was mixed, some acknowledging that, as many boys had future responsibilities as landowners, it was the duty of the school to teach these subjects; others saw a threat to established physics and chemistry, and disputed the ability to provide suitable practical work in geology.[84] Two years later M.D. Hill (Eton) questioned the axiom that, for its proper study, biology depended on a prior foundation of chemistry and physics, a suggestion which was categorized by the APSSM President, Sir J.J. Thomson, as 'revolutionary'; 'a man could not be a physiological chemist unless he knew chemistry', Thomson asserted, 'although biology and physical subjects should not be kept in separate compartments'. They should be brought closer together, like mathematics and physics.[85] At the same meeting, E.I. Lewis (Oundle) made the case for plant biology as an essential ingredient of liberal education, again linking his argument to the future responsibilities of many public school boys as landowners, estate managers, and farmers. Experimental work could be extended to practical gardening. In the discussion which followed, Lewis' headmaster, F.W. Sanderson, warned that 'biological boys' were 'most extraordinary creatures' who dug up and manured land intended for tennis courts; were never available for cricket and football, being on their allotments with their spades instead; and who were liable to be missing from their dormitories in the middle of the night because they were undertaking studies of plants in the absence of light.[86] Multiple and diverse evaluations of these experiments in 'middle school' science left members without any clear guidance, merely a persistent impression that something needed to be done.

This sense of deficiency led G.W. Hedley (Cheltenham College) in 1910 to propose that the Association should set up a sub-committee to consider the feasibility of drawing up a syllabus suitable for public schools.[87] This was done, but, after deliberation, the sub-committee could only report that 'the time was not yet ripe for such a syllabus to be published'. The varied contexts and purposes of science teaching made a general curriculum solution unattainable at that stage. In 1913, under Hedley's chairmanship, the General Committee returned to the problem.[88] On this occasion the instigator was Dr E.H. Tripp, one of the Association's few German trained chemists, with experience of teaching in a maintained grammar school and a technical college before being appointed to Bedford Modern School. In Tripp's view the limited survey of science teaching undertaken by Latter in the summer of 1908 needed up-dating and supplementing by a more thorough-going review of present-day conditions. At the annual meeting in January 1914 Tripp read a long paper, warning against complacency and offering evidence that much still remained to be done. Of 108 headmasters of schools represented on the Association only six were science graduates; science teaching was still under-staffed and the Cinderella of the curriculum. As science masters themselves had little power to effect change, they should more actively cultivate the support of learned scientific societies and bodies such as the British Science Guild.[89] In many ways Tripp was preaching to the converted; the discussion which followed was inconclusive though Tripp was not alone in becoming a member of both the British Association and the British Science Guild at this time.

More than any other single factor the tragic events of the war gave point to the argument that science was still far from being a central component in the education of those who might become civil and military leaders. A much cited administrative blunder was the continued export of lard to Germany, unprevented, according to a nescient member of the Government, because it had only recently been discovered that glycerine (used in the manufacture of explosives) could be obtained from lard.[90] As Arthur Smithells, a professor of chemistry in charge of the organization of anti-gas training lamented, it was 'nothing less than appalling to a man of science to watch the sacrifice of life . . . all the time knowing that as little knowledge of science as corresponds to knowing what an adverb is in grammar . . . would have saved all this'.[91] When, in October 1915, Tripp again brought before the APSSM General Committee the question of improving the status of science teaching in public schools, it was agreed to open a press campaign on the subject, M.D. Hill (Eton), F.M. Oldham (Dulwich) and Tripp to act as a sub-committee with this objective.[92]

Their first step was to draft a letter which was sent to a number of leading scientists asking for their signatures in support. A problem which arose here was that of getting a wording 'to suit all tastes', the original being pronounced by some as 'not crisp enough'. One of those approached, Hill's old mentor, Sir Ray Lankester, and a former President of the APSSM, produced an alternative draft. When this situation was reported to the APSSM General Committee, it was agreed that 'if a minimum of three "big wigs" would sign' a revised letter, Hill was to proceed with publication in any way thought best. Failing this, the Association would act on its own.[93]

In the event, after consultations between the APSSM members, Lankester and Professor H.H. Turner, their President-elect, it was agreed that a new letter should be prepared. This was published in *The Times* on 2 February 1916 under the heading 'The Neglect of Science' and over the signatures of thirty-six eminent men of science and industry. No member of the APSSM was a signatory, though Hill served for a time as a member of a Neglect of Science Committee established to superintend the campaign for reform. As the APSSM General Committee acknowledged in May 1916, matters had passed out of the hands of its sub-committee; the initiative now lay with those distinguished men of science who were interesting themselves in curriculum and examination change.[94]

The Neglect of Science letter was published again, in *The Times Educational Supplement* on 7 March 1916, accompanied by letters from scientists, headmasters and others. Its concern was unashamedly the education of a civic and military élite. Once the education of those from whose ranks the higher and lower grades of public service were filled was established on the right lines, it was assumed that 'the education of the democracy . . . would follow the change in the direction of the wealthier classes'.[95] Despite the fact that the large public schools had spent considerable sums of money on laboratories and scientific equipment in recent years, action was needed because old vested curriculum interests retained their dominance.

The objectives of the Neglect of Science Committee were embodied in a series of resolutions passed at a conference held in the Linnaean Society's rooms on 3 May 1916. First, natural sciences should be made an integral part of the curriculum in all the great schools of the country and should form part of the entrance examinations of the Universities of Oxford and Cambridge, as well as of the newer universities. This was essential for national efficiency. Secondly, natural sciences should be assigned 'capital importance' by the government in the competitive examinations for the Home and Indian Civil Service. Thirdly, some knowledge of the natural sciences should be required from all candidates for admission to Sandhurst, probably the only military institution in Europe where science was not included in the curriculum.[96]

Before examining further the involvement of the public school science masters in the Neglect of Science Campaign, it is necessary to allude to contemporaneous developments involving their Association. 1916 was a seminal year for science education and a number of initiatives, additional to the Neglect of Science Campaign, were launched or began to bear fruit. Important amongst these was the Board of Education's proposal to rationalize the complex system of external school examinations by the introduction of the School Certificate Examination. Although Circular 849, in which the proposals were embodied, was issued in 1914, it was not until two years later that the General Committee of the APSSM accepted the invitation of F.B. Stead, HM Staff Inspector of Secondary Schools, to express their views on the examination of science in the new arrangements.[97] The report of a discussion in the General Committee on 22 May 1916 is particularly illuminating in relation to the distinction which was being drawn between 'general science' and 'formal science', and is quoted at length.[98]

> It is becoming recognized more generally that science must form part of a more liberal education and whereas in the past most of the boys who took up this subject intended to continue their studies in it, now the majority of them will drop the subject on, or before, leaving school. In many Public schools some study of science is compulsory for boys.
>
> In some schools this change of conditions has led to a change in practice; instead of teaching just those elements of science which will be most useful for future study, an attempt is made, by self-contained courses, to awaken interest in and an appreciation of the possibilities of natural science; and only the specialists who separate out from the bigger groups are required to go through the grammar of science.
>
> It was thought unanimously that the 16-year-old examination in science should be framed in such a way as not to penalize those who had been taught along the lines indicated. But there was not the same unanimity as to the means to reach this end – one of the difficulties is the variety and range of subjects taught in this way in the Public schools. It was recognized that if papers were set in this more general science there must be either a big choice of subjects or else a good choice of questions in the general papers.
>
> There was much divergence of opinion as to whether candidates

who offered science should be made to choose between papers in what may be called formal science (i.e. heat, chemistry, etc.) and those in general science, or whether they should be required to take both classes of papers. Some considered that general science (and that only) should be compulsory for candidates in science, 'in order to avoid examining and early specializing'. Some had a strong preference for formal science, 'since general science is uneducational and is a poor examination subject'. Most would approve of an option between general and formal science, 'for in that way no teacher would be restricted in his methods'. Many (including some of those in classes 1 and 2) would be willing, as a compromise, to have a combination of the two types of paper, some in general science and some in formal science.

At this point, then, the science masters had mixed views on the kind of science teaching most appropriate for examination at age sixteen. Imminent events were to encourage crystallization of a firmer position.

In August 1916, Prime Minister Asquith appointed a Committee 'to enquire into the position occupied by Natural Science in the Educational System of Great Britain'.[99] The chairman was Sir J.J. Thomson, PRS, a past-President of the APSSM and a leading scientist who had not signed the Neglect of Science memorandum in *The Times*. The opportunity to make known its views to this potentially influential body was not one the Association could afford to miss and on 7 October 1916 a statement of 'fact, principle and policy' on science education in public schools was approved to serve as a text for a deputation which appeared before the Thomson Committee on 12 December. Much of the earlier opinion on the examination of science at sixteen was reiterated in this document. Now that science was being taught increasingly to *all* boys, a 'perhaps unwise' emphasis on scientific method and 'a certain disregard' of general knowledge of natural phenomena in previous courses should be rectified by attempts to arouse appreciation of the value and scope of science. This might entail drawing upon a range of subjects including astronomy, biology, geology and physiology; alternatively, science might be approached through its applications in engineering and agriculture. Such work would often run alongside a reduced component of 'logical experimental courses in physics and chemistry'.[100]

A similar dualism, incorporating both formal and general components in non-specialist science courses, marked the conclusions of another group deliberating on secondary school science at this time. Within a month of the announcement of the Prime Minister's enquiry, the General Committee of the British Association, meeting at Newcastle-upon-Tyne, had initiated an investigation, under the chairmanship of Professor R.A. Gregory, into 'the method and substance of science teaching in secondary schools, with particular reference to its essential place in general education'.[101] Composed almost entirely of men and women science teachers, this committee was not seen as duplicating the work of the Thomson committee which had industrial and professional interests to consider as well as educational ones. Indeed, the Thomson Committee had been criticized for not including 'a single person of either sex who was a present-day teacher of science in secondary schools'.[102]

The British Association committee had as its secretary Dr E.H. Tripp, by this time one of the joint secretaries of Section L, Educational Science. Indeed the committee was to undertake the survey which he had earlier advocated, extending it to boys' maintained schools and girls' secondary schools. It also included three other APSSM men (D. Berridge, Malvern; G.F. Daniell, London University Day Training College; A. Vassall, Harrow) as well as two women from the Association of Science Teachers (Dr Lilian J. Clarke, James Allen's Girls' School, Dulwich; Miss C.L. Laurie, Cheltenham Ladies' College). At this period the overlapping of membership between the teachers' associations and the B.A. was considerable. Professor R.A. Gregory, a leading figure in Section L and editor of *Nature*, was elected a member of the APSSM in May 1916 and Professor H.H. Turner, the APSSM's President-elect, was General Secretary of the B.A. Not surprisingly, the report of the B.A. committee reflected APSSM views in its recommendation that 'every pupil should undergo a course of training in experimental scientific inquiry as a part of his general education' along with 'courses of descriptive lessons and reading broad enough to appeal to all minds and to give a general view of natural facts and principles not limited to the range of any laboratory course or detailed lecture instruction, and differing from them by being extensive instead of intensive'. Variety in provision and the opportunity for a school to construct its own syllabuses lay at the heart of the proposals, with a concomitant requirement for decentralized examination arrangements. Seven schemes of work, reflecting different contexts in which science teaching might take place, were included in the report as exemplars. Amongst these pride of place was accorded to an outline of 'Science for All in a Public School' by Archer Vassall (Harrow).[103]

Vassall's account was based on a report by a sub-committee of the APSSM the previous year. Immediately following the Neglect of Science meeting on 3 May 1916, *The Times* carried a letter written to prevent 'a false and one-sided impression being made on the public mind'. Over the signatures of distinguished men of letters (and some scientists – one of whom had previously signed the science memorandum!) it warned that discussion on the school curriculum in the special circumstances of wartime might ignore elements vital to the formation of national character. Specifically, it expounded the educational benefits of classics, and challenged the view that scientific method was a 'peculiar property of physical science', arrogating it for its own field, indeed for 'all branches of knowledge rightly understood'.[104] Over the next few months the academic forces of science and of humanistic studies were progressively marshalled in defence of their curriculum claims. A Council of Humanistic Studies was established to coordinate the British Academy's educational interests with those of the five 'humanistic' subject teaching associations (Classical, English, Geographical, Historical and Modern Language). On the science side, the Royal Society set up a Conjoint Board of Scientific Societies whose Watching Committee on Education eventually superseded the Neglect of Science Committee as the chief spokesman for the interests of science. Its membership included A. Vassall, F.W. Sanderson and Professor R.A. Gregory, with Sir Ray Lankester as convenor.[105]

In August 1916, following a joint meeting of the five 'humanistic' associations, the gauntlet was thrown down to the representatives of science with an invitation to define the aims of science teaching.[106] Towards the end of a long (seven hours) meeting of the APSSM General Committee on 7 October, 'every member who had survived to this late stage . . . attempted this without satisfying himself or anyone else'. Vassall, as chairman, undertook to consolidate their points into a statement which was later published over his name and that of the President of the APSSM, Professor H.H. Turner. It emphasized that science was complementary to 'humanistic' studies in the curriculum, meeting two needs in particular. First, it made a distinctive contribution to the search for truth based on evidence rather than on authority, the history of science being 'a plain record of the search for truth for its own sake'. Second, every educated man needed to be familiar with 'certain facts and ideas in the world of natural science' because of their utility: it was the business of science in education to bring this knowledge within the range of all.[107]

At the same committee meeting, Vassall brought to his colleagues a request from the Neglect of Science Committee for advice on the kind of science which they thought should be made general in public schools. A sub-committee of Vassall, W.D. Eggar (Eton) and F.M. Oldham (Dulwich) was appointed to supply the detail.[108] Their report, *Science For All*, was published, with the committee's *Report for 1916*, as a separate pamphlet, and also, in part, in the report of Gregory's British Association committee. In no sense intended to be prescriptive as a strict syllabus, it offered a set of principles to govern the design of broadly-based science courses which emphasized the human aspects of the subject; within these principles the teacher was free to construct courses according to his particular circumstances. The dual aims of 'training in scientific method by experimental inquiry' and 'conveying useful information' were central, and scientific knowledge was to be related wherever possible to its applications in daily-life phenomena, machines, and agricultural processes.[109]

The term 'General Science' to describe a subject of examination was by no means new when it became current in the APSSM and SMA discussions around 1918. There had been a paper on General Elementary Science in the London University Matriculation examination as far back as 1899. Although it consisted mainly of physics and chemistry, there were doubts that it would prove 'too eclectic and discursive'. While the Mechanics it displaced 'scourged us with whips, the General Elementary Science will scourge us with scorpions', one headmaster wrote.[110] Three years later, in a restructuring of the examination, it appeared.

Now, however, General Science as an examination subject based on the *Science For All* proposals, appeared to be a possible solution to many of the problems of incorporating science in the curriculum of public schools and in the education of military and civil leaders. It consolidated the previously separate branches of science that had bedevilled curriculum planning in the middle forms of public schools, offering a broad foundation for future specialist studies and a general education for all. It provided a remedy for over-specialization in the upper school and in university entrance examinations. Thus the Historical Association was in favour of allowing a knowledge of science to count in History scholarship examinations; and Vassall was of the opinion that the standard of the papers in science scholarship examinations should be lowered, 'and a larger knowledge of General Science required'.[111]

In discussions with the University of Oxford over a proposal to make science a compulsory subject of examination for Responsions, it was reported that the examination would be exclusively upon General Science, based on *Science for All*. In connection with the Neglect of Science Committee's resolutions that entrants to Sandhurst should have demonstrated a knowledge of science and the Thomson Committee's strictures on the view that 'Infantry Officers did not require to have a knowledge of science',[112] General Science now offered the prospect of progress. 'Formal science' such as was required for Woolwich was unsuitable for Sandhurst, but 'General Science' became an optional subject in the entrance examination for Sandhurst from 1921.[113] As for Civil Servants, when the Treasury's Committee on the Class 1 examination reported in 1917, a paper on General Science, testing 'general principles, methods and applications of science' was made a requirement for all candidates, the allocation of marks giving it parity with other compulsory subjects in the examination.[114] Finally, after pressure from the science masters, and in accordance with the views of the Headmasters' Conference, the Oxford and Cambridge Schools Examination Board introduced General Science as an additional science subject into the School Certificate Examination in 1921.[115]

Inevitably, General Science became framed more sharply by association with examinations, the provisional and exemplary schemes in the APSSM report being transformed into precise syllabus requirements. Overall, however, it was the institutional context in which General Science was wrought that was the major determinant of this new curriculum species. Unable to assume anything in the way of prior knowledge of science from boys entering public schools, their masters required a self-contained, two-year course which would not only interest boys but which could be adorned with an appropriate rhetoric of educational justification. As the report of Gregory's B.A. committee noted, such rhetoric could no longer invoke mental training in scientific method: general transfer of acquired abilities was not automatic.[116] Instead, utility, as evidenced by the events of war, assumed greater importance, especially when associated with humanistic aspects of science, including romance and wonder, but also such qualities as 'self-sacrifice, persistence, courage, duty, accuracy, humility and hope', all of which were 'abundantly exemplified from the careers of men of science'.[117]

Gregory's hagiography, *Discovery or The Spirit and Service of Science*, published in 1916 at a time when humanists and scientists had gathered their forces in a posture of confrontation, did much to counter a view of the scientist as 'callous necromancer' lacking 'the compassionate heart of a full life'.[118] Following Gregory, the science masters claimed that their subject, like the humanities, could be taught so as to 'cause young men to see visions'. The educational value in a study was to be judged by the intensity of the stimulus it gave to the imagination. The formal study of a special science rarely appealed to these ends, but a 'broad and generous' course of General Science was 'a prophylactic against pedantry' which enabled a boy to 'preserve his humanity'.[119]

9 Science Education for the Rank and File

Changing contexts for General Science

The impressive benefits associated with General Science were, of course, much too attractive to be the prerogative of the few. With the broadening of the Association's membership, in January 1919, *Science for All* was re-interpreted by the SMA as science for all boys in secondary grammar schools. The context of science teaching in the new aided and maintained secondary schools was, however, markedly different from that in public schools. 'Neglect of science' applied to the former meant something very different from its application to the latter. As the Incorporated Association of Assistant Masters had stated in its evidence to the Thomson Committee, in the maintained schools science was an established and integral part of the curriculum, in no way inferior to any other subject. The science teaching problems in these schools arose more from inadequate material resources and staffing than from lack of time and status for the subject.[1] Furthermore, apart from secondary schools in some rural areas, there was little pressure to include biological knowledge in the general curriculum for boys because of their landed and agricultural interests. The functional sciences were physics and chemistry, studied as pre-professional, vocationally significant subjects which, in addition, lent themselves admirably to training in scientific method. There was some disquiet about too early specialization and a failure, especially in physics, to provide a sufficiently broad course representative of all branches.

But Gregory's plea for 'much more of the spirit and less of the valley of dry bones',[2] if it drew a response from science teachers in maintained grammar schools, did not lead inexorably to General Science. A more urgent need was for General Physics, a balanced course in the essentials of the various branches of physics to provide 'what every educated citizen ought to know'.[3] The main proviso here was that General Physics should be accepted by university authorities for matriculation examinations in place of their more specialized syllabuses in separate branches of physics. At this stage the maintained schools had relatively little advanced work and few connections with the older universities comparable to those of the public schools; hence the leaving certificate examination played a different role in their scheme of things.

If their institutional context inclined maintained grammar schools to view General Science as a less than obvious solution to their science curriculum problems, there were others who opposed the innovation on more fundamental grounds. In January 1917, Professor H.H. Turner, Savilian Professor of Astronomy at Oxford, uttered words of warning in his Presidential Address at the APSSM annual meeting which followed the publication of *Science for All*. 'It seems to be pretty clear', Turner remarked, 'that the expectation of any fundamental change in the *majority* of mankind towards physical science is doomed to disappointment. We might as well expect a similar change in their attitude towards music'. The present enthusiasm for teaching science to everybody left him 'lukewarm if not even cold'. His judgement was that the main energies of reformers should be directed towards 'the discovery and training of those few who show some aptitude for science rather than to broad schemes for the general diffusion of scientific knowledge'.[4]

The opposite view was provided by Gregory at the same meeting when, later in the day, he opened a discussion on 'Science for the Rank and File'. For those many students who would not proceed to scientific and industrial careers something more was needed than laboratory training in scientific method; the syllabuses outlined in *Science for All* pointed the way.[5] In support of this, the Members' Exhibition, for the first time, included a section on General Science. In contrast to Turner whose position was that 'natural science is *intrinsically uninteresting* to the vast majority'[6] (they would all look down a telescope once, out of curiosity, but few returned for a second peep, and fewer still to make a systematic study of the heavens), Gregory and the leaders of the APSSM held that interest could be stimulated by work which was also 'truly educational', imparting a lasting effect.

The pamphlet *Science for All* was twice revised and reprinted by the SMA in the 1920s.[7] The original version was said to have given rise to misconceptions about the nature and aims of General Science; accordingly, an improved syllabus, suggestions for practical work and specimen examination questions, having survived much criticism in the General Committee, were incorporated. Following the Oxford meeting of January 1921, at the suggestion of Brigadier-General Harold Hartley and the SMA President, Archer Vassall (Harrow), a Liaison Committee including both university and SMA representatives was established.[8] For a number of years this body exerted significant influence on examination boards to achieve improvements in science examinations. By 1932, six examining bodies – Bristol, Cambridge Local Examinations Syndicate, Durham, Oxford Local Examinations, Oxford and Cambridge Joint Board and the Central Welsh Board – had introduced General Science papers into their School Certificate examinations, and the Civil Service Commissioners set a similar paper in Part 1 of the Army Entrance Examination.[9]

As evidence of progress in establishing General Science as the most appropriate science subject up to the stage of the School Certificate, however, this situation was illusory. A Board of Education *Report of an Enquiry into the Conditions affecting the Teaching of Science* in 39 large urban secondary schools, published in 1925, concluded that the SMA's advocacy of General Science 'had had little or no influence on the work of Secondary Schools generally'. As an editorial in *The School Science Review* noted at the time, 'Upon the suitability of General Science as a course for all Certificate and Matriculation candidates opinion is known to be divided, but why the division should fall so decidedly as it does between schools examined by the Oxford and Cambridge Joint Board and schools that take other Certificate examinations remains to be investigated'.[10] In fact the reason was not too difficult to discern. The Joint Board served Headmasters' Conference schools predominantly; in the maintained sector, as one member of the SMA had pointed out earlier, especially in the newer secondary schools with developing advanced course work leading to the Second (Higher Certificate) Examination, *Science for All* did not provide 'a really sound elementary knowledge of the basic sciences'; it was 'a miscellany of odds and ends'. 'Real stimulus' to pursue the study of science could come from 'genuine work with the mind continually on the stretch' quite as much as from 'passive arm-chair lecture entertainment'. The case for abandoning the study of 'the most useful and stimulating branches of chemistry and physics' had not been made, although, to the extent that time permitted, the inclusion of biographical and historical material was to be encouraged.[11]

Further confirmation of lack of progress, if it were needed, came in 1928 from the report of a British Association committee under Gregory's chairmanship and including SMA members. Whilst reiterating the arguments for a broader science course in schools, the report was severely critical of the Oxford and Cambridge Joint Board's General Science syllabus and of its interpretation by the examiners whose questions betrayed 'a misconception of what general elementary science or science of everyday life should signify'. By way of exemplification, the committee appended the science schemes which had accompanied the B.A. report of 1917.[12] Not without some justification, given the superannuated status of several members of the B.A. committee, the SMA reaction was that the report provided evidence of 'that loss of faith so common with advancing years'. To fall back, as the committee had done, on syllabuses drawn up at the dawn of the General Science movement indicated that 'one must not look to the British Association for inspiration'.[13]

Possibly a similar charge of failure to inspire, or at least give a lead, could have been directed at the SMA around this time. The Board of Education's Consultative Committee had commenced an enquiry in 1924 into 'the education of the adolescent', meaning children in full-time attendance up to the age of fifteen in schools other than secondary schools. Not only did the Association decide in 1926 against widening its membership to include science teachers in Central

Schools, but also, in contrast to other subject teaching associations such as the Mathematical, Historical and Geographical Associations, it did not submit evidence on curriculum matters to the Committee.[14] The Hadow Report's recommendations on science teaching, although they had features in common with the general science courses which the SMA espoused, were not in any direct sense influenced by the Association. A harbinger of a broader concept of secondary education, the publication of the Hadow Report passed largely unnoticed by the SMA apart from a review in *The School Science Review* by Hugh Richardson,[15] a retired Quaker science master. Eight years later, when the Consultative Committee under Will Spens returned to the organization of post-elementary education, the Association was obliged to address seriously 'Science in the Hadow Report'. At this earlier stage, other contextual considerations pressed more strongly.

A major characteristic of General Science as a projected curriculum innovation was its lack of precise definition. This was at once both a weakness and a strength. Uncertainty about what was entailed made implementation difficult. On the other hand, the vagueness which resulted from a generalized rhetoric of justification and a plurality of examples enabled diverse interests to discover in General Science something that might serve their ends. For Gregory, concerned to present science as a humanity, it offered opportunities for the incorporation of informational and biographical material calculated to inspire. For others, such as E.J. Holmyard (Clifton) the wider treatment was concordant with aesthetic ideals; it enabled boys to appreciate to the full 'the serene joys of the intellectual life',[16] a view from which his colleagues on the SMA General Committee sharply dissented because of Holmyard's discounting of the utilitarian outcomes of learning science.[17] By the late 1920s another lobby had begun to see in General Science a vehicle for its purpose, in this case the inclusion of biology in the grammar school curriculum.

In October 1928 representatives of the SMA attended a Board of Education Conference on the extension of biology teaching in secondary schools. Concern on this matter had its origins in the Ministry of Agriculture and the Colonial Office, from where evidence came of a great shortage of biologically-trained men for work in the colonies.[18] The matter had already been broached at the Annual Meeting in Imperial College, earlier in the year,[19] and J.W. Stork (Charterhouse) and A. Vassall (Harrow) were deputed to represent the Association at a meeting to discuss the school teaching of biology with university teachers of botany and zoology at Cambridge.[20] The teaching of biology as Natural History posed problems with regard to organizing adequate field work and there were obvious difficulties in small schools where the staff was not large enough to carry a biologist. The erosion of time for chemistry and physics was also feared. Clearly if universities would accept a general science syllabus in their matriculation examination, a possible way forward might be to include biology under this umbrella.

To ascertain members' opinion on these and related matters an informal discussion was planned for the Annual Meeting in London in January 1930. At the same time a sub-committee of A. Vassall, E. Barrett (Dursley), F. Fairbrother (Cedars School, Leighton Buzzard) and I.M. Bankes-Williams (Harrow) was instructed to revise the General Science pamphlet.[21] Their task was given additional point by the news that a British Association committee had been established to consider the teaching of General Science with special reference to the teaching of biology.[22] In his capacity of Chairman of the SMA General Committee, Fairbrother led a discussion on General Science at the Birmingham Annual Meeting in January 1931, expressing surprise and pleasure in his summing up that the opponents of General Science had retired from the field of battle.[23] His reaction was not unjustified in the light of comments made on that occasion, and in view of opinion to be expressed elsewhere.[24] Though the enemy without might have been quelled, there remained, however, the enemy within. As Fairbrother acknowledged, it was still difficult to provide an exact description of General Science. In attempting that task in the years following, the SMA committee was to uncover competing definitions of general science for the rank and file.

Reshaping General Science

The revised General Science pamphlet, containing outlines of two courses, one for a large school and the other for a small, more rural, school, was distributed in December 1932.[25] It drew an immediate response from the stormy petrel of the General Science movement, H.S. Shelton, a teacher of chemistry and general science at Farnham Grammar School, Surrey, who submitted a critical article for publication in *The School Science Review*. Before its acceptance, Shelton was summoned to discuss his ideas with the General Committee and his paper, when it appeared in print, was accompanied by some defensive observations from the Committee.[26] Outspoken, opinionated and abrasive, Shelton condemned the SMA pamphlet as lacking any clear theory as to what General Science should be. The Committee 'occasionally tell us what General Science is not,' he wrote, but 'nowhere do (they) tell us what it is'. Their syllabus was impossibly long and needed pruning by about one-third. The chemistry was much too difficult, amounting to at least half that for a school certificate course in the subject, and the physical science material was not integrated.

Shelton was but one voice; his dissent, though voluble, might have been contained by a firm line. However, the SMA General Science proposals were challenged simultaneously by another body, whose prestige and authority could not be ignored. In the autumn of 1932 the Panel of Investigators appointed by the Secondary School Examinations Council reported on the School Certificate examinations held in 1931.[27] The importance of this major review had been underlined by the Chairman of the Council, Cyril Norwood, Head-master of Harrow, leading the investigation. Of the 23 members of the panel, those with special responsibility for the science examina-tions were: F. Fairbrother, headmaster of the Cedars Schools, Leighton Buzzard; F.A. Meier, senior science master, Rugby; E.G. Savage, HMI; F.B. Stead, HMI, and Dr Marie Dawson, HMI. All the men were members of the SMA, Fairbrother being one of the group which had produced the 1932 pamphlet.

The investigators criticized the single subject science papers currently available in the School Certificate examinations as narrow-ing; the best hope for improvement seemed to be found in experi-ments with General Science syllabuses, though the Oxford and Cambridge Joint Board's paper was not a model they could commend. Instead, it was recommended that a new syllabus and examination in Elementary Science should be developed and made compulsory for all candidates desiring a pass in science. This could be supplemented by optional papers, one in each of physics, chemistry and biology, so that schools wishing to do so could give science a prominent place in the curriculum. The new paper was to be both general and element-ary, but with the emphasis on the latter.[28] To this extent it differed from the SMA General Science proposals which were returned to the drawing board when a new sub-committee was appointed in March 1933 'to consider the aims, content and method of general science regarded as suitable for the elementary science suggested by the investigators' panel'.[29]

The SSEC Panel's proposals went well beyond the design of a new science syllabus and examination, however. Fundamental changes involving the separation of the School Certificate from university matriculation examinations were recommended. These brought into question the status of Elementary Science in the School Certificate examintion and specifically whether it was intended to be a mere qualifying subject in the science group or whether it would carry a credit, on a par with the single sciences. The original theory of the School Certificate had been that the examination would serve two purposes; conducted on the principle of 'easy papers and a high standard of marking' it was possible to award a pass for the (leaving) Certificate, and a mark of credit, at an appreciably higher standard, for university matriculation purposes. In time, however, the certi-ficate had become commercialized, matriculation certificates (i.e. credits in five subjects at one and the same sitting) being of consider-able value in the job-market for those who had no intention of going on to university.[30] A period of grievous economic depression such as that prevailing when the SSEC report was published was not one when a debasement of the currency could be contemplated and it was essential that Elementary Science should lead to a credit in any new arrangements.

The SMA's annual Report for 1932 contained detailed recom-mendations for an examination in Elementary Science involving *two* papers, a credit being possible by taking either both of these, or one, plus the examination in one of the single sciences. These proposals came from a newly-established Examinations Sub-Committee, set up at Fairbrother's instigation shortly after his appointment to the SSEC Panel.[31] At the Annual Meeting in Bristol in 1933 the recommendations were the subject of extensive debate, a record of the discussion being printed and circulated to all SMA members.[32] No decision was reached, the intention being to re-open the question at next year's meeting, thus allowing time for a thorough ventilation of important matters which could determine the shape of school science for the foreseeable future.

When members re-assembled at Imperial College, London, in January 1934, considerable opposition had developed to the idea of a *compulsory* paper in Elementary Science, even to the extent of critical comment being sent to the SMA Secretary by some of those unable to attend.[33] Compulsion would oblige the science curriculum to follow the examination, whereas the inverse relationship should hold. Nevertheless, dissatisfaction with existing syllabuses and recognition that a broader course had attractions, not least the opportunity to introduce biology, enabled the meeting finally to resolve in favour of an obligatory paper in Elementary Science for all taking the School Certificate examination.[34] The unreality of this centralist proposition was brought home to representatives of the SMA at a meeting with officials from four of the larger Examining Bodies (the Northern Universities Joint Board, London, Oxford Local and Cambridge Local) the following April. The Delegacy of the Oxford Local examinations had considered the matter of compulsion and reported their view that, without a pronouncement from the Board of Education, they had no authority to impose such a requirement. The best they could do would be to revise their science syllabuses and offer an examination in Elementary Science which was as close as possible to that advocated by the SMA. After general agreement on this point and further discussion, it was recommended that the Examining Bodies would revert to the title 'General Science', abandoning 'Elementary Science', and that 'General Science' would be used only for a subject which included biology as well as the physical sciences.[35]

This excursion by the SMA into the politics of examination reform, the issue of central control versus teachers' freedom of choice sharply dividing the membership, was time-consuming and resulted in the work of the General Science sub-committee, appointed in March 1933, being largely overtaken by events. The secretary and convenor of this group was F.W. Turner (Thames Valley County School), the other members being G.H.J. Adlam (City of London School), Dr T.J. Baker (King Edward VI High School, Birmingham), I.M. Bankes-Williams (Harrow), C. Bispham (King's School, Grantham) and F. Fairbrother (The Cedars School, Leighton Buzzard).[36] Turner's approach to the work of the sub-committee was empirical and pragmatic, in contrast to the idealism of previous reports. He proposed a detailed survey of what schools actually did under the heading of General Science, employing a questionnaire to all SMA members. Only when this data-base had been established did he think the committee could embark on the second stage, the formulation of a realistic policy for General Science, including a precise definition of its aim, details of content, teaching methods, the qualifications and training of teachers and a scheme of examination.[37]

Not surprisingly his comprehensive proposals failed to win the support of his fellow members who, having amended the title of the sub-committee to Elementary Science, concentrated on a new list of contents and a sample examination paper. The main innovation here was the setting of the draft examination paper, Part 1 of which included objective-type questions, for candidates in the schools of committee members, the results of this trial leading to modifications and, eventually, on a tight vote in the General Committee (five for, four against), to publication.[38]

Even before the pamphlet had been distributed to members, the General Committee had begun to redefine the problem of implementing its policy for the widespread teaching of General Science. In a preamble to the report from Turner's sub-committee it acknowledged that 'the philosophical background of General Science has not yet been developed'. A new strong sub-committee had been appointed 'to consider the fundamental basis on which the study of science should be built' and 'a substantial memorandum' was promised.[39] The 1934 report was, in effect, discounted as it was published. The general view (not shared by Shelton, however[40]) was that it was a disappointing effort, its principal merit being that it stirred into activity some important newcomers to the cause of General Science.[41]

Ideals and realities

Before embarking on the next stage of their campaign the SMA Committee paused to take stock; an ad-hoc group of the officers together with C. Bispham (from the now defunct Elementary Science committee), S.R. Humby (Winchester) and J.A. Lauwerys (University of London Institute of Education) was appointed to consider the constitution and terms of reference of a new General Science Sub-Committee.[42]

Lauwerys was one of the newer members of the SMA who had reacted adversely to the 1934 report and was instrumental in relating views on 'the transfer of training' to the justification for teaching General Science. Within the British Association it had recently been shown that 'the extravagant claims made in the past for the unique value of certain subjects from the point of view of mental training' could not be sustained. Experimental evidence from psychology appeared to cut the ground from under the feet of those who argued for intensive specialization involving the study of a single science. A narrow curriculum could no longer be justified by the claim that it trained boys to think and to appreciate 'Scientific method'.[43] As a lecturer in the methods of teaching science in the London Institute of Education, Lauwerys was able to bring a more theoretical perspective to bear on the teaching of General Science and his application of the transfer evidence made him a welcome recruit.

The views of the ad-hoc group were considered in February 1935 when a new General Science sub-committee was constituted.[44] It was an intriguing combination of experience and youth; public schools and maintained schools; headmasters and assistant masters; and of Oxbridge and provincial university backgrounds. Only in relation to geographical distribution did the membership betray a clear bias, with seven of the tweve men working in, or close to, London.

C. Bispham, BA (Cantab.) Recently senior science master, Berk-hamsted School Headmaster, King's School, Grantham.

C.L. Bryant, MA (Cantab.) Harrow School. An active APSSM member and officer. (Chairman)

J. Ellison, senior science master, Trinity County School, Wood Green.

W.J. Gale, BSc (Kings College London) senior science master, Bec School, Tooting.

W.G. Greaves, MA (Cantab.) Headmaster, Ledbury Grammar School.

J.A. Lauwerys, BSc. Lecturer and tutor in methods of science, University of London Institute of Education. (Convenor)

A.J. Price, MA (Oxon.) Science master, Berkhamsted School and, from 1936, headmaster, St Peter's School, York.

W.H. Reynolds, BSc (Imperial College) Headmaster, King's Norton Secondary School, Birmingham.

H.S. Shelton, BSc. Science master, Farnham Grammar School, Surrey.

L.G. Smith, BSc. Science master, Marylebone Grammar School.

A. Vassall, MA (Oxon.) Past-President of the SMA, one of the authors of the original *Science for All* proposals in 1916, and recently retired to Oxford from his post as senior science master, Harrow School.

C.J.R. Whitmore, MA (Cantab.), HMI, who joined the sub-committee 'in an advisory capacity' from its second meeting.

Bryant, Gale, Vassall and Whitmore had all been members of the APSSM; Reynolds, Bispham and Ellison were early recruits to the SMA after the widening of membership in 1919; Price, Greaves and Shelton joined in the late 1920s; L.G. Smith and Lauwerys in 1933. Bispham, Bryant, Gale, Reynolds and Vassall had all served on previous SMA General Committees. Greaves was a late addition to the sub-committee, recruited because his letter to the secretary of the SMA, about the 1934 Report had indicated 'ideas and experience' which could be useful.[45] In the event his contribution was a major factor in determining the committee's mode of operation. Not all were as active as Greaves. Price, on the point of promotion to his first headship, was prevented by 'an accident' from attending the inaugural meeting and, in a letter typed at 2 o'clock in the morning, cried off the second because of over-work.[46] These were critical meetings for the formation of the sub-committee's views; once the framework had been agreed, much of the detail was settled by correspondence. As for Shelton, his inclusion may have been an attempt to recruit the opposition. If so, it failed abysmally. He deluged the committee with papers, apparently unaware how out of tune his opinions were with those of his fellow members. 'Poor old Gale got landed with Shelton and had an awful time', Greaves wrote after the second meeting when members had divided into subject groups. 'He has some sort of fixed idea as to what should be taught and just obstructed all the morning.' Afterwards Whitmore suggested to Greaves that the General Committee should be asked to remove Shelton, a step which Bryant took reluctantly in the interests of progress.[47] Shelton's association with the sub-committee did not extend beyond the first two meetings and his membership of the SMA, though not his interest in General Science,[48] lapsed after 1936.

Apart from internal considerations, two contextual circumstances encouraged the sub-committee to make their review of the SMA's position on General Science both fundamental and detailed. First, the Consultative Committee to the Board of Education, then considering the organization of secondary education with special reference to grammar schools and technical high schools, had indicated that the SMA's opinion on science teaching would be welcomed.[49] Second, the SMA had recently entered into an agreement with the Incorporated Association of Assistant Masters to prepare 'an exhaustive memorandum on the teaching of science'. Both Lauwerys and L.G. Smith were amongst the SMA's team of eight who, together with twelve IAAM members, eventually produced a draft of a volume, *The Teaching of Science in Secondary Schools*, only for publication to be prevented by the outbreak of war.[50]

The terms of reference given to the General Science sub-committee were:

To consider the problems presented to teachers in Secondary Schools by the introduction of courses in General Science as a constituent of general education, and to make specific suggestions about
1   the aims to be kept in view,
2   the basic principles of the subject, an appreciation of which should be inculcated,
3   the material to be included in such courses,
4   methods of development and treatment of the material,
5   timetable requirements at different stages.[51]

For Bryant, chairman of the sub-committee, the first priority was to 'clarify our aims in presenting science in a general way' and to 'launch and maintain a persistent campaign in favour of our ideals – a sort of evangelizing mission'.[52] Vassall, equally, in his capacity as 'elder statesman', supported the notion of burnishing the ideal; it was not the job of the committee to be 'practical'; there were many roads to success and they should 'leave it to the state, Examiners, Masters and Universities to follow your lead'. The syllabus mattered little provided the spirit in which the work was executed was sound. As for examinations, his 'old man's dream' was of a School Certificate from which *all* science subjects, including General Science, had been abolished.[53]

In sharp contrast, Shelton urged that they should begin with point 5 in the terms of reference, the demands that would be made on the time-table. Content could then be settled under two broad headings, physical and biological: in his experience it was not always easy to unify these fields. As for aims and ideals, these were best presented to teachers by concrete proposals from which the theoretical basis could be inferred.[54]

Shelton's approach carried the day, but his victory was short-lived. When the sub-committee considered the issue of time there was a division of opinion. All agreed to develop a *minimum* syllabus, as opposed to an extensive one; a school could always expand the minimum if it had resources to do so. It was asserted that previous reports had suggested that 'sixteen-year-periods' (e.g. 4 periods per week for 4 years) might suffice for a minimum syllabus and it was proposed from the chair that this should be adopted. Shelton's amendment of 'eighteen-year-periods' was defeated, his being the only vote in favour.[55]

In fairness to Shelton it has to be said that 'sixteen-year-periods' (3 hours per week) was *less* than the time allocated for General Science in most previous reports and certainly below the Thomson Report's recommendation. There was some justice in his later comment that the committee had bound themselves to the time-table situation in 'classical schools'. In the larger maintained secondary school, nine periods per week ($6\frac{3}{4}$ hours) for the two sciences (chemistry and physics) were not unusual. It was his view that they had been asked in their terms of reference to pronounce on 'time-table requirements' and had not faced up to this responsibility. In consequence he dissociated himself from the committee in this matter indicating that it would not be possible for him to sign a report. Instead he intended to write a minority report to show the 'failings and weaknesses' of what had flowed from this critical decision on time.[56]

Better progress was made with syllabus construction. Here Greaves described his earlier experience of drafting a General Physics syllabus. First, a list (A) was drawn up of 'things a boy wants to know, the questions a boy wished to be answered'. Then, a list (B) was compiled of fundamental scientific ideas which it was believed every boy should know. The two lists were then compared to extract common material (list AB). Every item on this could be justified on two grounds: it helped a boy to an intelligent appreciation of his environment as well as to an understanding of underlying scientific principles. This approach to syllabus construction, in terms of pupil interests and the structure of the disciplines, was adopted for General Science.[57]

On the morning of the second meeting, the sub-committee met in subject groups of A men and B men. This was the ill-fated occasion when Shelton, volunteering to be a B man, apparently failed to stick to the rules of the game and tested Gale to the limit. 'Never did I see a man in such a difficult position handle it with such perfect tact,' Greaves wrote to him the next day. 'I got a dreadful shock when I entered the room and found his lordship there . . . unless we can get round him somehow the whole show will be ruined before birth.' Greaves' solution was to recruit another chemist, Ellison, 'a real General Science man', whose addition to the sub-committee was sanctioned at this point.[58]

Possibly if Price's duties with the Officers Training Corps had not prevented his attendance at the second meeting, events might have turned out differently. His reaction to the 'vexed question of time-table', expressed in a long letter to Lauwerys, was that if he and his 'rustic' colleagues at Berkhamsted had properly understood the 'metropolitan gem' of 'sixteen-year-periods', then he heartily agreed with Shelton. 'I think we should be erring very greatly if we allowed such a recommendation to go through', he wrote, and the report of the sub-committee, when published in 1936, carried a note of dissent from Price on this point.[59] Otherwise the three subject groups of A and B men worked steadily towards their minimum syllabuses which appeared in separate columns under the headings of physics, biology and chemistry in the final report.

Shelton fired two more salvos at the sub-committee before publication. In the first, a long memorandum, he condemned the approach to syllabus construction because it prevented 'the proper integration of the material on entirely different lines from the ordinary specialist science'; he deplored the decision to exclude geology and astronomy; and he feared that 'the hotch-potch' proposed was inferior to 'the present specialist science' which, in his view, was taught reasonably efficiently in most schools.[60] In the second, he returned to the issue, fundamental for him, of the time-table allowance. As Bryant had advised him that it would be better if he opposed the sub-committee from outside, rather than within, he used the columns of the journal of the Incorporated Association of Assistant Masters to ventilate his opinions on the inadequacy of the minimum syllabus, urging science teachers to state unanimously they would have nothing to do with it. Here Lauwerys effectively defended the sub-committee's stance in a prolonged exchange.[61]

On the important question of integration, the sub-committee had struggled with ways of synthesizing their separate biology, chemistry and physics syllabuses into 'a really and truly one subject'. It fell to Greaves, as syllabus coordinator, to take the initiative here; when the members forgathered after the long vacation of 1935, he described how he had tried and failed. Integration in terms of scientific principles was unsatisfactory because there were, for example, parts of biology which had no parallels in chemistry and physics. It seemed 'stupid' to adopt a system which led to exclusion of those parts of biology which were specifically biological. The method did not produce what was required and was rejected as unsatisfactory. As for the 'topic' method, which he favoured as a 'short and snappy' teaching device, it synthesized some things but not all, even when one employed links which were 'hocus-pocus': the 'Human Body' as a topic could lead to the study of the electric bell but only by forced articulation through the human finger exerting force on a white button and causing a buzzing noise in the kitchen! Even if topics were devised which unified the three sciences, they would still have to be arranged in a rational and practical teaching order. A sequence which might be possible and rational for mechanics need not necessarily be so for botany.

Greaves concluded that the topic as a synthesizing mechanism was 'a snare and a delusion'; the sub-committee should abandon all attempts at synthesis beyond arranging content in an order so that each part helped each other part as much as possible. Maybe an alternative interpretation in terms of topics could be offered later, if 'a keen topicist' could be found. Quoting his colleague L.G. Smith, Greaves ended by asking, 'Is it not a fact that the only thing biology and physics have in common is the attitude of mind of the biologist and the physicist?' If, as he suspected, this were so, then the only true synthesis had to be based on an attitude of mind which, in the schools, would appear not in the syllabus but in the master.[62] After nine months' work, the sub-committee appeared to have arrived at a position close to that outlined by Vassall in their first meeting.

The Teaching of General Science was published as an interim report of the Sub-committee in 1936. In the view of the SMA General Committee it 'was one of the most substantial pieces of work for which the Association has at any time been responsible'; a view which *Nature* endorsed, suggesting that 'it may become a landmark in the history of science education'.[63] Introducing a discussion on the report at the Annual Meeting in Manchester, in January 1937, Bryant addressed two questions to the assembled masters. 'Is General Science preferable to Specialized Science in the pre-Certificate stage?' and 'Is this the sort of General Science we want?' The response was mixed; some argued that General Science was not the best preparation for the Higher School Certificate; others that the General Science syllabus, though a minimum, was too long; and, from a physicist, that although the shelves of the chemists certainly needed dusting the sub-committee appeared to have swept them clean – surely there were new aspects of chemistry that needed stressing.[64] Not surprisingly, the Institute of Chemistry took a similar view, fearing that chemistry was being ignored, except as 'the handmaiden of biology'.[65] Though the general proposal for a less specialized science course in the School Certificate Examination commanded wide support, once the idea became concrete, opinion divided. Over the following months the pages of *The School Science Review* contained many contributions to the debate.

As for the sub-committee, it returned to its labours with the object of producing a course for *eight* periods a week, with a total of 750 teaching periods as against the 450 periods of the minimum syllabus.[66] This was eventually published in 1938, though not without a hint of a disclaimer from the General Committee which resolved that the report should be adopted because 'school science teaching should not rest on a narrow basis' and 'General Science meets this requirement and can be taught along the lines of the report'.[67] This cautious approval was not unconnected with a recent complaint from SMA members that 'certain Inspectors had been using the minimum syllabus as a means of compelling teachers to introduce General Science'. A deputation of W.G. Greaves (now Chairman of the General Committee), S.V. Brown (Liverpool Institute and SMA General Secretary) and G. Fowles (Latymer Upper School) met C.J.R. Whitmore HMI and Senior Chief Inspector E.G. Savage at the Board of Education on 25 March 1938 to discuss the matter. An account of their exchange, and an assurance that the Board's policy was not to force any subject into the curriculum and never to prescribe a syllabus, was printed in the annual report of the SMA for that year.[68]

Evidence of resentment on the part of members at too blatant a promotion of General Science did not prevent one further development by the SMA at this stage. Early in 1939, a joint committee of the AWST and the AAM published a General Science examination syllabus, provoking 'considerable discussion' in the SMA General Committee. This led to the establishment of a sub-committee of Bryant, Lauwerys, Greaves, Fairbrother and Reynolds to frame an alternative examination syllabus based on the 1936 *Report*, as a matter of some urgency.[69] It was feared that the women's syllabus might unduly influence examinations boards, especially the Joint Matriculation Board, then constructing examination syllabuses in General Science. A draft report on an SMA examination syllabus was discussed at the May meeting of the General Committee, the sub-committee being empowered 'to make emergency use' of it, if the need arose, during the summer. At the same meeting it was decided not to accede to a request from the women that their syllabus should be published in *The School Science Review*.[70] Behind this action lay a recognition that examinations in General Science needed to be markedly different from the conventional type if they were to avoid 'a rigidity and a formalism' which would destroy the educational advantages of the course. The SMA's tentative proposals in Part 2 of *The Teaching of General Science* (1938) had included a greater use of teacher estimates, as well as 'objective type' tests and an essay paper.[71] Unfortunately, these early attempts at examination reform, including a detailed specification of objectives not unlike those associated with the Nuffield Foundation's science teaching schemes some 25 years later, were curtailed by the outbreak of war.

General Science for Girls

'There can be no doubt', the Thomson Committee concluded in 1918, 'that the problem of the curriculum is more difficult in girls' schools than in boys' schools'.[72] The reasons for this were several, but conflicting ideals of women's education lay at the heart of the matter.

Certainly, many of the contextual influences which had given rise to General Science as the recommended subject of study in boys' schools up to the age of sixteen, did not operate on girls' schools. As a result the perceptions of the problems of science education held by women science teachers were different from those held by men. For a start, the biological sciences, represented principally by botany, were the mainstay of the science curriculum in girls' schools where, in contrast to boys' schools, physics tended to be the neglected science. In so far as there were problems on the biological side, these arose, first, from a failure to teach botany as a part of biology, so linking it to general laws about all living things; second, from an over-emphasis on systematics which led to a neglect of the relevance of botany to agriculture, horticulture and medicine; and, third, from a perceived need to extend biological studies to include lessons on personal and social hygiene.[73] There were different resource constraints also in girls' schools, especially in relation to laboratory provision, where, generally, the situation was much less satisfactory than in boys' schools. As for the time-table, the AST's recommendation of around three hours per week, well below the minimum recommended for boys in the Thomson Report, was deemed feasible only in those girls' schools which worked a 24-hour week; in schools which had morning attendance only, less time was available.[74]

When the AST undertook its exercise of syllabus construction in 1915, in anticipation of the School Certificate examination, there was no hint of interest in General Science, or *Science for All*, in girls' secondary schools.[75] The framework adopted was the traditional one of chemistry, physics, botany, zoology and geology. Thereafter the curriculum concerns of the AST and AWST were focused largely on science subjects in the Higher School Certificate examinations and liaison with universities to ensure no duplication of teaching effort in advanced course work. Early specialization in the pre-School Certificate years also received attention, with history of science a favoured remedy, though perhaps a measure more advocated than practised.[76]

The adoption of General Science in girls' secondary schools was gradual, unheralded by policy pronouncements and provoking little comment. Quietly, and without controversy, it became an accepted curriculum alternative in the early years of secondary education for girls. By the time of the British Association survey in 1931, 69 per cent of the girls' schools responding (compared with 56 per cent of the boys' schools) 'took General Science', though not necessarily as an examination subject in the School Certificate.[77] It has to be added, however, that what constituted General Science varied considerably from school to school; for many it was a means of incorporating some physical sciences in a curriculum which had been largely biological.

This diversity of provision in girls' secondary schools, coupled with the heterogeneous membership of the AWST, made it more difficult for the women than for the men to formulate a policy on curriculum matters. Many of their early discussions were inconclusive, an airing of differences and of reactions to change in school situations, with no well-defined outcomes.[78] The report of the SSEC panel of investigators into the School Certificate examination of 1932 did, however, provoke a definite reaction when it was considered at the annual meeting in 1933. On that occasion, 'after much discussion', five resolutions were passed and sent on to the SSEC, and to the professional associations of men and women heads and assistant teachers. The resolutions expressed unqualified opposition to compulsion with regard to any science subject in the School Certificate examination and deprecated the proposed obligatory paper in Elementary Science. The preference of the women science teachers was for a 'less wide syllabus' at this stage in order to concentrate on 'understanding of the method of growth of scientific knowledge through observation, experiment, hypothesis and the building up of theory'. There was no objection to the Elementary Science paper as an option, however, and the style of questions, as well as the proposals for the setting and marking of examination papers were warmly welcomed.[79]

Opinion in the AWST was further stimulated when, in 1934, the University of London sought reactions to proposed changes in the science subjects in the School Certificate examination. Following the meeting between examination bodies and the SMA in April of that year, it was suggested that General Science, with a syllabus on the lines of that drafted by the SMA, should replace Elementary Science in the examination, and that the three branches of physics at present examined, should be consolidated into one subject. Though a majority at the AWST summer meeting in 1934 supported this, there was a strong minority in favour of retaining a paper in Physics-with-Chemistry. There was also a marked reactionary feeling that botany should not disappear as a School Certificate subject, it being the science most widely studied in girls' secondary schools.[80]

The need to retain alternative courses of study in science, and the inappropriateness of attempts to devise one curriculum 'suitable to all the varying abilities and tastes of the pupils now admitted into our Secondary Schools' was emphasized by the AWST in its memorandum of evidence to the Spens Committee in 1934. At that time the opinion of the members was 'almost equally divided as to the wisdom of following a course in General Elementary Science up to the age of 16'. A broad syllabus in the early years was strongly commended, but for the immediate pre-Certificate years, a narrower course of study was preferred by many women science teachers. Here, courses in the physical sciences, with appropriate laboratory work, were to a large extent replacing or supplementing descriptive botany, whilst in biological studies there was now 'a marked tendency to include some instruction in animal biology', a change with which the Association was 'in entire agreement'.[81]

Writing to Miss M.E. Birt, honorary secretary of the AWST, R.F. Young, secretary to the Spens Committee, had suggested headings under which the views on science teaching of her Association might be formulated. Two of these dealt with General Science, the first relating to modifications in the School Certificate examination and the second to 'repercussions' on science staff if General Science were 'adopted'.[82] External stimulus of this kind, coupled with the recognition that the SMA had already given much thought to the subject, led to suggestions from the women that they should cooperate more fully with the men. At a Committee meeting in March 1935 it was agreed to write to the Chairman of the SMA asking his Association to consider the establishment of a joint sub-committee to discuss matters of common interest. The response came back that the SMA officers were always prepared to act as such a committee.[83] It was left to the women to take the initiative, however. In the event their collaboration with the science panel of the Association of Assistant Mistresses took priority.

There had always been a close relationship between the two associations since the AST had sprung from the London branch of the AAM in 1912. Cross membership was common at all levels up to and including presidents. When in the autumn of 1935 the AWST formally approached the science panel of the AAM there was an encouraging welcome to the prospect of collaboration.[84] The position in girls' schools on the teaching of general science was the first matter on which views were exchanged.

In March 1936 several AWST members attended the conference in London organized by J.A. Lauwerys on behalf of the SMA and presided over by Sir William Bragg, President of the Royal Society. The following week Lauwerys attended a committee meeting of the AWST to open a discussion on science teaching in girls' schools; in the course of this he drew attention to the availability of a considerable dossier of material on the SMA General Science Syllabus, then under development. To the suggestion that a joint production would be of greater value, he countered that the SMA was already committed to collaboration with the IAAM; further joint activity was not a realistic possibility at that moment.[85] Subsequently, Lauwerys proposed that members of the AWST should be eligible for branch membership of the SMA, but the SMA committee 'felt that the time was not yet opportune for such a step'.[86]

It was left then to the women to move ahead on their own. A number of examination bodies were producing General Science syllabuses and seeking their reactions. Additionally, the SMA Interim Report appeared at the end of 1936 and clearly had to be evaluated. To this end a sub-committee was established to formulate an AWST response.[87]

This 'critique' of the Interim Report was published in *The School Science Review*, accompanied by comments from C.L. Bryant, chairman of the General Science sub-committee.[88] AWST members had expressed their views on the Interim Report at the Annual General Meeting in London, in January 1937; some branches and other individuals had also provided written comments. On the basis of these, the AWST sub-committee comprising Dr Marie Dawson (retired HMI), Miss E.M.M. Higgins (High School, Gloucester), Miss E.W. Hobbs (King Edward High School, Birmingham), Miss H.M. Jehan (Municipal Secondary School, Devonport), Miss N.G. Mulligan (Girls' High School, Wakefield) and Miss Mary Sutton (St Martin's High School, London)[89] prepared a report which met with the general approval of the membership and the 'complete agreement' of the science panel of the AAM.[90]

Whilst approving of much in the SMA document, the AWST nevertheless found the minimum syllabus much too long. It was pointed out that some girls' schools had less than the prescribed 'sixteen-year periods' for science work and many were handicapped further by lack of accommodation and equipment. Even if time was available, it did not seem credible that a girl would 'thoroughly understand' and 'use with ease' the knowledge indicated, particularly that which she would not meet outside the laboratory. It was recommended that much of the physics should be cut out; and here mechanics came in for severe treatment, as did parts of electricity, three lessons on the measurement of voltage by a high resistance ammeter being thought inappropriate for girls. Also, some biology, e.g. the study of insects, should be treated in less detail so creating room for more work on 'such important subjects as heredity and reproduction'. Behind this apparently piecemeal attack lay a principle, that 'the "normal interests" of the average girl' should guide the construction of the syllabus. The point was conceded readily by Bryant. 'I entirely agree', he wrote. 'The syllabus should be modified to suit girls. We were thinking of boys all the time'.[91]

Having performed so effectively, the AWST General Science sub-committee was put to work again. The General Committee instructed it to carry its critique to a logical conclusion by constructing a general science syllabus for girls, together with an examination paper. This exercise was to be part of a larger inquiry into the science equipment and teaching methods used in girls' schools.[92] The sub-committee had a mind of its own, however, being unwilling to embark on syllabus development although commending the matter of science equipment as worth investigation. It recommended its dissolution as a sub-committee of the AWST and that a joint committee with the AAM should be set up to compile the syllabus. As for the intriguing concept of 'the normal interests of the average girl', members were requested to collect what information they could in their own schools, with additional inquiries being directed to 'the Institute of Psychology'.[93]

The joint AWST/AAM committee duly produced a General Science examination syllabus 'of School Certificate standard', involving two two-hour papers covering both the physical and biological sciences. With minor amendments this survived the critical scrutiny of the AWST General Committee in November 1938, after which it was printed for distribution to examining bodies and teachers' associations including the SMA.[94] The expectation of the women that the syllabus would be published in *The School Science Review* was disappointed, as noted previously.[95]

The content of the examination syllabus was substantially less than that in the SMA minimum syllabus; no attempt at integration was apparent, items being listed in separate sections corresponding to physics, chemistry and biology. The same arrangement characterized a supporting pamphlet on 'apparatus essential for the equipment of one laboratory for General Science up to School Certificate' which the joint committee published later in the year.[96] Only the biology section of the AWST/AAM syllabus included content not in the SMA document; here sexual reproduction was mentioned more explicitly as a topic, along with reference to the 'gradual evolution of parental care'. It appeared that 'the normal interests of the average girl' had not led to a selection of examinable science content different from that appropriate to boys.

The extent to which this congruence was real was indicated by subsequent discussions on General Science within the AWST. Speaking to her colleagues at an extraordinary general meeting in March 1939,[97] Miss W.M. Casswell (Withington Girls' School, Manchester) explained how the AWST/AAM syllabus had been used as the basis for Paper 1 of the Northern Universities' Joint Matriculation Board's new General Science Examination. The syllabus for this had been drawn up by six school teachers of science, both men and women. They had planned that the minimum syllabus associated with Paper 1 could be taught in less than the number of periods which it was assumed would be available in most schools, so allowing time to bias the teaching in preferred directions. In Miss Casswell's opinion such bias was 'very essential . . . or else there will be something strangely wrong'. It did not follow that the bias had to be examined, but 'we do want to have time to put in things we think important'. By way of illustration, she described how she had not been allowed 'to put in sodium bicarbonate or any of the various things it does in cooking'. In her view, this was 'quite important' knowledge, 'but since the men did not think it was, I let it go.'[98] There had to be a margin of time, therefore, to develop the teaching of the minimum syllabus in ways appropriate to the interests of their pupils.

The construction of a General Science examination syllabus suited to both boys and girls appeared to involve, first, agreement on the highest common factor of scientific interests of boys and girls, and, second, a reduction of content to a minimum so that a margin of uncommitted teaching time was available for 'bias'. With regard to the first requirement, however, Miss Casswell went on to explain that inquiries into the scientific interests of young girls in her own school had led her to believe that the common ground was substantial. She had begun by thinking that 'the Science Masters' General Science was useful for boys but not for girls'. Her revised opinion was that girls did not have 'any essentially different outlook from boys'.[99] In the discussion which followed, no member of her audience challenged this view. With regard to the second, the ideal and the reality rarely corresponded. In practice, minimum examination syllabuses had a habit of filling the available teaching time. Even if 'bias' had been thought essential, the opportunity to develop it rarely existed. The exigencies of the examination system and the realities of classroom life had nullified both the arguments and the opportunities for sex differentiation of the General Science curriculum. From a perception that General Science for girls needed to be an organization of knowledge distinct from that recommended for boys, the AWST, in a matter of months, seemed to have conceded the case for a largely common course. The extraordinary meeting of March 1939, and, in particular, Miss Casswell's statement embodying the argument both for and against 'bias', represented a turning point.

Further developments were prevented by the outbreak of war. As the AWST *Annual Report* for 1939–40 expressed it, in commenting on the indefinite postponement of a conference of examiners for General Science, 'there the matter rests for the moment'.[100] The issues were revived briefly in 1942 by a questionnaire from the Norwood Committee, asking about the suitability of General Science as 'the science of the main school'. The AWST's qualified approval required that science teachers should have 'a wider outlook' than at present and that the syllabus should be appropriately demanding for the abler pupils, with sufficient chemistry included. At the same time, care was necessary 'to avoid any utilitarian aspect'. Apart from the lack of good teachers and adequate resources, the factor which most hampered the full development of science in girls' secondary schools was 'a tendency, growing less but still prevalent, to ignore the cultural aspect of science'.[101] Both in substance and in phraseology, this latter statement betrayed influences from the SMA's justification of General Science as given in the Interim Report and rang discordantly with previous pronouncements of the AWST.

The issue of 'General Science for girls' arose once more in the life of the AWST in the 1950s when the SMA began to turn its attention to the teaching of science in secondary modern schools. Part 1 of a report from the SMA's Secondary Modern School Sub-Committee, published in 1953, gave details of a possible syllabus. Amongst criticisms of this was the complaint that it was not suitable for girls. Accordingly, an invitation was extended to the AWST to contribute a statement of its views. Miss P.M. Legh (Palmers School, Grays, Essex) and Miss N.M. Whitworth (City of Leicester Training College) prepared a chapter on 'Science for Girls' which was published anonymously, without acknowledgement (in contrast to similar chapters) and with critical annotations from the chairman of the Secondary Modern School Sub-Committee in Part 2 of *Secondary Modern Science Teaching* in 1957.[102]

In essence, the AWST view at this time was that the contrast between science for girls and for boys was 'in emphasis rather than in syllabus content'. The influence on the teaching of science of differences in the science interests and needs of girls and boys was small compared with that of other factors.[103] The shortage of women science teachers was again emphasized along with 'a lack of faith' on the part of many in girls' schools in the educational value of science. Subjects such as art, music, domestic science and needlework pressed more heavily on the timetable in girls' schools than did their counterparts in boys'. Selection from the science syllabus was inescapable and one criterion to be employed in this task was that 'the topic should be the concern of the pupil as a future citizen'. 'The appeal of looking after small children, and that of presenting an attractive appearance' were thought to be 'fairly general' as was 'the future vocation of wife and mother, or at least of homemaker'. It was in 'the human' rather than 'the mechanical' direction that the need and emotional drive of girls tended to act and hence it was argued that the science syllabus for girls should be given a biological and, to some extent, a domestic bias.[104] The 'mechanics section' of the SMA syllabus was severely pruned. The lever and its application to muscles and simple domestic affairs survived, but only as a demonstration experiment. If girls undertook individual practical work on it, they were led into 'unfruitful expenditure of time on calculations with those tiresome figures that are so liable to crop up instead of the round numbers one would wish for'. The suggestion that some study of evolution and of sex education should be implicit in the work on biology drew the comment from the SMA Sub-Committee that 'the evolution approach to the teaching of biology (even if it were universally approved – which is not the case) would be too difficult for Secondary Modern School children'.[105] The AWST representatives thought that by the fourth year of the course, the different interests of boys and girls had become so marked that, in a co-educational school, it was probably wise to teach them separately. This was in part a recognition that vocational concerns had become important: some of the more able girls in Secondary Modern Schools would proceed to Technical Colleges, or take courses run by the Electrical Association for Women; others would become nursery or hospital nurses. The foundation of scientific knowledge on which they could build was available in the SMA syllabus, provided it was modified in the ways indicated.

There is little evidence that these views on science for 'secondary modern' girls exerted much influence on the curriculum. Simultaneously with their publication the SMA was turning to a fundamental revision of science for grammar school boys. Later, AWST representation on the subject panels for biology, chemistry and physics was invited,[106] following the publication of the SMA's Policy Statement in 1957; and an AWST sub-committee of Miss E.L. Buckley, Miss M. Going, Miss C.P. Jones, Miss J.K. Raeburn, Miss D.M. Scott and Miss N.M. Whitworth was appointed to prepare a statement on the place of science in girls' grammar schools When this appeared in 1959 it contained no reference to General Science.[107] The syllabus in the first three years of secondary education was to include 'the main science subjects' (physics, chemistry and biology) but its detailed organization was left to individual schools to decide in the light of their circumstances. In the fourth and fifth years flexibility was essential; the curriculum for future specialists needed to be more extensive than that for others, but all was expressed in terms of the separate science subjects. The institutional constraints on science education in girls' secondary schools still exerted considerable influence; the 'normal interests of the average girl', scarcely any.

Post-war reconstruction

The events of war elevated science to a position of undisputed national importance. Nevertheless, at the first full meeting of the SMA following the outbreak of hostilities, at Rugby School in April 1942, Graham Savage, then Education Officer of the London County Council, warned of a danger. Come the peace, science in schools might be relegated to its former position, though its claims as 'the core of educational studies' would be even stronger then than in war-time. Savage indicated the need for 'a post-war policy'.[108]

By the autumn of that year a sub-committee had been established with membership representative of 'several types of school . . . also the administrative side'. Those involved were S.R. Humby (Winchester, chairman and convenor), C. Sladden (Eton), F. Fairbrother (Cedars School), A.W. Wellings (Leamington College), L.F. Ennever (Braintree County High School), L.C. Comber (Edmonton County School) and J.K. Elliot (late North Manchester High School). Their terms of reference required them to report on 'Science in Post-War Secondary Education, including (a) science in the pre-specialist stage, (b) the general education of science specialists, (c) the scientific education of non-science specialists'.[109] Given the imminent prospect of universal secondary education, the Association's perception of post-war priorities might be criticized as inappropriately narrow, with its prime focus on the sixth form. Certainly a message from an undelivered but published Presidential Address by Frederick Soddy

FRS in 1943, that with universal education everyone was now 'a potential ruler', hence 'Science for Rulers' was 'conterminous with Science for Everybody', did not seem to have been received.[110] As has been noted earlier, the SMA widened its membership to include teachers in secondary technical and secondary modern schools only slowly after 1944.

The sub-committee's report was published in *The School Science Review* as a draft document for comment by members.[111] So far as pre-School Certificate Science was concerned it appeared to endorse General Science as 'the policy of the SMA', set out in the two published reports of 1936 and 1938. Its interpretation of General Science was unusually liberal, however; any school teaching 'physics, chemistry and biology separately under different teachers', and including some geology and astronomy in geography lessons, was deemed to be offering General Science to its pupils. Where the committee broke new ground was in its extension of the idea of General Science to the sixth form. Here a course on 'the effects of science on modern life', with possibly some history and philosophy of science, was recommended as an antidote to narrow specialization for both arts and science sides.

The report had a mixed reception from the membership. C.L. Bryant's view, shared by others, was that everything that needed to be said about pre-School Certificate science was to be found in more elegant form in *The Teaching of General Science*.[112] Two other leading members took exception to references to Christianity in the report and the implication that education was concerned with the training of Christian men and women. In the view of H.P. Ramage and Dr H.F. Boulind, 'an Association of Science Masters would be going quite outside its proper province if it committed itself to an official policy of support for one particular religion'. An alternative version of the offending paragraphs was offered in which 'readers will find that there is no reference to Christianity'.[113] Yet another critic, Dr J.M. Fletcher, one of the SMA's industrial members, noted a lack of concrete suggestions, a failure to consider adequately curricula 'for the age period 11–15 . . . for grammar, modern and technical schools', and a neglect of the interests of girls.[114] Not surprisingly, the draft policy statement was taken little further and eventually abandoned. Its principal legacies were, first, a sub-committee established to consider and report on 'science for non-science specialists'[115] and, second, a 'Science and Religion Group' which, it was agreed, should be 'informal and unofficial', at least for the time being.[116]

Simultaneously, and independently, the AWST was also giving attention to post-war reconstruction. Its views were published in 1944 in a report entitled *Science in Post-Primary Education*,[117] remarkable for the way in which it anticipated the changed context of school science following the 1944 Education Act.

In many ways the AWST was better qualified than the SMA to tackle the problem of *Science for All* in the comprehensive secondary school. From the start its membership had been broadly based, including representatives from schools of many different kinds, in contrast to the relative homogeneity of the SMA. Indeed, within one type of school, the secondary grammar school for girls, there was a long-standing tradition of concern for girls of very different types, the 'capable girl of more practical bent', the 'dull girl', as well as the 'high intellectual type'. As the Association of Head Mistresses stated in its evidence to the Spens Committee, even where a girl did not display intellectual talents, she was often 'through character and grace, one whom the school would not willingly be without'. In any case, such girls were as likely as any others to become wives and mothers in whose hands the early education of the next generation would rest. It was the opinion of the headmistresses that 'To deny them the best is humanly degrading' and 'a short-sighted policy'.[118]

Drawing on its membership in secondary grammar schools, central schools, technical schools and training colleges, as well as the Central Council for Health Education, the AWST established a sub-committee of considerable experience to devise a science course appropriate for a post-war situation in which all children up to the age of sixteen would, sooner or later, be given a secondary school education. The chairman was Miss D. Bailey (head mistress, Queen Mary School, Lytham). Other members were Miss L.M. Budden (The Central School, Guildford); Miss A.V. Crawley (science mistress, Brondesbury and Kilburn High School, London); Miss F.R.M. Peecock (science mistress, Southampton Grammar School for Girls); Miss D.M. Sackett (head mistress, Day Technical School for Girls, Fort Pitt, Chatham); Miss P.M. Taylor (late science mistress, Southend-on-Sea High School for Girls and now Woman Education Officer, Central Council for Health Education); and Miss M.E. Truman (lecturer, The Training College, Salisbury).[119]

Having outlined the qualities needed by citizens in a free democracy, the committee concluded that 'a social general science course' revolving round 'the interests and capacity of the child' should be planned. It would be 'less academic than usual' and marked by an emphasis on the applications of science to everyday life. A 'common core' syllabus for pupils aged 11 to 13 in all kinds of secondary schools was required so that late transfers could take place without difficulty. An examination of syllabuses used in different kinds of school established that 'a common core' did in fact exist, though masked by 'very great divergencies in methods of presentation'. Its basic topics, as presented by the committee, were: I The universe and its attributes of light, heat and gravitation; II Water; III Air; IV Land; and V People.[120]

The proposals for subsequent years up to age sixteen were premised on the supposition that 'the yoke' of external examination would be thrown off in the future and schools entrusted with the conduct of their own internal tests. The reconstruction of the science syllabus for these years required contributions from scientists to ensure that adolescents became 'happy craftsmen in the widest possible sense'. All pupils, irrespective of school type, would take a general science course, the more intellectually and scientifically inclined supplementing this with studies in an additional branch of science.[121]

The detail of this AWST syllabus, interesting in its own right, is less important, in retrospect, than the intention that lay behind it. Though the case for a general science course reflecting 'the natural interests of the average girl' had apparently been abandoned at this stage, the common course for girls and boys which the AWST devised differed markedly from the SMA syllabus in General Science for boys. It demonstrated a grasp of the significance of institutional context, and specifically multilateralism, as a determinant of the school science curriculum which eluded the men for the next two decades. That educational events moved less slowly than anticipated by the women does not invalidate their proposals as a bold and imaginative attempt to solve a problem which the Secondary Science Curriculum Review was eventually established to tackle in 1981.[122]

General Science abandoned

Support for General Science as 'the Science of the main school' was reaffirmed in 1942 by the SMA in its evidence to the Norwood Committee enquiring into the curriculum and examinations of secondary schools. When it reported, the Norwood Committee commended General Science as a development of 'great promise', 'much to be encouraged'.[123] Shortly afterwards the SMA General Science Sub-committee was reconstituted as a standing committee, one of its first tasks being to review the existing syllabuses and reports published by the Association to see if revision was necessary. Apart from a strong feeling that the broad science training necessary for a teacher of general science was not being provided by universities, the main features of the SMA programme were judged sound.[124]

Three years later the committee returned to the question of revision. The structure of external school examinations was then being reviewed by the Secondary School Examinations Council which eventually recommended the replacement of the School Certificate examinations by the General Certificate of Education. Under the chairmanship of W.H. Reynolds from the previous team, a sub-committee of 'new men' was constituted to reshape General Science for the 1950s.[125] The membership comprised:

W. Ashhurst (Physics) Epsom College.
E.H. Coulson (Chemistry and Physics) Braintree County High School.
G.B. Hindle (Biology) King's Norton Grammar School.
E. Lucas (Biology) Winchester College.
D.H.J. Marchant (General Science and Biology) Ilford County High School.

E.W. Moore (General Science) Thorne Grammar School.
R. Thurlow (Physics) Leigh Grammar School.
E. Yerbury (Biology and Chemistry) Liverpool Collegiate School.
H.P. Young (Physics and Biology) Whitley Bay Grammar School.

A revision of the two syllabuses in *The Teaching of General Science* and the preparation of a schedule of practical work was undertaken, members of the sub-committee working in three subject panels representative of biology, chemistry and physics. Several who were to be active in the Ordinary Level subject panels which led to the Nuffield Foundation's Science Teaching Project a decade later served their apprenticeship in this way. When they reported to the main Committee in August 1949 it was revealed that they had attempted to develop a section on science in secondary modern schools but had abandoned this after 'a meeting with HMIs'.[126] With minor amendments their report was approved for publication, one novel feature being the inclusion of a detailed 'Basic Syllabus of Science for Non-Science Specialists'.[127] Two years later the sub-committee delivered an O level examination syllabus to accompany the teaching syllabus in the 1950 report, at which point it was deemed that it had 'completed the tasks assigned to it'.[128]

These words from the SMA *Report for 1952* were unintentionally prophetic. The changed educational context of the 1950s was one which did not encourage the further growth of general science as an examination subject. Its eclipse, relative to other science subjects over the decade, is well illustrated by the following figures for O level entries.[129]

	General Science	Biology	Chemistry	Physics
1951	21,672	29,014	20,677	21,548
1960	26,431	83,989	59,643	68,080

By the mid-50s a 'Cold War' climate had heightened concern about national shortages of scientists and technologists to an extent that allowed opponents of general science to attempt the *coup de grâce*. W.S. James, an Association member who had taught chemistry at Rossall School before moving to a post of lecturer in chemical education in the University of Bristol, used the columns of *The Times Educational Supplement* and *The New Scientist* to launch the attack. Her Majesty's Inspectorate, rather than the SMA, was his initial target because, in his view, they had 'almost to a man been plugging general science . . . in the schools'. A great industrial nation depended upon scientists, engineers and technicians, James asserted, and the shortage was now so grave that 'the rot which had attacked many schools over the last 20 years' had to be stopped. His remedy was 'specializing from the start' in grammar schools, i.e. teaching the three separate sciences. A second, anonymous article, though clearly from James's pen, cited the near unanimous opinion of chemistry teachers attending a refresher course at Bristol, that general science was an inadequate foundation for sixth-form chemistry. It was not in the national interest that such a state of affairs should continue.[130]

Not all those who responded to James's articles supported him, but he found an effective ally in another science education tutor, L. Connell (Leeds University), who deployed evidence of a different kind to attack the theoretical justifications for general science.[131] Joining forces, Connell and James then wrote a root and branch critique of general science which was published in *The School Science Review* in March 1958.[132] For them 'the fact that nearly all science teachers prefer to teach either physical or biological science, but not both' had to be accepted as axiomatic. It followed that any attempt to bring about an overdue improvement in the standards of school science teaching, an essential for 'the continued existence of this country as a leading scientific and industrial nation', necessitated as a first step, the abandonment of general science and its replacement by separate courses in the main sciences. Their argument was both cogent and timely, coinciding with movements for curriculum reform in the UK and USA. From across the Atlantic it drew a request from R.H. Carleton, Executive Secretary of the National Science Teachers' Association, for permission to reprint the article in the NSTA journal, *The Science Teacher*, because the issues discussed were 'so much in line with concerns . . . on science teaching in the USA'.[133]

Within the SMA Committee the article by Connell and James provoked an extended discussion on the Association's position on general science.[134] The recently published *Policy Statement* (1957) had avoided the term 'general science', describing instead 'a broadly based course of Natural Science (physics, chemistry, biology and, probably, astronomy) taught on a topic basis' in the first two years of the grammar school course. Beyond this, and up to O level, the reference was to separate physics, chemistry and biology, with their interdependence emphasized.[135] A suggestion from some SMA members that a referendum should be held to test opinion on general science was rejected by the Committee on grounds of expense and also because the SMA was said never to have advocated a single-subject general science approach as the only way of teaching science. Even so, it was thought desirable to publish 'some sort of disclaimer regarding the attitude sometimes attributed to the SMA in regard to General Science'.[136]

In his capacity as chairman of the SMA Committee, Charles Holt (Harrow Weald County Grammar School) then prepared a statement intended for publication in *The School Science Review*. The SMA, he reminded his readers, was not like 'a professional organization or Union', governed 'by clear-cut resolutions passed into effect by members' ballot, or at an Annual Business Meeting, so as to become . . . a *programme*'. Specifically, it never had been and was not now 'committed', as a matter of programme, either to general science as a single-subject or to any other royal road in science teaching. 'General Science' was best understood not as a label in the restricted single-subject sense, but as a concept of a well-integrated school course embracing all three of the main sciences, however they were taught. In these terms, the transformation in school science since the 1920s, especially in relation to physics for girls and biology for boys, owed much to the concept.[137]

This rationalization did less than justice to the complex ancestry of general science and appeared to adopt an even-handed approach to the single-subject general science and the three separate sciences. On the latter point, certainly, it ran counter to a strong current of opinion in the membership. E.W. Chanter (Blundells School), who earlier had written to the Committee urging a referendum on general science, now gave notice that he and D.N. Underwood (Malet Lambert High School, Hull) intended to move a resolution at the next Annual Business Meeting 'that this Association disapproves of the continued teaching of General Science as a substitute for the separate sciences'.[138] On receipt of his communication the Committee decided not to proceed further with their statement, which was never published. A technicality in the Association's rules necessitated the substitution of 'meeting' for 'Association' in the resolution, which was subjected to further amendments when it was put to the Annual Business Meeting on 1 January 1959. The final version, 'That this meeting disapproves of the teaching of General Science on an inadequate time allowance' was carried with few dissentients.[139]

This reduction of a militant resolution to blandness was indicative that 'the general science issue' had passed an apogee. The Association had already embarked on new activities of major importance and was redefining its priorities in different terms. Nevertheless, general science cast its long shadow on the curriculum developments which followed the Policy Statement of 1957. 'We know only too well how the phrase "General Science" has caused many science teachers to rise up in wrath, they being specialists in Physics only, Chemistry only, or Biology only,' H.P. Ramage wrote to B.E. Dawson (The Coopers' Company School) in 1960. 'We have therefore carefully avoided the use of that provocative term in everything we have published in our present "Science-and-Education" effort'.[140] But general science had been abandoned in name only. Driven underground in the late 1950s, it was to re-emerge as integrated or combined science, with undiminished capacity to divide the opinion of science teachers.

10 Curriculum control: the work of the Science and Education Committee

The post-war environment of school science teaching

As the second half of the twentieth century opened, the social context of science education was undergoing dramatic change.

Within the schools, the system of external examinations was converted in 1951 from a group to a single subject basis with the establishment of the General Certificate of Education, a step which failed to alleviate, if indeed it did not exacerbate, the main curriculum problem of the decade ahead, that of premature and narrow specialization. From 1956 until 1959 the Central Advisory Council for Education (England), under Sir Geoffrey Crowther, was engaged in an inquiry into the education of boys and girls between the ages of 15 and 18, reporting two months after C.P. Snow delivered his Rede Lecture on 'The Two Cultures'.[1] Exposing the bankruptcy of our common vocabulary, the Crowther Report was obliged to neologize, coining the term 'numeracy' for 'the mirror image of literacy'; much of its concern was directed to the achievement of balance in the curriculum of the enlarged and still expanding sixth forms.[2] In formulating its views, the Council heard evidence from members of the Science Masters' Association, particularly on the oppressive accumulation of factual knowledge in science syllabuses and on the type of science course which might profitably be offered to sixth-form arts specialists.

Outside the schools, political pressure was growing for change in the organizational and administrative framework of secondary education. Expressions of dissatisfaction with a selective system provoked forebodings about the demise of grammar schools,[3] and brought reassurances such as that of the Conservative Minister for Education, Sir David Eccles, to a joint meeting of the IAAM and AMA, that, 'My colleagues and I will never agree to the assassination of the grammar school'.[4] Yet the broad pattern of the future was clear. Estimating that more than 11 per cent of secondary schools would be 'all-ability' by 1965, the Crowther Report, in a prophetic understatement, predicted that 'the shape of the English school system in 1978 will differ from that of 1958 – perhaps almost as much as that of 1958 did from 1938'.[5] Before the end of 1964, Michael Stewart, Secretary of State for Education in the new Labour government, had promised a clear lead in the reorganization of secondary education on comprehensive lines. The following July, Circular 10/65 was issued, the government's signal of its firm intent to speed the end of selection at eleven plus and to eliminate separatism in secondary education.

Economic and military influences were at work also. Industrial demand for scientists and technologists increased greatly in the years following the end of the Second World War. The ad-hoc Barlow Committee on Scientific Manpower, appointed in December 1945 and reporting the following May, urged that the output of scientists from universities should be doubled 'at the earliest possible moment'.[6] In fact this target was achieved within five years, though further increase in numbers was slow and the mid 1950s were marked by repeated expressions of concern from both industry and the schools about the shortage of science graduates.

An improved supply of scientific manpower depended crucially on the size and staffing of science sixth forms. Recognition that all was not well in this area led the SMA and the AWST to undertake a joint fact-finding survey in 1953.[7] The results showed that whilst the size of sixth forms had increased markedly since 1939, during the same period the proportion of science teachers in the schools had decreased. In the 990 grammar schools responding to the inquiry, 115 science posts were unfilled, whilst nearly 1000 science teachers had left these schools in the previous ten years for other posts in industry or administration. The SMA/AWST Report was a harbinger of worse to come; by 1957 it was estimated that approximately one-seventh of all science posts in maintained grammar schools were either unfilled of filled unsatisfactorily.[8]

International comparisons, prompted not only by economic competition from abroad but also by the 'Cold War', underlined the gravity of the situation. 'If this country is to survive as a great Power,' Dr Willis Jackson stated in 1955, 'it will be through its achievements in science and technology.'[9] An early warning of the potential of science in the Soviet Union, in Eric Ashby's book *Scientists in Russia* (1947), was endorsed repeatedly throughout the early 1950s,[10] perhaps most substantially by a detailed statistical account of the organization and size of the Russian educational system in Nicholas DeWitt's *Soviet Professional Manpower* (1955). Reviewing this work, Professor Solly Zuckerman, chairman of the newly established Committee on Scientific Manpower,[11] likened the nations of the world to competitors in a race, vying to transform themselves scientifically because of their realization that science and technology 'form the foundations of economic and military power'. The lessons of the Second World War had been well learnt.

Within the legislature at home, leading members of the Parliamentary and Scientific Committee, such as Austen Albu in the House of Commons and Lord Glyn in the House of Lords,[12] pressed for greater resources for scientific and technological education, employing comparative evidence to demonstrate Britain's increasingly inferior position in relation to the USA, the USSR and Western Europe.

In November 1955 an important independent initiative was taken when a number of companies engaged in the chemical, electrical and mechanical engineering fields of industry established the Industrial Fund for the Advancement of Scientific Education in Schools. By 1963, when the Fund was wound up, a sum of almost £3.25 million had been allocated for the building and equipping of physical science laboratories in over 200 independent and direct grant secondary schools.[13] Though comparable developments were promised by the Minister of Education for the maintained sector, the necessary resources were slow to materialize, with the result that the independent schools, by virtue of their superior material provisions, were at this time much better positioned to recruit science teachers from the limited stock available.

In collaboration with the NUT and the Joint Four Secondary Associations, the SMA and the AWST conducted a further survey of conditions affecting science teaching in May 1957, this time focusing on laboratory accommodation, technical assistance and equipment.[14] Of 373 maintained grammar schools responding to the inquiry, only 44 per cent had laboratory accommodation which reached the standard of provision at that time laid down by the Ministry of Education; the more exacting standards set by the assessors of the Industrial Fund were satisfied by a single school. Yet, as Dr Henry Boulind, the chairman of the joint committee, pointed out, the number of scientists and technologists which the country required could only be supplied by the maintained grammar schools.[15] When the questionnaire was reissued two years later, though it revealed that 486 laboratories had been built in maintained schools in 1958–59, the percentage of those schools in which laboratory accommodation reached the Ministry's standards was virtually unchanged.[16]

Formidable though they were, increased demands on the productivity of school science education and on the quality of its output, in a situation of worsening, or at best static, resources, were by no means the only problems confronting science teachers in the mid 1950s. Their science disciplines, into which many of them had been initiated in the inter-war years, had undergone major transformations.[17] Publication of the exponential growth curves of scientific knowledge, with a steady doubling of the index of quantity every 15 years, was a feature of the 1950s,[18] but recognition of the rate of advance of science and of the speed and vigour of its application in industry and elsewhere, did not depend on quantitative studies in the science of science. As Sir Alexander Todd reminded his audience, when delivering the presidential address to the SMA in January 1957, the interval between Otto Hahn's laboratory observations on the fission of the uranium atom in 1939 and the supply of electrical power from Calder Hall in 1956 was a mere 17 years.[19] In 1960, under Todd's chairmanship, the Advisory Council on Scientific Policy cited approvingly the view that up to 25 per cent of the content of school syllabuses in biology, chemistry and physics could be removed without any harm.[20] The need to make room for new material such as 'modern physics' was one desideratum, but, more fundamentally, the organization and structure of the various sciences had altered with the advance of knowledge. Both external and internal influences marked the time as ripe for a major revaluation of the aims and methods of science teaching.

The origins of the Science and Education Sub-Committee

The United Nations Educational, Scientific and Cultural Organization (UNESCO) was established in November 1946 to contribute to peace and security by promoting collaboration among its Member States in the fields of education, science and culture. Towards the end of 1949, the General Committee of the SMA received a request from UNESCO for views on ways in which collaboration between associations of science teachers in different countries might be fostered.[21] At that stage the SMA had few official contacts with counterparts elsewhere, though some of its members were also members of the National Science Teachers' Association (USA), links existed with science teachers in France and Norway, and some 3 per cent of its membership taught in schools overseas.[22]

In its reply, the SMA General Committee drew attention to the NSTA suggestion that there should be 'an international drive' to introduce more science into education, an undertaking which would only be of value if informed by 'a better conception of the nature and scope of science than sometimes exists today'.[23] Rejecting arguments for the inclusion of technology in school science teaching and for a greater emphasis on the physical sciences, the case was made for science as a vital contributor to the general education of all children. The recently revised version of the SMA report on *The Teaching of General Science*, due to be published in 1950, the Association's Jubilee Year, was cited as an example of a course of the type needed.

In the years immediately following, cooperation between organizations of science teachers was promoted by UNESCO in a variety of ways; exchange of publications was encouraged; ideas on laboratory experiments and exhibits were elicited; and personal contacts between leading science teachers were facilitated by invitations to international meetings. When, in October 1956, the SMA General Committee considered a request from UNESCO to nominate a member to take part in a conference in Hamburg on Science Curricula in Primary and Secondary Schools, it was agreed that the Association's General Secretary, Dr Henry Boulind, should go.[24] An account of the Hamburg Conference, 22–27 October 1956, was published in *The School Science Review* and a brief verbal report was made by Boulind to the General Committee at its meeting in December 1956. Subsequently, and in the light of discussions which had taken place during the 54th Annual Meeting of the SMA, 2–5 January 1957, held in the University of Cambridge, Boulind prepared a more detailed *Memorandum on Science Syllabuses* incorporating suggestions about possible action which the Association might take.[25]

Two conclusions of central importance had emerged from the Hamburg conference. First, delegates from every country represented there had emphasized that all pupils, even those whose formal education ended at fifteen, should know something of the production, nature, uses and possibilities of atomic energy. The problems associated with this aim were recognized. With school apparatus then available, little if any experimental work was possible; furthermore, the subject lay outside the everyday experience of most pupils and, indeed, of most teachers of science. Yet, such was the importance of atomic energy for citizens of the future, there was consensus that some knowledge of the subject was essential.[26]

Second, when considering a possible physics syllabus for all pupils aged 15 to 18 in a less specialized context than the English science sixth form, the delegates recommended content which went beyond that of a typical physics syllabus in England; their proposals incorporated some study of the methods of science, of modern scientific concepts, of the history of science and of social and technical applications. In Boulind's words, 'Perhaps a large part of such a syllabus . . . will seem very similar to present A level syllabuses, but the aims are totally different, namely, education in science and through science, rather than the teaching of science'.

In considering what steps the SMA might take, Boulind's Memorandum argued for a major redefinition by the Association of the ends and means of school science education, followed by pressure on the centres of curriculum control in order to bring about the intended changes.

> Adequate scientific education is essential for the whole population, and certainly for the 20 per cent of pupils of 'grammar-school type' who will become 'men of affairs' in administration, industry, business, teaching and other professions. It may be that education will in the future be centred upon science just as it has been centred upon classics in the past. The Association should take action, first, by proposing new aims, methods and syllabuses that will extend and revitalize science teaching and, more than anything else, enable this country to take a leading place in the world of the future, and second, by persuading the Ministry and the Examining Boards to accept new syllabuses and new aims.[27]

At a well-attended meeting of the General Committee on 2 March 1957, the Memorandum was discussed, one member, Harold Tunley, reporting that views similar to those of Boulind had been expressed at a recent meeting of the Institute of Physics. It was clear that the task of school science teachers 'needed to be thought out afresh from first principles'. Accordingly a sub-committee was formed with terms of reference 'to inquire into the aims, scope and content of science teaching in grammar schools, with special reference to the part that science can play in general education'.[28] Its members were:

Dr H.F. Boulind (Physicist), Chairman and convenor, Lecturer, Department of Education, University of Cambridge.

H.F. Broad (Physicist), Headmaster, The Cedars School, Leighton Buzzard.

E.H. Coulson (Chemist), Braintree County High School, Essex.

W.H. Dowdeswell (Biologist), The College, Winchester.

E.W. Moore (Chemist), Boys' Grammar School, King's Norton, Birmingham.

H.P. Ramage (Biologist), Gresham's School, Holt.

H. Tunley (Physicist), Merchant Taylors' School, Great Crosby, Liverpool.

With the exception of Dowdeswell all were, or had been, members of the SMA General Committee; several were officers. In anticipation of the heavy burden of work ahead, Boulind relinquished the post of General Secretary, Broad taking over these duties.

The historic first meeting of this Science Teaching Sub-Committee, soon to be renamed the Science and Education Sub-Committee, was held over two days, 23 and 24 April 1957, in the Department of Education at Cambridge. So was inaugurated the train of events leading to the Nuffield Foundation Science Teaching Project five years later.

A policy for grammar school science

According to *The Shorter Oxford English Dictionary*, policy is 'a course of action adopted and pursued'. In this sense, it might be said that the curriculum policy of the SMA during the inter-war years, and beyond, was one of advocating General Science. Thus, in response to a question from the Norwood Committee in 1942, 'Is General Science to be adopted as the Science of the main school?' the SMA replied, 'Assuming that General Science means a broad course comprising at least Physics, Chemistry and Biology, and perhaps also Astronomy and Geology, then it *should* be adopted as the science of the main school.'[29] A year later, a draft report intended as the basis for a general policy for the Association asserted that, 'For the pre-School Certificate course in secondary schools the policy of the Science Masters' Association is General Science as set out in the two reports, *The Teaching of General Science*, . . . 1936 and 1938'.[30] By this stage, however, the government's White Paper on Educational Reconstruction, foreshadowing the 1944 Education Act, had made it clear that the time was inopportune for crystallization of a position on the teaching of science in secondary schools and further work on the draft report was postponed.

In the spring of 1949 a new, 'exploratory' sub-committee was established, not to produce a policy statement, but to clarify what was implied for the Association by enunciation of a policy, and to examine ways and means of formulating one.[31] The changed conditions of the post-war years had made General Science a less acceptable candidate for support and its relative popularity as a School Certificate examination subject had already begun to decline.[32] Although the SMA sub-committee on General Science in 1950 affirmed the soundness of the principles underlying the earlier reports of 1936 and 1938, it was clear that retention of General Science as a central plank in the Association's educational policy would be out of tune with the times and with the views of many members. No record of a report from the 'exploratory' sub-committee has been traced,[33] but its terms of reference indicate a concern with the problem of establishing a policy which was representative of opinion amongst the rapidly growing membership, over 4000 in number by 1950, an increasing percentage coming from secondary modern and secondary technical schools.[34]

The members of the Science and Education Sub-Committee began their work, therefore, with little to constrain them from earlier policy considerations. Indeed, their purpose was altogether more ambitious than anything the Association had attempted previously. It was nothing less than to redefine fundamentally school science education, making it appropriate to the changed context of the mid-twentieth century, and having formulated new aims and syllabuses, to secure their widespread adoption by the exercise of persuasion and influence.

As a first step in this process, following Boulind's report on the initial meeting of his sub-committee, the General Committee decided to draw up and publish a draft statement of Association policy on secondary school science.[35] The groundwork for this had already been completed by the Science and Education Sub-Committee at its two-day meeting in Cambridge, 23–24 April 1957, and the statement was quickly produced. At the General Committee's October meeting it was adopted on a vote, with two members opposing.[36] Copies were printed and distributed to all SMA and AWST members with the November 1957 issue of *The School Science Review*. Additionally, copies were sent to the Ministry of Education, science departments of universities, the Royal Society, the British Association, the Headmasters' Conference, the Joint Four Secondary School Associations, and all LEA Education Officers and the headmasters of grammar schools.

At the heart of the 1957 Policy Statement was the proposition that science should be a 'core' subject in the grammar school curriculum, alongside English and Mathematics. A common course of science for all pupils up to the statutory school leaving age of fifteen was recommended, this being planned in two stages. After an introductory phase of two years, during which a broadly based course of natural science was to be taught on a topic basis, there followed a three-year intermediate phase leading up to GCE Ordinary level. The work in this latter period was to be composed of 'physics, chemistry and biology', the expectation being that the more able pupils, at least, would be examined in each of these 'three main branches of science'. By the end of this stage, the last period for formal instruction for many, pupils should have acquired some appreciation of the methods of science and of 'the scientific attitude', being able 'to comprehend science as a major manifestation of the human spirit'.[37]

With Professor N.F. Mott's future 'men of affairs' very much in mind, the Advanced Phase, covering the sixth-form or 'pre-university years', was characterized by dual provision. First, all sixth-formers, irrespective of chosen specialist subjects, were to follow 'a broadly based course embracing the history and philosophy of science, its present-day social and technological consequences and its future possibilities'. Work under this heading was to be subject to examination, first as part of General Papers, and also as an optional subject at A level. It was envisaged that in time, the examination would become compulsory. Second, the existing pattern of specialized studies involving A level science subjects was endorsed, subject to reduction in the width of the factual knowledge required.[38]

Public reaction to the Policy Statement was favourable, though its applicability to schools in Scotland and Northern Ireland was questioned and the AWST produced an alternative statement in 1959, reflective of the problems faced by those who taught in girls' schools.[39] Whilst endorsing much in the SMA document, the AWST preferred an introductory common course of three years' duration followed in years four and five by a variety of schemes constructed according to the interests and intentions of the girls. Again, at sixth-form level, though strongly supporting the need to reduce factual content in A level science syllabuses, the AWST recommendations differed from those of the SMA. Separate provision was thought appropriate for the Arts specialists, in contrast to a common cultural course for all sixth-form boys. Furthermore, the existence in the sixth-forms of many girls' schools of those who would not be following a full A level course, necessitated the provision of 'less academic General courses which may lead to Ordinary Level examinations'.[40]

In the month of its publication the SMA Policy Statement served a timely function when the Association was invited to send a delegation for an informal discussion with Mr Geoffrey Lloyd, the Minister of Education and members of his staff. Six members[41] met the Minister, the first occasion on which the Association had been so consulted; and the opportunity was taken to explain the main themes of the Policy Statement and to elaborate views on the revision of content necessary in A level science syllabuses.

During the following year, some 15,000 copies of the Policy

Statement were distributed. Comments were received from branches and individual members of the SMA; further discussions with Her Majesty's Inspectorate took place at the Annual Meeting in Leeds, January 1958; members of the Science and Education Committee gave evidence before the Crowther Committee in May 1958, particular points of discussion being the time allowance needed for three science subjects up to O level and the content of the proposed non-specialist sixth-form courses in science; and a delegation of SMA members met representatives of the Secondary School Examinations Council for exploratory talks on the possibility of reducing the factual content of A level science syllabuses. As Boulind reported, *Science and Education* had been very widely read and approved, press notices with one exception (*The Teachers' World*) being uniformly good. As a result, knowledge of the Association and of its work was greatly increased in many influential quarters.[42]

The main effort of the Science and Education Committee was directed now towards implementation of its recommendations, though revision of the Policy Statement continued alongside, with the object of achieving a version acceptable to both the SMA and the AWST. When this appeared in 1961[43] it was described as 'mainly concerning grammar schools', though its more general aspects were said to be applicable to all secondary schools. The introductory and intermediate phases were no longer so precisely defined in terms of years, in order to accommodate the variations in patterns of science teaching in girls' schools and also in secondary schools in Scotland. The SMA recommendation that *all* sixth-formers should study some science was unchanged, but the requirement that all pupils should follow the *same* course up to the end of the fifth-form year was now modified to one involving 'a balanced course of science subjects'. In a new introductory section of the Statement, the relationship between science and technology and the rôle of technology as an intermediary in the influence of science on society were commented upon, though the 'deeper ways' in which science affected people were said to be through the new insights and conceptions which it provided. Finally, the timetable implications of the recommendations for the first five years of secondary education were analysed in an appendix, the result being the need for more time than most schools then allocated. Bearing in mind the importance which society was currently placing on the supply of scientists and technologists, the moment could scarcely have been more propitious for staking a claim for increased time for science. The intractable nature of school curriculum forces had been underestimated, however, and this was one aspect of the Associations' policy on which little progress was to be made in the years ahead.

Looking back on the work of the SMA and AWST in this period, the production of a Policy Statement can be seen as a step of major significance in the associations' attempt to acquire recognition as the authoritative voice on the theory and practice of school science.

Social, economic and technical changes, as well as other factors, were forcing the pace of educational adaptation to an entirely unprecedented extent when the Science and Education Sub-Committee was called into being. Writing in 1963 about the need for a national body which could stimulate and coordinate school curriculum developments in such a situation, Derek Morrell, one of the main architects of the Ministry of Education's Curriculum Study Group (1962) and a future secretary of the Schools Council (1964), diagnosed 'a vacuum in curriculum matters' created by a long tradition of *laissez-faire* in this field.[44] So far as school science education was concerned, the events of the late 1950s and early 1960s can be interpreted as a positive and responsible effort to fill this vacuum by the two professional associations of science teachers.

Blue prints for the future

Four years of intense activity followed the publication of the 1957 Policy Statement, the recommendations in which raised formidable problems of syllabus construction, of teaching methods, of suitable training for science teachers and of examination design.

It was to syllabuses that the Association turned first, setting up panels in November 1957 for each of biology, chemistry and physics, a 'fourth panel' being established in January 1958 with responsibility for the innovatory course of science in sixth-form general education. Each panel was under the chairmanship of a member of the Science and Education Committee (H.P. Ramage – 'Biology' and 'Science in Sixth Form General Education'; E.W. Moore and, after July 1961, E.H. Coulson – 'Chemistry'; H. Tunley – 'Physics'). From the first, members of the AWST served on the panels. Meetings were held regularly, usually on Saturdays, the Chemistry panel, for example, convening nine times in the two-year period 1958–59, often in the Great Northern Hotel, King's Cross, to facilitate travel arrangements for its members. Between meetings, much work was done by correspondence, although not until the acquisition of a permanent headquarters in 1960 was clerical assistance available from the Association to support the panels.

Progress was most rapid in biology, the panel of six having a syllabus in draft form and ready for comment by the end of 1958. The work of the chemists, involving a complete reappraisal of the teaching of chemical theory in the O level course, entailed consultation with the physicists about the development of ideas on atomic structure. Furthermore, the panel having decided that one criterion for the inclusion of factual content was its relation to processes of everyday or industrial importance, the new O level syllabus incorporated more organic chemistry than had been customary hitherto.[45] By November 1959, however, a draft of both O and A level chemistry syllabuses was ready for the printer.

Although the need for reform in physics was perhaps most obvious, and to a considerable extent had initiated the work of the Science and Education Committee, the physics panel did not hold its first meeting until the end of 1958. Nevertheless, a draft O level scheme was completed in time for distribution the following December, the companion A level syllabus following later. 'Physics for All', not 'Physics for the Future Specialist', was claimed to be the hallmark of the O level syllabus which incorporated a substantial section on Atomic Structure and Nuclear Energy not previously included in work at this level.[46]

The draft syllabuses were discussed at the Annual Meeting of the SMA on 1 January 1960 at Southampton and by March of that year the Association was able to report that 518 copies of the biology syllabus, 715 of the chemistry syllabus and 742 of the physics syllabus had been distributed to members.[47] In the light of comments received, emendation of the drafts continued during 1960 with a view to publication at the end of the year, the revised Policy Statement and the three panel reports comprising Part I of the Science and Education Committee's blueprint for revitalized science teaching.

The 'Fourth Panel', meanwhile, was also preparing a report though clearly the content of a general course of science for all sixth-formers was bound to be influenced by the foundation of work laid in the first five years of secondary education. Hence, the main effort of the 'fourth panel' had to wait the formulation of views by the other panels in December 1959. Exploratory meetings were held before this date, however, the first of which, convened by Boulind in January 1958, involved not only future panel members, but also university specialists in the history and philosophy of science and others interested in the possibility of establishing a Science Greats course at Cambridge.[48] In the words of W.H. Dowdeswell, recorder for this inaugural meeting, 'The discussion covered a wide range of topics and ideas, veering so rapidly in different directions that it is difficult to compile anything which remotely resembles a chronological record of proceedings.'

The proposal to 'teach about science' as distinct from 'teaching science' was, according to Boulind, a comparatively new thing in English education'[49] and Recommendation 2 of the 1957 Policy Statement had attracted the attention of a number of universities, especially Leeds and Oxford from each of which came offers to collaborate with the SMA in the provision of in-service courses for sixth-form teachers.[50] Eventually a draft report from the Fourth Panel was printed and made available for comment in 1961–2, a substantially revised version being published in 1963 as a section of Part II of the Science and Education Report.

In the three years following the publication of the 1957 Policy Statement the panel activities threw up many problems. In connection with the syllabuses a major area of difficulty was the teaching approach for atomic structure and nuclear energy. A small number of innovative science masters such as J.L. Lewis (Malvern College), a member of the physics panel, had begun the task of developing courses with experimental work by pupils, often in the context of sixth-form general studies. In the spring of 1961 Lewis visited schools in Germany and the USSR bringing back information about the emphasis placed on atomic and nuclear physics, the impressive demonstration apparatus available from firms such as Leybold and Phywe, and the substantial funds allocated to schools of all types (e.g. approximately £2 million from the Federal Ministry of Atomic Energy) for the purchase of equipment for teaching modern physics.[51]

As far back as 1945, following a lecture at the Oxford Annual Meeting by Dr Grove of the Radiochemical Centre, Amersham, the SMA had established a sub-committee to devise experiments involving radioactive isotopes.[52] Under the chairmanship of W.G. Rhodes, this group had done sound work although the tendency was to view the experiments as suitable only to the upper levels of science teaching because 'the introduction of techniques based upon theoretical concepts that are not understood is of doubtful value'. In contrast to the German schools which Lewis had visited, there were virtually no neutron sources in British schools. Stringent conditions laid down by the Radiological Protection Service governed the use of radiation sources in schools.[53] The general position, as reported by Rhodes to the General Committee in June 1959, appeared to be that those who had drawn up the Ministry of Education pamphlet on the use of radioactive substances in schools were looking to the SMA for guidance on future possibilities.[54] In effect, the question of use of radioactive materials was then referred to the three subject panels and the work of the radioactive substances sub-committee allowed to lapse.[55] When Rhodes resigned from the chairmanship some short time later, the way was open to adopt a proposal from the physics panel that J.L. Lewis should act as convenor of a new sub-committee on the use of atomic and nuclear science in the teaching of physics and chemistry.[56] On Lewis's suggestion the committee's title was broadened to become the Sub-Committee on the Teaching of Modern Physical Science with terms of reference 'To devise experimental work necessary for the teaching of modern physical science and to suggest suitable courses'.[57] The activities of this committee were to play an important part in the Studley experiment, a pilot scheme involving some 30 schools in the examination of a modern physics course at O level, and later in the Nuffield Foundation Physics Teaching Project.

The Studley experiment was so called because of its origin in discussions at Studley College, Warwickshire, between members of the AWST and SMA chemistry and physics panels, on the one hand, and the Science Panel of the Secondary School Examinations Council and members of HM Inspectorate, on the other. The formal position was that the Secondary School Examinations Council was required to approve the new syllabuses before they could be implemented. The

Studley Conference was significant in a number of ways. It obliged the Associations to produce their stoutest defence of the syllabuses in the face of a powerful challenge from Dr R.A.R. Tricker, Staff Inspector for Science, that the teaching of modern atomic theory could not be based on convincing experimental evidence at GCE O level and would degenerate into the transmission of dogma. It brought about the Studley experiment as a controlled trial of the new physics course and it led to closer collaboration between the Associations and the Inspectorate, not only in the monitoring of the experiment but also in the work of apparatus development undertaken by Lewis's modern physical science committee.

A second problem arising from the work of the panels and one which had became particularly pressing by the autumn of 1960 was how best to accelerate the production of supporting materials for the syllabuses, especially teachers' guides. Change in the practice of science teaching was unlikely to follow publication of the syllabuses unless guidance on teaching methods and on the training of teachers was available in some considerable detail. A concerted attack on this was necessary if momentum was not to be lost; the cottage industry and part-time approach which had characterized activity so far was too slow. What was needed, Boulind argued to the General Committee in November 1960, was an unbroken period where all concerned might meet to address themselves to the issues, uninterrupted by the daily routine of their professional lives. A week at Barrow Court, an old manor close to Bristol, during August or September of the following year was suggested as a possibility.[58]

Such a proposal, though modest in comparison with the summer schools Boulind had visited in the USA the previous summer, nevertheless had major financial implications. When to this was added the cost of publishing Part I of the Science and Education Report, it was clear that the Association had begun to increase the scale of its activities beyond anything that could be financed from the revenue then available to it. It was agreed that an approach should be made to the Gulbenkian Foundation for a grant of £5000 to assist towards the production, printing and publication of Part I and Part II of the Report. As E.W. Tapper remarked to his colleagues on the General Committee, this was the first occasion in its history on which the Association had sought outside financial assistance.[59]

Barrow Court

1961 was a year of signal importance for the SMA and AWST. It saw the official opening of a headquarters building for the SMA at Cambridge, the appointment of a full-time, salaried General Secretary, E.W. Tapper, and the first formal steps towards unification of the two associations. It was also the year in which proposals were formulated for the implementation on a national scale of the new science teaching schemes.

For the Science and Education Committee, the conference at Barrow Court, 28 August – 2 September 1961, proved to be a watershed.[60] At a meeting of the 'Planning Committee' held on the first evening, it was explained by Boulind that the SMA was not able to finance much more than the publication of the Policy Statement and the three subject syllabuses. Beyond that there were no cut-and-dried plans; indeed a main purpose of the conference was to explore how best to carry matters forward. With this end in mind, the Science and Education Committee, now augmented by four members from the AWST (Miss B.G. Ashton, Miss F.M. Eastwood, Miss M. Going and Miss J.D. Ling) and by two additional SMA members (J.L. Lewis and E.W. Tapper), had invited representatives from the Ministry of Education, the Royal Institute of Chemistry and the Institute of Physics to join them.[61] These, together with selected members of the various panels established by the Committee, made up the thirty-three persons who came together in 'weather ideal' and surroundings which 'were perfect' to assess progress and explore options for the future.

In terms of subject interests, the membership of the conference was anything but balanced; almost all the physics and modern physical science panel members attended, with a high proportion of the chemistry panel, but only one representative on the biology panel, W.H. Dowdeswell. H.P. Ramage, chairman of the biology panel and of the panel reporting on science in sixth-form general education, was absent, though new names drawn from those on the panel for 'The Introductory Phase', established in January 1961, were included. The object of this group, under the chairmanship of E.W. Tapper (and later B.E. Dawson), was to produce 'an example of an integrated scheme' drawing upon the reports of the three subject panels.[62]

Discussion in the Planning Committee revealed widespread agreement that financial help should be sought, possibly from government, in order to produce teachers' guides, to provide in-service courses for teachers, and to establish a centre or research institute where apparatus could be developed and teaching techniques evaluated.[63] There was evidence of ample goodwill from the Royal Institute of Chemistry and the Institute of Physics, the representatives present, D.G. Chisman and N. Clarke, both offering practical assistance. J.L. Lewis reported on the activities of the Scientific Instrument Manufacturers' Association in the field of apparatus development and on the support received for the idea of a research institute, when broached with Professor Mott of Cambridge. Such an institute would need a full-time Director, adequate laboratories and technical assistants, with science teachers being seconded to it on a regular basis. Churchill College, Cambridge, had been mentioned as a possible location and Chisman made the tempting suggestion that members of the panels should be the first to enjoy a sabbatical year there. More realistically, on the grounds that many teachers would not wish to relinquish their classes for this length of time, part-time secondments were also considered.

At the end of the day L.R.B. Elton made a definite proposal that money should be sought for the objectives which had been under discussion. This was agreed, a triple approach from the SMA/AWST, the Institute of Physics and the Royal Institute of Chemistry being regarded as the best strategy for success. The SMA and the AWST had been successful in securing grants in aid of previous activities, the Gulbenkian Foundation having assisted with the cost of publishing reports and Esso Petroleum Company contributing to the costs of the Barrow Court conference. Possible sources of additional grant were mentioned, including the Nuffield Foundation, the Leverhulme Trust and ICI.

The four days which followed were devoted largely to discussion of teaching methods following reports from the panels on the Introductory Phase, the teaching of Modern Physical Science and the training of graduate science teachers. Priorities for further work by the separate subject panels were established. There was also a discussion on the important subject of the present system of GCE examinations in chemistry and physics. Introducing this, E.H. Coulson contrasted the GCE arrangements with which schools were familiar with those used for the award of Ordinary and Higher National Certificates in Technical Colleges. The possibility of adapting the National Certificate scheme for use in schools was raised, with a view to achieving a teacher-based examination. It was agreed that a special sub-committee be set up to consider this, the members being Miss Eastwood, Chisman, Coulson (Chairman) and Tapper. The draft report of this sub-committee was finally submitted to the General Committee at its meeting in November 1961.[64]

When the Science and Education Committee met again at the end of the week, panel chairmen reported that, though much had been achieved, there seemed little prospect that the work which lay ahead could be accomplished on the basis of the customary Saturday meetings. The situation in biology, especially, was commented on, other bodies such as the Institute of Biology, the Nature Conservancy Board, as well as the University of Keele, being increasingly active in this field. It was Dowdeswell's opinion that the original biology syllabus 'needed breaking down and each section examined in the light of modern approaches to the study of the subject.' If the SMA and the AWST did not take a lead in this matter, and in the preparation of guides for teachers, some other body would.[65]

As to future action, informal approaches to learned societies and professional scientific organizations had revealed that the SMA and AWST were regarded as the most suitable bodies to put forward proposals for the implementation of the new syllabuses. 'The two Associations had initiated the venture and their knowledge and experience must be used to see it through'.[66] It was agreed that Boulind should seek a meeting with Sir Alexander Todd, Chairman of the Advisory Council on Scientific Policy with a view to enlisting the Council's aid in securing:

(a) The conditions (adequate finance, seconding of teachers, secretarial assistance, office and laboratory accommodation, etc.) necessary to enable the Panels to finish their work and to publish their conclusions.

(b) The organization of a comprehensive and large scale programme of teachers' courses to implement the work of the Panels.

(c) The establishment, as a long-term project, of a permanent Institute to guide future developments and to undertake research into matters which affect science teaching.[67]

Beyond this, the important matter of examination reform was taken forward by a decision of the General Committee that the draft report of Coulson's Sub-committee should be sent to all branches of the Association for comment.[68] A final point related to the Introductory Phase. Two schemes had been outlined in the Interim report presented at Barrow Court. After discussion the panel was instructed to prepare a third scheme with a more physical bias and with preparatory schools in mind.[69] This postscript to the long week's deliberations was a reminder that independent schools were disproportionately represented at the Conference; of nine boys' schools with science masters present, six had been beneficiaries of the Industrial Fund.

The Association and the Foundation

Immediately on returning from Bristol, Boulind wrote to Sir Alexander Todd at the Chemical Laboratories, Cambridge and a meeting was arranged for 26 September.[70] Previous studies of the background to Nuffield Science have located the first suggestion that the Nuffield Foundation be approached for funds as coming from Sir Alexander Todd to E.H. Coulson and D.G. Chisman, *en passant*, at the official opening of the new headquarters of the SMA in Cambridge on 30 September.[71] Possibly the idea was relayed on separate occasions both to Boulind and to Coulson and Chisman. Be that as it may; on 2 October Boulind wrote formally to R.A. Becher, an Assistant Director of the Nuffield Foundation, presuming that Todd in his capacity as a trustee of the Foundation would have already spoken with Becher seeking an urgent meeting. His letter was accompanied by the revised Policy Statement, the syllabuses of the three subject panels and the report on the Barrow Court conference.

The response was immediate and positive. On 9 October Boulind travelled to Nuffield Lodge where he outlined the SMA/AWST objectives to the Director, Dr L. Farrer-Brown and R.A. Becher. The outcome was a request from the Foundation for a formal proposal, setting out the needs and the means necessary for their satisfaction.

There followed a month of intense activity. By 12 October the first draft of a document headed *SMA/AWST School Science Project:*

Grammar-Type Schools, prepared by Boulind, had been sent to Coulson and Elton, representing the chemistry and physics panels, and to Tapper, as secretary of the Science and Education Committee. On 27 October an amended second draft was despatched to all members of the Committee, as well as to Chisman and Clarke.[72] By 15 November, Boulind was able to report to Becher that the proposals were in their final stages and likely to reach the Foundation after they had been seen by the SMA General Committee at its meeting on 25 November. In fact, at Becher's request, advance copies of the proposals were sent before this date, followed by further copies when the General Committee had given approval in principle. The paper was received in time for circulation to the trustees of the Nuffield Foundation before their meeting on 8 December 1961.

As has been described elsewhere, the Nuffield Foundation's interest in educational innovation had been kindled well before this approach from the SMA and the AWST.[73] In the early 1960s a number of independent requests had been made to the Foundation for help in connection with the reform of science teaching, some being concerned with separate disciplines, others with the teaching of science as a core subject in primary as well as secondary schools. The position in the autumn of 1961, summarized at an informal meeting between J.L. Lewis, N. Clarke, Farrer-Brown and Becher, was that should realistic and coordinated proposals be received, the Foundation might be 'closely interested and prepared to come in with large scale support.'[74] At that stage it seemed possible that an approach might be forthcoming from the newly-established National Committee on Physics Education, of which Professor N.F. Mott was chairman, Clarke, secretary, and Lewis a member.

At the meeting of the Foundation's trustees on 8 December 1961, two papers prepared by Farrer-Brown were the subject of discussion, in addition to the SMA/AWST application. The first document raised issues of general policy, suggesting that support of research and experiment in education should become a central feature of the Foundation's programme.[75] The second, entitled 'The teaching of science and mathematics', took matters further by exploring the strategy and tactics of intervention in the designated subjects. It was proposed that support up to £250,000 might not be excessive for a project of 'urgency and importance' in the field of science. Whilst the overall goal should be school science at every level, the proximate objective should be the reform of O level courses in biology, chemistry and physics, with physics the 'spearhead of the campaign'.[76] Subject to further consultations, particularly with the Ministry of Education, the trustees agreed that the Foundation should extend its support to schemes for the advancement of education in schools, and, more specifically, that it should move ahead itself with plans for a major project in the field of science teaching.

On 11 December, Becher informed Boulind that the trustees had found the SMA/AWST memorandum 'a valuable starting point for discussion'. Further time was needed to look into the scheme in more detail, however. This 'holding letter', acknowledged by Becher later as characterized by 'somewhat cryptic and oblique wording', drew from Boulind a request for clarification. 'I take it', he wrote on 14 December, 'that while the Foundation would not wish to commit itself until something more concrete has been worked out, yet there is every intention of seeing the project through. I shall not, therefore, take any immediate steps towards seeking finance from other sources.' A consortium of industrial organizations, a new Industrial Fund, was then mentioned as a possible alternative to Nuffield. In conclusion, Boulind emphasized that the SMA and AWST, though the initiators of the proposal, in no sense expected to be the grantee if the Foundation decided to provide funds. 'I do not envisage that the Associations could or should run it', he stated. 'It would be a Nuffield undertaking, presumably overseen by a Nuffield Steering Committee on which the Associations might be represented.' This was not a view shared by all SMA members. Replying, Becher confirmed that there was every intention 'of seeing the science teaching project through'. As to the steering committee, it would be chosen by the Foundation, though 'it would be very surprising if no members of the Associations were given a place' on it.

On 22 January 1962, Becher again wrote to Boulind informing him that the trustees had given approval to a concrete scheme for O level physics teaching as the first part of a comprehensive project for the teaching of science as a whole. Details could not be announced until the organizer of the physics teaching project had been appointed and the membership of the advisory committee agreed, but the SMA would be kept fully informed. Informal lines of communication were undoubtedly active over the next month, but by the date of the meeting of the Science and Education Committee on 17 February, no official news had been received. 'Most of what we know or surmise', Boulind wrote complainingly to Becher on 19 February, 'has come from casual conversations with other people who have greater knowledge of what the Foundation is doing.' 'The complete lack of consultation between the Foundation and our Associations, especially over such an important matter as the organizer of the physics teaching project' was a matter of considerable concern. Outlining the contributions which the Associations had already made to the development of new syllabuses, the revision of examinations and the devising of suitable experiments for new work, all of which had 'the general support and sympathy of the Minister and Ministry', Boulind emphasized the wide backing which the Associations' work had received throughout the country. 'What we now fear', he continued, 'is that you have in mind some scheme which is quite separate from anything we have proposed . . . What we do *not* want, and would strongly oppose, is "physics for the future honours physicist".' In the Associations' view, 'Physics for the educated citizen' was the requirement for the O level stage, and 'physics for the future *scientist*' (not necessarily a physicist) for any later A level work.

A confidential and conciliatory reply from Becher came by return. The long delay had been due to the extensive consultations in which the Foundation had felt obliged to engage. 'There were so many other bodies besides yourselves whose interests had to be taken into account.' The support of Professor Mott's National Committee on Physics Teaching had to be ensured, as well as that of the Scottish Advisory Committee on Physics Teaching. The backing of the Ministry of Education was also essential. 'Their initial attitude was to some extent hostile', but after 'a series of somewhat arduous discussions . . . they are now fully satisfied about the merits of the approach we propose to adopt'. Reassurances were offered that the prime concern was still 'physics for the educated citizen' and that 'it was no part of our trustees' intention to carry out this work in the absence of close collaboration with the SMA and the AWST.' Finally, for Boulind's eyes only, the name of the organizer whose services were being sought was divulged, Donald McGill, HMI, of the Scottish Education Department.[77]

McGill's release from the SED was not achieved until 1 May 1962, but, in time for the next meeting of the Science and Education Committee on 3 March, Becher provided Boulind with 'a very encouraging piece of news that we only got yesterday.' Professor Nevill Mott FRS had agreed to act as chairman of the Consultative Committee to the Physics 11–15 Project. On 10 March, Boulind was able to respond that the SMA General Committee was very pleased to hear what he was able to tell them and satisfaction was expressed with the interim report.

The details of the Nuffield Foundation Science Teaching Project were first publicly announced in the House of Commons in April 1962 by the then Minister of Education, Sir David Eccles. When the Physics 11–15 Project[78] officially commenced on 1 May 1962 the membership of the Consultative Committee included

Dr C.W.W. Read, Chief Education Officer, West Sussex, a member of the SMA since 1932

J.L. Lewis, Malvern College, Chairman of the SMA's Modern Physical Sciences Committee

Sister St Joan of Arc, La Retraite High School, Bristol, a member of the AWST

W.K. Mace, King Edward VII School, Sheffield, a member of the SMA since 1951.

The work of the project was organized on a regional basis with team leaders, all of whom were SMA or AWST members, including E.J. Wenham and M.J. Elwell (Birmingham), Sister St Joan of Arc (Bristol), Dr H.F. Boulind (Cambridge), Dr J. Goodier and J.M. Osborne (London), J.L. Lewis and D. Chaundy (Malvern), R. Stone and G.E. Foxcroft (Manchester), R.D. Harrison (Northumbria), W.

Ritchie and J.T. Jardine (Scotland) and D. Layton (Yorkshire).

The Foundation's Chemistry 11–15 Project followed, commencing on 15 September 1962. H.F. Halliwell, a member of the Chemistry Panel, was appointed Organizer, with E.H. Coulson and D.G. Chisman serving on the Consultative Committee. Coulson was also seconded to work on the project as Deputy Organizer and subsequently (1965) as Organizer of the Advanced Chemistry Project.

The situation in biology was less straightforward. *Biology for Grammar Schools* had been the subject of critical comment and it was the Foundation's view that of the three syllabuses produced by the SMA, 'the biology proposals were by far the least satisfactory and are, perhaps, best forgotten'.[79] Though not referring specifically to the SMA schemes, in the opinion of J.W.L. Beament, Professor of Zoology at Cambridge, 'The elder half of our schoolmasters were trained in the attitude of the nineteenth century towards biology' and 'it would mean disaster for the future of biology if schoolmasters with such an outlook were allowed for any reason – political or otherwise – to have a determining power over the school curriculum'.[80]

Recognition of deficiencies in their biology proposals led the Science and Education Committee to propose a new panel on 'The Teaching of Modern Biological Science', which was established in March 1962. Its terms of reference were 'To select themes from the report *Biology for Grammar Schools* and to develop them in such a way as to help teachers to present them scientifically, in harmony with modern biological procedures and thought'. W.H. Dowdeswell was asked to be chairman.[81] In fact the work of the panel was overtaken by events. In its efforts to ensure that biology should not lag behind physics and chemistry, the Nuffield Foundation convened a meeting on 2 May 1962 attended by Professors Waddington, Pringle and Valentine, Dr J. Brierley HMI, and four SMA representatives, J.J. Bryant (Quarry Bank High School, Liverpool), B.M. Jones (Dulwich), J. Peirson (Rugby) and W.H. Dowdeswell (Winchester). Reporting back to the General Committee of the SMA, Dowdeswell recorded his belief that 'something really worthwhile is going to come of all this . . . There is no doubt that the SMA has an important part to play in the development of the new biology syllabuses even if we are not the "prime movers" as in physics and chemistry'.[82]

Should none of the SMA representatives at the meeting be involved in the Nuffield Foundation Biology Project, it was Dowdeswell's suggestion that the new panel on Modern Biological Science ought to undertake the task of scrutinizing and commenting upon the various proposals that emerged from the Nuffield unit. In fact Dowdeswell was appointed Organizer of the Foundation's Biology Project and by the autumn Coulson was reporting to the General Committee, on behalf of the Science and Education Committee, that the work of the original Biology Panel was now complete and that the work of the new panel should await a progress report from the

Nuffield Foundation Biology 11–16 Project.[83] At the same meeting, on the recommendation of the Science and Education Committee, it was unanimously resolved 'That the scope of the present Science and Education Committee be broadened to cover schools of all types.' The full implications of the 1944 Education Act had at last been faced.

Action and reaction

Amalgamation of the SMA and AWST in 1963 provided an occasion for a review of the rôle of the Science and Education Committee. Under the new constitution its name was changed, becoming simply the Education Committee, and its membership was formalized to include a chairman and three members appointed by Council, together with representatives of each of the sub-committees which it had established. Its chairman was *ex-officio* a member of Council and its meetings were to be attended by the General Secretary. In consequence of the extension of the scope of its work, the existing grammar school sub-committees (Introductory Phase, Biology, Chemistry, Physics, 'Fourth Panel', and Modern Physical Science) were supplemented by others for Modern School Science, Technical School Science, Primary School Science, Science Teaching Aids, Laboratory Technicians and Examinations.[84] Though new names emerged amongst its membership as a result, the contribution of the original core of the SMA and AWST Science and Education Committee remained seminal, with Boulind as chairman until 1967.[85]

In the years immediately following the establishment of the Nuffield Foundation Science Teaching Project, the involvement of many leading members of the ASE in aspects of the development work perhaps left little time for reflection on larger issues of policy, though the 1961 Policy Statement was eventually revised to make it applicable to schools of all types.[86] By that date, however, the publication of materials from the 11–16 Project was in sight, and the need for stocktaking was further underlined by the government's declaration to end selective secondary education. Other influences on the school curriculum were at work also, notably pressure for the teaching of applied science and technology. Within the Association itself there were organizational matters causing concern. With a membership approaching 11,000, the mechanisms for involving as many as possible in discussion and formation of policy were in need of urgent examination. At the 1964–65 Annual Meeting in Imperial College, London, the lecture theatres had been packed to over-crowding when expositions of the Nuffield schemes were given, the discussion at Annual Meetings, once an important source of members' views for the Executive, was now almost impossible. There was also a general recognition of the need to involve a new generation of younger members in the work of the Association;[87] many of the stalwarts of the post-war years, having been recruited to science teaching in the 1930s, were coming within sight of the end of their careers.

A first skirmish with some of these issues occurred in May 1965 when the Education Committee, together with the officers of the ASE, held a two-day Conference at Cambridge on new ideas on the teaching of science. The speakers and topics were:

H.F. Halliwell and Dr J.E. Spice. Physical Science (Structure and Properties of Matter)
D.I.R. Porter, HMI. Engineering Studies
Mrs H.E. Misselbrook. Secondary Science
E.J. Machin. C.S.E.
Miss V.J. Evans. Teaching Science in a large Girls' School
Dr H.F. Boulind. Minority time
C.L. Williams, HMI. Developments in the teaching of science.[88]

In considering how the information provided in the talks might best be disseminated to the Association's membership, and how the reaction of members might most effectively be expressed, it became clear that branch meetings had a crucial part to play. Strong support was given to the idea of holding a follow-up Conference the next year on a subject which had previously been discussed at branch level, one or two members of each branch, selected for their ability to represent the views of their fellow members, being invited to attend. Such a development clearly had financial implications which would need to be taken into account in the Association's annual estimates.

At a meeting of the Education Committee on 18 September 1965, after discussion of a letter from Boulind and of a general survey by the General Secretary of present trends in science teaching, it was decided to recommend these proposals to Council and to request an additional sum of £500 to cover the attendant expenses. Suitable topics for discussion at the Conference were invited from any source, the intention being to submit them to branches for reaction. In fact, though a number of suggestions came forward from individuals, they tended to be of a specific and ad hoc nature, ranging from the design of laboratories and the duties of laboratory technicians, on the one hand, to proposals for liaison with the Schools Council over the evaluation of new science courses, on the other. A more coordinated viewpoint was expressed in a memorandum from J.L. Lewis, follow-ing a meeting of members of the physics and chemistry panels during the Cambridge Annual Meeting.[89] As much of the work of the original panels had now been incorporated into the various Nuffield science teaching projects, Lewis recommended the disbanding of the physics and chemistry panels. Similarly, the Modern Physical Science Committee was thought to need new terms of reference which confined its actitivies to apparatus development and experimental work, though this should now extend to classical as well as 'modern' topics. To meet the needs of the future, a new Secondary School

Science Panel should be established with responsibility for the publication of a series of monographs on methods of science teaching; these publications should be used to encourage new ideas and younger teachers. These proposals, together with an alternative set from H.P. Ramage, were sent to all members of the Committee for consideration before meeting at the 1966 Cambridge Conference.

By this stage the membership of the Education Committee had grown considerably, being more than twenty in number with not infrequent changes as representatives of the various sub-committees altered. At an extra-ordinary meeting of the Committee held immediately after the March 1966 Conference to review conclusions, the view was expressed that the present Committee was too large and lacked the necessary continuity for it to function effectively in the realms of policy formation.[90] A smaller group of six, together with the Association's Chairman and General Secretary, might be more appropriate for this task and it was agreed that Broad, Boulind and Tapper should examine this possibility and report back at the next meeting.[91] On this occasion, the need to involve more younger members was emphasized and another Conference was proposed for the autumn to which 'younger teachers with interest and drive' would be invited to address the question 'What are the most urgent and serious problems in school science education today and what should the ASE do about them?' The teachers in mind could come from any type of school, primary or secondary; they did not need to be graduates, nor, indeed, ASE members.[92]

Further to this, and following Lewis's proposals, it was resolved that the four existing secondary panels should be disbanded, and that the Modern Physical Science Committee should become a Physical Science Apparatus Committee, with a parallel Biological Apparatus and Materials Committee established. As if to underline the views of several members of the Education Committee that the Association should be concerned with wider problems arising from the teaching of science than in the past, the same meeting received a Memorandum from the National Foundation for Educational Research on research projects in the area of science teaching, including reference to the interest of the Science Committee of the Schools Council in the evaluation of the new O level schemes, and the Foundation's own work in connection with the International Evaluation of Achievement project and the measurement of pupils' attitude towards science.[93]

The rôle of the Education Committee continued to be a subject of discussion over the next year. The December Conference of 'younger members', for whom the typical school was comprehensive, ranged over a bewildering set of problems, including shortage of material resources, the gulf between school science and technology, teaching science to mixed-ability classes, and the conditions of service of over-burdened science teachers, a matter which the Trust Deed excluded from the objects of the ASE.[94] The final speaker, Jon

Ogborn, brought the work of the Education Committee into sharp focus again, however. In his opinion the initiative in curriculum development held by the Association around 1960, having passed to the Nuffield groups, was now about to return to the ASE to make of it what it could. An ASE curriculum development committee might be what was needed.

The presence of other bodies in the curriculum field, notably the Schools Council, made unilateral action impolitic, however, and at the May 1967 meeting of the Education Committee there was considerable discussion as to how the ASE could maintain satisfactory liaison with the Schools Council on whose committees it had no formal representation. It was resolved that the General Secretary should ask the Minister of Education to allow an observer, with power to report back to the ASE, on each Schools Council committee or panel concerned with science. At the same time, inquiries were to be directed to other subject teaching associations to establish whether they were satisfied with the present representation on School Council committees.[95]

The annual Education Conference, by now a regular feature on the ASE calendar, was held at Nottingham in 1967. At its conclusion, the Education Committee met to review its position and resolutions for its reconstitution were carried. An Executive Committee of about six members, four of whom would be elected at the annual Education Conference, was to coordinate activities with Working Parties, established by the Executive as necessary for whatever specific purposes were deemed important, reporting back to it. The composition of the first of these 'task forces' was approved, its business being to explore with NFER ways in which the ASE might assist with educational research projects in the period 1967–68, and to select three projects which the Association might carry out, possibly in collaboration with another institution. It was further recommended that Council should consider the appointment of a full-time salaried Research Coordinator, at least for a limited period.[96]

Before the next meeting of the Education Committee E.W. Tapper prepared a report on its composition and functions: discussion of this led to an amended composition for the proposed Executive Committee and clarified the relationship of the Committee to Council. Even so, some disquiet remained that the new proposals, whilst well designed to fulfil the important function of looking ahead, and deciding the topics towards which the ASE should direct its efforts, would nevertheless be unable to deal effectively with the many routine inquiries received at Headquarters. It was also not clear where responsibility lay for the publication of reports and the dissemination of information to members.

To examine these matters, a meeting between Boulind, as Chairman of the Education Committee, J.J. Bryant, chairman of the ASE, the Vice-Chairmen of the Association and E.W. Tapper, General Secretary, was held in Cambridge on Sunday, 2 July 1967, when it was decided that two Education Committees were needed.[97] The first, to be known as the Education (Research) Committee, would be responsible for work previously assigned to the proposed Executive Education Committee. The second, the Education (Coordinating) Committee, would deal with enquiries from members, the appointment of representatives of the ASE on other bodies and the reports from these representatives, and the coordination of the work of sub-committees other than those of a 'research' nature. This committee also had an important part to play in relation to the involvement of Branches in discussion of aspects of science education. Approved by Council at its Autumn meeting, the detailed implementation of the dual arrangement was completed at the final meeting of the Education Committee on 11 November 1967. A new organizational structure had been created, and the names of the members of the Education Committees signified that the hand-over or responsibility to a new generation of the Association's membership was under way.[98] In view of 'the large reserve of untapped talent within the Association', the Education Committee agreed that 'no member of the Association should, as far as possible, be actively engaged with more than one project of either the Education (Research) or Education (Coordinating) Committee.'[99]

As the trustees of the Nuffield Foundation were reminded when reviewing the work of their science teaching projects, 'In the intricate and tangled pattern of organization which constitutes the English school system, it is extremely difficult to determine where the main responsibility for curriculum development lies.'[100] Control over the curriculum of secondary schools in England and Wales was, throughout the period under consideration in this chapter, uniquely diffused. Simultaneously with the Nuffield Foundation's intervention in the field of school science education, the Ministry of Education established a new unit, the Curriculum Study Group. The hostile response to this development, especially from local education authorities, who interpreted it as a move by central government to usurp their freedom in curriculum matters, led to recognition of the need for more acceptable cooperative machinery in the field of school curriculum and examinations and the establishment of the Schools Council in 1964.[101]

Leaving aside the views of those who regarded the Nuffield Foundation's actions, following the submission of proposals for the SMA/AWST School Science Project, as a 'take-over',[102] the events of the early 1960s represented a set-back to the ASE in its legitimate aspirations to achieve recognition as an organization which could pronounce authoritatively on what should be taking place in school science teaching. Developments in the mid- and late-1960s, including the launching of the Schools Council Project Technology and the creation of the Schools Science and Technology Committee,[103] further demonstrated the complexity of the influences which bore on the school science curriculum.

By 1966, however, the energies of the Association had been marshalled for recovery. 'I had the chance of a general talk with Boulind about the ASE's future plans,' R.A. Becher wrote to the coordinator of the Nuffield Science Projects in August of that year. 'It appears that the ASE Education Committee is anxious to re-establish itself as one of the main forces for ideas on science teaching and fears that unless it takes some positive move now it will be overshadowed by bodies such as the Schools Council and the Professional Scientific Associations'.[104] The constitutional reforms of 1967 and the involvement of a new generation of science teachers were fundamental to this end. After a decade of activity unprecedented in the history of the Association, Boulind handed over the chairmanship of the Education Committee to R. Schofield (Education (Research) Committee) and Miss M.E. Tilstone (Education (Coordinating) Committee). At the Annual Business Meeting on 4 January 1968 he was elected an Honorary Member of the ASE in recognition of his services.

11 The challenge of technology

The manpower imperative

In his address to members of the Science Masters' Association at the Annual Meeting in London on 30 December 1952, one of the Association's most supportive and far-sighted Presidents, Sir Graham Savage C.B., identified two ideas which had characterized science teaching in England. The first concerned the development of individual character; the second, the service which science could offer to the country. In urging that this second ideal should be given greater prominence in the future, the technologist's question, 'How can it be used?', being as important as the pure scientist's 'Is it true?', the President drew attention to an unrequited demand by industry for those who could apply science to the satisfaction of human needs. Specifically, he advocated that workshop practice and engineering drawing should find a place more commonly in schools, even in the sixth-forms.[1]

Such a proposal ran contrary to the cultural justification for the teaching of science which had previously characterized the pronouncements of the SMA. Indeed, Sir Graham Savage was in advance of his time in attempting to draw together the threads of two distinct traditions of science teaching in England and Wales, the first developed in public and grammar schools and the second in technical and vocational institutions. At the time of his address and throughout the 1950s the prevailing view was that school science education should be general, unspecialized and non-vocational. On this matter education, science and industry appeared to speak with a common voice. Reflecting the opinions of many witnesses, the Central Advisory Council for Education asserted in 1959 that science was 'a suitable instrument of a liberal education' provided syllabuses were revised and were no longer regarded simply as 'the first stages in the vocational training of a scientific worker'.[2] A similar prescription came from the joint session of Sections A (Physics and Mathematics) and L (Education) of the British Association for the Advancement of Science in 1955; in a discussion on 'the education of the physicist', speakers were unanimous in their preference for a broadly based, general education as the most appropriate foundation for a university course in science.[3] In so far as industry had a uniform voice on educational matters, it was concordant with the preference for a general education, at least at this stage. Though the scarcity of good applicants for university engineering departments was a matter of concern for the Education Committee of the Federation of British

Industries from the early 1950s, there was no expectation that the schools would teach engineering. Rather, the emphasis was upon mathematics and pure science as a basis for specialized technological and applied studies later.[4] Likewise, the Trades Union Congress in a memorandum on Technical Education submitted to the Select Committee on Estimates in 1953 was clear that 'technical education should not begin too soon' and 'the job of the school up to the statutory school leaving age is to give general education'.[5]

The efficacy of these judgements was increasingly called into question, however, by evidence on the limited extent to which able boys and girls chose to study applied science and engineering after leaving school and, subsequently, to seek employment in the world of industry. 'The success of a country in the modern world depends almost entirely on its success in scientific research and in the speed and vigour with which it applies its results in industry and commerce', Sir Alexander Todd told his audience of science teachers in January 1957. 'The nation that neglects science and technology has no future as a great power'.[6] In this connection, figures showing the recent output of graduates in science and technology (the latter being mainly engineers) in Russia, the USA and the UK gave cause for considerable disquiet.

Table 11.1   Graduates per million of population (1954)[7]

	Science	Technology	Total
USSR	56	280	336
USA	144	137	280
UK	105	57	162

The national response to this situation is a well-documented story.[8] Provision for higher technological education was expanded both within the university sector, the Imperial College of Science and Technology being developed into a major centre, and within the further education sector, ten Colleges of Advanced Technology being designated between 1957 and 1961.[9] Unfortunately, this increased capacity was not matched by pressure from school leavers for places, the quantity and quality of applicants remaining matters of concern into the 1960s and beyond. Measures to remedy the state of affairs can be categorized broadly under three headings:

(i)   attempts to improve the supply of science teachers and the physical resources available for their work;
(ii) attempts to improve the image and status of technology and engineering as occupations;
(iii) curriculum measures designed to counter the imputed effect of grammar school education in directing boys and girls away

from the concrete and the mechanical to the abstract and the pure.

The involvement of the Association in each of these is examined below.

The supply of science teachers and resources for school science

An adequate supply of suitably qualified teachers of science was crucial to the success of any national scheme for increasing scientific and technological manpower. Attention was directed early, therefore, to the difficulties which schools were experiencing in competing effectively with industry for able graduates. At a conference on Industry and the Universities, convened by the Federation of British Industries in November 1949, it was reported by headmasters present that 'incompetent people' were being appointed as science teachers and that some schools were having to drop scientific subjects from their curriculum.[10]

In an effort to obtain a clearer picture of the extent of the shortage, the General Committee of the SMA, in collaboration with the AWST, instituted its own inquiry in March 1953. The results, from a sample of almost 1000 grammar schools in which the Associations had members, were published the following year, copies of a report being distributed to major scientific, educational and industrial organisations.[11]

Though the evidence of overall shortage and of inadequate technical support for science teachers was disturbing, the SMA/AWST survey indicated that the problems were less severe in independent than in maintained schools. Certainly a year later, when consideration was being given by a number of industrial companies to measures which might increase the future supply of scientists and technologists, the shortage of science teachers was deemed to be a less critical problem than lack of money for capital projects in the independent and direct grant secondary schools.[12] In consequence, the Industrial Fund for the Advancement of Scientific Education in Schools was established in November 1955 to offer assistance by way of grants for building, modernizing and equipping science accommodation in these schools. The chief assessor for this scheme was Sir Graham Savage and the 'approved list' of apparatus for use by public and direct grant schools in the teaching of chemistry, physics and geology – the science subjects which the Fund supported – was compiled with the help of prominent SMA members.[13] When the Executive Committee of the Industrial Fund held its final meeting in 1963 a sum of £2000 from the surplus was allocated to the (by then) ASE, part of this grant to be spent on 'closer liaison with the practice and teaching of technology'.[14]

Laboratory provision in the maintained sector of secondary education never achieved the same level as in the independent sector during the 1950s. Though much building did take place, information collected by the SMA, AWST, National Union of Teachers and the 'Joint Four' Secondary Associations in 1957 and 1959 showed that a serious disparity remained between the maintained grammar schools on one hand, and the direct grant and independent schools on the other, in relation to laboratory facilities, as well as to technical assistance and annual expenditure on science work.[15] The situation in girls' schools was especially disturbing.

Discussions on science teacher shortages were dominated throughout the 1950s by references to the demographic abstractions known as 'the bulge' and 'the trend', i.e. the post-war increase in births and the tendency for children to stay at school beyond the leaving age of fifteen, respectively. Though the output from universities of graduates in pure science increased by more than 50 per cent between 1950 and 1960, the number recruited by the maintained schools failed to keep pace with the rate of expansion of the educational system; additionally, there was a decline in the quality of new science teachers, as measured by class of degree held. This was a period when science education in secondary grammar schools was largely sustained by the core of high quality graduates recruited in the period of over-supply between the wars.

Whilst the SMA and the AWST could draw attention to the extent of the problem in the schools, measures to improve the supply inevitably brought under consideration matters such as salaries, financial inducements, career structures and conditions of service. Reference to these was inescapable in discussions between representatives of the SMA/AWST and other bodies such as the Advisory Council for the Training and Supply of Teachers and a statement on possible remedies for the shortage was prepared by the General Committee of the SMA in 1954;[16] but for the Associations to have taken matters further would have involved entering forbidden territory. The Trust Deed of the newly formed ASE in 1963 made explicit what had been clearly understood previously, that the regulation of relations between employers and employees, and the provision of pecuniary benefits for members were not objects which the Associations were free to pursue.

Arguably, however, the efficient use of qualified science teachers with its corollary, the provision of adequate laboratory technician support, whilst bearing on 'conditions of service', nevertheless fell within the Associations' legitimate sphere of action. Certainly, the SMA had a long-standing concern for the effective administration of school science laboratories, in its evidence to the Norwood Committee[17] emphasizing the 'inadequate (sometimes a complete lack of) laboratory assistance' as an important factor impeding the full development of science as a secondary school subject. The supply and training of laboratory technicians were matters to which the Associations returned repeatedly in the 1950s and 1960s.

The ability of the SMA and AWST to provide information about, and to advise on, the shortage of science teachers undoubtedly led to an enhancement of their status and to the extending of communication channels with centres of power and influence in the 1950s. Links between professional scientific organizations and the SMA had existed for many years, and these were augmented and strengthened. In 1952 the Royal Institute of Chemistry invited the science masters to nominate two representatives to attend future meetings of its Education Committee,[18] following this a year later with a request for ideas on means of increasing collaboration with the SMA. The General Committee agreed to recommend that branches of the Association should explore the possibility of joint meetings with local sections of the R.I.C. and the Institute of Physics.[19] The Royal Institution, following discussions between its Director, Sir Lawrence Bragg, John Oriel of Shell Petroleum and SMA officers, made new educational provisions for both sixth-form students and science teachers, members of the London branches of the SMA and AWST being involved in the planning.[20] Following another initiative by Oriel, in collaboration with Dr C.G. Williams, head of Shell Research, the Royal Society introduced a scheme to aid teachers wishing to pursue scientific research in their schools. A joint committee of the Royal Society and the SMA was established to supervise the scheme which was supported by grants from several industrial companies.

However, the most significant extension of the Associations' links during this period was the closer, direct collaboration with industrial organizations. Following a meeting between industrialists and educationalists sponsored by the Federation of British Industries in January 1954, the General Committee of the SMA decided to invite industrialists to the next Annual Meeting.[21] The following year, a similar invitation was extended to the Secretary and members of the Executive Committee of the Industrial Fund,[22] and to representatives of Esso Petroleum seeking to provide financial aid for school science teaching.[23] The Esso 'Junior' Loan Service of Scientific Apparatus, inaugurated in 1959, provided support for the teaching of elementary science in preparatory schools. A 'Senior' Loan Service followed. It was at this time that a number of industrial concerns began to offer short courses of in-service education for teachers. After a meeting with representatives of the SMA in 1954, the British Iron and Steel Federation provided two courses, in Sheffield and Glasgow, on the applications of science in the iron and steel industry, the SMA addressograph facilities being made available to the B.I.S.F. for the distribution to members of free copies of *The Steel Review*.[24] In April 1957 the Shell Petroleum Company organized a three-day conference at University College, London, attended by over 250 science masters and mistresses.[25] Liaison between industrial organizations and science teachers also led to the production of resource materials including films and booklets. Unilever, ICI, Shell and BP were amongst several companies active in this way. In 1960 the budget figure for Unilever's science booklets was £61,000, a not inconsiderable expenditure for those days.[26]

It was not until 1970 that the ASE elected its first industrialist President – John Rose, Research Director of ICI. However, national concern over the supply of graduates with scientific qualifications and the related issue of the shortage of secondary school science teachers brought the SMA and AWST into prominence in the 1950s and led to the establishment of relationships with industry which were progressively developed over the following two decades.

Changing the image of technology

The 1957 Policy Statement of the SMA had made only limited reference to applied science, a knowledge and understanding of the implications of modern scientific and technological developments being included as one of several aims of school science teaching.[27] This position was affirmed by the ASE, and was well summarized by its General Secretary, E.W. Tapper, in 1964:

> The ASE is . . . interested in the supply of better applied scientists to Universities and Colleges of Advanced Technology. Consultation has taken place with the Royal Society and the Engineering Institutes . . . Every organization we have consulted is quite firm that technology should not be taught in schools and here the Policy Statement agrees.[28]

In fact opinion on the nature of school science was shifting even as Tapper wrote. Certainly by 1964 there were influential voices pressing for greater attention to the application of science subjects to real-life engineering problems and for the introduction of applied science laboratories in schools.[29] In similar vein, H.R.H. The Prince Philip, in his first address to the Association as its Patron, had taken science teachers to task for a too marked predilection for the fundamental, as opposed to the practical and applied, in their teaching.[30] Independently, the case for a school curriculum development project in applied science and technology was being pressed with some success by leaders of the Association of Heads of Secondary Technical Schools.[31]

To appreciate the Association's position, it has to be remembered that, until Tapper's appointment in January 1962, the SMA was administered entirely by part-time officers, at that stage much exercised with other matters including the establishment of a permanent Headquarters office, amalgamation with the AWST and the strenuous activities leading up to and resulting from the Nuffield Foundation's science teaching projects. The time did not seem ripe for a major shift in policy emphasis. In any case, the problem of securing the interest of able boys in a career in engineering had been examined in 1958 when H.E. Dance HMI, Staff Inspector for Engineering in the Ministry of Education, who had broached the matter, was invited to a meeting of the SMA General Committee.[32] Speaking on behalf of the Institution of Mechanical Engineers, in particular, Dance had indicated that there was no wish to interfere with existing general education in science; there was, however, a need to foster the interest of boys in engineering. A background paper outlined the SMA's view that, whilst recognizing the problem, the Association was opposed to engineering and technology in the school curriculum if this was likely to lead to a reduction in time for science studies. The incorporation of technological applications as exemplary material in the teaching of science was, however, approved. A subsequent meeting between representatives of the SMA and the Education Committee of the Institution of Mechanical Engineers ratified this position as did advice received by the ASE, six years later, in discussions with representatives of the Royal Society and the Engineering Institutions Joint Council. The outcome then was that, 'in general, technology cannot, and indeed should not, be included as such in school curricula. It was more important to ensure a high standard in the teaching of basic science and mathematics'.[33] As Sir Patrick Linstead, Rector of Imperial College of Science and Technology, had emphasized in his Presidential address to the SMA in 1962, in his institution, as in other leading centres, the formal education of engineers was becoming increasingly an education in engineering sciences.[34] The emphasis was on the fundamental principles of the subject and the best preparation for this was through the study of science and mathematics in the sixth form. At the same time, too many of 'the clever boys . . . with scientific and mathematical ability' were going into pure science and not enough into applied science and engineering. What was required was that science and mathematics teachers should exert 'that gentle and persuasive pressure for which they are so rightly famous' to direct more able students towards engineering, metallurgy and similar subjects.[35]

This role of propagandist for applied science was not one which many teachers were equipped to assume, even if willing to do so. Most had been trained in the tradition of pure science with only limited knowledge of industrial applications and of possible careers in engineering and technology. Even with appropriate training and relevant curricula[36] at their disposal, many teachers would have interpreted their professional responsibilities in the same way as a correspondent to the ASE *Bulletin*. In his experience, few sixth-formers had made up their minds firmly about their future careers by the time of entry to university; in such circumstances it was not for the science teacher to intervene. Rather he was likely to suggest the degree course which left open most options, rather than recommend a narrower field.[37]

As for the officers of the ASE, they were caught in a dilemma. Powerful new allies were pulling them in one direction and, as representatives of an organization with ambitions to guide the development of science education, they acknowledged national responsibilities to improve the supply of engineers and technologists. On the other hand, the officers were the servants of the membership and could only lead where their constituents permitted. E.W. Tapper, the full-time General Secretary, used the newly founded *Bulletin*, of which he was editor, to sound opinion on the part which the ASE should play, especially in refurbishing the image of technology. The response from members, following a request for comments on the place of technology in schools, constituted anything but a clear mandate for a revision of policy.[38]

Steps were taken, however, to stir the members to action. Publications on engineering science and technology were advertised, and a detailed account by Tapper of 'The place of technology in schools' was printed in the *Bulletin*.[39] At the President's dinner in May 1964, representatives of the Engineering Institutions were invited to meet industrialists and ASE officers, Sir Graham Savage speaking for the ASE. It was agreed that industry needed to make closer contact with the science teachers and assist in their re-education. 'It is . . . up to us to do something about it,' Tapper urged his readers, 'to learn what is this image of technology and to put across to pupils in our teaching, and in discussions as to future careers, what technology is all about.'[40]

Following a conference of headmasters and headmistresses arranged by the Royal Society and the Engineering Institutions Joint Council at Cambridge in March 1965, and at which the ASE's royal Patron delivered the opening address,[41] a booklet on *The Challenge of Engineering as a Career* was written on behalf of the ASE. Teacher Fellowships and extended visits to industrial centres were offered by a number of organizations; the Shell three-day Easter conferences in 1964, the eighth and ninth in the annual series held in University College, London, were devoted to the subjects of Applied Science and Problem-Solving, respectively.[42] Indeed the extent of industrial intervention elicited a warm appreciation in the *Bulletin*, written by the ASE's Treasurer, of the substantial contribution of 'our friends in industry'.[43]

The most significant initiative taken at this stage by the Association itself was unquestionably related to the programme of the Annual Meeting. As early as 1961, shortly after his appointment as Annual Meeting Secretary of the SMA, D.W. Harlow had been approached by Sir Harold Hartley, an Honorary Member and Past President, on the subject of the low esteem in which careers in engineering and technology were held by sixth-formers. Hartley, like Savage, was a long-standing supporter of the Association, having been instrumental in arranging the first Annual Meeting to be held at Oxford in 1921.[44] In addition to being a university chemist of distinction, he had considerable industrial interests and influence; he had also played a major part in securing for the Association the patronage of H.R.H. The Prince Philip. It was put to Harlow that the Annual Meeting was an occasion to remedy the tarnished image of technology and, specifically, that the next Annual Meeting, due to be held in the

Imperial College of Science and Technology, provided an opportunity to plan a programme rich in contributions about engineering sciences and technology.[45] Accordingly, the London meeting of January 1962 included a much higher proportion of lectures on applied science than previous meetings and this bias was maintained throughout the five years for which Harlow held office as Annual Meeting Secretary. At the Manchester College of Science and Technology in January 1963, there was a special exhibition of 'Science and Industry', whilst on the occasion of the unusually rapid return to Imperial College in December 1964, a similar exhibition on 'Applied Science' was mounted. Next year at Cambridge, a large Government Exhibition on the theme Innovation in Technology was opened by the Rt Hon. R.E. Prentice, Minister of State, Department of Education and Science.[46]

Looking back on this period it was Harlow's judgement that the Annual Meetings had stimulated an initial enthusiasm for the applications of science amongst those attending, but that this was followed by a falling off in interest and a reaction from some of the Association's regions that the Committee was trying to 'force applications down their throats'.[47] By 1967 there were clear signs that the dissemination of information about technology and industrial careers was having little effect on the dispositions of science teachers and on the choices of sixth-formers. Provision of the Shell Easter Conferences ceased in that year as did publication of the magazine *Science and Technology*.[48] More significantly there was growing evidence, about to be published in the Dainton Report, of a swing away from the study of physical sciences in the sixth forms;[49] the future of pure science, as well as that of applied, appeared to be in jeopardy.

Throughout this period of the mid-1960s, the Association failed to achieve a clear view of the place of technology in education. Unquestionably, something had to be done to remedy the national shortage of engineers and the general opinion that the cure entailed changes in the schools was never seriously challenged by the Executive Committee. The membership, however, clung to educational and cultural justifications for the teaching of science, and seemed little disposed to acknowledge the economic and vocational functions of schooling. Notwithstanding much prompting behind the scenes by influential figures like Linstead, Savage and Hartley, and despite a financial incentive from the Industrial Fund to establish 'closer liaison with the practice and teaching of technology', the Education Committee was obliged to report in 1965 that 'so far the ASE has not been advised as to how it (the Industrial Fund grant) might best be spent.'[50] In December 1964, Savage and Boulind appeared before the Parliamentary and Scientific Committee when that body was considering 'Teaching of science in schools, with particular reference to the future application of science'. Beyond general collaboration with other agencies and encouragement to its members to become more aware of industrial applications, it did not seem that the Association had identified a clear course of action. Boulind did suggest, however, that there was need for a new project, additional to Nuffield, 'based more jointly on physics and mathematics, possibly with engineering and possibly with electronics.'[51] The opportunity for initiatives by the Association in this direction had already been forestalled, however. Others, working outside its orbit, were developing alternative approaches to the teaching of science in schools and beginning to command resources for attempts at curriculum reform.

The counter-culture of technology

An 'alternative road' through secondary education, with an emphasis on making, doing and problem-solving, in contrast to the academic and bookish studies of the grammar school curriculum, had been commended by the Crowther Report in 1959.[52] The idea of a more practical education, uniting hand and mind, was, of course, not new, but few of its manifestations had been full-time and divorced from occupational requirements. The construction of a new form of full-time and intellectually demanding practical education, the best model for which was to be found in the sixth forms of technical secondary schools, was, in the judgement of the Crowther committee, a major task facing English education.[53]

It was from this alternative tradition of secondary education that new initiatives in science education began to emerge. In the early 1960s, D.W. Hutchings, science tutor in the Oxford University Department of Education, convened a number of important conferences on the subject of technology and the sixth-form student, as well as carrying out research into the attitudes of sixth-formers towards engineering and technology. At the second conference in June 1961, an account was presented of the curriculum devised at Nottingham High Pavement School[54] where boys took A level Mathematics (Pure and Applied), Physics and Technical Drawing at School, whilst simultaneously following courses in Applied Heat and Applied Mechanics for one half-day each week at Nottingham Technical College. In addition, new ways of teaching Physics and Applied Mathematics were being explored in collaboration with Professor J.A. Pope of Nottingham University. In his firm, Tecquipment, Pope had developed small-scale apparatus which students could use to illustrate how fundamental scientific principles were applied to technology. The necessity for this followed from his belief that there was 'a world of difference between being able to apply theoretical principles to answer examination questions and having such a confidence in the principle that . . . you will risk your professional reputation by applying it to actual design'.[55] It was the opinion of the headmaster of High Pavement School that a 'technical stream' should exist in every large secondary grammar school; in this connection he thought it 'unfortunate' that the new physics syllabus proposed by the SMA offered so few opportunities to use the approach developed by Pope.

High Pavement School was by no means alone in its attempt to introduce applied science and engineering activities into the school curriculum.[56] In 1964, the Education Committee of the Institution of Mechanical Engineers set up an 'Applied Science in Schools Panel' to supervise a fact-finding enquiry into the nature and extent of these activities. The resulting 'Page Report'[57] described an impressive range of project work and syllabus development not only in technical secondary schools, but also in a number of pioneering independent, direct grant and other grammar schools. Of 239 schools responding to a question about whether they subscribed to the 'alternative road' thesis, 96 per cent said that they did, although only 37 per cent thought it was applicable to their most able sixth-formers.[58]

Another outstanding sixth-form engineering course was that developed at Ealing Grammar School as a voluntary, unexamined and after-school activity. The work was formal, involving theory lectures as well as practical work, with an emphasis on the applications of scientific principles in the subjects of fluid flow, heat engines, strength of materials and electronics. In the words of the Page Report, the Ealing approach was 'concentrated and closed-ended . . . at the opposite extreme of the spectrum to project work'.[59] Again, Professor J.A. Pope assisted with the design of suitable small-scale apparatus, notably an hydraulics bench, while Dr C.G. Williams, the chairman of the Institution of Mechanical Engineers' Applied Science in Schools Panel, designed, built and presented to the school a miniature engine test-bed.[60]

A different approach, involving an applied science project in the A level Physics examination of the Cambridge Local Examinations Syndicate, was employed with considerable success at Dauntsey's School by G.B. Harrison, the engineering master.[61] The Cambridge Local Examinations Syndicate had also accepted for examination an A level syllabus in the elements of engineering design, developed over a five-year period by staff at Doncaster Technical Grammar School, along with an O level syllabus in the applications of physics.[62] Perhaps more than any other school, Doncaster, under its head Edward Semper, had committed itself to the philosophy of 'the alternative road'. Sixth-form projects, each lasting for two years, were used extensively in the science teaching and the school also included 'investigations' in the A level course, each boy tackling four investigations which were assessed both internally and externally.

The Page Report revealed the extent to which versions of school science education existed which nevertheless were unacknowledged as a resource for the national curriculum developments then taking place. Before looking in more detail at the activities in this field which led to the establishment of Project Technology, it is necessary to turn briefly to the national context of science and technology where important changes were taking place in the 1960s.

Reference has already been made to the views of Sir Patrick Linstead on the education of engineers in universities.[63] This emphasis on scientific principles, 'the engineering sciences' in Linstead's phrase, was not viewed by all as an unmitigated good. Some distinguished engineers, including many who had received a more practical training, feared that the university courses did less than justice to design awareness and creativity.[64] Even so, there was little pressure from either camp for schools to depart from a general education in physics, mathematics and chemistry, or physics and double mathematics, for prospective university engineers. Professor J.T. Allanson expressed the view of most engineers at a conference on 'Technology and the Sixth-Form Boy' when he said, 'The question generally asked us is "Would you prefer boys in the sixth-form to take that subject called 'mechanical engineering science' or something like that, and 'engineering drawing'?" and the answer to that one is far as I am concerned is a very firm "No".'[65]

The debate over analytical and scientific versus design and creative approaches in engineering education, though dividing opinion, was overshadowed by a unifying concern for the status of engineering as a profession. In 1965 the Council of Engineering Institutions came into being 'to promote and coordinate . . . the development of science, art and practice of engineering'. The title 'Chartered Engineer' (C Eng.) was introduced, CEI laying down the levels of education, training and responsibilities required. One difficulty facing the new body was that the term 'engineer' had no precise meaning to the general public and was in popular use in a variety of ways. As the Finniston Report was to point out, some years later, British engineers were 'ill-served by a generic title not specifically associated with and reserved to a highly-educated and vital professional group in society.'[66] Another difficulty was 'the misleading national tendency to regard engineering as a subordinate branch of "science" '.[67] Engineering was different from science and the founding of the CEI signalled a move in the direction of intellectual autonomy.

Reorganization of the administration of science in Britain in the early 1960s and, in particular, the decision in 1964 by Harold Wilson's Labour government to establish a Ministry of Technology, separate from the newly-created Department of Education and Science, similarly emphasized the difference.[68] Schools, universities and the support of scientific research now came under the DES, whilst support for applications of science and development work came under the Ministry of Technology. This organization was in contrast to the recommendation in the Robbins Report that higher education and all research, pure and applied, should be under one ministry, with separate provision for schools.

In his second Presidential Address to the ASE in December 1964, Linstead spoke critically of the new arrangements,[69] stressing the essential unity of method and outlook of scientists and technologists, and hence the need to postpone differentiation between the two groups at least until the stage of university education. As to the proposal then being canvassed for the creation of a Royal Society of Technology, to do for technology what the Royal Society did so well for science, this was despatched as thoroughly harmful, institutionalizing 'a cleavage which should be sealed and not widened', and ineffectual, the proposed new body being inescapably 'a second best and poor relation'.[70] In his view, the Royal Society had taken the right step with its decision to increase its annual election to the Fellowship from 25 to 32, so allowing for the election of more technologists and retaining for itself the authority to speak for both pure and applied science.

The position, then, of the ASE was uncomfortably interjacent, its traditional allies from the world of 'high science' pulling in one direction whilst 'new friends' from industry and other voices such as those of Savage, Hartley and its Royal Patron, indicating the need for contrary developments. The establishment of The Engineering Council, whose inaugural policy statement affirmed a determination 'to encourage the development and teaching of mathematics, science *and technology* in schools' was still some years away,[71] but the seeds of autonomous technology were being sown in the early 1960s and the curriculum developments described in the Page Report were a harbinger of things to come.

Travellers down the alternative road

The Association of Heads of Secondary Technical Schools (AHSTS) came into being in 1951, formalizing regular gatherings and Northern and Southern regional meetings of headmasters which had been held since 1947.[72] Its aims were to secure equality of provision and parity of esteem for secondary technical schools within the tripartite system which characterized English secondary education in the post-war years. Cardinal within this programme was the development of a distinctive curriculum with an emphasis on the intellectual stimulus and theoretical insights that could be derived from problem-solving activities and investigations centred upon modern technology.

In June 1961 the annual conference of the AHSTS was held in Doncaster, where detailed consideration was given to Chapter 35 of the Crowther Report, dealing with the 'alternative road.'[73] The conference agreed that curriculum research was urgently needed into the construction of syllabuses, teaching methods and improved means of assessment. To finance this work, the President and Secretary of the Association, together with Edward Semper, headmaster of Doncaster Technical Grammar School, were delegated to approach the Education Committee of the FBI, the British Employers' Confederation and the Committee of Principals of Colleges of Advanced Technology. From each of these bodies they obtained an encouraging response, and were urged to draw up a precise set of proposals, costed realistically, with which to approach the Ministry of Education and various foundations for financial support.

By December 1962, a national Development Committee had been established by Semper, then on a four-month secondment to the Sheffield University Institute of Education. Membership of this committee included representatives of universities, colleges of advanced technology, training colleges, the AHSTS, FBI, British Employers' Confederation, ASE, examining boards, Youth Employment Service, the Association of Inspectors and Organizers of Handicraft, the Association of Hospital Matrons and the Ministry of Education. At a meeting in London in January 1963 it was agreed by the development Committee 'to promote a programme of research in the teaching of applied science and technology in secondary schools', a sub-committee being appointed to draw up detailed plans.

It was shortly after this that Semper wrote to the ASE to inquire if there was interest amongst its members in the development of a new approach to science teaching based on problem-solving activities and experimental investigations drawn from applied science. Details of his proposal were printed in the *Bulletin*, though without reference to Semper or the AHSTS, and interested ASE members were invited to respond to their General Secretary.[74] Over thirty people replied, including some who 'became quite prominent names in later years', convincing evidence to Semper that there was within the ASE a body of support for the curriculum development being planned.

One ASE member, G.B. Harrison, in following up the *Bulletin*'s note, submitted for publication in *The School Science Review* an account of the project work he had developed at Dauntsey's School, urging that 'the ASE should take a definite line on this subject and make some positive steps towards promoting a wider interest amongst science teachers in the applications of their subject.' Harrison cautioned that 'if we do not do this, we may find ourselves being made to look very narrow in our outlook by the activities of the several progressive bodies now searching for ways and means of producing more and better applied scientists and technologists'.[75] Tapper's discussion paper on 'The Place of Technology in Schools' can be seen as a response to Harrison's warning.[76]

In the meantime, representatives of industry on Semper's Development Committee had marshalled financial support, though only to an extent which permitted a modest local project.[77] When Semper approached the joint-secretaries of the newly established Schools Council early in 1965, they urged the need for a more general, national initiative. 'If you want to go it alone, we will give you pound for pound for what you can raise', D.H. Morrell was reported to have informed Semper. 'If, on the other hand, you hand it over to us, we will put a very substantial sum of money into it.' In Semper's words, 'Put in those terms, there was only one choice.'

In February 1965, Semper, with his fellow headmaster W.S. Brace (Elgin Secondary Technical School and Honorary Secretary of the

Association for Technical Education in Schools, as the AHSTS had by then become) attended a meeting of the ASE Education Committee to inform the Association of the developments afoot.[78] To the Council of the ATES in May, this meeting was reported as having been 'cordial and instructive'; members were also informed that leadership of the curriculum research project had now passed to the Schools Council where plans for a feasibility study of 'Engineering Science as a Sixth-Form Subject' were being laid.[79]

Following a conference in May 1965 to discuss a paper prepared by D.I.R. Porter, a member of Her Majesty's Inspectorate with special responsibilities for craft subjects,[80] the Schools Council agreed that a pilot scheme should be organized with the object of publishing a description of a range of tested possibilities for engineering science courses. A Consultative Committee was established under the chairmanship of Dr J. Topping, Principal of Brunel College of Advanced Technology, and chairman of the Council's subject committee on Craft, Applied Science and Technology.[81] Provision was made for wide representation by bodies including the Royal Society, the CEI, the engineering institutions, the ASE (Tapper) and the ATES (Semper). By November 1965 it had been agreed that G.B. Harrison, recently moved from Dauntsey's School to a post at Loughborough College of Education,[82] should be the organizer of the pilot project, with the possibility ahead of a major project to develop in greater detail the guidance needed by schools wishing to broaden the scope of their work in the field of engineering science and technology.

Crossed lines and strained relations

The total grant in support of Project Technology, covering its pilot year (1966), the period of -the main project (1967–70) and of extension (1970–72), amounted to £270,000. By all standards then applying, this was a major investment in curriculum change. Something of the difficulties of a project which attempted to resist classification within a subject area, its impact being intended to bear upon the total curriculum, has been recounted elsewhere.[83] What follows is limited to an examination of its relationship to the ASE.

Early in 1966, Tapper wrote to Harrison inviting him to speak on 'Schools and Technology' within the programme of the ASE 'Easter' Education Conference at Cambridge.[84] Harrison's contribution, emphasizing the importance of creative design aspects in science teaching, his self-styled 'hobby-horse', gave members of the Education Committee and ASE officers present a clear indication of the directions in which Project Technology would move.[85]

Possibly the recognition that major developments were occurring outside the ASE, together with a recovered determination to exert influence in the shaping of school science, led the Executive Committee of the Association to decide in January 1967 to hold a major two-day conference in London in the autumn on the theme of Schools and Applied Science.[86] The Royal Patron was to be present and the purpose of the Conference was ostensibly to give members an opportunity to assess the various schemes 'by which some ASE members, and other bodies, were endeavouring to interest school pupils in Applied Science'. Naturally, a contribution was sought from the Schools Council project.

At the meeting of the Executive Committee on 24 June, D.W. Harlow, the Annual Meetings Secretary, on whom the main burden of planning fell, reported on 'certain difficulties with the progress and the publicizing of the Autumn Conference.' The nature of some of these was made clear in a letter to Harlow from J.A.G. Banks, the Schools Council officer associated with Project Technology.[87] It was proposed that the Council's contributions to the objectives of the meeting would be:

(i) to make science teachers fully aware of the plans for Project Technology so that they could establish contact, through their L.E.A.s, with it; and

(ii) to elicit public support for the Council's proposal for financial support from industrial firms for the technology project.

The letter went on to imply that the project would be the principal topic in the programme for the final morning of the conference. It was also clear that the Schools Council saw the ASE as a possible liaison body between schools and industry in organizing, 'perhaps within the context of the project', courses for teachers on industrial applications of science. A draft letter from Banks to local educational authorities, informing them of the ASE conference and requesting release of teachers who might wish to attend, was appended.

Harlow's reply, though discreetly worded, made explicit the tensions that existed.[88] First, there was no question that the whole of the final morning could be devoted to the Council's Technology Project. What the ASE had planned was a short opening talk by G.C. Sneed (Ealing Grammar School for Boys) followed by a similar contribution from F.J. French (Bromley Technical High School for Boys), both men speaking 'as direct guests of the Association', on activity already proceeding in schools. G.B. Harrison would then follow to explain, 'in the limited time at his disposal . . . the latest moves through the Schools Council Technology project.'[89]

As for using the meeting to encourage financial support from industry for Project Technology, this was unacceptable 'within the context of our Association meeting'. The whole point of the occasion, Harlow continued, was 'to launch an ASE-inspired programme', an aim which could not be equated with Banks' proposal.

The draft letter to the LEAs also posed a problem because it would be wrong for information about the meeting to reach members before they had received a communication from the ASE. Banks was asked to hold up the despatch 'until I have clearance from the Palace and we as an Association can notify our members'. At a final planning meeting early in September, Harlow revealed the fine details of the programme to Banks and Harrison. Matters were presented as having already been agreed by 'the Palace' and, as Harrison later recorded, no manoeuvrability remained.

Those attending the two-day conference in November – in reality, Friday afternoon and Saturday morning – heard H.R.H. Prince Philip in his Opening Address declare himself 'personally convinced that the present science courses in schools should be augmented by some applied science instruction.'[90] Sir Harold Hartley also spoke, urging science teachers to recognize that the economic future of the country, which lay largely in their hands, turned on the effective education of creative engineers and technologists. Contributions followed from distinguished university and industrial engineers and applied scientists. Closing the proceedings at the end of the afternoon, H.R.H. Prince Philip identified a number of problems raised in discussions, including practical matters such as the availability of appropriate apparatus in schools and the need for more effective liaison between industries, universities and schools.[91] These could not be left to solve themselves. A follow-up committee was needed to work on them after the Conference was over and, in this context, references made to the need for 'another industrial fund'. He then announced the formation and membership of an Action Group of five engineers and five members of the ASE who were charged to report back to him, at which stage 'we can get down to brass tacks'.[92]

At the final session on the Saturday morning, J.J. Bryant, the Chairman of the ASE gave an 'Outline of the Association's Plans', which included three new developments to 'increase our influence and efficiency'. The first was the prospect of a purpose-built headquarters on the site of a college of technology within easy reach of London. Second, the organization of the ASE branches had been overhauled to improve communication between the membership and the executive. Groups concerned with particular interests and topics were also being set up; in this connection the establishment of a group on Applied Science would have been a priority, had not the existence of the Action Group, with its wider scope and greater influence, now made that unnecessary. Finally, the Education Committee had been reorganized into separate Education (Research) and Education (Coordinating) Committees. In these ways the ASE was attempting to meet the challenges that faced it: there was, in Bryant's opinion, every reason to hope 'that the ASE would continue to play a major role in education development in every field of science'.[93] It appeared that, in relation to newer entrants into the science education arena, the ASE had carried the day.

Behind the scenes, however, there were problems. The Confederation of British Industries had been associated with Project Technology from its pilot stage, S. Moore-Coulson, Secretary of the CBI, being a member of the Consultative Committee.[94] When the major project was established in 1967, the CBI encouraged member firms to assist in practical ways such as developing equipment, making films and linking schools and industry.[95] Some time later, following the decision of the Schools Council General Purposes Committee to endorse an approach to industry for financial help towards the work of Project Technology, the CBI gave 'its blessing to the proposed appeal by the Schools Council to industry for advice, loans, gifts and financial support from firms.' 'This will be known to all our Regions', Moore-Coulson informed Banks in October 1967, 'and can be acted on in all appropriate ways'.[96] The full weight of the CBI's support had therefore been committed to Project Technology a few days before the ASE's November Conference.

The failure of communication between the several organizations working on the problem of recruitment of engineers, and particularly the disunity between the agencies of science and of industry, as well illustrated in a letter from Sir Harold Hartley, himself a scientist with strong industrial interests and indeed on this occasion writing from the Central Electricity Generating Board's Research and Development Department, to the Honourable Montague Woodhouse, Director of Education and Training for the CBI. Hartley's letter followed immediately the decision of the CBI to support Project Technology. 'I am ashamed to say that I did not know of your activity', he candidly acknowledged. 'I have been active in that field myself so the sooner we meet the better.'[97]

Much of Hartley's detailed information about Project Technology and certainly about CBI's financial support for it came from Moore-Coulson via Woodhouse. It was not surprising then, given his 'Socratic friendship'[98] with H.R.H. Prince Philip that Hartley should 'strongly advise' Woodhouse, on the eve of the November Conference, that the CBI should 'hold its hand'. The reference in Prince Philip's speech to the need for a new Industrial Fund 'to provide apparatus such as Mr Sneed's' must have been doubly alarming to supporters of Project Technology.[99] Not only was Sneed's approach very different from that of the Project; but, more important, a decision had already been taken by the CBI to recommend its members to support the appeal from the Schools Council in aid of Project Technology.

When, following the first meeting of the Action Group, C.G. Williams, one of its leading members, wrote to the CBI requesting that it hold back its appeal to members so that coordination of effort could be agreed, Woodhouse's comment to Moore-Coulson was 'I am sure . . . you will give this very short shrift.' There was to be no countermanding the decision already announced; the launching of the Action Group and the appointment of Lord Jackson as its chairman 'seem to have been cooked up by the CEI without consulting us' Woodhouse complained, reflecting a view that the Council of Engineering Institutions, eager to prove itself as a new organization, appeared reluctant to work in parallel with the CBI.[100]

In the event, a headlong collision was avoided, though this lack of coordination over financial support placed severe limitations on the ability of the Action Group to influence events.

Disagreement over funding was accompanied by discord over curriculum aims. In this connection, relations between the ASE and Project Technology were not improved by the publication of an article, based on an interview of E.W. Tapper and F.C. Brown, in *The Times Educational Supplement*, shortly before the Annual Meeting in London.[101] Under the headline 'Doubts on relevance of technology project' the ASE was reported as being sharply critical of the Schools Council's work in this field, in part because the bias was 'too much towards craft activities.' At a time when the ASE was claimed to be striving to increase its membership in all types of maintained schools, 'one senses a hint of envy', the reporter, William Luckin, wrote, 'at the Schools Council's greater potential to inject its ideas into the state system.' Reference was made to the ASE involvement with the Action Group, from which 'something pretty hot' was to come next September as a result of the ASE, the engineering profession and industry mounting 'a joint assault on technological ignorance in the secondary schools.'

Luckin's article drew a strongly worded response from G.B. Harrison, protesting at misrepresentation of the work of his project and urging that the ASE and Project Technology had common objectives.[102] 'The ASE has been invited on more than one occasion to join forces with the Schools Council Project in Technology in promoting the applied science interest', Harrison wrote. 'This invitation has so far been ignored, or even actively opposed, the ASE leading one to believe that they are about to launch a programme of their own inspiration.'[103] Another respondent, M.T. Deere of the Technical Education Unit, University of Reading, similarly upbraided the ASE, fearing that it would 'pin its faith on the "Ealing Grammar School" approach' which, in his view, failed to develop pupils' ingenuity and creativity. Deere also questioned why the ASE had not voiced its criticisms previously as it was represented on the Consultative Committee of Project Technology.[104]

The following week a letter from Tapper was printed in the *TES* suggesting that Luckin had been unduly selective in drawing from the wide range of issues discussed during his meeting with Tapper and F.C. Brown. 'The ASE does not clash with the Schools Council Science Project or with the plans of its director', Tapper asserted. 'It will not appeal for funds from industry and it has taken steps to involve its membership in the problems involved' by seeking means to introduce 'technology (but not under that name) as an integral part of science courses'.[105]

Even before Tapper's letter appeared, he and Harrison had met in Cambridge in an endeavour to heal the breach. Harrison's summary of a long and constructive meeting was that 'the General Secretary and I obviously see eye to eye on pretty well all the questions which were discussed'.[106] Tapper's role as General Secretary was that of 'a very efficient administrator who does not have to, and is not expected to, make decisions committing the ASE to any new line of policy.' In any case, matters had now moved very much into the hands of the Action Group, which itself was likely to be discharged in the not too distant future in favour of a more permanent body, better suited to address the longer term problems of bringing boys and girls to an improved understanding of the importance of technology.

The Action Group held its first meeting on 10 November 1967 and its last on 20 March 1968, reporting to H.R.H. Prince Philip at the end of February. Its recommendations included a new survey on what was being done in schools to introduce applied science considerations and a four-day national Summer School at Imperial College where selected science teachers, of proven skill and enthusiasm, would demonstrate to their colleagues how they were enlivening their teaching through science applications. F.C. Brown, as Chairman of the ASE, urged branches to provide information for the survey, the intention being to review findings at the Spring Education Conference; individual members of the Association were exhorted to offer their services as demonstrators for the Summer School.[107]

In fact neither enterprise quite measured up to expectation. The planning of the summer exhibition by the School Science and Technology Committee, the successor to the Action Group, was plagued by financial uncertainties (it cost some £2000 more than estimated) whilst the letter inviting schools to attend was not received in some areas until after the end of the summer term. At a late date it was decided to persuade industrial firms to exhibit, as well as schools; in consequence there were almost as many items from universities, colleges and industry as from the schools. Space for display was at a premium and the amount of information to be absorbed in the course of a visit was great.[108] Moreover, by the autumn of 1968, other initiatives had been taken to provide courses and exhibitions of applied science for school teachers, so that the Imperial College venture was not unique, except possibly in scale. It was not repeated.[109]

As for the ASE's fact-finding survey of 'good practice', little more was heard of this, the main item at the Spring Education Conference being the report of the Dainton Committee, with its alarming account of a sharp swing away from science in the sixth-forms. D.T. Kelly, a science teacher from Semper's school and a member of the ASE, recently recruited by Harrison to be responsible for the science coordination work of Project Technology, spoke about engineering science and project work in the schools, but the reports of regional representatives were more centred on the lack of laboratory technicians and the effects on science teaching of external examination syllabuses than upon 'good practice' in school technology.[110]

Reshaping policy

The end of the sixties brought a hiatus in the ASE's attempts to accommodate or react to influences from 'the alternative road'. At national level the Action Group gave way, in turn, to the Schools Science and Technology Committee (1967–71) and to the Standing Conference on Schools Science and Technology (1971 onwards). The former body, under the chairmanship of H.R.H. Prince Philip, included F.C. Brown and J.J. Bryant from the ASE, as well as G.B. Harrison and E. Semper, amongst its members. Under its sponsorship the Imperial College Summer School of 1968 was organized. It initiated collaboration with the British Association; spent much time in considering the strategy for an appeal to industry for financial support; and contributed to the development of Project Technology through the encouragement of regional centres. Increasingly, the importance of these local initiatives was recognized and, correlatively, the need for a national coordinating agency, the Standing Conference, which held its inaugural meeting in January 1971, the ASE being one of a large number of member organizations.

The breathing space provided to the ASE membership by these national developments gave time for reflection on classroom problems associated with the teaching of engineering science and the use of projects. In a critical review,[111] two London teachers pointed out that the types of project which were feasible in most schools, given the constraints of resources and time, did not bear much relationship to professional engineering and design activities and so were unlikely to provide a sound basis for vocational choice; that organizational and timetable problems often prevented close liaison between science and craft departments; that the present schemes of examination of school engineering courses did not seem to test skills much different from those tested in science examinations; and that the reasons for student reluctance to enter university departments of engineering were probably more complex than advocates of 'creativity' in science teaching appeared to allow. A complementary analysis of problems was offered by Deryk T. Kelly,[112] from the staff of Project Technology, who emphasized the difficult role of the teacher in guiding pupils engaged in project work, as well as fears about mounting expenditure if projects involving construction were embarked upon. For Kelly, as for many others, however, the major problem was that of instituting a simple, fair and objective system of project assessment which would yield comparative results from one school to another. Additionally, there was the matter of links with industry. Though many schools reported favourably on their attempts to enter into relations with local industries, not all had found a ready welcome to their approaches.

Much of this grass-root reaction to the implementation of a technological dimension in science teaching was stimulated by the publication in *Education in Science*, from February 1967 until

September 1969, of a 'Project' supplement. The origin of this was a request to the ASE from J.A.G. Banks of the Schools Council for help in disseminating ideas on project work.[113] In terms of professional pressures, however, the claims of technological applications could not have ranked high in the experience of most science teachers. Secondary school reorganization, with the attendant problems of mixed ability classes; the science curriculum projects from the Nuffield Foundation and the Schools Council; interminable debate about the structure of sixth-form studies and examinations; the shortage of technical supporting staff, to say nothing of concerns about SI units and chemical nomenclature, were all prior claimants on the attention of many.

To some extent the Dainton Report, with its prediction of empty science sixth-forms by 1984,[114] brought the ASE ship back on course, if, indeed, it had been in danger of drifting into uncharted waters. When, at the end of the sixties, the Association turned to updating its Policy Statement and to the submission of comment to the Secretary of State for Education for consideration when revising the Education Acts, the emphasis was firmly on 'science as the vehicle for carrying the aims of a general education.'[115] A recommendation in a policy discussion paper that science teachers should 'refresh themselves . . . with periods in industry and technological institutions'[116] did not survive into the final agreed statement. Here specific reference to technology was limited to a concluding section on 'The Future', in an Annexe to the Policy Statement.[117] Asserting that the laboured insistence on 'discovery' in recent curriculum innovations had left 'no time for applying the discovered principles to the real situations and problems in applied science and technology', the need was acknowledged for experimentation with new types of science courses. Beyond this the Association appeared unwilling to go in 1971.

The technology issue was not so easily shelved, however. A year later, when detailed consideration was being given to the science education of children aged 13 to 16 years, the role of technology was addressed in detail. In the resulting report,[118] from a sub-committee of the Education (Coordinating) Committee under the chairmanship of Professor E.H. Coulson, members were reminded that 'for many pupils technological subjects provide the easiest and most convincing approach to a knowledge of scientific principles.' It was not surprising, therefore, that at the Spring Education Conference at Nottingham in 1973, 'Science and Technology in Schools' appeared again as a major item on the agenda.[119] Following lectures by Dr Frank McKim (Marlborough College) and Peter Dutton (Sheffield Science and Technology Centre), discussion groups met and reported unanimity on the need to include some technological content in school science courses. Furthermore, all groups urged that the ASE should make a statement on its attitude towards technology.

When, following the work of another sub-committee of the Education (Coordinating) Committee, the statement was published as a discussion document,[120] it emphasized in a way no previous policy utterance had done, the 'important and creative objective' of teachers in relation to 'the evaluation of the applications of science through technology'. 'Above all', it asserted, 'science teaching must aim to develop effective decision-making in maturing adults. Real experience in decision-making is achieved through the appreciation of technology and through practical experience of problem-solving in the design and construction of a device or system, however simple, to serve a need.' The real worth of this activity was achieved only if it was carried through, beyond the constructional stage, to a critical evaluation, including an assessment of 'the ways in which it affects, for good or ill, the quality of life'. Whilst recognizing that science teachers need help in preparing for this 'extended approach', the Association declared itself as welcoming any initiative to develop interdisciplinary approaches to the appreciation of technology and the creation of technological capability.

This ambitious statement, both embracing technology and, at the same time, taking a wider view of it than most of its proponents, was too marked an advance on previous doctrine for it to have immediate impact on practice. Curriculum experimentation continued, but its scale remained largely unchanged until external stimulus was applied in the autumn of 1976.

Mr James Callaghan's speech on education, delivered at Ruskin College, Oxford, in October 1976, and inaugurating the 'Great Debate', included a specific reference to science teaching.[121] In the view of the Prime Minister, it needed 'a more technological bias' that would 'lead towards practical applications in industry rather than towards academic studies'. The refrain was scarcely new, but it was now orchestrated within a deliberate movement to obtain increased central control over the content of the school curriculum. As had been argued in the Yellow Book,[122] the DES's briefing memorandum for the Prime Minister, the time was ripe for a greater emphasis on the economic functions of education and on the provision of more practically based courses linking schools and industry. An identical message came from the CBI which had recently initiated a project on *Understanding British Industry* and whose Director-General, John Methven, had called for a greater stress on applied as opposed to pure studies in schools.[123] A Schools Council *Industry Project* sponsored by the Trades Union Congress and the Confederation of British Industries followed in 1977.

Capitalizing on what they rightly sensed as a marked change in the political context for science education, G.B. Harrison, by then Director of the National Centre for School Technology at Trent Polytechnic, and P.E. Dutton, of the Sheffield Regional Centre for Science and Technology, threw down the gauntlet to the ASE in a provocative article entitled 'The challenge of including technological activities in school science.'[124] 'How will you react now?' they asked, with reference to the statements by the Prime Minister and the

Director-General of the CBI. Their article provoked critical letters from some members including H.P. Ramage,[125] but the Association at large had already begun to respond. A new sub-committee on Science and Technology was established. At the Education Conference at Nottingham in April 1977, 'Science, Design and Craft Education' and 'Science and Technology' were main themes,[126] discussion groups focusing particularly on the initiatives which the new sub-committee might take for the benefit of members. In addition, the Association collaborated with the Council of Engineering Institutions in a curriculum development project, *Science and Society*, directed by John Lewis (Chairman of the ASE in 1977) and designed to provide teachers with resource materials to show the relevance of science to the world outside the classroom. The Association secured for its President in 1977 Sir Alastair Pilkington FRS, a distinguished industrialist and energetic advocate of closer relations between education and industry. An ASE Award Scheme was inaugurated to encourage developments in areas of special concern, the first prize going to a submission on 'Technology in a Primary School'; two years later, when the scheme was again offered, the theme for the Awards was 'Science/Industry Links and Science Teaching'.[127] The Department of Industry was approached for funds to support a review of physics examination syllabuses, the ASE's Regional structure to be used to assist the development of technological approaches to topics and the modification of examination papers to incorporate technological aspects.[128] Finally, before the year was out, the Education (Research) Committee set up a Working Party to produce a document as the basis of Association policy in science education into the 1980s.[129]

Detailed evaluation of the consultative document, *Alternatives for Science Education*, and of the resulting Policy Statement, *Education through Science*, is outside the scope of this book. What can be said is that there are no precedents in the Association's history for the extent of the activity since 1976 in the field of educational and industrial cooperation. Frequent accounts appeared in *Education in Science*, and elsewhere, of the help which professional institutions and industrial agencies were offering to schools and of the experience of science teachers who had availed themselves of this.[130] By the early 1980s, the title of the Science and Technology Sub-Committee had become the Science, Industry and Technology Sub-Committee, with a suitably enlarged membership.

Yet this formal acknowledgement of a liaison between science and technology in the service of industrial ends concealed problems which were inadequately addressed in the ASE's Policy Statement. A hint of these was given by Sir James Hamilton, Permanent Secretary to the Department of Education and Science and a former engineer, speaking at the Association Dinner during the Annual Meeting at Hull in 1980.[131] Referring to *Alternatives for Science Education* and to a recent HMI survey of secondary education,[132] he drew attention to the over-academic science curriculum offered to many fourth and fifth year secondary school pupils. Whether the solution lay in the direction of 'courses in technology' or of more knowledge of scientific concepts in real-life practical situations was uncertain for him. Nothing must be done to 'erode the understanding of fundamentals'; 'an ill-taught course in technology' was not to be preferred to a 'well-taught course in the basic science.'

A related issue arose at the Autumn Conference of the Standing Conference on Schools' Science and Technology in October 1980 when, following a talk by Dr Frank McKim on the problems of examining the applications of scientific knowledge, T. Dodd, an adviser in Design and Technical Studies, challenged the assumption that the main road to technological understanding for pupils was through science.[133] Instead, the alternative route, through courses in technology, was advocated. In practice, as a subsequent HMI report[134] showed, technology courses in secondary schools were not yet sufficiently well established to make them a realistic alternative to science, though the Inspectorate was in no doubt that 'a course in technology merits consideration for a place in the curriculum of all pupils up to the statutory leaving age'.[135] That a newcomer had truly arrived on the curriculum scene was confirmed by the *Policy Statement* of the new Engineering Council, Finniston's 'engine for change', in its declared intent to promote a higher standard of technological literacy within the educational system. To this end it would 'encourage the development and teaching of mathematics, science and technology in schools in a way which is relevant to the needs of society, industry and the engineering profession'.[136]

A change in the curriculum relationships of science and technology from alternatives to uneasy partners, carried implications for the roles of each which, from the science side at least, need more detailed exploration. In April 1982, the Science, Industry and Technology Sub-Committee confronted the membership with the question, 'Does the Association need a new view of school science and technology?', urging that much might be gained from increased cooperation between science teachers and their colleagues with 'a formalized technology brief.'[137] Depending on the response of members, a document might be published 'as a legitimate extension of the Association's recent Policy Statement *Education through Science*'.

All this was a far cry from the Association's reluctance in the 1960s to admit the word 'technology' into its policy deliberations. From origins of neglect and inferiority, a cuckoo in the nest of science education, autonomous school technology had emerged. In the course of its development it had changed the character of school science and had severely tested the Association's ability to adapt to external forces.

12 Facing the Future

The quest for influence

Various explanations have been offered to account for the lack of central control over the content of secondary school education in the post-war years, a period which was exceptional in this respect. One speculation, not altogether serious, is that those who drafted the 1944 Education Bill quite simply forgot about the curriculum, such was their concern with other aspects of the settlement. Alternatively, and more convincingly, they may have recognized that the curriculum implications of 'secondary education for all' were so momentous that they would have engendered controversy without limit if exposed at that stage. Again, it has been argued that diffused responsibility for the curriculum was a deliberate strategy to prevent rapid reversal of educational decisions following a change in political power at the centre. Whatever the explanation, Derek Morrell's diagnosis of 'a vacuum in curriculum matters' was unquestionably accurate in the late 1950s.

Viewed in this light, the Policy Statements of 1957 and 1961 can be seen as deliberate and well-timed initiatives on the part of the SMA and AWST, designed to fill the vacuum, at least as far as the science curriculum was concerned. They were a clear bid for authority to define the place and content of science in grammar school education. The events which followed have already been related in Chapter 10 above. The outcome was a project firmly under the control of the Nuffield Foundation, the Associations suffering a set-back in their attempts to influence the direction of curriculum change. Their authority was over-ridden by other sources including professional science and the Ministry of Education, though it should be added that individual members of the SMA and AWST played important parts in the various teams responsible for the Nuffield Projects.

The formation of the Ministry's Curriculum Study Group was announced in the House of Commons by Sir David Eccles two days after he had informed Members about the launching of the Nuffield Science Teaching Project. In the face of local education authority wrath at centralist intervention into curriculum matters, the Study Group was soon disbanded, leading to the establishment of the Schools Council. Although much was made at the time of the extent to which teachers controlled the new Council's committees, representation was largely in terms of teacher unions. Subject teaching associations were not, as a matter of right, guaranteed a voice and the ASE (as by this time it had become) found itself constitutionally excluded from the deliberations of the Science Committee of the Schools Council.

In many ways this development was of more significance than that involving the Nuffield Foundation. The Nuffield intervention, though powerful, had from the first been seen as transient. Having attended to school science the Trustees would eventually seek other needful recipients for their largesse. In contrast, in the mid-sixties the Schools Council had all the appearances of a permanent feature on the educational landscape. It commanded resources beyond anything the ASE could hope to match and its mechanisms for the articulation of its products with the schools seemed superior. Through it, alternative versions of school science might be manufactured and distributed to the classroom, irrespective of ASE opinion.

As we have seen, by 1967 the Association had braced itself for recovery and, especially after revision of the policy of the Education (Research) Committee in the early 1970s, began to pursue the quest for curriculum influence with renewed vigour. Rebuffed as an instigator of curriculum change when it had sought resources in the 1960s, the Association now adopted a policy of 'do-it-yourself', sponsoring the development of projects such as LAMP in the mid-seventies. Subsequently, with increasing confidence, it turned again for external funding for curriculum projects, this time successfully, from bodies such as the Department of Energy, the Industry/Education Unit of the Department of Industry and from commercial and industrial organizations. It attempted to enhance its authority to pronounce on matters of science education by engaging in research activities. Although its bid for the contract to conduct the national monitoring of children's scientific attainments, in connection with the DES's Assessment of Performance Unit, was unsuccessful, it did receive a substantial grant from the Schools Council for a project involving 'Case Studies in Decision Making'. By 1977, also, it had negotiated constitutional representation on the Science Committee of the Schools Council. The culmination of this line of development, as indicated in Chapter 5, was the establishment of the Secondary Science Curriculum Review in 1981 with strong ASE representation on the Steering Committee and, as Director, an ex-chairman of the ASE who had been a leading architect of the proposal for the Review.

Parallel and complementary to this direct involvement with the curriculum, the Association embarked on a further initiative in 1981. Both the Consultative Document *Alternatives for Science Education* (1979) and the subsequent Policy Statement (1981) had laid great stress on the need for in-service education of science teachers. Even before the Policy Statement had been agreed, a paper from Dr R.W. West and Professor J.J. Thompson on Validation and Accreditation had been considered by the ASE Council and a Working Party established to report on the case for, or against, ASE involvement in the validation of in-service courses for science teachers.[1] This working party, under West's chairmanship, concluded that 'a strong case exists for the Association to become a Validating Body in the field of in-service education', a view which Council later endorsed. An important argument in reaching this decision, and 'the prime justification for embarking on validation' was that unless the Association entered the field it would be 'entirely in the hands of the training institutions and existing validating bodies when it comes to the implementation of its own policy recommendations'. Criteria for courses leading to a Diploma in Science Education were drafted, it being recommended that each course should include 'detailed discussion and consideration of the aims of science education, and the context to which they relate, as presented in the 1981 Policy Statement. On the financial side of this development and in the light of experience of the Mathematical Association which already offered a Diploma, it was estimated that within a few years of entering the validation field, the ASE might expect to be in receipt of an income from validation fees which was well in excess of related expenditure.[2] A Validation Board was established under the chairmanship of Sir Norman Lindop, the recently retired Director of Hatfield Polytechnic and an ex-President of the ASE. Initial plans included the offer of a Certificate in Science Teaching (Primary) and a Diploma in Science Education (Primary), with a later phase of work to deal with science education at secondary level.[3] By establishment of its Validation Board the Association had acquired a mechanism for influencing the in-service education of science teachers in the direction of its own policy objectives.

Taken together, the series of developments since the early 1970s, embracing increased curriculum intervention, research involvement and control over professional qualifications, represents a pattern of growth not unfamiliar to students of the natural history of occupations. It corresponds to a transformation from amateurs to professionals, and to the explicit acknowledgement of power as the end in view – power, that is, in the sense of controlling an occupation – in specific terms, of making the ASE an institution for the collegiate determination of what counts as valid teaching of science in schools. Extrapolating, it leads into issues such as conditions of service, levels of salaries and the setting of standards of entry into the profession; ultimately to unionization which the Association's Trust Deed forbids.

Here then is a contemporary dilemma for the ASE. Recognizing the political nature of curriculum decisions, and that what takes place under the name of science education is the outcome of complex interactions between the many competing interest groups which have transformed the curriculum vacuum into a high pressure system, it is being obliged to pursue activities which led along a road to the end of which it can never go. In no way could a subject teaching association be envisaged as an effective rival to the existing teacher unions as, for example, a negotiator of the salaries of its members. Such ambitions and available instrumentalities are incommensurate.

The future role of the ASE was the subject of debate at the first Yorkshire Region Science Education conference in 1973, an occasion attended by the Chairman of the Association in that year, W.F. Archenhold (University of Leeds) and the General Secretary, B.G. Atwood. Speakers offered views on the implications of contextual changes resulting from the growth not only of non-selective secondary schools, but also of teachers' centres and of science centres under the auspices of the professional scientific institutes. The development of local education authority Advisory Services was also commented on. It seemed that many regional activities, previously only available through the ASE, were now being offered by other agencies. Rather than compete, it was suggested that the ASE should re-define its role and direct its energies into new fields.[4]

The theme was carried forward to the Education Conference at Nottingham the following year. Here one contributor, B.R. Chapman (University of Leeds) whose earlier paper to Yorkshire Region was amongst those circulated at Nottingham, urged that in the future the ASE should aim 'to have some say in giving academic validation and professional recognition to science teachers'. This might include power to prevent the unqualified from teaching science and to protect members from being required to teach unfamiliar subjects without prior in-service education. A different suggestion was that the ASE should establish a fellowship grade to which meritorious science teachers might aspire.[5]

In the course of discussion it was made clear that the Trust Deed imposed considerable limitations on the scope of the Association's action. Additionally, however, the idea of alliances with the teacher unions to aid the quest for influence over the professional welfare of members commanded relatively little support. Most regions were in favour of the status quo as far as the aims of the Association were concerned. The role of 'licensing body' was seen as neither realistic nor appropriate at this stage.[6]

Nevertheless change was taking place, and the ASE was departing noticeably from the 'learned society' role which had characterized much of the activity of the AWST and the SMA. New relationships were being made with Her Majesty's Inspectorate, industry, commerce, examinations boards and professional science.[7] In this connection the background of those recently serving as President is revealing. Until 1977 there was little departure from the custom of electing a Vice-Chancellor or science professor from the university which was host to the Annual Meeting. In that year the ASE's third industrialist President was appointed; those who followed are listed in Table 12.1.[8]

It is too early yet to evaluate the consequences of this closer association of the ASE with industry and with other bodies having a stake in science education. Important benefits have no doubt accrued, not least financial. At the same time effective partnerships require that both partners derive continuing satisfaction from the relationship without too great a loss of independence for each. In its multifarious relationships one question for the ASE concerns the extent to which it is 'an

Table 12.1   Presidents of the ASE

1977	Sir Alastair Pilkington FRS Chairman of the Pilkington Group of Companies
1978–9	Norman Booth Recently retired Senior Staff Inspector (Science), DES
1980	Sir Norman Lindop MSc, FRIC Director, The Hatfield Polytechnic
1981	Sir Denis Rooke CBE, FRS, FEng Chairman, British Gas Corporation
1982	Sir Hermann Bondi, KCB, FRS Chairman, Natural Environment Research Council and a former Chief Scientific Adviser to the Ministry of Defence
1983	Sir Robert Clayton, CBE, F Eng Technical Director, General Electric Company PLC
1984	Sir James Hamilton KCB, MBE Permanent Secretary, DES until his retirement in April 1983

instrument being played' or 'a voice to be heeded'. Another is whether there is sufficient common ground between the aims and purposes of new partners to enable the Association to maintain a consistent point of view. Could it sustain alliances with both the Royal Society and the Engineering Council, for example, if it was found that these bodies expressed divergent opinions about the place of technology in the school curriculum? The challenge for the Association is to contribute to and derive benefits from partnerships, whilst retaining for its membership both independence and a capability for expressing a radical point of view.

Women in the Association

When the ASE came into being in 1963 the ratio of men to women in the membership was approximately 3.7 to 1. This value has not changed greatly over the years. It might be reasonable, therefore, to expect that the presence of women in the offices and committees of the Association would be reflective of their presence in the membership at large.

Over the twenty-one-year period, 1963 to 1983, the chairman of the ASE has been a woman on four occasions, as against seventeen for men. There has never been a woman Honorary Treasurer, Honorary Annual Meeting Secretary or Editor of *The School Science Review*. Two of the five Honorary Minuting Secretaries have been women. As for the important Education Committees, the Research Committee has had one woman and five men as chairman; the Coordinating Committee has had two women and three men. There has been one woman President of the ASE.

Whether this is an acceptable distribution of offices between the sexes is a question which cannot be answered on the basis of such limited data over a relatively short time scale alone. Nevertheless, concern about the position of women in the Association has been expressed from time to time. It was a central issue at the time of amalgamation. Similarly in 1967, when the Branches Sub-Committee recommended to Council the abolition of the office of Honorary Secretary for Girls' Schools, it simultaneously expressed the opinion that in the newly-designated Regions 'Women members should be represented on all committees'.[9]

The position of women in the Association is not unrelated to their position in the science community at large where their under-representation has generated concern. Much effort has been expended in attempts to overcome the apparent reluctance of girls to study the physical sciences and to take up careers in science and engineering.[10] In this connection the records of the AST and AWST make a unique contribution to the discussion. The exclusion of women from the APSSM and the SMA brought into being a separate association of women science teachers who, for some fifty years, conducted their affairs, established their priorities and expressed their curriculum preferences largely uncontaminated by male influences. From a study of the Minute books and other records of the AST and AWST during the period 1912 to 1962 it is clear that the interests, preferred modes of organization and conceptions of school science of women science teachers had characteristics which differentiated them clearly from those of men. Indeed, the prospect arises of a distinct 'women's science education'.

In terms of concerns, the women had fewer formal contacts with the major institutions of professional science and with distinguished luminaries of the research world than did the men. Their President was, typically, a headmistress in contrast to the men's FRS. Their focus within science tended to be more on its applications and its interactions with everyday life than on abstract theory and technique. Thus, the fine detail of apparatus design and new ways of performing school experiments, a major attraction of the Members' Exhibition at the men's Annual Meetings, held little interest for the women. They rarely entered into agreements with scientific apparatus manufacturers for demonstrations and exhibitions, as did the men. Whereas the men, from the first, limited their external relations to a narrow range of bodies, such as universities and examination boards, which they wished to influence, the women were more open, entering into communication with a much wider range of organizations such as the Electrical Association for Women, the English Speaking Union, the British Film Institute, the British Social Hygiene Council and the Central Council for Health Education.

The women had from the first a stronger teacher-training element in their membership than did the men. This brought perspectives into their work which had few counterparts in the deliberations of the

SMA. Thus, ideas from educational psychology on the nature of the child and of children's learning were included early in the women's discussions, a concern for educational theory contrasting markedly with the pragmatic approach of most male science teachers.

An indication of the differences between women's conceptions of school science education and those of men is provided by the repeated complaints from members of the AWST that, although they were obliged under their rules to subscribe to *The School Science Review*, the journal failed to cater for their needs. Few women contributed to its pages, despite requests from the (male) editor. Their preferred mode of communication about professional problems of common concern was the *conversazione*, rather than the scientific paper or publication. Their annual meetings incorporated a distinct social dimension, fears about the loss of this being one obstacle to amalgamation.

At the level of curriculum there is evidence that the conception of 'general science' outlined in discussion and in reports of the women science teachers in the 1930s had emphases which made it a distinct entity from the version recommended by the SMA. To take but one example, topics such as 'the gradual evolution of parental care' did not intrude into the syllabus for boys. Eventually, for reasons which have been made clear earlier, men and women science teachers were drawn into closer working relationships which led to an amalgamated Association. With this convergence, alternative definitions of school science were brought into interaction and conflict, the resulting curriculum recommendations being the product of impositions of meaning which substantially modified 'women's science education'.

No doubt many of the differences in curriculum prescriptions can be explained in terms of the different institutional contexts within which the women and men science teachers worked, especially in the inter-war and immediate post-war years. Changes in the social context, notably with respect to the social role of women as 'home-makers', also contributed in time to the lessening of differences. But when due allowance is made for contextual and social influences on the curriculum preferences, agenda and organizational practices of the women science teachers, as revealed in their Minute books, reports and records of meetings, the impression remains of unexplained, residual differences. In particular, their preferred model of sharing experiences, bolstering confidence and mutually supporting each other in the common task of teaching science represent a distinct aspect of the women's activity which differentiated them from the men. Unquestionably the decision to unite with the men in 1963 brought many benefits to the women. But those who predicted that a price would be paid were correct. Amalgamation entailed adaptation of organizational practices and support systems which had sustained the women in their associations for half a century.

Problems of scale

Historically, association has had many purposes including protection from hostile forces; power and influence for the achievement of common goals; and a sense of identity and status for those involved. Whatever the purpose, it is an act which is premised on the existence of common values, interests and aspirations which bind the members together. In the case of the APSSM and for much of its life, the SMA – to a lesser extent the AWST – homogeneity of interests, narrowly defined, was a zealously-guarded characteristic of the membership. With the rapid increase in numbers which the ASE experienced in the sixties and seventies, institutional diversity and geographical dispersion exacerbated old problems and created new ones. There was need to keep under constant review the ways in which a membership representing a much increased range of special interests could be held together. The greater involvement of the Association in deliberations on science education at national level and the need to formulate authoritative responses to government papers and other reports placed strains upon the established methods of consulting the opinion of members. Indeed, the general problem of communication between the membership, on the one hand, and the officers and the burgeoning committee structure of the Association, on the other, brought the workings of Council under formal review in 1976.

W.J. Kirkham, Chairman in that year, was provoked sufficiently by the situation to issue a note to Council members expressing concern at their lack of involvement in deliberations about policy. The Regions, for him, were 'the strength of the Association' and the only committee on which they were fully represented was Council. It followed that Council should 'set the pace of the Association'. Instead, it had become 'a rubber stamping organization'. 'Are the meetings too short?' 'Does the agenda appear too cut and dried?' 'Do the Region representatives and elected members come without ideas?' Kirkham asked.[11]

At the next meeting of Council, after 'considerable discussion', a Working Party was established to report on the structure and function of Council. This group went about its business energetically; a questionnaire was sent to ASE members, all Regions and some 700 individuals responding. The major finding of the investigation, reported the following year, was that between the 'scattered members and the elected national officers and committees' there was 'a potentially enormous gap'. Various measures were proposed to improve communications and some immediate changes followed. A new Publications Committee was established to coordinate all the various publishing activities of the Association. The calendar of Council meetings was revised to provide more time for meetings and arrangements for the circulation of papers were improved to permit Region Representatives greater opportunity to consult locally.[12]

Within the Working Party's report was a strongly-expressed view that the Executive Committee had become the prime initiator of policy and activity in the Association, a role not in accord with the Rule that it should 'manage the affairs of the Association in accordance with the policy determined by Council and under the supervision of Council'. This criticism drew a sharp retort from Kirkham's successor, J.L. Lewis, writing as Chairman of the Executive Committee, first, that the Working Party had exceeded its brief in making such references, its allotted task being to look into the workings of Council; and second, that the Executive Committee's activities were fully reported to Council, but when an opinion was sought on possible courses of action 'the response we get is negligible'.[13]

Behind this exchange was a genuine problem arising from the voluntary nature of participation in the affairs of the Association. Region Representatives, all of whom would be in full-time employment, had not always found it easy to consult fully in their regions in the time between receipt of Council papers and the date of the meeting. Some reluctance to express a firm opinion on critical issues was perhaps understandable in the circumstances. Similarly, the burden on honorary officers, also serving on a voluntary and part-time basis, had grown considerably. Yet the Association's ability to exert influence on developments at national level depended on a fast response to approaches and initiatives by external bodies. In such a situation, the concentration of power in a relatively small number of officers was difficult to avoid. Concurrently, the opportunity for increase in the influence of the permanent, salaried officials became greater. Repositories of the long-term collective memory of Council and Executive, they were also, by virtue of their full-time appointments, more readily available to represent the Association at short notice. In this connection, the Working Party recommended that consideration should be given to the possibility of the ASE paying for the part-time secondment of the Chairman from his normal employment during his year of office.

The extent to which democratic impulses can counteract bureaucratic and oligarchic drift remains to be seen, as the ASE continues to grow. There are financial, apart from other, limits on the number of occasions in a year when Council can meet. Also the time scales for democratic consultation and for necessary action are not always compatible. The period can be considerable for news of Council's deliberations to travel to the Regions, and within Regions to local Section committees, and then, in the reverse direction, for an expression of opinion to be formulated and transmitted from Sections back to Council. At an earlier date, when the SMA was negotiating with the Nuffield Foundation there was some evidence that the time-consuming consultations between members of the General Committee had contributed to the Foundation's decision to keep the management of the Science Teaching Project firmly under its own control. The contemporary problem for the ASE is whether there is not a contradiction between its disposition to openness and involvement of members in its approach to policy formation and curriculum review, and its need for crisp, centralized decision-taking which its quest for influence entails.

A not unrelated problem of scale is the extent to which the membership, with growth, has become more segmented. The danger here is the erosion of common values which bind the members together. Officer priorities and perspectives may not always match those of the grass-root members. For the latter, as has been the case since the origin of the Associations, the most prized benefits of membership are usually the comradeship and support which they have found in local and national meetings and the information in publications of direct relevance to practical, everyday aspects of school science teaching. Thus, advice about laboratory safety, examination changes and curriculum and apparatus development is highly prized and remains an important part of the Association's work. Additionally, however, for the Association's officers new priorities have emerged, such as the need to make and maintain alliances necessary for the implementation of policy and to ensure the forceful representation of the Association's views in important national arenas. Quest for influence and provision of a service to members are not necessarily incompatible, but may be a source of tension not least in relation to the allocation of the Association's resources.

Segmentation occurs along other dimensions also. Primary school teachers and specialist teachers of biology, chemistry and physics working with students in the 16–19 age range, to take but two examples, do not have the same requirements of the ASE. Their definitions of science education may differ profoundly, the latter perceiving it in terms of pre-professional training and the former as one contributor only to children's intellectual, emotional and physical development. Even within one of these groups there may be different senses of mission, technique and student-teacher relationships. The experiences of those teaching GCE A level sciences in a vocationally orientated college of further education are not necessarily the same as those teaching the same subjects in an 11–18 comprehensive secondary school.

The ASE's claim to be an Association for *all* science teachers has considerable validity in terms of its expanded membership. At the same time it requires a practical recognition of the diversity of its membership in the services it offers, as well as a sensitivity to the fact that the diversity is dynamic, in continual change. In such a situation the tendency is for any programme of planned activities to focus on the elements which are common to a number of groups, with the unique and special taking second place. Careful judgements are required here in the disposition of finite resources; thus, it was decided in 1983 that the publication of a journal for primary school science teachers could not be justified on grounds of expense.[14] If diversity increases to a point when the importance to particular segments of the membership of what is unique to them is greater than that of common components provided, the history of associations suggests that disintegration results. Splinter groups emerge in independent or symbiotic existence. The Association of Teachers of Geology, founded in 1967,[15] and the Association for Astronomy Education, 1981,[16] may be seen as cases in point, the former having a joint sub-committee with the ASE's Education (Coordinating) Committee.

Impediments to change

It has been said that we shape our institutions which in turn shape us. Viewing the Associations from an historical perspective it is possible to detect examples of this proposition at work. Thus, the continued influence of the independent and grammar school teachers who had established the Associations in the early decades of the century was a contributory factor to the slowness with which the concept of 'science for all' was grasped in the 1960s. As late as 1973 a chairman of the ASE was unable to go beyond a reference to *the potential* of the Association to become one for all teachers of science.[17]

Similarly, relationships with the science departments of universities and with leading organizations of professional science, such as the Royal Society, undoubtedly assisted the APSSM and the SMA in their declared aim of improving the teaching of science. At the same time, and despite the efforts of the ASE's Patron, and other influential figures such as Sir Harold Hartley and Sir Graham Savage, these affiliations disposed the Association in the 1960s to a view of technology which made difficult a *rapprochement* with developments taking place elsewhere.

With regard to the school curriculum, it might be questioned whether the establishment of subject teaching associations has not contributed to educational divisiveness. Boundary insulation around subject territories has been strengthened, making more difficult the construction of, and acquisition of status by, new organizations of knowledge. School technology and environmental education might be cited as examples where attempts have been made to establish new subjects, so far with only limited success. Neither has been accommodated readily within the ASE and, like Domestic Science, each has had to established its own association of teachers.

This is not to say that a problem has not been recognized. A significant step to reduce boundary insulation and to facilitate an exchange of views was taken by the ASE in 1971 when the Chairman, B.G. Atwood, convened a meeting of representatives of twenty subject teaching associations at Hatfield. It was agreed on that occasion to form a Council of Subject Teaching Associations as a means of increasing their involvement in decision and policy making at all levels, and of improving communication between them. The administration of the affairs of COSTA was carried out by the ASE until 1977, when the Historical Association assumed responsibility. It was largely as a result of pressure from COSTA that the Schools Council constitution was amended in 1975 to permit the inclusion on its subject committees of representatives of subject teaching associations.[18]

Looking to the more distant future it could be that, as the idea of life-long science education becomes a reality with developments in informal science education and new institutional provisions for the learning of science by adults, the ASE's historical focus on schools will be a limiting factor on its influence. Because science and technology are now so much part of the economic and social fabric it is essential that improved means be developed to enable adults to acquire the knowledge and skills necessary for the formation of opinions on contemporary issues. School science courses alone can never provide all that citizens will need throughout their lives to understand a changing world and to influence decisions about the many social issues which have a science and technology component. The necessary articulation of school and adult learning was mentioned briefly, and for the first time, in the ASE's Policy Statement *Education through Science* (1981)[19] but the conception of school courses as a foundation for subsequent informal learning of science in relation to an unpredictable future remains, as yet, an unacknowledged challenge.

Ultimately, two related factors above all others are likely to determine the ability of the ASE to capitalize on opportunities presented by future contextual change in pursuit of its goal of pronouncing authoritatively on science education. The first of these is finance and the second the opinion of the ordinary membership.

In connection with finance, a central question is whether the Association's policies and capabilities are appropriate to, and sufficiently supportive of, its evolving roles. Considering annual turnover, and allowing for subscription increases, comparative figures for the period 1965–66 to 1982–83 are indicative of impressive growth (Table 12.2).[20] At the same time, the critical index of effective management, the ratio of salary costs to turnover, has been held fairly constant, its average value over the period being 16.5 per cent and this despite growth of the Headquarters' establishment (Table 12.3) and the laudable determination of the ASE in later years to pay 'the rate for the job' to all its staff.

Within this broad picture of healthy expansion, the policy has been for activities of direct benefit to the membership to be financed from annual subscriptions, up to approximately 80 per cent of total expenditure. Beyond this, there are financially self-supporting services to members, including publications other than the journals, and general activities in which the Association engages in its quest for the improvement of science teaching.

One question for the future arises from the increased diversification of interests within the category of Ordinary Member. To supply direct satisfactions for *all* kinds of science teachers clearly entails additional provisions, both regionally and nationally, with the implication of additional costs. The involvement of primary school teachers is a case in point. The publication of a separate journal devoted to the needs and interests of such teachers could not be contemplated because of

Table 12.2   *Turnover and Salary Costs (£)*

	Turnover	Salary Costs
1965–6	36,691	6,019 (16.4%)
1973–4	157,725	22,647 (14.4%)
1982–3	901,148	151,110 (16.8%)

Table 12.3   *Headquarters Staff*

	Professional	Clerical and Ancillary (full- and part-time)
1965	1	9
1973	3	13
1983	5	28

the expense. The news-sheet *ASE Primary Science*, initially aided by grant from the Department of Industry, became a net cost to the Association from 1983 when the grant ended.

Another question is whether there is sufficient flexibility in the Association's budgetary arrangements to enable it to respond promptly and effectively to major contextual changes such as the Technical and Vocational Education Initiative sponsored by the Manpower Services Commission in 1983. A large fraction of the ASE's expenditure at present goes on inescapable, continuing commitments. Maybe, if the proportion of income from publications and validation work grows in the future, a greater potential for manoeuvrability will be achieved. The availability of 'investment and venture capital' to ensure leadership in new areas of potential importance, such as technology and adult science education, is essential if influence in traditional areas is to be retained.

A third question, related to the heavy dependence of the ASE's finances on the annual subscriptions of ordinary members, is whether membership levels can be improved. Recruitment of science teachers to the profession has decreased in recent years. This factor, in conjunction with the age structure of the school science teaching force, generates a constant pressure to recruit more members to the ASE. In the early 1980s, perhaps one in three 'science teachers' in the UK was a member. Much room for expansion therefore remains, but this is likely to be achieved only if the Association can make itself more attractive to the reluctant 'two-thirds'. Again, there are financial implications and although the present subscription is generally regarded as a modest price to pay for the services members receive, there is clearly a practical limit on what the Association can expect its ordinary members to pay.

The perceptions and priorities of the ordinary member, then, constitute the other and most fundamental determinant of the future of the ASE. The history of associations, not only those of teachers, provides numerous instances of leaderships and memberships parting company with disastrous consequences for the body to which they belong. here the ASE faces its greatest challenge. It has established itself as 'the most important repository of knowledge and experience of teaching science to the pupils in our schools'.[21] For many ordinary members, over many years, it has offered 'a constant source of guidance, support and inspiration'.[22] Its meaning to them is admirably captured in the words of the ASE's first woman Chairman, Frances Eastwood, who described it as 'a group of PEOPLE with common interests, common problems and common aims, pursued in a spirit of friendship sufficiently strong to welcome and survive sharp differences of opinion'.[23] Expansion and changed circumstances have now made the Association more pluralistic and professional. Can it travel further, maintaining old roles, but offering also an example of 'teachers taking responsibility for their own professional development'[24] in directions which they themselves have been largely instrumental in determining?

References

1 The Association of Public School Science Masters

1 R.H. Tawney, Educational Ideals and Social Realities, Presidential address to The New English Fellowship (English Section), 3 Jan. 1934. *Report of the Twenty-Second Annual Conference of Educational Associations* (Edinburgh 1934) p. 168.

2 See e.g. *The School World, 1* (1899) pp.44–5, 86, 124, 170–1, 211–13. Also: T.W. Bamford, *Rise of the Public School* (London 1967) pp. 226–66.

3 G. Baron, The Origins and Early History of the Headmasters' Conference, 1869–1914, *Educational Review, 7* (June 1955) pp. 230–1.

4 See e.g. A.J. Meadows and W.H. Brock, Topics fit for gentlemen: the problem of science in the public school curriculum, in: B. Simon and I. Bradley (eds.), *The Victorian Public School* (Dublin 1975) pp. 95–114.

5 Both Huxley and Tyndall were members of the X-Club, founded in 1864 and in its day 'the most powerful and influential scientific coterie in England'. The nine members of this social network also included Sir John Lubbock, appointed one of the Public School Commissioners in 1868; Dr William Spottiswoode, mathematician and Queen's Printer, governor of Westminster School from 1869; and George Busk, retired naval surgeon, governor of Charterhouse from 1872. All were Fellows of the Royal Society.

6 A.J. Meadows and W.H. Brock op.cit. p.111.

7 E.C. Mack, *Public Schools and British Opinion since 1860* (Columbia 1941) Chapter 7.

8 The Modern Language Association, established in 1892, included amongst its aims:
   (a) To raise the standard of efficiency in the teaching of Modern Languages, and to promote their study in schools, universities, and in the country generally.
   (b) To improve the status of Modern Languages as a subject of education.
   By 1904 it had 500 members.
   The Geographical Association, established in 1893 at Oxford by a meeting of public school masters, aimed to improve the teaching of geography and was open to all teachers of geography and other persons interested in the teaching of geography.
   The Classical Association was constituted in December 1903.

9 *Report of the Committee appointed to consider the education and training of officers of the Army* (London HMSO 1902) Cd. 982 x. 193
   Evidence 1902. Cd. 983 x. 347
   See also: Frank S. Russell, Our uneducated officers, *The Nineteenth Century and After, 52* (July 1902) p.87.

10 *Report of the Board of Visitors appointed by the Secretary of State for War for the inspection of The Royal Military College, Sandhurst in the year 1897* (London HMSO 1898) C.8744 p.6. Appendix B.

11 O. Lodge, Our Public Schools as a Public Peril, *The Nineteenth Century and After, 52* (Dec. 1902) p.950.
   In his book, *Public Schools and the Public Needs* (London 1901) p. 134, G.G. Coulton, who had been Army class master at both Sherborne and Dulwich,

agreed that the public schools taught boys 'the very opposite of all that Baden–Powell insists on for a soldier. Want of observation, want of intelligent reasoning power, disbelief in professional training, belief in amusement, neglect of book-learning – are not these precisely the faults which our officers, high and low, have too often shown in this war, side by side with their finer qualities?'

12 M.J. Wilkinson, The Office of Special Inquiries and reports: Educational Policy–Making under Michael Sadler, *History of Education, 8* (Dec. 1979) p. 282.

13 P.H.J.H. Gosden, The Board of Education Act 1899, *British J. of Educational Studies, 11* (Nov. 1962) p. 51.

14 The full sentence, from Sadler's *Memorandum on the Future Organisation of the Internal Departments of the Board of Education* to the Duke of Devonshire, President of the Council (7 July 1899) is, 'There is every sign of growing indignation at the very idea of an organisation of the Board of Education which would degrade and weaken the position of the great public schools and of Oxford and Cambridge.'

15 P.H.J.H. Gosden, op. cit. p.52.
    See also: K.D. Roberts, The Separation of Secondary Education from Technical Education, *Vocational Aspect of Education, 21* (1969) pp.101–5.

16 Association of Public School Science Masters: A short history of the steps taken to promote a meeting of science masters in public schools. 14 May 1900–Dec. 1903. Unpublished account, held at ASE Headquarters, Hatfield.

17 Detailed accounts of the Conferences are given in:
    London Technical Education Gazette, 5 (1899) pp.1, 22–30, 325, 328. LCC Technical Education Board, Minutes of Proceedings. Report of the Science, Art and Technology Sub-Committee, 15 Feb. 1899.
    London Technical Education Gazette, 6 (1900) pp. 33–44, 63–9, 82–3, 94–104. LCC Technical Education Board, Minutes of Proceedings. Report of the Science, Art and Technology Sub-Committee, 25 Feb. 1900.

18 *The School World, 1* (1899) p.64. The editor of the *School World*, from whose pen the suggestion for a National Association came, was probably A.T. Simmons, who collaborated with Richard Gregory in the establishment of this monthly journal for secondary schoolteachers.

19 APSSM, Report of General Meeting 1916, p.23.

20 Roscoe to Hill. Letter dated 10 July 1900.

21 APSSM, A short history . . . Account of meeting on 19 Jan. 1901.

22 For details of Porter see: *Journal of the Chemical Society, 1933*. Part 2, pp.1650–2.
    J.R. de S. Honey, *Tom Brown's Universe* (London 1977) p.137.
    J.L. Heilbron, *H.G.J. Moseley: The Life and Letters of an English Physicist 1887–1915* (London 1974) pp.23–5.

23 Porter's studies on the phenomenon of flicker are published in three papers in the *Proceedings of the Royal Society* (1898, 1902 and 1912). He determined the relative retinal stimulation by light of different colours and the time during which that stimulation lasted undiminished. The speed with which the black and white sectored disc must be driven in order that flicker may just vanish was found to vary with the logarithm of the illumination: this relationship came to be known as Porter's law.

24 For details of Eggar's life see:
    J.A. Venn (compiler), *Alumni Cantabrigiensis* (CUP 1944)
    J.L. Heilbron, op. cit. pp. 21–2.
    J. Huxley, *Memories* (London 1970) p.50.
    L.E. Jones, *A Victorian Boyhood* (London 1955) pp.195–7.
    SSR, 27 No.102 (March 1946) p.277.

25 J.L. Heilbron. op.cit. p.153.
Despite Moseley's view of him, Eggar later wrote a verse to accompany a com-memorative plaque put up at Eton and recording Moseley's first exposure to X radiation.

> The rays whose path here first he saw
> Were his to range in order'd law.
> A nobler law made straight the way
> That leads him 'neath a nobler ray.'

Heilbron, op.cit. p.125.

26 For details of de Havilland, see:
J.A. Venn (compiler), *Alumni Cantabrigienses* (CUP 1944)
The Times, 30 May 1952, p.8.

27 *SSR, 39* No.139 (June 1958) p.511
de Havilland was a not undistinguished amateur historian who collaborated with C.H.K. Marten and E.H. Carter in the writing of *Elementary Histories*, first published by Blackwell in 1915, and still used in schools, in an 11th edition in 1952.

28 For details of Hill see
SSR, 39 No.139 (June 1958) pp.511–12.
M.D. Hill, *Eton and Elsewhere* (London 1928)
The Hills and Hazelwood School in: W.A.C. Stewart, *Progressives and Radicals in English Education. 1790–1970* (London, Macmillan 1972) pp.54–67.
J.L. Heilbron, op.cit. p.23.

29 M.D. Hill, op.cit. p. 164.

30 Webb does not appear to have been a graduate, but passed the University of London Intermediate Examination, with Class 2 Honours in Zoology in 1889, being listed next to H.G. Wells who went on to take his BSc with Class I Honours in Zoology in the following year. The Selborne Society, founded in 1885, had as its aim the promotion of the study of Natural History and the preservation of plants and animals from needless destruction. Lord Avebury (John Lubbock) was its President. Its publication, *Nature Notes*, appeared monthly.

31 The ten schools were Eton, Harrow, Charterhouse, Cheltenham, Brighton, Exeter, Radley, Weymouth, Felsted and University College School. The numbers from each school were Eton 4, Harrow 2, Charterhouse 2 and the rest, one each.

32 In the event, the programme circulated listed six papers although only five of these were delivered.

33 Included amongst these was L. Cumming of Rugby School, the oldest master present, who had been seventh wrangler in 1865. Cumming continued in active membership of the Association of Public School Science Masters throughout the life of that body, serving on the committee for a period before the First World War when he must have been approaching seventy years of age.

34 *Royal Commission on Scientific Instruction and the Advancement of Science* Sixth Report. 1875. Appendix. p.152. [C.1279] xxviii

35 W.H. Brock, Geometry and the Universities: Euclid and his modern rivals 1860–1901, *History of Education, 4* (1975) pp.21–35.

36 In January 1902 a letter on the teaching of mathematics in public schools was printed in both *The Mathematical Gazette* and *Nature* over the signatures of twenty–two teachers (the original letter has, in fact, twenty–three signatures to it). Of these Holmes, Payne and Saunders (all of Merchant Taylors'), Hurst (Eton) and Slater (Charterhouse) attended the 1901 meeting of public school science masters.

37 These were by no means the only front-rank public schools missing e.g. Marl-

borough, St Paul's, Shrewsbury and Tonbridge were all absent. Of these four, all but St Paul's were represented at the next conference in 1902.

38 The phrase is that of the Director General of Military Education, cited by W.J. Courthope, the Senior Civil Service Commissioner in charge of the Army entrance examinations, in his evidence to the Akers-Douglas Committee in May 1901. *Report of the Committee appointed to consider the Education and Training of Officers of the Army*. (London HMSO 1902) Minutes of Evidence p.9. For the evolution of this view of the education of Army officers see: Trevor Hearl, Military education in the school curriculum 1800–1870, *History of Education, 5* (Oct. 1976) pp.251–64.

39 Charles G. Steel, Assistant Master at Rugby, in describing the Modern Side in his School, referred to the varying content of the curriculum of the Army Class which had to keep in alignment with the changing schemes of examination for entrance to Sandhurst and Woolwich. Board of Education. Educational Pamphlet No. 7 *Modern Sides of Public Schools (ii) Rugby* (London HMSO 1907) p.2.

40 T.W. Bamford, op.cit. p. 219.

41 Board of Education: Educational Pamphlets No. 16. *Modern Sides of Public Schools, (viii) Bedford Grammar School* (London 1909) p.2.

42 Board of Education: Educational Pamphlets No. 15. *Modern Sides of Public Schools, (vi) Clifton* (London 1909) p.2.

43 J.R. de S. Honey, op.cit. p.138.

44 Board of Education: Educational Pamphlets No. 8. *Modern Sides of Public Schools (iii) Eton* (London HMSO 1907) pp.1–6.

45 Board of Education: Educational Pamphlets No. 3. *The Modern Side at Harrow: The working of an educational experiment* (London HMSO 1905) p.5.

46 Winston S. Churchill. *My early life* (London 1959) cited by: J. Smyth. *Sandhurst* (London 1961) p.105.

47 *45th Report of His Majesty's Civil Service Commissioners* (London HMSO 1901) pp.lxxv–lxxvi.

48 *Report of the Board of Visitors appointed by the Secretary of State for War for the Inspection of the Royal Military Academy, Woolwich in the Year 1900*. (London HMSO 1901) p.3 Appendix B.

49 E. Nightingale, 'Sir Cyril Ernest Ashford, MA, KBE, CB, HVO' *SSR, 33*, No. 119 (Nov. 1951), pp.109–10.

50 Cited by Trevor Hearl, Military Education and the School Curriculum 1800–1870, *History of Education, 5* (1976) p. 264.

51 D. Newsome, *A History of Wellington College 1859–1959* (London 1959) p.9.

52 For biographical detail on Talbot, see: *The School Masters' Yearbook and Directory 1922* (London 1922) p.484.
    Haileybury was to combine with the Imperial Services College, Windsor, in 1942.

53 For details of Rintoul's life see: *SSR, 1*, No. 1 (June 1919) p.32 and *1*, No. 3 (Feb. 1920) pp.109–10.

54 *Report of the Committee appointed to consider the Education and Training of Officers of the Army*. Cd. 982 (London HMSO 1902) Minutes of Evidence, p.162.

55 Biographical information on science masters has been derived from a number of sources including:
    J.A. Venn (compiler) *Alumni Cantabrigiensis* (Cambridge 1922–54).
    J. Foster *Alumni Oxoniensis* (Oxford 1887–92).
    The Cambridge University Calendar (Cambridge, annually).

The Historical Register of the University of Oxford (Oxford 1900).
University of London, *The Calendar*. (London annually).
The Schoolmasters' Yearbook and Directory (London, 1903–, annually).
Obituary notices in *The School Science Review* and elsewhere.

56 A. Vassall, Some Aspects of Science and Education, *SSR, 2*, No. 7 (Feb. 1921) p.252.

57 Conference of Public School Science Masters. Papers read at the meetings held in the rooms of the University of London, on 19 Jan. 1901 and on 18 Jan. 1902. pp.10–14.

58 Ibid., pp.19–21.

59 Ibid., pp.6–10.

60 Ibid., pp.1–5.

61 Ibid., p.5.

62 Ibid., p.20.

63 *Short history of the steps taken to promote a meeting of Science Masters in Public Schools*. Notes on meeting on 23 Nov. 1901.

64 Ibid.

65 Ibid., Report on conference 18 Jan. 1902.

66 Ibid.

67 Ibid., APSSM, *Memorandum of Association*.

68 D.S.L. Cardwell, *The Organisation of Science in England* (London, revised edition 1972) p.208.

69 See e.g. E.W. Jenkins, *From Armstrong to Nuffield* (London 1979) pp.222–3.

70 *The Schoolmasters' Yearbook and Educational Directory 1914* (London 1914) p.xxi.

71 APSSM, *Report of the General Meeting 1909*. Rule 10, pp.12–13.
This rule defining eligibility for membership remained unchanged until 1918, the final year in the life of the Association, when the reference to 'similar status' was deleted and the final sentence amended to read 'or in which, in the opinion of the Committee, the aims and interests of the science masters are similar to those of the members of the Association.'

72 APSSM, Minute Book, Committee Meeting, Saturday 23 Oct. 1909.

73 Table compiled from lists of members in *Reports of the General Meeting* for the years in question. Membership figure for 1903 is taken from *Nature, 67* (Jan. 1903) p.284.

74 The issue had, in fact, been raised in previous discussion at the General Meeting held in Jan. 1917.

75 APSSM, Minute Book, 7 Oct. 1916.

76 Final membership of the BA committee differed from that listed in the *Report of 86th Meeting* (London 1917) p.lix and included Prof. R.A. Gregory (chairman), Dr E.H. Tripp (secretary), Mr W. Aldridge, Professor H.E. Armstrong, Mr D. Berridge, Mr G.D. Buckmaster, Dr Lilian J. Clarke, Mr G.F. Daniell, Miss I.M. Drummond, Mr G.D. Dunkerley, Miss A.E. Escott, Mr R. Cary Gilson, Miss C.L. Laurie, Prof. T.P. Nunn, Mr F.W. Sanderson, Mr A. Vassall and Prof. A.M. Worthington.

77 APSSM, Report of General Meeting 1918, p.38.

78 APSSM, Minute Book, 18 May 1918.

79 In practice the percentage of these 'special members' never exceeded 6% of the Association's total membership in any one year.

80 Professor H.E. Armstrong and Professor W.A. Tilden both attended regularly before their election as President of the Association. W.C. Fletcher, Chief Inspector of Secondary Schools, Board of Education, and F.B. Stead, Staff Inspector (and Secretary to J.J. Thomson's Committee) were frequent attenders, as was C.W. Kimmins, Science Inspector to the LCC.

81 Jackson was 8th Wrangler and Ashford 11th Wrangler in Part 1 of the Mathematical Tripos in 1889.

82 Short history of the steps taken to promote a meeting of Science Masters in Public Schools, 18 Jan. 1902.

83 Short history . . . 17 Jan. 1903. Talbot would appear to be the first officer to use a typewriter.

84 APSSM, Minute Book, 5 Oct. 1907.

85 Ibid., 10 Jan. 1912.

86 Ibid., 20 Feb. 1915 and 27 April 1915.
APSSM, Report of General Meeting 1915, pp.25–6.
APSSM, Report of General Meeting 1916, p.22.

87 Berridge had been a member of the British Association since 1894 and was a Secretary of Section L, Educational Science, in 1912, 1913 and 1915.

88 Information on which the analysis of committee membership is based has been derived from the APSSM Minute Books, annual Reports of the General Meetings from 1900 to 1918 inclusive, and accounts of the Association's work in the *Schoolmasters' Yearbook and Directory, Nature, The School World* and The *Journal of Education.*

89 Of the Presidents formally elected after the adoption of the constitution in January 1902, and up to the change in constitution in January 1919, twelve of the sixteen were, or shortly became, 'Scientific Knights'. Of the science presidents, only H.E. Armstrong, H.B. Baker and H.H. Turner failed to gain knighthoods.

90 The meeting was being held in Westminster School.

91 The Association had been in correspondence with Mr Haldane throughout 1906 on the subject of the qualifying examination for Army entrants.

92 Ewing had delivered a notable address on the education of naval cadets at the Annual Conference of the Preparatory School Association in December 1906.

93 Professor A. Smithells, in reviewing Armstrong's book *The Teaching of Scientific Method,* referred to the author as 'vigorous almost to violence, red hot, scathing, scornful, uncompromising and incessant'. *Nature,* 69 (21 Jan. 1904) p.290.

94 Ross's address was printed in *Nature,* 102 (9 Jan. 1919) pp.376–8.

95 *The Neglect of Science*: Report of Proceedings of a Conference held in the Rooms of the Linnaean Society, Burlington House, Piccadilly, W. on Wednesday, 3 May 1916. (London 1916) pp.25–7.

96 For further details on W.W. Vaughan, see: David Newsome, *A history of Wellington College* (London 1959) esp. Chapter 8, pp.273–312.

97 M.D. Hill, for example, was secretary of the Lucretian Club, a group of about a dozen zoologists who met to dine once a month in London. Sir Ray Lankester was invariably present; microscopic preparations were shown and 'the talk ran entirely "to shop".' M.D. Hill, *Eton and Elsewhere* (London 1928) p.102.

98 *Year-Book of the Royal Society of London 1903,* (London 1903) pp.190–5.

99 Ibid., p.193.

100 Ibid., pp.194–5.

101 *Year-Book of the Royal Society of London 1904* (London 1904) p.45.

102 The letter sent to universities, together with the committee's statement, are printed as an Appendix in: Sir W. Huggins, *The Royal Society or, Science in the State and in the Schools* (London 1906) pp.119–22.

103 Ibid., pp.109–17.

104 Ibid., p.116.

105 Ibid., p.113.

106 Criticisms of unlimited transfer of training were still in their infancy and it was natural for proponents of scientific studies to justify them in the terms currently employed for the justification of classics and mathematics.

2   The Association of Science Teachers

1 See e.g. Margaret Bryant, *The Unexpected Revolution* (London 1979)
Josephine Kamm, *Indicative Past* (London 1971).
Nonita Glenday and Mary Price, *Reluctant Revolutionaries* (London 1974).
Rita McWilliams–Tullberg, *Women at Cambridge* (London 1975)
Vera Brittain, *The Women at Oxford* (London 1960)
For a more specific account of the scientific education of girls, see: E.W. Jenkins, *From Armstrong to Nuffield* (London 1979) esp. Chapter 5, pp.170–214 and for university science education: Roy Macleod and Russell Moseley, Breadth, Depth and Excellence', *Studies in Science Education, 5* (1978) pp.85–106.

2 R. Macleod and R. Moseley, op.cit. pp.91 and 103.

3 Details derived from: Board of Education. *Report of the Consultative Committee on differentiation of the curriculum for boys and girls respectively in secondary schools* (London 1923) p.42.

4 Cited by Sara A. Burstall, Rise and development of Public Secondary Schools for Girls, 1850–1910, in: Sara A. Burstall and M.A. Douglas (eds.) *Public Schools for Girls* (London 1911) pp.8–9.

5 Ibid., p.19.

6 Ibid., p.8. In 1861, 46% of women in the 20–34 age group were unmarried. R. McWilliams–Tullberg, *Women at Cambridge* (London 1975) p.229.

7 Cited by Burstall op.cit. p.9.

8 *Natural Science in Education, being the report of the Committee on the Position of Natural Science in the Educational System of Great Britain.* (London 1918) p.36.

9 The objectives cited are ones to which prominence was given in a paper by M.A. Douglas, Chairman of the Curricula Sub-Committee of the Association of Head-mistresses, in 1910.
Burstall op.cit. p.278.

10 Helen G. Klaassen, 'The Teaching of Physics in Girls' Schools', *The Journal of Education, 23* (ns) Nov. 1901 p.689. The writer was on the staff of Newnham College, Cambridge.

11 *The Record of Technical and Secondary Education, 14*, No. 59 (1905) p.357.

12 The 'special provision for girls' in the Regulations initially referred to an approved course in 'Practical Housewifery'. This was later changed to 'Domestic Subjects'.

13 Sara A. Burstall and M.A. Douglas (eds.), op.cit.

14 Ibid., p.132.

15 Nonita Glenday and Mary Price, op.cit., p.71.

16 See e.g. C.S. Bremner, King's College for Women. The Department of Home Science and Economics, *The Journal of Education, 35* (ns) (1913) pp.72–4.

17 A detailed study of Smithells' contribution is to be found in: A. Flintham, The contribution of Arthur Smithells, FRS (1860–1939) to the development of science education in England. Unpublished MEd dissertation, University of Leeds, 1974.

18 Four Girton and Newnham Tutors, Science Teaching in Girls' Schools, *The Journal of Education, 32* (ns) (1910) pp.36–8.
The four tutors were: Agnes Bell Collier, Director of Mathematical Studies and Staff Lecturer in Mathematics, Newnham College, Cambridge; Ida Freund, Director of Studies (Physical Sciences) and Staff Lecturer (Chemistry) at Newnham College, Cambridge; M.T. Meyer, Director of Mathematical Studies and Lecturer in Mathematics, Girton College, Cambridge; M. Beatrice Thomas, Director of Studies in Natural Sciences and Lecturer in Chemistry, Girton College, Cambridge.

19 See e.g. her evidence to the Consultative Committee in their *Report on Practical Work in Secondary Schools*, (London 1913) pp.312–16.

20 Wife of Professor Henry Fawcett, Professor of Political Economy at Cambridge, the future Dame Millicent Garrett Fawcett was a founder of the Association for promoting the Higher Education of Women in Cambridge. Her daughter, Philippa Fawcett, was classed 'above the Senior Wrangler' in Part 1 of the Mathematical Tripos in 1890.

21 Mrs Sidney Webb, English teachers and their professional organisations, *The New Statesman*, Special Supplement, *5*, No. 129, 25 Sep. 1915, p.16.

22 *The Journal of Education, 30* (ns) (1908) pp.151–2.

23 Both papers were later published in *The School World, 2* (1909) pp.66–8 and 140–3.

24 *The Journal of Education, 32* (ns) (1910) p.106.

25 Ibid., *33* (ns) (1911) p.140.

26 Ibid., *34* (ns) (1912) p.147.

27 Minute Book, General Meetings of the AST, 23 Nov. 1912. Committee meetings of the AST had been held from July 1912.

28 *The Journal of Education, 34* (ns) (1912) p.681.

29 *Report of the Conference of Educational Associations, January 1914* (Edinburgh 1914) p.239.

30 The Association of Women Science Teachers was united with the Science Masters' Association to form the Association for Science Education in January 1963.

31 APSSM Minute Book, 8 Jan. 1913 and 31 May 1913.
The Conference was established in 1913 as 'a British Association of Education' in an attempt to draw together the many annual conferences of special groups of teachers and, in particular, to counteract the centrifugal influence on the curriculum of separate subject teaching associations.

32 AST, Minutes of General Meetings, 23 Nov. 1912.

33 Miss Lees, for example, was the opening speaker at a discussion on methods of

teaching physical science at a conference organised in 1900 by the Association for the Education of Women in Oxford. *The Journal of Education, 22* (ns) (1900) p.374. She was also, by all accounts, a severe task-mistress. As one of her junior science colleagues recalled, 'she expected them to come to school on Saturday mornings to set up and try out experiments for the week'. AWST, *A short history* (1962) p.5.

34 Josephine Kamm, *Indicative Past* (London 1971) pp.144–5.

35 Board of Education. *Report of the Consultative Committee on Practical Work in Secondary Schools* (London 1913) pp. 74–84, 321–4.

36 Education offered not only an occupation and income, but a way of life, to the large number of unmarried middle class educated women at this time. In 1915, of the 373 headmistresses in membership of the Association of Headmistresses, six only were married women or widows.

37 See e.g. Kenneth C. Bailey, *A history of Trinity College Dublin 1892–1945* (Dublin 1947) p.12 and Alice Gardner, *A short history of Newnham College, Cambridge* (Cambridge 1921) pp.111–12.

38 Miss Pearson's connection with the AST was, however, short-lived. She resigned from the committee after one year's service.

39 Miss Lees was a Past President of the AAM (1911–2) and an active committee woman of that body, as were Miss Jackson and Miss Mitchener.

40 A proposal at the inaugural general meeting that AAM members should pay a reduced subscription rate was defeated and a flat rate for all agreed.

41 AST, Minutes of Committee Meetings, 6 Jan. 1916.

42 *The Journal of Education, 38* (ns) (1916) p.83.

43 AST, Minutes of Committee Meetings, 11 March 1916.

44 AST, Minutes of General Meetings, 26 May 1916.

45 The figures are derived from AST and APSSM records and from 'The Directory of Educational Associations' published in *The Journal of Education* for the years in question.

46 The women differed markedly from the men in their handling of those who 'overlooked' payment of their subscriptions. Whereas, after a decent interval, the men quietly dropped the defaulter, omitting his name from the list of members and ceasing to send communications, the women published the names of 'back-sliders' as an appendix to the list of members in the printed annual report of the Association.

47 AST, Minutes of General Meetings, 23 Nov. 1912.

48 Evelyn Sharp, *Hertha Ayrton 1854–1923. A Memoir* (London 1926).

49 See e.g. Barbara Stephen, *Emily Davies and Girton College* (London 1927) p.369.

50 Minutes of the London Branch of the AST and AWST, 29 June 1928.

51 The original provision was for three ordinary members to be elected, but this was increased to five when the Articles were revised in 1916. AST, Minutes of General Meetings, 26 May 1916.
Branch representatives were added to the Executive Committee from 1918.

52 *Dictionary of National Biography*, Second Supplement, (London 1912).

53 Stoney's son, George Gerald, also achieved distinction in the field of science being elected FRS and, until 1912, managing the turbine works of Sir Charles Parsons.

54 See e.g. Alice Gardner, op.cit. p.38.

55 *The Journal of Education, 32* (ns) (1910) pp.36–8.

56 R.M. Scrimgeour (ed.) *The North London Collegiate School 1850–1950* (London 1950) pp.92–106.

57 *Natural Science in Education, being the report of the committee on the position of natural science in the educational system of Great Britain* (London 1918) see e.g. pp.37, 50 and 99.

58 Letter from G.H.J. Adlam to C.L. Bryant, 5 Dec. 1944.

59 Here, and elsewhere, membership figures are derived from the Minutes of General Meetings and Minutes of the Committee Meetings of the AST.

60 Biographical details of Dr Delf and other members of the Association are taken from *The Directory of Women Teachers and other women engaged in Higher and Secondary Education*, (London 1913 and subsequent issues).

61 Minutes of the London Branch of the AST, 1915–1922.

62 Ibid., 28 March 1919.

63 AST, Minutes of Committee Meetings, 6 Jan. 1916.

64 Ibid., 9 July 1915. Attempts to form a Northern branch began during the presidency of Mrs Bidder, herself a former pupil of Bradford Grammar School.

65 Ibid., 19 Dec. 1917.

66 The Association had produced a report on *School Laboratories* and another on *Botanical References*, both of which had been much praised by members and well-received in the educational press.

67 AST, Minutes of General Meetings, 3 Jan. 1918.

68 It is not entirely clear why this category of branch member was introduced. Most probably it was seen as a way of enabling those already forming into a separate Association in Yorkshire, to remain together whilst at the same time drawing them into union with the AST.

69 Yorkshire Natural Science Association, *Annual Report for 1918–1919* (Leeds 1919), p.5.

70 AST, Minutes of General Meetings, 19 June 1920.

71 Although Wager was never listed as a member of the APSSM or SMA, on his death *The School Science Review* printed an extensive obituary notice and full-page portrait of him. *SSR, 12*, No. 45 (Oct. 1930) pp.1–6.

72 Circular letter from M.E. Birt, dated 9 June 1930. By this date Miss Shove had moved from Leeds to a post at the Maria Grey Training College in London.

73 Miss Heaton had strong Yorkshire connections, having been educated at Leeds Girls High School. She left her post at Bedford College in 1920 and some time later was appointed Science Mistress at the Mount School, York.

74 AST, Minutes of General Meetings, 19 June 1920.

75 SMA, Minutes of Committee Meetings, 21 Feb. 1920.

76 Ibid., 16 Oct. 1920.

77 See e.g. Review of the Year, in: *The Schoolmasters' Yearbook and Educational Directory 1919* (London 1919) p.lxii.

78 Figures are taken from the *Annual Reports* of the Board of Education for the years in question.

79 Ibid.

80 F.W. Oliver's father, Daniel Oliver FRS, had also held the chair of botany at University College London. It was Daniel Oliver to whom the manuscript of J.S. Henslow's unfinished book on *Practical Lessons in Systematic and Economic Botany* was passed on Henslow's death in 1861, and who converted the work into a best-selling school text, *Lessons in Elementary Botany*, in the Macmillan's 'Elementary Class Book' series.

81 Accounts of the discussion were printed in: *Nature, 102* (30 Jan. 1919) pp.436–7. *The Journal of Education and School World, 51* (Feb.1919) pp.131–4.

82 AST, Minutes of Committee Meetings, Dec. 1918.

83 SMA, Minutes of Committee Meetings, 8 March 1919. In fact lines were beginning to get slightly crossed. The Incorporated Association of Head Masters also had the question of coordination of school and university work under consideration, although not merely from the standpoint of science. Again, the SMA had a Liaison Sub-Committee to deal with matters requiring coordinated action by schools and universities. In July 1921, the AST felt obliged to write to General Hartley at Oxford, a prime mover in the establishment of the SMA Liaison Sub-Committee, asking him if this body was not duplicating the work of the Consultative Council of University and School Science Teachers, of which he was a member. Association of Science Teachers, Minutes of Committee Meetings, 9 July 1921.

84 AST, Minutes of Committee Meetings, Autumn 1919 (not dated).

85 This at least was the view of the science masters as recorded in *Report for 1924*, p.42. Again, in their annual *Report for 1932*, after the Council had been revived, the account of the meeting held on 12 February 1932 recorded that 'very few representatives attended'. The difficulties facing the Council were, of course, considerable. It had no funds of its own. In matters such as the undergraduate curriculum, the universities were autonomous, whilst on questions relating to entrance requirements, the science departments within a university could not act unilaterally.

86 SMA, Minutes of Committee Meetings, 11 Oct. 1919 and 6 Jan. 1920.

87 AST, Minutes of Committee Meetings, 21 Oct. 1921.

88 AST, Minutes of General Meetings, 3 Jan. 1922.

89 G.H.J. Adlam to C.L. Bryant. Letter dated 24 Nov. 1944.

90 The phrases 'SMA property' and 'stave off' were Adlam's, used in his letter to Bryant. Ibid.

91 AST, Minutes of Committee Meetings, 24 March 1922.

92 AST, Minutes of General Meetings, 8 July 1922.

93 Ibid.

94 Honorary membership has also been offered to Professor Oliver, who appears to have declined, and to Mr D.H. Nagel, Trinity College, Oxford, who accepted, but died shortly afterwards.

95 SMA, Minutes of Committee Meetings, 10 March 1923.

3   The Association of Women Science Teachers

1 The writer was Miss Eileen M. Bull (Westcliff High School for Girls), *SSR, 27* (March 1946) p.291. Miss Bull was Honorary Treasurer of the AWST but was writing in a private capacity, her views not being shared by others on the AWST Executive Committee. AWST, Minutes of Executive Committee, 29 Sept. 1945.

2 AWST, Minutes of Executive Committee, 16 June 1928.

3 AWST, *Report for 1945* (1946) p.11.

4 AWST, Minutes of Executive Committee, 9 May 1948.

5 Ibid. 24 March 1922.

6 Twenty-five overseas countries were represented in the list of members for 1962.

7 At the time of the Annual General Meeting in January 1962 it was reported that 500 subscriptions were outstanding for the current year.
AWST, *Report 1960–61* (London 1962) p.15.
See also: *Report 1950–51* (1952) p.15. Miss Higson, the Association's secretary sent out 'reminders' to about 25% of the membership each year at this stage. Two printed reminders and a letter cost approximately one shilling, the annual subscription being 15 shillings.
For discussion of the 'Black List' see AWST, Minutes of Executive Committee 19 May 1939.

8 Miss R. Stern, Miss R.V. Shove and Miss M.B. Thomas, all founder members and active workers on the committees of the Association, were amongst those whose deaths were recorded.

9 By 1962, this category of member had virtually disappeared.

10 Miss M.W. Sutton, Presidential Address to the AWST, 3 Feb. 1951. AWST, *Report 1949–50* (1951) p.15.

11 In 1958 the Executive Committee considered a suggestion from one of the Association's teacher-training members, Miss E.S.M. Phillips, that a separate section should be formed to cater for the interests of those employed as training college lecturers. Whilst unwilling to subdivide the Association, cooption of a representative of such interests was agreed. AWST, Minutes of Executive Committee, Jan. 1958.

12 AWST, Report 1949–50 (1951) p.12.

13 AWST, *Report 1934* (1935) pp.4–5.
AWST, *Report 1935–36* (1936).

14 AWST, *Report 1943–44* (1944) p.5.

15 AWST, Minutes of Executive Committee, 6 May 1944.

16 Ibid., 9 September 1944 and AWST, *Report 1944–45* (1945) p.6.

17 AWST, Minutes of Executive Committee, 29 Sept. 1945.

18 Ibid., 8 Dec. 1945.

19 Ibid., 3 Jan. 1946.

20 Miss Higson had been a member of the AWST since 1923. In addition to teaching experience in a variety of schools, in the North of England and in London, she had considerable experience of committee work as a former Secretary and President of the London Branch of the Association of Assistant Mistresses.

21 AWST, *Report 1958–1959* (1960) p.8. Miss Higson retired on 30 Sept. 1959, being succeeded by Miss A.E. Kemlo who remained in office until amalgamation with the SMA in January 1963.

22 AWST, *Report 1949–50* (1951) p.20–1, and *Memorandum and Articles of the Association of Women Science Teachers* (Revised 1951).

23 AWST, Minutes of General Meeting, 3 Feb. 1951.

24 A further point of some significance was to make the AWST financial year correspond with *The School Science Review* year; by so doing, the expense of sending copies to resigned or lapsed AWST members was hopefully avoided.

25 *SSR, 22* (March 1941) p.336.

26 Ibid., *24* (Nov. 1942) pp.100–1.
    25 (Nov. 1943) pp.126–8.
    25 (Feb. 1944) pp.259–60.

27 AWST, Minutes of General Meeting, 4 Jan. 1946.

28 AWST, Minutes of Executive Committee, 19 Nov. 1938. On this occasion the proposal was sent to the branches for consideration with a view to discussion at the Annual General Meeting in 1940. In the event, no meeting was possible because of the circumstances of war.

29 AWST, *Report 1949–50* (1951) p.15.

30 AWST, *Report 1951–52* (1953) pp.6–7.

31 Though listed as a 'school' President, Miss P.M. Taylor had taken up the post of women education officer to the Central Council for Health Education in 1944.

32 AWST, *Report 1949–50* (1951) p.22.
    By this stage, joint meetings were common and the Association also wished to encourage the attendance of Secondary Modern School science teachers who were not members of the SMA.

33 AWST, Minutes of General Meeting, 5 Feb. 1930.

34 Ibid., Jan. 1936.

35 AWST, Minutes of Executive Committee, 22 Nov. 1929.

36 The 'Summer Meeting' became titled the 'Summer Conference' in 1955.

37 In 1926, over 92% of the membership of 460 was on a branch list. The later figure of 60% is based on formal membership of a branch; annual reports from branches made frequent reference to the fact that 'active membership', as evidenced by attendance at branch meetings, was much less than formal membership.

38 AWST, *Report 1950–51* (1952) p.24.
    The branch was 'unofficial' because it failed to satisfy the requirement in the Articles that 'not less than twenty members' should be involved in an application to form a branch.

39 *SSR, 7* (June 1926) p.302.

40 AWST, *Report 1936–37*.

41 AWST, *Report 1944–45* (1945) p.23.

42 AWST, *Report for 1947* (1948) pp.24–5.
    SSR, 28 (March 1947) p.259.

43 AWST, *Report 1947–48* (1949) pp.24–5.
    AWST, *Report 1948–49* (1950) pp.23–4.

44 AWST, *Report 1948–49* (1950) p.27.

45 AWST, *Report 1943–44* (1944) p.9.

46 AWST, Minutes of the Executive Committee, 2 Oct. 1943.

47 *SSR, 26* (June 1945) p.386.

48 *SSR, 35* (June 1954) pp.440–1.
    AWST, *Report 1953–54* (1955) pp.33–4. From the AWST Miss K.M.H. Chapman (President 1953–4) and Miss J.K. Raeburn (President 1955–6) were headmistresses of Essex schools; from the SMA, E.H. Coulson (Braintree County High School) was chairman in 1953, having previously served as a committee member and treasurer; D.H.J. Marchant (S. West Essex Technical School) had been a committee member, librarian, and chairman in 1952.

49 The formation of a South Midland Joint Branch had been announced in 1950 [*SSR, 31* (June 1950) p.414] but the number of women members did not reach twenty and the title of the branch reverted to the South Midland Branch of the SMA. Constitutionally, a joint branch had to satisfy the separate requirements of each of the two Associations for the formation of a branch. No attempt was made to devise a new requirement to cover joint enterprises.

50 AWST, *Report 1949–50* (1951) pp.31–2.

51 Ibid.

52 Other branches had similar problems of poor attendance at meetings. At its Annual General Meeting in December 1956 the Liverpool Area Branch considered whether it should continue its existence because 'of poor response of members in replying to circulars and attending meetings.'
AWST, Liverpool Area Branch. Minutes, 8 Dec. 1956.

53 AWST, Northern Ireland Branch. Minutes of Annual General Meetings, Secretary's Report 1960–1.

54 AWST, Minutes of Executive Committee. 12 Feb. 1949.

55 AWST, *Report 1949–50* (1951) p.6.

56 The absence of an Oxford Branch is notable.

57 Edith A. Lewis, The Welsh Branch of the Association of Women Science Teachers, *Collegiate Faculty of Education Journal*, University College of Swansea (1966) pp.28–31.

58 *SSR, 35* (March 1954) p.170. The percentage return on the 512 forms sent out by the AWST was 48%.

59 Informal, because business was rarely conducted at the Summer Meeting. Many members of the AWST were also members of the British Association for the Advancement of Science and the peripatetic summer meeting was probably modelled on the BA's practice. When the turn of the London Branch came to be responsible for a summer meeting, a highly successful and popular innovation in 1958 was a visit to the International Exhibition at Brussels. Sixty-four members, led by the President and Secretary of the London Branch (Miss D.J. Alexander and Miss F.M. Eastwood, respectively) spent five days in Brussels, where their itinerary included a meeting with the Belgian Science Teachers' Association. AWST, *Report 1957–1958* (1959) p.6.

60 Irrespective of size, each branch only had one representative although in 1937 the North Western Branch asked for, and was granted, a second representative at the Annual Meeting, its membership having reached 100. AWST, Minutes of Executive Committee, 13 Nov. 1937.

61 AWST, Minutes of Executive Committee, 2 Feb. 1951.

62 Ibid., 28 Jan. 1961.

4   The Science Masters' Association

1 SMA, Minute Book, 21 Sep. 1925.

2 SMA, *Report of Committee and Balance Sheets, 1960*, p.43.

3 SMA, Minute Book, 4 Jan. 1927 and 2 June 1951.

4 SMA, *Report for 1920*, p.36. The phrase was amended later to read 'restricted to matters arising out of the *teaching* of Natural Science'.

5 Yorkshire Natural Science Association, *Annual Report for 1918–1919* (Leeds 1919) p.5.

6 SMA Rule 11, *Report for 1920*, p.38.

7 SMA, Minute Book, 12 March 1921, 18 March 1922, 27 May 1922.

8 SMA, *Report for 1922*, p.51.

9 SMA, *Report for 1926*, p.58 and Minute Book, 5 June 1926 and 2 Oct. 1926.

10 SMA, Minute Book, 13 Oct. 1934 and 24 Nov. 1934.

11 Ibid., 16 May 1936, 10 Oct. 1936, 5 Jan. 1937, 6 Feb. 1937.

12 Ibid., 1 Jan. 1936, 15 Feb. 1936, 28 Nov. 1936, 25 May 1940.

13 Ibid., 29 May 1937.

14 Ibid., 4 Feb. 1939.

15 Ibid., 6 Jan. 1945.

16 Ibid., 4 Jan. 1946.

17 SMA, *Report of Committee and Balance Sheets, 1951*, p.1.

18 SMA, *Report of Committee and Balance Sheets, 1952*, p.2.

19 SMA, Minute Book, 14 Feb. 1948.

20 Ibid., 5 Jan. 1949.

21 Ibid., 24 Apr. 1949, 8 Oct. 1949, 21 Oct. 1950 and 26 Nov. 1960.

22 Ibid., 24 Sept. 1960.

23 SMA, *Report for 1935*, p.117 and Minute Book, 30 Dec. 1947.

24 Figures taken from annual reports and SMA, Minute Book, 3 March 1963 and 26 May 1962.

25 The appointment of a separate Membership Secretary was agreed at the SMA Annual Business Meeting in December 1931. Until the appointment of a full-time salaried Secretary in the autumn of 1961, when the work of the Membership Secretary was taken over by the Treasurer and an Assistant Secretary, the office of Membership Secretary being abolished, there were three holders of the office, all headmasters:
1932–46 F. Fairbrother, Cedars School, Leighton Buzzard.
1946–57 H.F. Broad, Cedars School, Leighton Buzzard.
1957–61 G.S. Brown, Grammar School. Tewksbury.

26 Information about the schools represented by the SMA is provided in the published membership lists of the Association.

27 Interviews with SMA members including Mr I.G. Jones (Doncaster) and Mr. J.C. Siddons (Bradford).

28 The figures are obtained by representing the SMA schools as a percentage of secondary schools on the Board of Educations grant list plus schools not on the grant list but recognised as 'efficient'. Other ways of calculating the total number of secondary schools which might have been represented yield higher figures e.g. SMA, *Report for 1928*, p.67.

29 SMA, *Report of Committee and Balance Sheet, 1959*, p.1.

30 SMA, *Membership List*. Correct to 31 Dec. 1960.

31 SMA, *Rules* (revised to 4 Jan. 1962) p.1.

32 SMA, Minute Book, 28 Nov. 1959. See also 29 Nov. 1958 for a preliminary discussion on the Association's interest in science in primary schools.

33 SMA, *Report for 1920*, p.36.

34 SMA, *Report for 1926*, p.59.

35 SMA, *Rules* (revised to 31 Dec. 1946), Rules 4 and 5.

36 SMA, *Report for 1926*, p.61 and *SSR, 7*, No. 25 (Sept. 1925) pp.1–3.

37 SMA, Minute Book, 3 Oct. 1931 and 12 March 1932.

38 SMA, *Report of Committee and Balance Sheets*, 1939, p.3 and Minute Book, 25 May 1940.

39 SMA, Minute Book, 28 Dec. 1955 and 3 March 1956.

40 Ibid., 5 March 1960.

41 Ibid., 28 May 1960, 11 Sept. 1961 and 25 Nov. 1961.

42 The information about membership, holders of offices and periods of service is derived from annual reports, General Committee minutes, and *The School Science Review*.

43 SMA, Minute Book, 7 Dec. 1935.

44 See, e.g. SMA, Minute Book, 8 Oct. 1949.

45 Biographical material on SMA officers has been drawn from a variety of sources including obituary notices and entries in *The Schoolmasters Yearbook and Directory*.

46 *SSR, 38*, No. 134 (Nov. 1956) p.125.

47 Oscroft was in his late 50s when appointed as Treasurer: he retired from Uppingham two years later and died in December 1933. See: *SSR, 15*, No. 59 (March 1934) p.292. Neville's term of office was extended, exceptionally, for a fifth year: SMA, *Report for 1936*, p.122. See also *SSR, 23*, No. 91 (June 1942) p.252.

48 SMA, Minute Book, 3 Oct. 1931 and *Report for 1931*, p.83.

49 *SSR, 22*, No. 87 (March 1941) p.336.

50 Ibid., *24* No. 93 (Feb. 1943) pp.229–30.

51 Ibid., *24*, No. 92 (Nov. 1942) p.95.

52 See Chapter 10.

53 *SSR, 43*, No. 149 (Nov. 1961) p.3. The announcement was made on 30 Sept. 1961 on the occasion of the official opening of the SMA's new Headquarters at Cambridge. See also: SMA, Minute Book, Officers meeting, 4 Jan. 1961.

54 See Chapter 11. Also: G. McCulloch, E.W. Jenkins and D. Layton, *Technological Revolution? The politics of school science and technology since 1945* (Falmer Press 1984).

55 *SSR, 6*, No. 23 (Feb. 1925) pp. 177–85 and 197–200. Arising from the debate at Leeds the SMA established a sub-committee on the relationship between schools and universities in the teaching of science. Professor Arthur Smithells of Leeds University was an influential member of this body which recommended the establishment of a branch organisation for the SMA. See: SMA, *Report for 1925*, pp.47–8.

56 SMA, *Report for 1925*, pp.53–4.

57 SMA, *Report for 1927*, p.65.

58 SMA, *Report for 1929*, p.72.

59 *SSR, 12*, No. 45 (Oct. 1930) p.78.

60 SMA, *Report for 1935*, pp.119–20. Also, see above Chapter 2, pp.53–4.

61 SMA, *Report for 1925*, p.48.

62 SMA, *Memorandum and Rules of the Association*. Revised to 31 Dec. 1946.

63 SMA, *Report for 1929*, p.65.

64 SMA, Minute Book, 22 May 1960.

65 SMA, Minute Book, Meeting of Officers and Branch Representatives, 18 March 1961; General Committee Meeting, 10 June 1961.

66 SMA, *Report of Committee, 1944*, p.4.

67 SMA, *Report of Committee, 1946*, pp.4–9.

68 SMA, *Report of Committee, 1947*, p.6., *Report of Committee, 1948*, p.13. See also: *SSR, 29*, No. 109 (June 1948) pp.352–4.

69 SMA, Minute Book, 9 Oct. 1948.

70 *SSR, 41*, No. 145 (June 1960) pp.538–9.

71 *SSR., 42*, No. 148 (June 1961) p.548.

72 SMA, Minute Book, 24 Sept. 1960.

73 *SSR, 35*, No. 127 (June 1954) pp.440–1.

74 SMA, Minute Book, 25 Nov. 1961 and *SSR, 43*, No. 151 (June 1962) pp.675–6.

5   The Association for Science Education

1 *Science Education*. A Policy statement issued by the Science Masters' Association and The Association of Women Science Teachers (John Murray 1961).
The provision and maintenance of laboratories in grammar schools. 1961.
The training of graduate science teachers. A section of Part II of the Science and Education Report issued by the Science Masters' Association and The Association of Women Science Teachers (John Murray 1963).

2 AWST, Minutes of Executive Committee, 6 Jan. 1962.

3 Miss E. Lois Buckley (President, AWST) to members, 7 Feb. 1962.

4 AWST, Minutes of Executive Committee, 6 Jan. 1962 and 17 March 1962.

5 SMA, Minutes of General Committee, 25 Nov. 1961.

6 *SSR, 43* (June 1962) p.676.

7 AWST, Minutes of Executive Committee, 6 Jan. 1962.

8 Notes of a meeting of a working party of representatives of the SMA and the AWST on amalgamation of the two Associations . . . 27 Jan. 1962.

9 Memorandum on the proposed merger. Messrs Bircham and Co. undated.

10 Notes and comments on the proposed merger. Prepared by E.W. Tapper (General Secretary, SMA) for a meeting of the Steering Committee, 6 Oct. 1962.

11 SMA, Minutes of General Committee, 22 Sept. 1962.

12 Draft Trust Deed and Rules of the British Science Teachers' Association, Bircham and Co. 1962. W.H. Dowland, Chairman of the SMA in 1962, and Miss M. Going, Vice-President of the AWST were the two Trustees.

13 SMA, Minutes of the meeting of Branch Officers and the General Committee, 1 Jan. 1963.
Minutes of the Annual Business Meeting, 3 Jan. 1963.
Minutes of the Final Committee Meeting, 4 Jan. 1963.
AWST, Record of the Inaugural Business Meeting, 5 Jan. 1963.
Minutes of Annual General Meeting, 4 Jan. 1963.
ASE, Record of the Inaugural Business Meeting, 5 Jan. 1963.

Dr B.V. Bowden, Principal of the Manchester College of Science and Technology and President of the SMA in 1962, was later to become Lord Bowden and serve as Minister of State in the Department of Education and Science in the Labour Government of 1964.

14 ASE, Record of the Inaugural Business Meeting, 5 Jan. 1963.

15 ASE *Trust Deed and Rules*, Jan. 1963. p.4.

16 Ibid.

17 Ibid., pp.14–15.

18 Ibid., p.15.

19 Ibid., p.16.

20 The work of the Education Committee is the subject of Chapter 10.

21 SMA, Minutes of General Committee, 28 Nov. 1959 and Hugh P. Ramage, A Science Education Centre, Nov. 1959.

22 SMA, Minutes of General Committee, 5 March 1960 and interview with F.C. Brown, Cambridge, 31 Oct. 1980.

23 Ibid.

24 Interview with F.C. Brown, Cambridge, 31 Oct. 1980 and correspondence between the County Planning Officer; Messrs Few and Kester, Solicitors; and F.C. Brown, April/May 1960.
SMA, Minutes of General Committee, 28 May 1960.

25 SMA, Minutes of General Committee, 28 May 1960 and interview with F.C. Brown, Cambridge, 31 Oct. 1980.

26 SMA, Minutes of General Committee, 24 Sept. 1960. This was the first occasion that the General Committee had met in the new Headquarters.

27 SMA, Minutes of meeting of Headquarters Management Committee, 6 Nov. 1960.

28 Ibid., 11 Feb. 1961.
SMA, Minutes of General Committee, 4 March 1961.
SMA, Minutes of meeting of Officers, 10 June 1961.

29 SMA, Minutes of meeting of Officers, 10 June 1961.
SMA, Minutes of General Committee, 10 June 1961.

30 SMA, Minutes of General Committee, 16 Sept. 1961.

31 *SSR, 43* (March 1962) p.483.

32 *SSR, 43* (Nov. 1961) p.3.

33 SMA, Minutes of General Committee, 25 Nov. 1961.

34 ASE, Report of meeting of the H.Q. Committee, 18 Dec. 1965.

35 ASE, Minutes of meeting of the H.Q. Site Committee, 5 Feb. 1966, and Agendum 6, ASE Council, 9 Oct. 1965, being a motion from the Midland Branch in support of Birmingham as a base.

36 ASE, Minutes of meeting of the H.Q. Site Committee, 26 Feb. 1966. See also: *Education in Science*, No. 41 (Feb. 1971) pp.13–15.

37 ASE, Minutes of Executive Committee, 28 Feb. 1967; 25 Feb. 1967; 29 April 1967.

38 New Headquarters for the Association for Science Education. Appeal Brochure, signed by R.S. Nyholm (President) and F.C. Brown (Chairman), 1968.

39 E.H. Coulson, 'A Personal Appeal', *Education in Science*, No. 32 (April 1969) p.11.
    E.H. Coulson and E.G. Breeze, 'The Appeal Fund', *Education in Science,* No. 34 (Sept. 1969) p.13.

40 ASE Annual Report 1969. *Education in Science.* No. 41 (Feb. 1971) pp.18 and 23. In fact the Association received a sum of £5000 from DES towards the Headquarters fund. ASE Minutes of Council, 9 May 1970.

41 ASE Annual Report for the Year ended 31 July 1977, *Education in Science*, No. 75 (Nov. 1977) p.11.

42 J.A. Darby, The ASE Building and Development Fund, *Education in Science*, No. 81 (Jan. 1979) p.10. A list of contributors is given.

43 Income Tax Relief could be claimed on the whole of the annual subscription, the ASE having negotiated an agreement with the Inland Revenue in April 1963. See ASE *Bulletin*, No. 5 (April 1963) pp.11–12. There was also a reduced subscription for the first year of membership.

44 ASE, *Trust Deed and Rules*, Jan. 1963. The reference to teachers in Further Education, as distinct from Colleges of Higher Education, came later.

45 ASE, Record of the Inaugural Business Meeting, 5 Jan. 1963. 46 men and 15 women were elected as Honorary Members of the ASE. The number of Honorary Members over the two following decades remained at the same level i.e. approximately 60.

46 Memorandum on Membership, prepared by the General Secretary, 1968, and paper on New Grades of Membership. See also: *Education in Science*, No. 31 (Feb. 1969) p.16.

47 ASE, Annual Report for the year ended 31 July 1982, *Education in Science*, No. 100 (Nov. 1982) p.23. Also *Education in Science*, No. 98 (June 1982) pp.11–12.

48 Memorandum on Membership, prepared by the General Secretary, 1968.

49 ASE, Report from Science and Education committee, Meeting held 19 Jan. 1963.

50 *Bulletin*, No. 7 (Nov. 1963) pp.18–21. The statement was also published by the School Natural Science Society in *Natural Science in Schools*.

51 *Education in Science*, No. 18 (June 1966) p.18.

52 ASE, Minutes of Executive Committee, 28 Jan. 1961.

53 ASE, Minutes of Education (Coordinating) Committee, 20 Nov. 71. *Education in Science*, No. 51 (Jan. 1973) p.15. Dr Collis had been a member of the previous sub-committee.

54 ASE, Minutes of Education (Coordinating) Committee, 26 Sept. 1970 and 21 Nov. 1970.

55 *Education in Science,* No. 65 (Nov. 1975) p.18.

56 *Education in Science*, No. 90 (Nov. 1980) p.14 and No. 100 (Nov. 1982) p.22. Production of the news-sheet was aided by a grant from the Industry/Education Unit of the Department of Industry. An example of the news-sheet was printed in *Education in Science*, No. 97 (April 1982) centre pages.

57 *Education in Science*, No. 100 (Nov.1982) p.22 and No. 103 (June 1983) p.9.

58 *Education in Science*, No. 49 (Sept. 1972) p.13; No. 51 (Jan. 1973) p.15.

59 *Education in Science*, No. 55 (Nov. 1973) p.20.

60 *Education in Science*, No. 57 (April 1974) pp.18–20.

61 *Education in Science*, No. 62 (April 1975) pp.20–1.

62 *Education in Science*, No. 63 (June 1975) p.21 and No. 77 (April 1978) p.11.

63 H.R. Jones, Science in Further Education. A brief sketch of the provision in England and Wales, *Education in Science*, No. 93 (June 1981) p.17.

64 *Education in Science*, No. 82 (April 1979) p.12.

65 See e.g. articles by W.A. Tovell, H.R. Jones and R. Marks in *Education in Science*, No. 92 (April 1981); No. 93 (June 1981); and No. 96 (Jan. 1982) respectively.

66 *Education in Science*, No. 9 (Sept. 1966) p.9 and No. 21 (Feb. 1967) pp.27–8.

67 *Education in Science*, No. 55 (Nov. 1973) p.16 and No. 60 (Nov. 1974) p.18.

68 *Education in Science*, No. 77 (April 1978) p.14 and SMA Minute Book, 1 Jan. 1936, 15 Feb. 1936, 28 Nov. 1936 and 25 May 1940.

69 ASE, Minutes of Executive Committee, 19 Jan. 1963 and 22 Feb. 1963.

70 Ibid., 7 March 1964.

71 ASE, Minutes of Council, 13 Oct. 1967.

72 Details of the names of office holders are published in each issue of *The School Science Review*.

73 ASE, Minutes of Executive Committee, 30 Nov. 1963 and 18 Nov. 1964. AWST, Minutes of Annual General Meeting, 3 Jan. 1963.

74 *Education in Science*, No. 70 (Nov. 1976) p.25.

75 ASE, Minutes of Council, 13 Oct. 1967.

76 *Education in Science*, No. 70 (Nov. 1976) p.16 and No. 75 (Nov. 1977) p.12.

77 Ibid., No. 75 (Nov. 1977) p.14.

78 Ibid., No. 80 (Nov. 1978) pp.13 and 18.

79 See Chapter 10.

80 *Education in Science*, No. 21 (Feb. 1967) p.35.

81 H.F. Boulind, Brief History of the Education Committee; J.J. Bryant, The new Education Committees of the ASE, *Education in Science*, No. 26 (Feb. 1968) pp.18–19.

82 *Education in Science*, No. 40 (Nov. 1970) p.13.

83 Ibid., No. 52 (April 1973) pp.21–3. See also: *Education in Science*, No. 46 (Feb. 1972) p.16.

84 See, for example, *Education in Science*, No. 71 (Jan. 1977) pp.18–20; No. 76 (Jan. 1978) pp.19–22; No. 81 (Jan. 1979) pp.17–20; No. 91 (Jan. 1981) pp.17–20; No. 101 (Jan. 1983) pp.20–9.

85 *Education in Science*, No. 101 (Jan. 1983) pp.20–2.

86 H.F. Boulind and J.J. Bryant writing about the old and new committees in: *Education in Science*, No. 26 (Feb. 1968) pp.18–19.

87 R.W. West, The Education (Research) Committee of the Association for Science Education: Roles and Problems, *Studies in Science Education*, 1 (1974) p.87.

88 ASE, Minutes of Education (Research) Committee, 12 Sept. 1970. Appendix.

89 *Education in Science*, No. 41 (Feb. 1971) p.19.

90 R.W. West, Discussion notes on the future role of the ASE Education (Research) Committee, 9 Sept. 1971.

91 R.W. West, The Education (Research) Committee of the Association for Science

Education: Roles and Problems, *Studies in Science Education*, *1* (1974) p.89.

92 *Education in Science*, No. 60; (Nov. 1974) pp.19–20.

93 *Education in Science*, No. 80 (Nov. 1978) p.18.

94 Ibid. Dr J. Spice was Chairman of the Schools Council's Science Committee.

95 *Education in Science*, No. 93 (June 1981) p.11, and No. 99 (Sept. 1982) pp.29–31.

96 Professor Thompson had also been chairman of the Working Party established under the auspices of the Education (Research) Committee which prepared the Consultative Document *Alternatives for Science Education* (ASE 1979) leading to the Policy Statement, *Education through Science* (ASE 1981). J.C. Heaney was chairman of the Policy Group which produced the statement, other members being W.F. Archenhold, J. Nellist, J.J. Thompson and R.W. West; Heaney was also Chairman of the ASE in 1980. He resigned from the Review's Steering Committee in March 1983 being replaced by G.C. Hill, the ASE's Honorary Liaison Secretary and an ex-secretary of the Education (Coordinating) Committee.

97 H.F. Boulind, 'Brief history of the Education Committee', *Education in Science*, No. 26 (Feb. 1968) p.18.

98 C.M. Wilson, 'The role of the Association in the work of the Review', *Education in Science*, No. 103 (June 1983) pp.15–16.

99 Martin Baxter, 'No time for the ASE?', *Education in Science*, No. 78 (June 1978) p.27.

100 *Education in Science*, No. 101 (Jan. 1983) pp.20–29.

101 B.G. Atwood, Branch Re-Organisation, *Education in Science*, No. 26 (Feb. 1968) pp.23–24.

102 *Education in Science*, No. 102 (April 1983) p.12 and No. 104 (Sept. 1983) p.9.

103 Ibid., No. 87 (April 1980) p.11.

104 Ibid., No. 64 (Sept. 1975) p.11.

105 SMA, Minutes of General Committee, 26 May 1962 and 24 Nov. 1962.

106 SMA, Minutes of Meeting of Branch Officers and General Committee, 1 Jan. 1963.

107 ASE, Report of Branches Sub-Committee, Feb. 1967.

108 ASE, Minutes of Executive Committee, 26 Oct. 1963, 11 Dec. 1965 and 7 May 1966.

109 Ibid., 27 July 1963. ASE, Minutes of Meeting of Officers and Branch Chairmen, 31 Dec. 1963.

110 ASE Minutes of Council, 8 Oct. 1966.

111 B.G. Atwood, Branch Re-organisation, *Education in Science*, No. 26 Feb. 1968, pp.23–4.
See also: Report of Branches Sub-Committee discussed at the meeting of Council on 18 March 1967.

112 J.J. Bryant, Report to Council of the comments of the Executive Committee upon the Report of the Branches Sub-Committee, 4 Mar. 1967.

113 The elected members were generally regarded as being free from Regional allegiance and, as independent members of Council, able to express a national point of view. Their recommendations for change are discussed later: see pp.286–7.

114 *Education in Science*, No. 87 (April 1980) p.11.

115 ASE, Report of the Regions Sub-Committee Chairman to Spring Council, 8 Mar. 1969.

6   Communications (i) Conference and communion

1 *Report from the Select Committee on Scientific Instruction* (London 1868) C. 432. p.v.

2 *Natural Science in Education* (London, HMSO 1918) p.90.

3 Ibid., p.91.

4 A. Smithells, Schools and University Science, *SSR, 5*, No. 19 (Feb. 1924) p.134.

5 Ibid., pp.130–1.

6 APSSM, Minute Book, 21 Oct. 1905. Also: *Agenda and Abstract of Papers*, Annual Meeting, 20 Jan. 1906. Westminster School. *The Journal of Education, 29* (ns) (Feb. 1907) p.106.

7 APSSM, Minute Book, 5 October 1907.

8 APSSM, Report of the General Meeting 1909, p.18.

9 APSSM, Minute Book, 9 May 1908.

10 APSSM, *Catalogue of Exhibition of Scientific Apparatus and Books at Annual Meeting*, (London 1911) p.98.
Ibid., (London, 1916) p.40.

11 APSSM, *Catalogue of Exhibition of Scientific and Military Apparatus and Books at Annual Meeting, Eton College, Windsor* (London 1917) pp.16–21.

12 APSSM, *Catalogue of Exhibition of Scientific Apparatus and Books at Annual Meeting* (London 1910) pp.82–95.
The four publishers were Geo. Bell and Sons; Cambridge University Press; Macmillan, and Methuen.
ASE *Annual Meeting 1983*, University of Manchester, pp.63–5.

13 APSSM, *Catalogue of Exhibition of Scientific Apparatus and Books at Annual Meeting*, (London 1910) pp.9–18.

14 SMA, *Report for 1936*, pp.7 and 24–5.

15 *SSR, 32* No. 118 (June 1951) p.336. The speaker was Sir Graham Savage.

16 See e.g. the Presidential Address by Professor J.S.B. Stopford, 'Aims of biology in education', in: SMA, *Report for 1936*, pp.8–14.

17 *SSR, 6* No. 22 (Dec. 1924) p.127.

18 SMA, *Report for 1937*, pp.29–32.

19 See Chapter 11, pp.261–2.

20 *Education in Science*, No. 31 (Feb. 1969), p.12.

21 ASE, Minutes of Education (Coordinating) Committee, 27 Sept. 1969.

22 ASE, Study Series, *Annual Meeting 1974: Educational Proceedings* (Hatfield, ASE 1974) pp.3 and 9–21.

23 See Chapter 5, pp.124–6.

24 ASE, Study Series No. 4, *Annual Meeting 1975: A report* (Hatfield, ASE 1975) p.55.

25 B.M. Presst to Dr W.J. Kirkham, letter dated 11 Jan. 1977.

26 *Education in Science*, No. 94 (Sept. 1981) pp.17–18. Details of the ASE's activities in connection with validation of in-service causes are given in Chapter 12.

27 *Education in Science*, No. 60 (November 1974) p.17.

28 ASE, Minutes of Executive Committee, 13 Nov. 1976.

29 SMA, *Report of Committee and Balance Sheets*, 1948, p.3.

30 See e.g. E.O. Tancock, 'General Impressions of the Oxford Meeting', *SSR, 2* No. 7 (Feb. 1921) p.307.
Also: ASE, *Annual Meeting 1983* (St Albans 1983) p.73.

31 ASE, Minutes of Education (Coordinating) Committee, 27 Sept. 1969.

32 *Education in Science*, No. 64 (Sept. 1975) p.11.

33 See Chapters 3 and 4, pp.72–8 and 99–103.

34 *SSR, 8* No. 30 (Dec. 1926) p.118.

35 I.G. Jones, 'Forty years on in Yorkshire', *Education in Science*, No. 54 (Sep. 1973) pp.16–19.
SMA, Yorkshire Branch, Minutes of Committee Meetings, 24 Nov. 1934.

36 SMA, North-Western Branch, Minutes of Committee Meetings, 28 Feb. 1930.

37 SMA, East Midlands Branch, Meeting of Science Teachers, 7 Oct. 1961.

38 AWST, London Branch, Minutes of Branch Meetings, 22 Nov. 1952; 14 Nov. 1953; 27 Nov. 1954; 20 Feb. 1956; 1 Dec. 1956; 12 Feb. 1957; 20 Feb. 1958.

39 SMA, North-Eastern Branch, Minutes of Committee Meetings, 27 May 1967.

40 *SSR, 29* No. 108 (Mar. 1948) p.238.

41 SMA, Northern Ireland Branch, Minutes of Committee Meeting, Feb. 1957.

42 *SSR, 12* No. 47 (Mar. 1931) p.193 and private communication from Miss Beryl G. Ashton, 9 Jan. 1980. Miss Ashton was a leading member of both the AWST and the Midland Branch of the ASE.

43 SMA, South Wales Branch, Minutes of Meetings, 26 Oct. 1929; 25 Oct. 1930.

44 ASE, West Midlands Region, Minutes of Committee Meetings, 1 March 1977 and 11 May 1977.

45 E. Nightingale, HSTA. The first eleven years, *Hartshorn*, The Bulletin of the Hertfordshire Science Teachers' Association, No. 12 (March 1960) pp.4–5. See also: No. 31 (Dec. 1969) pp.3–5.

46 SMA, *Report of Committee and Balance Sheets* 1950, p.6. Ibid., 1951, p.8.

47 ASE, London Region, Minutes of Committee Meetings, 12 June 1969 and 19 Nov. 1974.

48 Leeds Science Teachers' Association, *Journal*, Volume 1 (June 1963) p.i.

49 ASE, West Midland Region, Minutes of Committee Meetings, 20 Nov. 1974; and 17 Nov. 1976.

50 Ernest Nightingale, H.S.T.A. The first twenty one years *Hartshorn*, No. 31 (Dec. 1969) p.3.

51 ASE, North-East Region, Questionnaire sent to all members in the Region, Spring 1971, and Analysis of the replies to the Questionnaire, Minutes of Commitee Meetings, 13 Oct. 1971.

52 See pp.129–133.

53 For details of the review of the structure and function of Council see Chapter 12, pp.286–8.

54 ASE, Midland Branch, Minutes of Committee Meetings, 29 Nov. 1966.

55 ASE, London Region, Minutes of Committee Meetings, 22 Oct. 1968 and 23 Jan. 1969.

56 ASE, London Region, Minutes of Annual Business Meeting, 4 Jan. 1964.

57 ASE, London Region, Minutes of Committee Meetings, 21 Sept. 1965 and 17 March 1969.

58 *Education in Science*, No. 16 (Feb. 1966) p.18.

59 Ibid., No. 38 (June 1970) p.12.

60 Details of the proceedings of Education Conferences are given in *Education in Science*, usually the June issue of the year in question.

61 Education in Science, No. 73 (June 1977) p.12.

62 International Council of Scientific Unions. *Newsletter from the Committee on the Teaching of Science*, No. 10 (Sept. 1982) p.8.

63 *SSR, 37* No. 132 (March (1956) p.270.

64 ICSU, *Newsletter from the Committee on the Teaching of Science*, No. 6 (Aug. 1980) pp.2–9.
    ASE, *Education in Science*, No. 54 (Sept. 1973) p.35 and No. 96 (Jan. 1982) p.30.

65 Robert H. Carleton, *The NSTA Story 1944–1974*, (National Science Teachers Association, Washinton D.C. 1976) p.161.

66 ASE, Study Series No. 4, *Annual Meeting 1975. A Report* (Hatfield 1975) pp.54–60.

7   Communications (ii) Publications and pronouncements

1 *The correlation of mathematical and science teaching*. Report of a joint committee of the Mathematical Association and the Association of Public School Science Masters. (London 1910).

2 *Natural Science in Education*. Being the report of the Committee on the position of natural science in the educational system of Great Britain. (London, HMSO 1918) pp.96–7.

3 APSSM, Minute Book, 18 May 1918.

4 APSSM, Minute Book, 13 July 1918.

5 G.H.J. Adlam to C.L. Bryant, letter dated 24 November 1944.

6 Ibid. Adlam's letter was the basis of Bryant's contribution, 'The hundredth number', in *SSR, 26* No. 100 (June 1945), pp.256–9.

7 G.H.J. Adlam to John Murray, letter dated 26 October 1918.

8 Sir Ronald Ross KCB, FRS to John Murray JP CVO, letter dated 28 October 1918. Ross edited *Science Progress*, a quarterly review published by John Murray.

9 G.H.J. Adlam to C.L. Bryant, letter dated 24 November 1944.

10 Ibid.

11 SMA, Minutes of General Committee, 12 November 1921.

12 In fact the SMA reverted to the appointment of members as Advertisement Editor in the 1950s, R.H. Dyball serving from 1952 to 1955 and Charles Holt from 1955 to 1959. On Holt's retirement from the office due to ill-health in 1959, Mrs Farquharson took over the duties again. SMA *Report of Committee 1960*, pp.3–4. See also *Education in Science*, No. 60 (Nov. 1974) p.17.

13 SMA, *Report of Committee 1942*, p.2

14 *SSR, 28*, No. 104 (October 1946) pp.2–4.

15 ASE, Minutes of Executive Committee, 14 Sept. 1963 and 30 Nov. 1963.

16 ASE, Minutes of Joint Meeting of *The School Science Review* and Publication Committees, 10 July 1965.
The 'honorarium' paid to the Editor was substantially greater than that which previous Editors had received. Humby had received £250 in 1946 and Dyball £250 in 1962 and £300 in 1963. Payments in excess of these figures were deemed to raise question about the ASE's position as a charity.

17 G. Fowles, A Past Chairman's Reminiscences of Three Editors, *SSR, 47* No. 163 (June 1966) p.847.

18 Andrew Bishop, Fifty years on: the Editor's view, *SSR, 50*, No. 173 (June 1969) p.713.

19 G.H.J. Adlam to C.L. Bryant, letter dated 24 November 1944.

20 G.H.J. Adlam to C.L. Bryant, letter dated 5 December 1944.

21 E.G. Savage, *SSR, 26*, No. 100 (June 1945) p.261.

22 AWST, *Report for 1944–45*, p.10.

23 The writer was F.B. Finter (Clifton College). *SSR, 11*, No. 43 (March 1930) p.282.

24 By the 1940s the British Council was taking 500 copies of *SSR* for distribution overseas. See e.g. SMA, *Report of Committee 1942*, p.2.

25 G. Fowles, op.cit. (note 17) p.848.

26 G.H.J. Adlam to C.L. Bryant, letter dated 5 December 1944.

27 G. Fowles, op.cit (note 17) p.849.

28 C.L. Bryant, Science and the Spens Report, *SSR, 21*, No. 82 (Dec. 1939) pp.781–790.

29 See e.g. Cyril Burt, Formal Training, *SSR, 20*, No. 81 (Oct. 1939) pp.653–666.

30 SMA, Minutes of General Committee, 10 June 1961.

31 SMA, *Bulletin* No. 1 (April 1962), From the Editor (unpaginated).

32 ASE, *Bulletin*, No. 13 (April 1965), pp.10–14.

33 The Branch replies and Council's observations were considered in detail at a meeting of the Joint *SSR* and Publications Committee, 4 June 1966.

34 ASE London Branch, Minutes of Committee Meeting, 21 Sept. 1965.

35 ASE Midland Branch, Minutes of 3rd Annual General Meeting, 12 March 1966.

36 *Education in Science*, No. 19 (Sept. 1966) pp.9–10.

37 ASE, Minutes of Executive Committee, 28 June 1969.

38 *Education in Science*, No. 86 (January 1980) p.9 and No. 87 (April 1980) p.11.

39 *SSR, 57*, No. 201 (June 1976) p.780.

40 Brian Matthews, The School Science Review – Is it the Journal members want? *Education in Science*, No. 72 (April 1977) pp.15–16.

41 Ibid., p.17.

42 *Education in Science*, No. 76 (Jan. 1978) pp.13–14.

43 The series also included a report on *Laboratory Assistants* (1938).

44 SMA, *The teaching of General Science* (John Murray, 1936).

45 At a later date a joint publication of the SMA and AWST, *Safeguards in the*

Laboratory, appeared (1947), a second and third editions following in 1950 and 1957.

46 *SSR, 8* No. 32 (June 1927) p. 286.

47 SMA, Minutes of General Committee, 16 May 1931.

48 John Murrays to G.H.J. Adlam, letter dated 26 Oct. 1936.

49 G.H.J. Adlam to H.E. Wilmott (John Murray), 17 Nov. 1944.

50 This was replaced by *Teaching Science at the Secondary Stage. A Handbook on the Teaching of Science to the Average Pupil* (John Murray, 1967).

51 SMA, *Report of the Sub-Committee on Laboratory Technicians 1955* (John Murray, 1955).

52 All the Policy Statements up to 1965 and the reports in the Science and Education series were published for the Association by John Murray.

53 *Education in Science*, No. 35 (Nov. 1969) pp.13–14.

54 ASE, Minutes of Education (Research) Committee, 29 Jan. 1977.

55 ASE, *Education through Science. Policy Statement.* (1981) p.2.

56 *Education in Science*, No. 80 (Nov. 1978) p.13.

57 *Education in Science*, No. 75 (Nov. 1977) p.15. *Safeguards in the School Laboratory* had achieved an 8th edition by 1981.

58 All these reports and pamphlets were published by the ASE and distributed from Headquarters.

59 *Education in Science*, No. 106 (Jan. 1984) p.18.

60 Information about ASE projects and publications is drawn from Annual Reports, from the minutes of relevant committees and from details of publications in *Education in Science* e.g. No. 60 (Nov. 1974) p.19; No. 75 (Nov. 1977) p.16; No. 92 (April 1981) pp.14 and 45; No. 106 (Jan. 1984) pp.18 and 27.

61 ASE, Minutes of Publications Committee, 18 March and 28 October 1978. ASE, Minutes of Coordinating Committee, 24 June 1978.

62 *Education in Science*, No. 60 (Nov. 1974) p.15; No. 80 (Nov. 1978) pp.13–14; No. 105 (Nov. 1983) p.16.

63 The view of professionalism here and elsewhere is much influenced by: Terence J. Johnson, *Profession and Power* (London, 1972).

8   Science education for an élite

1 See e.g. Harry Butterworth, 'The Science and Art Department Examinations: origins and achievements'. In: Roy MacLeod (ed.) *Days of Judgement* (Nafferton Books, 1982) pp.27–44.
Also: D.R. Stoddart, 'That Victorian Science: Huxley's Physiography and its impact on geography', *Transactions of the Institute of British Geographers, 66* (1975) pp.17–40.

2 *The Schoolmasters Yearbook and Directory* (London 1904) pp.330–1.

3 Ibid., p.389. The Advisory Board on Military Education and Training was appointed by the Secretary of State for War in April 1903.

4 A.T. Simmons, 'Physics in state-aided secondary schools'. In: The Physical Society of London, *The Teaching of Physics in Schools* (London 1918) pp.26–30.

5 These problems, specific to public schools, provided the main items on the programmes of the first two conferences held by the public school science masters in

1901 and 1902, and were recurring themes at annual meetings thereafter.

6 W.A. Shenstone, Science Teaching in Preparatory Schools, *The Preparatory School Review*, 2, No. 7 (July 1897) pp.75–6.
   Archer Vassall, The teaching of science, *The Preparatory School Review*, 2, No. 8 (Dec. 1897) p.107. Also: Natural science in preparatory schools, *The Preparatory School Review*, 2, No. 10 (July 1898) pp.37–8.

7 Archer Vassall, op.cit. (1898) p.38.

8 *The Journal of Education, 26* (ns) (1904) p.412.

9 APSSM, Minute Book, 13 May 1904.

10 *The Preparatory School Review, 5*, No. 30 (March 1905) pp.212–16 and 225–31.

11 O.H. Latter, Science at the beginning and end of the curriculum, *The School World, 18*, Nov. 1916, pp.401–3.
   O.H. Latter, *Report on science teaching in public schools represented on the Association of Public School Science Masters*. Board of Education. Educational Pamphlets No. 17. (HMSO 1909) p.13.

12 O.H. Latter, op.cit (1909) p.19.

13 APSSM, *Report of General Meeting, 1911*. Report of the Committee (1910) p.16.
   APSSM, Minute Book, 12 Feb. 1910.

14 Ibid., 28 May 1910.

15 Ibid., 28 Oct. 1911.

16 Ibid., 22 May 1916 and 7 Oct. 1916.

17 *Natural Science in Education*. (London HMSO 1918) p.30.

18 APSSM Minute Book, 18 May 1918.

19 *The Journal of Education and School World, 55* (Feb. 1923) p.120.

20 H.C. King, 'Common Examination for Entrance to Public Schools', *The Journal of Education and School World, 56* (Sept. 1923) pp.646–7.

21 *SSR, 1*, No. 1 (June 1919) pp.29–30.

22 Archer Vassall, Some aspect of science and education, *SSR, 2*, No. 7 (Feb. 1921) p.242.
   See also: *SSR, 1*, No. 2 (Oct. 1919) p.59.

23 F.W. Sanderson, Work in Preparatory Schools, *The Preparatory School Review, 7*, No. 66 (March 1917) pp.269–72. Sanderson was not a member of the APSSM.

24 V.S. Bryant, Science teaching in the early stages. *SSR, 1*, No. 3 (Feb. 1920) pp.87–90.

25 Anthony West, *Observer*, 4 Jan. 1976, p.15.

26 *Foundations: A reconsideration of the aims of teaching in preparatory schools*. The report of a committee appointed by the Council of the Incorporated Association of Preparatory Schools. Chairman: H.J.G. Collis. (1959) pp.29–31.

27 *Science in Preparatory Schools*. A report on the IAPS science refresher conference held at Worcester College, Oxford, April 1961. (Esso Petroleum Co. Ltd) p.25.

28 Ibid.

29 *Guide to Science teaching in the Preparatory Schools*. A recommended course for preparatory schools approved by the Science Panel appointed by the Joint Working Party of HMC and IAPS on the Common Entrance Examination. Nuffield

Foundation Science Teaching Project. (1966) p.3.

30 Ibid. Revised edition. (1973) The chairman of the Common Entrance Science Panel was J.L. Lewis (Malvern) and members of the biology, chemistry and physics panels in 1973 included other leading members of the ASE.

31 J.W. Headlam HMI reported in 1902 that 'Greek had practically disappeared' and 'In English subjects' . . . 'the very first elements of good work are absent'. Board of Education. *General Reports on Higher Education, 1902*. Report on the Teaching of Literary Subjects in some Secondary Schools by J.W. Headlam. In December 1902, the H.M.C. passed a resolution that the first care of a Secretary of Secondary Education (in the Board of Education) 'should be to redress the balance which now weighs in favour of scientific studies against literary studies'. *The Schoolmasters Yearbook and Directory 1904* (London 1904) p.180.

32 G.C. Bourne, The teaching of natural science. In: C. Cookson (Ed.). *Essays on Secondary Education*, (Oxford, 1895) p.146.

33 The account of the Oxbridge scholarship examinations which follows is drawn from a number of sources, but reflects principally the perceptions of difficulties for public school science masters as recounted by C.G. Falkner (Weymouth) and M.D. Hill (Eton) in papers delivered at the conferences in 1901 and 1902. Conference of Public School Science Masters, *Papers read at the Meetings held . . . on Jan. 19, 1901 and on Jan. 18, 1902*. pp.14–18 and 28–32.

34 The phrase was Hill's. Ibid. p.30.

35 G.C. Bourne. op.cit. p.147.

36 APSSM, Minute Book, 14 May 1902.

37 Ibid., 8 Nov. 1902.

38 *The Times*, Friday, 13 Feb. 1903.

39 *The Times*, Monday, 16 Feb. 1903.

40 See Chapter 1 above, pp.31–2.

41 See e.g. *The School World*, 6 (Dec. 1904) pp.469–70.

42 *The School World*, 7 (1905) pp.27–28 and 146–7.

43 APSSM, *Report of General Meeting 1916*, p.23. See also: C.M. Stuart, The Reform of Examinations, *The School World, 9* (June 1907) p.214.

44 APSSM, *Report of General Meeting 1918*, p.20. The report of Bryant's meeting with a Committee of the Hebdomadal Council was printed as an Appendix, pp.24–5.

45 Ibid. and pp.25–8, 50–3.

46 APSSM, Minute Book, 3 Oct. 1908.

47 Ibid., 23 Oct. 1909, 12 Jan. 1910, 29 Oct. 1910, 27 May 1911.

48 Ibid., 11 May 1912, 12 Oct. 1912, 8 Jan. 1913, 31 May 1913, 10 Jan. 1914.

49 Ibid., 23 Oct. 1915.

50 Ibid., 3 Jan. 1916, 22 May 1916, 7 Oct. 1916.
F.B. Stead had been educated, and had taught science, at Clifton College. He was Secretary to the Prime Minister's Committee, under the chairmanship of Sir J.J. Thomson, appointed in 1916 to report on the position of natural science in the educational system of Great Britain. The APSSM Committee in Jan. 1918 decided 'to consider . . . Mr. Stead . . . as honorary member of the Association so far as regards the sending of publication'. Stead was formally elected in 1923 though he had been active in APSSM meetings earlier during his teaching years at Clifton. At the annual meeting in January 1905 he gave a paper on teaching

'scientific method' to boys on the literary side who had no time for a regular course in chemistry and physics. *The School World, 7* (1905) p.64.

51 Board of Education. Educational Pamphlets, No. 17. *Report on science teaching in Public Schools represented on the Association of Public School Science Masters.* (General ed: O.H. Latter). (HMSO 1909) p.7.

52 Science and Art Department, *27th Report* (London, 1880) pp.86–7.

53 For an account of the theory of military education in nineteenth century England see: T. Hearl, Military education and the school curriculum, 1800–70, *History of Education, 5*(3) (1976) pp.251–64.

54 See chapter 1 above, pp.11–13.
The Board of Education's Office of Special Inquiries and Reports published a series of accounts of *Modern Sides of Public Schools* from 1905, beginning with Harrow and including *The Army Class at Eton* (1907), *The Modern Side at Clifton College* (1909) and *The Civil and Military Department at Bedford Grammar School* (1909).

55 *Report of the Committee appointed to enquire into the entrance examinations (in non-military subjects) of candidates for commissions in the army.* C.7373. (London, HMSO 1894).

56 Ibid. p.ix.

57 *The Schoolmasters' Yearbook and Directory 1903* (London, 1903) pp.213–4.

58 Conference of Public School Science Masters. *Papers read at the meeting held . . . on Jan. 19, 1901 and on Jan. 18, 1902.* pp.22–8.

59 Ibid. p.26.

60 *Nature, 64* (1901) pp.55–6.

61 *Report of the Committee appointed to consider the education and training of officers of the Army.* Cd.982. (London HMSO 1902) pp.3–4.

62 *Nature, 69* (26 Nov. 1903) p.86.

63 The appointed President for the year was in fact Sir Michael Foster, a member of the Akers-Douglas Committee on the education of Army officers. Foster, however, became ill and Dr. Gow deputised. APSSM Minute Book, 14 January 1905. Dr. Gow was chairman of the Examinations Committee of the Head Masters Conference as the time of his address. Two years later, when the APSSM secured the services of another leading headmaster and non-scientist as their President (Rev. the Hon. Edward Lyttelton, recently appointed to Eton College) there were further expressions of support for science teaching. See e.g. *The Journal of Education, 29* (ns) Feb. 1907) p.106.

64 Leonard Blaikie was elected a member in Jan. 1903.

65 APSSM, Minute Book, 2 May 1906, 24 Nov. 1906, 5 Oct. 1907. In fact Haldane never served as President.

66 *The Schoolmasters Yearbook and Directory 1904*, (London, 1904) pp.247 and 359.

67 APSSM, Minute Book, 13 May 1904, 14 Jan. 1905, 17 May 1905.

68 Ibid., 24 Nov. 1906.

69 *The Journal of Education, 26* (ns) (Feb. 1904) p.174.

70 R.E. Thwaites, Conditions of science work in secondary schools, *The School World, 9* (Sept. 1907) pp.347–8.

71 Board of Education. Educational Pamphlets, No. 17. op.cit.

72 Ibid., p.12.

73 Ibid., p.10.

74 APSSM, *Report of the General Meeting 1913*, pp.20–1; and Minute Book, 31 May 1913, 18 Oct. 1913, 18 May 1918.

75 APSSM, *Report of General Meeting, 1916*, pp.20–2, 45–7.

76 C.L. Bryant, School Instruction in Science for Military Purposes, *The School World, 18* (April 1916) pp.133–5.

77 APSSM, *Catalogue of exhibition of scientific and military apparatus and books.* (Eton College, Windsor. 1917) pp.16–21.
    Ibid., (The City of London School, 1918) pp.18–20.

78 *The Journal of Education, 38* (ns) (Feb. 1916) p.83.

79 APSSM, Short history of steps taken to promote a meeting of science masters in public schools. Record of meeting on 8 Nov. 1902.
    An account of the influence of medicine on science education in England is given in a paper by A.L. Mansell, *History of Education, 5* (June 1976) pp.155–68.

80 APSSM, Minute Book, 2 Nov. 1907; 13 Jan. and 9 May, 1908; 15 May and 23 Oct. 1909. Also: *Report of the General Meeting 1909*, pp.32–4. *Report of the General Meeting 1910*, pp.15–16.

81 APSSM, Minute Book, 27 May and 28 Oct. 1911; 11 May 1912. Report of the General Meeting 1912, p.18.
    Sir Henry Morris, The recognition of the public schools, *The Lancet*, (16 June 1911) pp.1594–5.

82 APSSM, Annual meeting, Westminster School, 20 Jan. 1906. Abstract of Papers. See also: *The School World, 8* (1906) p.70.

83 G.H. Martin, Science for the Classical Side, *The School World, 11* (1909) pp.50–1. APSSM, *Report of the General Meeting 1909*, pp. 31–2.

84 APSSM, *Report of the General Meeting 1910*, pp.48–50.

85 APSSM, *Report of the General Meeting 1912*, pp.21–3.

86 Ibid., pp.24–5.

87 APSSM, Minute Book, 28 May 1910.

88 Ibid., 31 May 1913.

89 APSSM, *Report of the General Meeting 1914*, pp.40–4.
    The Journal of Education, 36 (ns) (1914) pp.567–9 and 694–6.

90 *The Neglect of Science*. Report of Proceedings of a Conference held in the Rooms of the Linnaean Society, Burlington House, Piccadilly, W. on Wednesday, 3 May 1916. (London, 1916) p.3.

91 A.S. Smithells to Major-General Sir Cecil Lowther, Dec. 1918.

92 APSSM, Minute Book, 23 Oct. 1915.

93 Ibid., 3 Jan. 1916.

94 Ibid., 22 May 1916.

95 *The Neglect of Science* op.cit. p.4.

96 Ibid., p.7.

97 F.B. Stead was a former member of the APSSM being listed in 1902 when on the staff of Clifton College. On moving to the Board of Education his membership lapsed, but from 1911 he was a 'non-member entitled to receive the publications

of the Association.' In 1923 he was elected an Honorary Member. See ref. 50 above.

98 APSSM, Minute Book, 22 May 1916.

99 *Natural Science in Education*, Being a report of the Committee on the Position of Natural Science in the Educational System of Great Britain. (London, HMSO., Cd.9011, 1918)

100 APSSM, *Report of General Meeting 1917*, pp.26–7. The APSSM memorandum was also published in full in *The School World, 19* (March 1917) pp.94–7.

101 British Association for the Advancement of Science, *Report of the Eighty–Sixth Meeting, 1916* (London 1917) p.lix.

102 See e.g. *The Journal of Education, 38* (n.s.) (Oct. 1916) p.575; and E.H. Tripp, The Government Committee on Science in Secondary Education, *The School World, 18* (Oct. 1916) pp.369–70.

103 British Association for the Advancement of Science, *Report . . . 1917* (London 1918) pp.123–207.

104 *The Times*, 4 May, 1916. The letter was also published in: F.G. Kenyon (ed.) *Education, Scientific and Humane*. A report of the Proceedings of the Council for Humanistic Studies (London 1917) pp.5–8.

105 Conjoint Board of Scientific Societies. Aims, objects and results of the first year's work, 1916–1917. pp.14–16.
For the details of conferences between the Conjoint Board and the Council for Humanistic Studies, see: F.G. Kenyon, *Education: Secondary and University* (London 1919).

106 F.G. Kenyon (ed.) *Education Scientific and Humane* (London 1917) p.10.

107 Ibid., pp.11–12.

108 APSSM, Minute Book, 7 Oct. 1916.

109 APSSM, Report of General Meeting 1917, pp.32–43.

110 Rev. Canon Fowler, The Matriculation Examination of the University of London. In: C. Cookson (editor), *Essays on Secondary Education* (Oxford 1898) p.246.

111 F.G. Kenyon, *Education: Secondary and University*. (London 1919) pp.24 and 44.

112 *Natural Science in Education*, op.cit. p.163.

113 *The Journal of Education, 53* (1921) p.81.

114 Civil Service. Class 1 Examination. Copy of Report dated 20 June 1917, of the Committee appointed by the Lords Commissioners of His Majesty's Treasury (London HMSO, 1917) Cd.8657, pp.15–16 and 32.

115 The Headmasters' Conference had previously passed resolutions in support of General Science. See R.A. Gregory, Science for the Rank and File, *The School World, 19* (Feb. 1917) p.49.

116 British Association for the Advancement of Science, *Report . . . 1917* (London 1918) p.134.

117 R.A. Gregory, *Discovery or The Spirit and Service of Science*, (London 1916) pp.v–vii.

118 Ibid.

119 G.H. Adlam, Science for All. A plea for General Science, *SSR, 2* No. 6 (Dec. 1920) pp.197–202, especially pp.198, 201.

9 Science education for the rank and file

1 Science in Secondary Education, *The School World, 19* (June 1917) p.196.

2 R.A. Gregory, Science for the Rank and File, *The School World, 19* (Feb. 1917) p.50. Gregory's address was given at the annual meeting of the APSSM held at Eton College on 3 Jan. 1917.

3 See e.g. A.T. Simmons, Physics in state-aided secondary schools. In: The Physical Society of London, *The teaching of physics in schools*. (London 1918) p.27s.

4 H.H. Turner, The embarrassments of the investigator. In: APSSM, *Report of General Meeting 1917*, pp.44–61.

5 APSSM, *Report of General Meeting 1917*, pp.62–7. See also the published version of Gregory's paper, ref. 2 above.
Details of the Members Exhibition are in *Catalogue of Exhibition of Scientific and Military Apparatus and Books at Annual Meeting, Eton College, Windsor*, 3 and 4 Jan. 1917.

6 In a letter of Professor Arthur Smithells, 20 Jan. 1917, Turner developed his ideas by critical annotations on an article by Smithells (The Place of Natural Science in a General Education, *The School Guardian*, 18 Nov. 1916, pp.3–4 and 16 Dec. pp.27–8). Smithells attended the APSSM Annual Meeting at which Turner delivered his address and joined in the discussion on Gregory's paper, supporting the humanising of school science.

7 SMA, Minute Book, 15 May 1920; 16 Oct. 1920; 3 Jan. 1924; 8 March 1924; 10 May 1924; 11 Oct. 1924. Also: *Report for 1924*, p.42.
The 1920 revision was published in *SSR, 2*, No. 6 (Dec. 1920) pp.197–212, including A Plea for General Science (pp.197–202) written by the editor, G.H.J. Adlam (City of London School). It also appeared as a pamphlet.

8 SMA, Minute Book, 12 March 1921.
The membership of the Liaison Committee was:
SMA: J.R. Eccles (Gresham); E.R. Thomas (R.G.S., Newcastle-upon-Tyne); A. Vassall (Harrow).
Universities: Dr Irvine Masson (London); H. Thirkill (Clare College, Cambridge); Brig. Gen. H. Hartley (Balliol College, Oxford).
Its business was 'to discuss matters of policy and curriculum which affect schools and universities'. SMA, *Report for 1921*, p.50. It was described by the SMA as 'one of the most important' of its sub-committees (*Report* for 1922, p.54); although much of its business was concerned with the Higher School Certificate examinations in science, it also pressed strongly for General Science in the School Certificate; see e.g. *Report for 1924*, p.42. Brigadier-General Hartley, later Sir Harold Hartley FRS, had a life-long interest in the work of the science masters: he was President of the SMA in 1926 and was still actively involved in the 1960s (See Chapter 11). The introduction of General Science into the School Certificate Examination of the Oxford and Cambridge Joint Board against strong opposition was probably much due to his influence; SMA, Minute Book, 21 Feb. 1920 and *SSR, 1*, No. 2 (Oct. 1919) p.55.

9 SMA, Educational Pamphlet No. 3. *General Science. Outlines of Two Courses. Suggested Practical Work*, Revised (1932), (London, 1932) p.20.

10 Conditions for Effective Science Teaching, *SSR, 7*, No. 26 (Dec. 1925) p.70–1. A deputation of the officers of the SMA went to the Board of Education to 'confer over points' in the Board's *Report* on which the SMA did not agree. SMA, Minute Book, 31 Jan. 1925.
Board of Education, *Report of an Enquiry into the Conditions affecting the Teaching of Science in Secondary Schools for Boys in England*. (London HMSO 1925)

11 G.N. Pingriff, Science for All – Some Criticisms, *SSR, 2*, No. 8 (June 1921) pp.323–6.

12 Science in School Certificate Examinations. British Association for the Advancement of Science, *Report 1928* (London 1929) pp.443–532.

13 *SSR, 9*, No. 43 (March 1930) p.236.
Eight of the 14 members of the B.A. Committee had served also on the 1917 committee. Of the six SMA members, only one had recent experience of the work of the Association's General Committee, and several were retired.

14 SMA, Minute Book, 2 Oct. 1926.
The Hadow Committee also received evidence from the British Social Hygiene Council and the Association of Teachers of Domestic Subjects. Individual members of the SMA presented evidence e.g. G.W. Olive, a biologist and headmaster of Dauntsey Agricultural School, Wiltshire.

15 Hugh Richardson, Education of the Adolescent, *SSR, 8*, No. 32 (June 1927) pp.272–6.

16 E.J. Holmyard, School Science, *Nature, 123*, (8 June 1929) pp.861–3.

17 SMA, Minute Book, 5 Oct. 1929 and *SSR, 11*, No. 43 (March 1930) p.238, where the committee endorses the occupational value of science teaching.

18 A report of the meeting is given in: SMA, *Report for 1928*, p.70.
See also: Rt Hon. W. Ormsby Gore, Colonial Appointments, *SSR, 10*, No. 38 (Dec. 1928) pp.81–85.
Prof. A.G. Tansley, Botany as a university subject for candidates for colonial appointments, *SSR, 10*, No. 39 (March 1929) pp.179–183.

19 See report of discussion at the Annual Meeting, *SSR, 9*, No. 35 (Feb. 1928) pp.157–62.

20 SMA, Minute Book, 24 November 1928 and *Report for 1929*, pp.71–2.

21 *SSR, 11*, No. 42 (Dec. 1929) p.91. SMA, Minute Book, 2 Jan. 1930.

22 British Association for the Advancement of Science, *Report 1929*. (London 1930) p.xxxv.

23 *SSR, 12*, No. 47 (March 1931) pp.255–263.

24 The British Association committee's report, when it eventually appeared, came out strongly in support of General Science; *Report 1933*. (London 1934) p.329.
See also the Presidential Address to Section L by W. Mayhowe Heller the previous year; *Report 1932*, (London 1932) p.216.

25 SMA, Educational Pamphlet No. 3, op.cit.

26 H.S. Shelton, Essay-Review. General Science, *SSR, 14*, No. 56 (June 1933) pp.458–67.

27 *The School Certificate Examination* being the report of the panel of investigators appointed by the Secondary School Examinations Council to enquire into the eight approved School Certificate examinations held in the summer of 1931. (London HMSO) 1932.

28 Ibid., pp.120–4.

29 SMA, Minute Book, 25 March 1933.

30 See the editorial contribution (by G.H.J. Adlam) on: Matriculation and the School Certificate Examination, *SSR, 14*, No. 56 (June 1933) pp.452–7.

31 SMA, *Annual Report 1932*, pp.85–7 and Minute Book, 12 March 1932.

32 SMA, Report of discussion at the General Meeting, 1933, of the recommendations made in the Committee's Report on the Content of School Certificate Science, pp.1–8.

33 Amongst the letters received was one from F.W.G. Ridgewell, Senior Science

Master at Surbiton County School and IAAM Executive Member for Surrey. 'I strongly deprecate making any science subject compulsory', Ridgewell wrote. 'The effect of the new proposals will be to make the school syllabus follow the new examination syllabus, one of the things we most wish to avoid'. Ridgewell was not an opponent of General Science and taught it in his school. The IAAM Council was debating a resolution condemning *compulsory* General Science almost simultaneously with the SMA discussions.

34 See e.g. D. Thompson, General Science – Its Origins and Growth, *SSR, 40*, No. 140 (Nov. 1958) p.119.
R. Hitchcock, Science – as a whole, *SSR, 15*, No. 60 (June 1934) p.532.

35 School Certificate Examinations. Record of a Conference held on April 16, 1934. *SSR, 16*, No. 61 (Oct. 1934) p.125.
Also: *SSR, 15*, No. 60 (June 1934) p.525.

36 SMA, Minute Book, 25 March 1933. Baker declined to serve.

37 F.W. Turner: letter dated 13 April 1933 to members of the sub-committee on General Science.

38 F.W. Turner to A.E. Foot, General Secretary, SMA, 9 Jan. 1935.
SMA, Minute Book, 20 May 1933; 26 May 1934; 24 Nov. 1934.

39 The pamphlet, *Revised Report of the General Science Sub-Committee with Specimen Paper*, was sent to SMA members and headmasters with a covering letter from the General Secretary, A.E. Foot, Eton College, on 9 Jan. 1935. The preamble is on p.1.

40 H.S. Shelton, *The theory and practice of General Science*. (London 1939) p.32.

41 C.L. Bryant (chairman of the new General Science sub-committee) in a letter to J.A. Lauwerys (convenor), 24 Jan. 1935.

42 SMA, Minute Book, 1 Jan. 1935.

43 See e.g. J.A. Lauwerys, The teaching of physical science, *SSR, 17*, No. 66 (Dec. 1935) p.164.
British Association for the Advancement of Science, *Report 1929* (London 1930) pp.302–9.

44 SMA, Minute Book, 16 Feb. 1935.

45 S.V. Brown, General Secretary of the SMA in a letter to J.A. Lauwerys, convenor of the sub-committee, 18 Feb. 1935.

46 SMA, General Science Sub-Committee, Minutes, 23 March and 1 June, 1935.
A.J. Price to J.A. Lauwerys, 30 May 1935.

47 W.G. Greaves to C.L. Bryant, 2 June 1935.
C.L. Bryant to W.G. Greaves, 3 June 1935.
SMA, Minute Book, 12 Oct. 1935.

48 Shelton's book, some parts of which were based on articles of his which had appeared in *The Schoolmaster and Woman Teacher's Chronicle*, was published in 1939. H.S. Shelton, *The theory and practice of General Science*. (London 1939).

49 SMA, Minute Book, 26 May 1934, and *Report for 1934*, p.125.

50 SMA, *Report for 1935*, p.117. Also: Incorporated Association of Assistant Masters, *The AMA* (Oct. 1935) p.266.

51 SMA, Minute Book, 16 Feb. 1935.

52 C.L. Bryant to J.A. Lauwerys, 24 Feb. 1935.

53 A. Vassall: paper submitted to the General Science Sub-Committee for its first meeting, 23 March 1935.

54 H.S. Shelton to J.A. Lauwerys, 28 Feb. 1935.
SMA, General Science Sub-Committee, Minutes, 23 March 1935.

55 SMA, General Science Sub-Committee, op.cit.

56 H.S. Shelton, Memorandum on the timetable requirements for General Science.

57 W.G. Greaves to S.V. Brown, 2 Feb. 1935 and 9 Feb. 1935.
W.G. Greaves: memorandum on construction of a General Physics syllabus.
Prepared for the first meeting of the General Science Sub-Committee.

58 W.G. Greaves to C.L. Bryant, 2 June 1935.
W.G. Greaves to W.J. Gale, 2 June 1935.

59 A.J. Price to J.A. Lauwerys, 30 May 1935.

60 H.S. Shelton, Memorandum on the General Science Syllabus (no date, but prepared after the sub-committee's second meeting on 1st June, 1935).

61 *The AMA* (May 1936) p.130: (June 1936) p.192: (July 1936) p.220: (Sept.
1936) p.248: (Nov. 1936) p.207.

62 W.G. Greaves, Memorandum on Integration and Synthesis, prepared for the
meeting of the General Science Sub-Committee, 9 Nov. 1935.

63 SMA, *Report for 1936*, pp.22 and 121.

64 SMA, Report for 1936, pp.22–3.

65 *SSR, 18*, No. 72 (June 1937) p.595.

66 SMA, Minute Book, 29 May 1937.

67 Ibid., 22 Oct. 1938.

68 Ibid., 5 Feb. 1938 and *Report for 1938*, p.129.

69 SMA, Minute Book, 4 Feb. 1939.

70 Ibid., 20 May 1939.

71 Science Masters' Association, *The Teaching of General Science*, Part II. (London
1938) pp.62–73.

72 *Natural Science in Education*. (London HMSO, Cd. 9011, 1918) p.38.

73 See e.g. AST, Minutes of General Meetings, 7 Jan. 1917. Miss I.M. Drummond
opened a discussion on the present position of science teaching in girls' schools, as
a preliminary to the submission of evidence to the Thomson Committee and the
British Association committee. She was, of course, a member of the latter.
AST, Minutes of General Meetings, 13 July 1918. Dr E.M. Delf, F.L.S., lectured
on necessary changes in the teaching of botany in schools. *The Journal of Education, 50* (Feb. 1918) p.125.
British Association for the Advancement of Science, *Report 1933*. (London,
1933) p.319.

74 *Natural Science in Education* op.cit. p.37. The Association of Headmistresses did
not find it possible to endorse the AST's recommendation of 3 hours per week
because 'it would be difficult to find the time for other subjects'.

75 AST, Minutes of Committee Meetings, 2 Jan. 1915.
Minutes of General Meetings, 13 Nov. 1915.

76 AST, Minutes of General Meetings, 6 Jan. 1919. The afternoon was given over to
a conference on relations between schools and universities in regard to science
teaching and a Consultative Committee of the university and school teachers was
established.
On history of science, see Miss M.B. Thomas's presidential address to the AST,
The Journal of Education, 53 (Feb. 1921) pp.117–8.

77 British Association for the Advancement of Science, *Report 1933*. (London, 1933) p.322.

78 See e.g. the discussion in 1918 on a resolution that Group 3 of the School Certificate Examination should contain only mathematics, and 'elements of physics and chemistry', all other science subjects to come under Group 4. The point of the resolution was to ensure that every girl should have studied the elements of physical science before leaving school. After 'a heated discussion' an amendment was carried, 27 votes to 17, that no candidate who offered a biological subject only in Group 3 could pass, unless it could be shown that she had followed also a satisfactory course in physics and chemistry. The practical problems of implementing this were ignored, and no change in practice was made. AST, Minutes of General Meeting, 13 July 1918.

79 AWST, Minutes of General Meeting, 6 Jan. 1933.

80 AWST, *Annual Report for 1934*, pp.10–12, 21.

81 Ibid., p.23.

82 Miss M.E. Birt to all members of the AWST, letter dated March 1934.

83 AWST, Minutes of Committee Meeting, 9 March 1935.
SMA, Minute Book, 25 May 1935.

84 Miss I.G. Lewis, (Wimbledon High School) to Miss M.E. Birt, 13 Oct. 1935.
AWST, Minutes of Committee Meeting, 16 Nov. 1935; 26 Jan. 1936.

85 AWST, Minutes of Committee Meeting, 28 March 1936.

86 SMA, Minute Book, 29 May 1937.

87 AWST, Minutes of Committee Meeting, 28 Nov. 1936.
Also: AWST, *Report 1936–37*, p.12.

88 *SSR, 19*, No. 13 (Oct. 1937) pp.134–6.

89 AWST, *Annual Report 1937–38*.

90 *SSR,* op.cit. p.135.

91 Ibid., p.136.

92 AWST, Minutes of Committee Meeting, 13 Nov. 1937.

93 Ibid. and 29 Jan. 1938.

94 *A General Science Examination Syllabus*. Compiled by a Joint Standing Committee of the Association of Assistant Mistresses (Science Panel) and the Association of Women Science Teachers. (1939)
AWST, Minutes of Committee Meeting, 19 Nov. 1938 and 5 Jan. 1939.

95 Ibid., 4 March 1939. Supra, p.213.

96 AWST, Minutes of General Meeting, 19 May 1939.

97 AWST, *Annual Report 1938–39*, pp.65–70.

98 Ibid., p.66.

99 Ibid., p.67. When the AWST was asked by Lauwerys, in connection with the SMA/AMA joint committee's work, for recommendations for the guidance of men teachers in coeducational schools, the reply was that 'with a good teacher no differentiation regarding content of courses or methods was either needed or desirable'. AWST, Minutes of Committee Meeting, 19 Nov. 1938.

100 AWST, *Annual Report 1939–40*, p.00.

101 AWST, Minutes of Committee Meeting, 17 April 1942.

102 Secondary Modern Schools Committee of the SMA, *Secondary Modern Science Teaching, Part 2* (London, 1957) pp.141–9.
AWST, Minutes of Committee Meeting, 12 May 1956.

103 SMA, *Secondary Modern Science Teaching, Part 2*, op.cit. p.141.

104 Ibid., p.143.

105 Ibid., p.147.

106 AWST, Minutes of Committee Meeting, 3 Jan. 1958. The representatives were: Miss F.M. Eastwood (Chemistry); Miss J.D. Ling (Physics); Miss P.M. Taylor (Biology); Miss L.E. Higson (Fourth Panel).

107 AWST, Minutes of Committee Meeting, 27 Nov. 1958.
AWST, *The Place of Science in the Girls' Grammar School*. (1959).

108 *SSR., 23*, No. 91 (June 1942) pp.337–8.

109 *SSR., 24*, No. 93 (Feb. 1943) p.229.

110 Frederick Soddy, Science for Rulers, *SSR, 25*, No. 95 (Nov. 1943) p.7.

111 Science in Secondary School Education, *SSR, 24*, No. 94 (June 1943) pp.344–8.

112 *SSR., 25*, No. 95 (Nov. 1943) p.119.

113 Ibid.

114 *SSR., 25*, No. 95 (Nov. 1943) pp.122–4.

115 SMA, Minute Book, 29 April 1944.

116 SMA, Minute Book, 9 June 1945.

117 Interim Report of a Sub-Committee of the Association of Women Science Teachers, *Science in Post-Primary Education with reference to the Scientific Education in schools of pupils of 11–18, and its relation to their subsequent training in Universities and Colleges* (London, John Murray 1944).

118 Cited by M. Hyndman, Multilateralism and the Spens Report: Evidence from the Archives, *British Journal of Educational Studies, 24*, No. 3 (Oct. 1976) p.245.

119 AWST., *Science in Post-Primary Education* (London 1944) pp.v–vi.

120 *Science in Post-Primary Education*, op.cit. pp.6–13.

121 Ibid. pp.13–14.

122 Secondary Science Curriculum Review, *Science Education 11–16: proposals for action and consultation* (London, 1983) p.1.

123 *SSR, 24*, No. 92 (Nov. 1942) pp.96–7. Board of Education, *Curriculum and Examinations in Secondary Schools* (London HMSO, 1943) p.109.

124 SMA, Minute Book, 29 April, 1944.
SSR, 26, No. 99 (Feb. 1945) pp.238–9.

125 SMA, Minute Book, 8 Feb. 1947 and *Report of Committee, 1947*, p.5.

126 SMA, Minute Book, 1 Aug. 1949.

127 SMA, *Report of Committee*, 1950, p.6.

128 SMA, *Report of Committee*, 1952, p.7.

129 E.W. Jenkins, *From Armstrong to Nuffield* (London 1979) p.94.

130 W.S. James, Grammar School Science. Specialising from the start. *The Times Educational Supplement* (27 April 1956) p.530.
See also: General Science on Trial. Pooling of ignorance, *The Times Educational*

Supplement (28 Sept. 1956) p.1171; a further article by James was published in *The New Scientist* (19 Sept. 1957).

131 L. Connell, *The Times Educational Supplement* (5 Oct. 1956) p.1199.

132 L. Connell and W.S. James, General Science Today, *SSR, 39*, No. 138 (March 1958) pp.277–285.

133 *SSR, 39*, No. 139 (June 1958) p.531.

134 SMA, Minute Book, 1 March, 1958.

135 SMA, *Science and Education. A Policy Statement* (1957) pp.6, 8.

136 Charles Holt (Chairman, SMA Committee): letter to committee members, 2 June 1958, and draft statement on General Science.

137 Ibid.

138 SMA, Minute Book, 4 Oct. 1958.

139 *SSR, 40*, No. 142 (June 1959) p.514.

140 H.P. Ramage to B.E. Dawson, correspondence dated 11 Jan. 1960. Ramage had analysed the teaching subjects of 2500 SMA members in a sample of 1000 Grammar Schools and found that almost 60% were 'one-subject' men. Only 21% taught a combination of subjects which included General Science.

10   Curriculum control: the work of the Science and Education Committee

1 C.P. Snow, *The Two Cultures and the Scientific Revolution* (Cambridge 1959).

2 Ministry of Education, *15 to 18. A report of the Central Advisory Council for Education (England). Volume 1. Report.* (London HMSO 1959)
By 'numeracy' was meant 'the ability to reason quantitatively' and 'some understanding of scientific method and some acquaintance with the achievement of science' (p.461). For evidence of the SMA see pp.265 and 278.

3 E. James, Grammar Schools in Danger, *Sunday Times*, Jan. 1954.

4 Sir David Eccles, address to the Incorporated Association of Assistant Masters and the Association of Assistant Mistresses, 30 Dec. 1954.

5 Ministry of Education, *15 to 18* (London HMSO 1959) p.27.

6 *Scientific Manpower*. Report of a Committee appointed by the Lord President of the Council. Cmd. 6824. (London, HMSO 1946) p.22.

7 K.M.H. Chapman and E.H. Coulson, An enquiry into the conditions affecting science teaching in grammar schools. *SSR, 35*, No. 126 (March 1954) pp.168–177.

8 A.W. Barton, The supply of science teachers, in: W.H. Perkins (ed.) *Science in Schools* (London, 1958) p.53.

9 Willis Jackson, 'The Supply of Scientists and Technologists, *The Financial Times Annual Review of British Industry* (1955) p.101. Dr. Willis Jackson, later Lord Jackson of Burnley, was chairman of the committee on Manpower Resources for Science and Technology in the 1960s.

10 The government's White Paper on Technical Education (CMD. 9703) (London HMSO 1956) announcing the expenditure of £100 million on technical education over a five year period, included details of technical manpower in the USA, Soviety Russia and Western Europe.

11 The Scientific Manpower Committee was established in 1952 by the Advisory Council on Scientific Policy.
Professor S. Zuckerman, Scientists and Technologists in USSR, *The Times Educational Supplement*, (30 Dec. 1955) p.1331.

12 e.g. Austen Albu, How science can help industry, *The Listener*. (29 April 1954) pp.729–30.
Editorial, *Nature, 175* No. 4449 (5 Feb. 1955) pp.223–6.

13 *Report on the Industrial Fund for the Advancement of Scientific Education in Schools* (London May 1957)
Final Report of the Executive Committee. Industrial Fund for the Advancement of Scientific Education in Schools (London December 1963)
The main purpose of the Fund was to improve the supply to industry of physical scientists and mathematicians.
The Science Masters' Association/Association for Science Education received a grant from the Industrial Fund to assist in the establishment of permanent headquarters, then at Cambridge.

14 Provision and maintenance of laboratories in grammar schools, *SSR, 39*, No. 139 (June 1958) pp.438–46, and *41*, No. 145 (June 1960) pp.461–73.

15 H.F. Boulind, Accommodation and Equipment, in: W.H. Perkins (ed.), *Science in Schools* (London 1958) p.68.

16 Provision and maintenance of laboratories in grammar schools (1959), *SSR, 41*, No. 145 (June 1960) p.465.

17 The problem was perhaps especially acute in the case of women teachers. At the Conference on Science in Schools, sponsored by the British Association in April 1958, Miss L.E. Higson, Secretary of the AWST, made an impassioned plea for a sabbatical year for the many older, single women science teachers (c.40% of the total, in her estimate) who needed to refresh themselves and come up-to-date in their subject. W.H. Perkins (ed.) *Science in Schools*. (London 1958) p.103–4.

18 See e.g. D.J. de Solla Price. Quantitative measures of the development of science, *Archives Internationales d'Histoire des Sciences, 14* (1951) pp.85–93. Also, The exponential curve of science, *Discovery* (1956), pp.240–3.

19 Sir Alexander Todd, The Scientist-Supply and Demand, *SSR, 38*, No. 135 (March 1957) p.161.

20 *Annual Report of the Advisory Council on Scientific Policy 1959–60* Cmnd. 1167 (London HMSO 1960) p.16.

21 *SSR, 32*, No. 116 (Oct. 1950) pp.113–116.

22 Ibid., p.114.

23 Ibid., p.115.

24 The conference at the Unesco Institute for Education, Hamburg, was also attended by Mr (later Professor) Brian Holmes of the University of London Institute of Education, who contributed a paper on the training of teachers of science.
Dr H.F. Boulind was at this stage university lecturer in the Department of Education, University of Cambridge, a post he had held from 1949. Having graduated from Cambridge in 1928 with first class honours in physics, he subsequently taught in grammar schools in Leicester and Cambridge. From 1945 until 1968, Boulind served as an officer of the SMA and, later, the ASE, being General Secretary from 1951–5, chairman in 1959 and chairman of the influential Science and Education Sub-Committee from 1956 to 1967. He wrote several books including a UNESCO handbook, *Teaching of Physics in Tropical Secondary Schools*. Dr Boulind died in 1970, at the age of 63, whilst visiting New Delhi.
The account of the Hamburg Conference is in *SSR, 38*, No. 135 (March 1957) pp.291–2.

25 At the Cambridge Annual Meeting, January 1957, members of the SMA heard two addresses, the first by Sir Alexander Todd and the second by Professor N.F. Mott, in both of which the case for less specialised courses in schools and univer-

sities was strongly argued. In particular, reference was made to a proposed 'Science Greats' course intended for future 'men of affairs', rather than professional scientists. See: *SSR*, *38*, Nos.135 and 136 (1957) pp.160–7 and 405–6.

26 Boulind's suggestion was that teaching about atomic energy should be a high priority item on the agenda of the SMA's recently reconstituted Secondary Modern Sub-Committee.

27 No copy of the Memorandum exists in the Minute Book of the General Committee of the SMA but a former Minuting Secretary, Mr I.G. Jones (Doncaster) kindly made one available from his personal papers.

28 SMA, Minutes of General Committee, 2 March 1957.

29 *SSR, 24* No. 92 (Nov. 1942) pp.96–7. Italics in original

30 Ibid. *24*, No. 94 (June 1943) p.346.

31 SMA, Minutes of Meeting of the Officers of the Association, 22–24 April, 1949. The sub-committee was unusually constituted. Its convenor and chairman was G. Fowles (Chairman, General Committee 1940–44); other members were E.H. Coulson (Treasurer since 1946), Richard Palmer, J.S. Arthur OBE and one other, unnamed, person to represent the Secondary Modern Schools. Neither Palmer nor Arthur had served on the SMA General Committee. Arthur, elected to the SMA in 1923, was close to retirement in 1949. Palmer, in the Department of Education, University of Liverpool at the time of his election to the SMA in 1937, worked with the BBC, Bristol in 1946. The inclusion of a representative of the Secondary Modern Schools is interesting, as indicative of an intention to examine policy for all secondary schools following the passing of the 1944 Act. Future policy statements of the SMA did not carry this intent forward until 1965.

32 See Chapter 9, p.225.

33 The sub-committee had been instructed to report by October, 1949.

34 Over the two year period, 1949 to 1951, the percentage of schools represented on the SMA in the secondary modern and secondary technical category increased from 14.7% to 26.1%, while those in the grammar school category declined from 75% to 62.5%.

35 SMA, Minutes of General Committee, 1 June 1957.

36 One dissenting voice was almost certainly that of a member from Scotland, F.G. Daldy. The printed Policy Statement was not sent to Scottish schools in the general distribution in November 1957 and the Scottish Branch was then invited to produce a separate document appropriate to the different educational conditions in Scotland. A similar request went to the Northern Ireland Branch, whose representative S.H. Dunlop also served on the SMA's General Committee at this stage and probably cast the second vote against the Policy Statement.

37 *Science and Education*. A Policy Statement by the Committee of the Science Masters' Association (Nov. 1957) pp.4–9.

39 *The Place of Science in the Girls' Grammar School*. A statement published by the Executive Committee of the Association of Women Science Teachers (1959).

40 Ibid., p.4.

41 W.G. Rhodes, Chairman of the SMA Committee; H.F. Boulind, Chairman of the Science and Education Committee; H.F. Broad and W.H. Dowland, Secretaries of the Committee; R.H. Dyball, Editor of *The School Science Review*; and E.H. Coulson, a leading member of the Science and Education Committee. In contrast to his predecessor, Lord Hailsham, and his successor, Sir David Eccles, Mr. Lloyd was able to describe himself 'as one in whose education science had taken a large part'. SMA, Minutes of General Committee, 30 Nov. 1957.

42 H.F. Boulind, Progress report, 'Science and Education'. Document circulated to the General Committee at its meeting on 1st March 1958.

43 *Science and Education*. A policy statement issued by the Science Masters' Association and The Association of Women Science Teachers (John Murray 1961)
The scope of the statement was widened when a further-revised version was published under the title *School Science and General Education* in 1965. This was intended to apply to *all* secondary school pupils, not just the minority in grammar schools.

44 D.H. Morrell, Proposed Schools Council for the Curriculum and Examinations. Typescript of draft dated 24 Jan. 1963 sent from the Curriculum Study Groups to Sir William Alexander, Association of Education Committees, for comment. AEC File 31(a).

45 SMA, Minutes of the Chemistry Panel, 25 Jan., 14 June, 25 Oct. 1958.

46 The Science Masters' Association, (Draft) Report of the Physics Panel to the Science-and-Education Committee (1959) p.2.

47 SMA, Minutes of General Committee, 5 March 1960.

48 Those present included:
H.F. Boulind, W.H. Dowdeswell, I.G. Jones, H. Lockett, H.P. Ramage, all of the SMA.
Miss L.E. Higson, Secretary, AWST.
Mrs. E.W. Parsons, Chairman, Cambridgeshire Education Committee
Dr W.G. Humphrey, Headmaster, The Leys School, Cambridge.
J.A. Ratcliffe, FRS, Cavendish Laboratory, Cambridge University.
Dr Peter Sykes, Cambridge University Chemical Laboratory.
Dr A.R. Hill, Lecturer in History and Philosophy of Science, Cambridge University
Mr K.G. Collier, St Luke's College, Exeter.

49 H.F. Boulind, letter dated 20 Jan. 1958 inviting members to the exploratory meeting at Cambridge from which the 'Fourth Panel' arose.

50 The work at Leeds by Professor Stephen Toulmin and Dr June Goodfield led to the establishment in 1960 of the Nuffield Foundation Unit for the History of Ideas which produced teaching materials for the history and philosophy of science. Though supported by the Foundation at the same time as the Nuffield Science Teaching Project, there is little evidence to suggest that the Unit and the Project interacted in any way. Dr Goodfield attended a meeting of the 'Fourth Panel' as an adviser on 15 March 1958, and the Yorkshire Branch of the SMA held a one-day conference, 26 April 1958, on the policy statement and on the place of history and philosophy of science in school teaching. The discussion was opened by Professor S.E. Toulmin.

51 J.L. Lewis, A report on a sabbatical term Jan.–April 1961. Printed for private distribution by Esso Petroleum Co. Ltd, Nov. 1961.

52 SMA, Minutes of General Committee, 13 March 1954.

53 In his report, J.L. Lewis stated that he knew of only two English schools with a neutron source in 1961, his own, Malvern College, and St John's, Leatherhead. Op.cit. (ref.51) p.G4.

54 SMA, Minutes of General Committee, 6 June 1959.

55 Ibid., 28 Nov. 1959.

56 Ibid., 24 Sept. 1960.

57 Ibid., 26 Nov. 1960.

58 SMA, Minutes of General Committee, 26 Nov. 1960.

59 Ibid.

60 Much of the work of organising the conference and preparing papers for the various committee meetings had been undertaken by Mr and Mrs E.W. Tapper and it was Tapper who wrote the report on the conference which was presented to the General Committee of the SMA at its meeting, 16 Sept. 1961. The report, with notes of the meeting of 'a Planning Committee', notes of a meeting to discuss examinations in physics and chemistry, including the special sub-committee's report, and minutes of the meeting of the Science and Education Committee, 2 Sept. 1961, provide the evidence on which this account of the meeting at Barrow Court is based.

61 V.J. Long, HMI, a physicist; N. Booth, HMI, a chemist; D.G. Chisman, Education Officer, Royal Institute of Chemistry; N. Clarke, deputy Secretary, Institute of Physics.
Others present included: Professor H. Lipson, FRS, Manchester College of Science and Technology, and Dr L.R.B. Elton, Battersea College of Technology, both members of the Physics Panel.

62 Association for Science Education, *Science in the Introductory Phase* (John Murray 1967) p.4.

63 This 'Planning Committee' of the Science and Education Committee consisted of H.F. Boulind (chairman), E.W. Tapper (Secretary), V.J. Long, HMI, N. Booth, HMI, D.G. Chisman, N. Clarke, E.H. Coulson, Miss F.M. Eastwood, M.G. Brown, H. Tunley, Professor H. Lipson, Dr L.R.B. Elton, and J.L. Lewis; eight physicists and five chemists.

64 Observations on the present system of examination for the General Certificate of Education and suggestions for possible modifications. A report of a special sub-committee of the Science and Education Committee.

65 The general point that if the SMA and AWST 'did not move quickly, there was a danger that others would forestall them' was made again by E.H. Coulson in commenting on the report on the Barrow Court Conference to the General Committee. SMA, Minutes of General Committee, 16 Sept. 1961.

66 SMA, Minutes of a meeting of the Science and Education Committee, 2 Sept. 1961.

67 Ibid.

68 SMA, Minutes of General Committee, 25 Nov. 1961.

69 SMA, Minutes of a meeting of the Science and Education Committee, 2 Sept. 1961.

70 Dr Henry Boulind's correspondence as chairman of the SMA/AWST Science and Education Committee, and covering the period 4 Sept. 1961 to 5 May 1964, has been made available to me by his widow, Mrs Joan Boulind CBE. Her generosity and help is gratefully acknowledged. As the dates of letters and names of correspondents are given in the text, citations from letters are not further referenced in this chapter.

71 See e.g. Mary Waring, *Social Pressures and Curriculum Innovation. A study of the Nuffield Foundation Science Teaching Project* (Methuen 1979) p.78.

72 All but one of the members of the Science and Education Committee approved the draft, and a similar dissenting voice was heard in the General Committee where Boulind's action in producing the document was endorsed, the voting being 17 for and 1 against. SMA, Minutes of General Committee, 25 Nov. 1961.

73 Mary Waring (1979) op. cit. pp.79–85.

74 Nuffield Foundation. File EDU/52. Note of discussion between Mr John Lewis, Senior Science Master at Malvern, Mr Norman Clarke, Assistant Secretary at the Institute of Physics, the Director and Assistant Director on 30 Oct. 1961.

75 Nuffield Foundation. Policy Paper 115/1. Educational Research and Experiment.

76 Nuffield Foundation. Policy Paper 115/2. The teaching of science and mathematics.

77 McGill had been a member of the SMA since 1947, but had not been active in the affairs of the Association. His death on 22 March 1963 was a severe set-back to the Physics Project, which was directed thereafter by Professor Eric Rogers as organiser and J.L. Lewis as associate organiser.

78 Both the physics and chemistry projects were styled '11–15' in a draft progress report sent to Lord Todd in October 9162 by R.A. Becher, for use in connection with the Advisory Council on Scientific Policy. When a *Progress Report* was published by the Foundation in October 1963 the nomenclature had changed to '11–16'. The membership of the consultative Committee had also increased by this date.

79 Nuffield Foundation. File EDU/52. 'Science Teaching Programme. Agencies concerned with school science curriculum reform.' Paper prepared for the information of the trustees (1963) p.2.

80 J.W.L. Beament, The experimental approach, in: *New Thinking in School Biology* (OECD, 1963) p.48.

81 SMA, Minutes of General Committee, 3 March 1962.

82 SMA, Minutes of General Committee, 26 May 1962 and W.H. Dowdeswell's written report to the Committee, dated 3 May 1962.

83 SMA, Minutes of General Committee, 24 Nov. 1962.

84 ASE, Minutes of meeting of Science and Education Committee, 19 Jan. 1963.

85 The 'new' Education Committee included six of the seven original members from 1957, E.W. Moore having retired due to ill-health in 1961. Boulind, Broad, Coulson, Dowdeswell, Ramage and Tunley of the SMA, together with Tapper in his capacity as General Secretary from 1962, and Misses F.M. Eastwood and B.G. Ashton of the AWST provided continuity in the work of the committee.

86 ASE, *Science and Education. School Science and General Education*. A Policy Statement introducing the Science and Education Reports issued by the Association for Science Education (John Murray 1965).

87 These points were made in Report of a Conference held by the Education Committee in Cambridge on 1 and 2 May, 1965, presented to the Education Committee at its meeting on 18 Sept. 1965.

88 Report of Conference held by the Education Committee in Cambridge on 1st and 2nd May 1965. ASE, Minutes of Education Committee, 18 Sept. 1965. Due to the non-availability of the speaker sought, Biology in the Sixth Form was an important omission from the programme.

89 ASE, Future of Education Committee Meeting, Cambridge, 29 Dec. 1965 and: John Lewis, Memorandum on Future ASE work. Both documents accompany Minutes of the Education Committee, 12 Feb. 1966.

90 ASE, Minutes of an Extraordinary Meeting of the Education Committee, 27 March 1966. Policy was, of course, the formal responsibility of the ASE Council, to which the Education Committee reported.

91 H.F. Broad was chairman of the ASE in 1966.

92 ASE, Minutes of meeting of the Education Committee, 21 May 1966. Report of special sub-committee.

93 The National Foundation for Educational Research. Memorandum for the Education Committee of the Association for Science Education. Research Projects in the area of Science Teaching. Document ED/66/3/2. Minutes of the Education Committee, 21 May, 1966.

94 A report of the December Conference was published in *SSR, 48*, No. 166 (June 1967) pp.761–70, under the title 'Looking into the Future'.

95 ASE, Minutes of meeting of the Education Committee, 20 May 1967. This initiative foreshadowed the founding of COSTA, the Council of Subject Teaching Associations, in 1971. The first secretary/treasurer of this new body was the General Secretary of the ASE and the ASE 'serviced' COSTA in its early years, meetings being held in the ASE Headquarters at Hatfield. Representation of the ASE on the Schools Council Science Committee took longer to achieve.

96 ASE, Minutes of meeting of the Education Committee, 16 April 1967. The proposal for a research officer was later deemed 'not a practical proposition', the funds of the ASE being heavily committed over the next five years and the salary for such an appointment being 'beyond our means'.

97 ASE, Report of a meeting of Chairman and Vice-Chairmen, Sunday, 2 July 1967. This report went to the Executive Committee of the ASE only in the first instance; on 15 August 1967 a document outlining the composition and functions of the two Education Committees was sent by Tapper to all members of the Education Committee, with a request for comments in writing by 9 September.

98 Education (Research) Committee: Chairman Mr R. Schofield
          Honorary Secretary Mr D.W. Harlow
          Honorary Editor   Mr A.A. Bishop
          Members: Mr J.F. Eggleston
                    Mr I.D.S. Robertson
                    Miss B.S. Beaumont
                    Dr D.J. Daniels
          Chairman of the ASE Mr F.C. Brown
   Education (Co-ordinating) Committee:
          Chairman   Miss M.E. Tilstone
          Honorary Secretary Mr E.W. Tapper
          Members: Dr G.M. Owen
                    Mr D.M. Chillingworth
                    Dr W.J. Hughes

99 ASE, Minutes of a special meeting of the Education Committee, 11 Nov. 1967.

100 Nuffield Foundation. Science Teaching Programme. Agencies concerned School Science Curriculum Reform. File EDU/52. Nov. 1963.

101 See, for example, Ronald A. Manzer, *Teachers and Politics* (Manchester University Press 1970) pp.90–7.

102 Mary Waring, Background to Nuffield Science, *History of Education, 8*, No. 3 (Sept. 1979) p.236.
and: Biological Science: Integration or Fragmentation? in: W.E. Marsden, (editor), *Post-War Curriculum Development: an Historical Appraisal*, (History of Education Society 1979) p.53.

103 See Chapter 11, following.

104 Nuffield Foundation. File EDU/53. Physics Project 1966. R.A. Becher to K.W. Keohane, 30 Aug. 1966.

11 The challenge of technology

1 *SSR, 34*, No. 124 (June 1953) pp.322–34.

2 Ministry of Education, *15 to 18. A report of the Central Advisory Council for Education (England)* (London HMSO 1959) p.265.

3 *Nature, 176*, (8 Oct. 1955). pp.678–9.

4 See e.g. the record of discussion in the FBI Education Committee, 1 Dec. 1953. Mss. 200/F/1/1/116.

5 Twelfth Report from the Select Committee on Estimates, *Technical Education* (London HMSO 1953) p.160.

6 Sir Alexander Todd, Presidential Address to the Science Masters' Association, 2 January 1957. The Scientist-Supply and Demand, *SSR, 38*, No. 135 (March 1957) p.161.

7 Ibid., p.162.

8 See e.g. S.F. Cotgrove, *Technical Education and Social Change* (Allen & Unwin 1958).
   Michael Argles, *South Kensington to Robbins* (London, Longmans 1964).

9 Ministry of Education for England and Wales, *Education in 1961* (London HMSO) pp.38–40.

10 *Report of the Conference on Industry and the Universities*. Federation of British Industries (London 1950) p.22.

11 K.M.H. Chapman and E.H. Coulson, Enquiry into conditions affecting science teaching in grammar schools, *SSR, 35*, No. 126 (March 1954) pp.168–77.
   SMA, Minutes of General Committee, 4 March 1953; 10 Oct. 1953; 29 Dec. 1953; 13 March 1954.

12 *Report of the Executive Committee of the Industrial Fund for the Advancement of Scientific Education in Schools* (London, May 1957) p.5.

13 *Apparatus Brochure. List of apparatus suggested for use in schools in teaching Physics, Chemistry and Geology* (The Industrial Fund for the Advancement of Scientific Education in Schools, 1957) Foreword.

14 *Final Report of the Executive Committee*. Industrial Fund for the Advancement of Scientific Education in Schools (London, Dec. 1963) pp.6–9. The total sum allocated to the ASE was £3000.

15 A detailed account of the joint committee's investigation is given in: E.W. Jenkins, *From Armstrong to Nuffield* (London 1979) pp.276–81, Chapters 6 and 7 of this book deal with 'The Supply of Teachers' and 'Laboratory Provision and Design'.

16 See e.g. SMA, Minutes of General Committee, 10 Oct. 1953. Shortage of Science Teachers in Secondary Schools: Policy Report of the General Committee, *SSR, 35*, No. 127 (June 1954) pp.309–12.

17 *SSR, 24*, No. 92 (Nov. 1942) p.99.

18 SMA, Minutes of General Committee, 1 March 1952.

19 Ibid., 14 March 1953.

20 Ibid., 3 March 1956.
   Sir Lawrence Bragg, The contribution of the Royal Institution to the teaching of science, *SSR, 40*, No. 141 (March 1959) pp.240–5.
   Sir Lawrence Bragg, 'Schools Lectures' at the Royal Institution. A new venture. *Discovery, 18*, No. 2 (Feb. 1957) pp.66–7
   John Oriel was a significant figure in the relations of industry and science education being one of the originators of the Industrial Fund; see the obituary notice in *Education in Science*, No. 29 (Sept. 1968) p.15.
   Details of the joint committee are given in *SSR, 39*, No. 137 (Nov. 1957) p.153.

21 SMA, Minutes of General Committee, 13 March 1954.

22 Ibid., 3 Dec. 1955.

23 The important five-day conference at Barrow Court in 1961, which led to the approach by the SMA to the Nuffield Foundation, was supported by a generous grant from Esso Petroleum Company. See above p.242.

24 SMA, Minutes of General Committee, 4 Dec. 1954.

25 *SSR, 39*, No. 137 (Nov. 1957) pp.128–9. This was the first of eleven such annual conferences sponsored by Shell International Petroleum Company Limited.

26 Personal communication from Miss Elizabeth McCreath, Education Section, Unilever Ltd.

27 *Science and Education*. A Policy Statement by the Committee of the Science Masters' Association (London 1957) p.11.

28 E.W. Tapper: letter to G.B. Harrison, Dauntsey's School. 23 June 1964.

29 See e.g. Dr C.G. Williams, Director, Shell Research Ltd, Discussion paper for the Education Committee of the Institution of Mechanical Engineers: Applied Science in Schools; 21 August 1963. Sir Frank Mason, *The Shape of Things to Come: a challenge to engineers* (1964).

30 *SSR, 45*, No. 155 (Nov. 1963) p.10.

31 Association for Technical Education in Schools, *Curriculum Research in Applied Science and Technology*. Report of a study conference Sheffield, April 1964.

32 SMA, Minutes of General Committee, 7 June 1958. An abridged version of the background paper was published in *SSR, 40*, No. 140 (Nov. 1958) pp.182–3.

33 ASE, *Bulletin* No. 10 (Sept. 1964) p.27.

34 *SSR, 43*, No. 150 (March 1962) pp.318–19.

35 Ibid.

36 In the judgement of J.L. Lewis, one of the major contributors to the Nuffield Science Teaching Project, the Nuffield curriculum programmes, particularly in physics, did not do enough 'to show the relevance of science to the world outside the laboratory in which the student will live'. John Lewis, Preface to *Teachers' Guide*. Science in Society Project (ASE, 1980) p.3.

37 ASE, *Bulletin*, No. 12 (Feb. 1965) p.35.

38 ASE, *The Bulletin*, No. 11 (Nov. 1964) p.11 and No. 12 (Feb. 1965) pp.35–9.

39 ASE, *Bulletin*, No. 9 (April 1964) p.26.

40 ASE, *Bulletin*, No. 10 (Sept. 1964) p.28.

41 ASE, *Bulletin*, No. 13 (April 1965) pp.10–14.

42 ASE, *Bulletin*, No. 14 (Sept. 1965) pp.38–9.

43 Ibid., p.39.

44 This was the first Annual Meeting of the SMA to be held outside London. When the Association returned to Oxford in 1927, Hartley was President and elected an Honorary Member.

45 Personal communication from D.W. Harlow. Also: ASE, Minutes of the Executive Committee, 7 March 1964, when Harlow reported on meetings with Sir Harold Hartley and Sir Willis Jackson regarding the urgent need to interest school leavers in 'technical education'. It was agreed by the Committee that Harlow, Tapper and F.C. Brown (Treasurer) should form a Sub-Committee to take such action as was deemed necessary to foster closer liaison with the practice and teaching of technology.

46 *SSR, 47*, No. 163 (June 1966) p.767.

47 Personal communication from D.W. Harlow.

48 *Education in Science*, No. 24 (Sept. 1967) p.28.
    Education in Science, No. 22 (April 1967) p.45.

49 Council for Scientific Policy, *Enquiry into the flow of Candidates in Science and Technology into Higher Education*. Cmnd. 3541. (London HMSO 1968).

50 ASE, *Bulletin*, No. 12 (Feb. 1965) p.14.

51 Parliamentary and Scientific Committee, *Annual Report 1964*, p.23.

52 Ministry of Education *15 to 18*. A report of the Central Advisory Council for Education (England). Volume 1, Report (London HMSO 1959) p.398.

53 Ibid., p.468.

54 *Technology and the Grammar Schools*. Report of a Conference held at the Oxford University Institute of Education, June 1961. pp.20–3.

55 Ibid., p.22.

56 Certain independent schools, notably Oundle and Dulwich (in each of which F.W. Sanderson's influence had been exerted), as well as others, especially schools with a strong Army and/or Navy connection, had well-established reputations in the teaching of workshop skills and engineering activities. E.W. Tapper had been a physics master at Dulwich before taking up his full-time post as General Secretary of the SMA/ASE.

57 G.T. Page, *Engineering among the Schools* (The Institution of Mechanical Engineers, 1965).

58 Ibid., p.32.

59 Ibid., p.80.

60 G.C. Sneed, The Ealing Experiment. *New Scientist*, 8 June 1967, p.598.

61 G.T. Page, op.cit. pp.95–101.
    L.J. Taylor. *Project work in 'A' level Physics? A report on the effects of project work introduced into 'A' level Physics at Dauntsey's School*. Schools Council Project Technology. Occasional Paper. 2. 1969.

62 G.T. Page, op.cit. p.72–3, 90–1, and 116–17.
    See also: S.M. Tuff, Investigations in Physics, *Bulletin*, No. 5 (April 1963) pp.34–46.
    E. Semper, Technology and the Sixth Form Boy – the teaching aspect. Lecture given at the Shell Science Teachers' Course, University College, London. April 1964.

63 *SSR, 43*, No. 150 (March 1962) p.318.

64 G.T. Page op.cit. p.28, where Sir John Baker, professor of engineering at Cambridge, is cited as concerned about engineering science at university 'killing design and creativity'.
    See also in this connection: D. Ragland, *J. of Engineering Education, 53* (1963), p.417.

65 British Petroleum Company. *Technology and the Sixth Form Boy*. Report of Conference held at the Kensington Palace Hotel, 26 Feb.–1 March 1964, p.25.

66 *Engineering our Future*. Report of the Committee of Inquiry into the Engineering Profession. Cmnd. 7794 (London, HMSO 1980) p.25.

67 Ibid.

68 For a detailed account of the changes see: Philip Gummett, *Scientists in Whitehall*

(Manchester University Press 1980).
Also: *Committee of Enquiry into the Organization of Civil Science.* Cmnd.2171 (London HMSO 1963).

69 Sir Patrick Linstead, Science and Technology – Separate or Together?, *SSR, 46,* No. 159 (March 1965) pp.281–93.

70 Ibid., p.292.
On the proposal to establish a society for applied scientists, see Sir Gordon Sutherland's letter to the *Guardian*, 30 Nov. 1963, and the editorial in *New Scientist*, 5 Dec. 1963.

71 The Engineering Council, established under Royal Charter in 1982 in response to recommendations in the Report of the Finniston Committee of Inquiry into the Engineering Profession, issued its Policy Statement in September 1982. Italics added.

72 The Association changed its name, and widened its membership, in 1964 to become the Association for Technical Education in Schools (ATES). A further change was made in 1973 when the name became the Association for Technological Education in Schools.

73 The information on which this account is based is drawn from a variety of sources including: ATES, *Curriculum research in applied science and technology.* Report of study conference, Halifax Hall, Sheffield, 9–11 April, 1974.
Personal communications from Edward Semper, OBE.
R. Walker. Project Technology. In: L. Stenhouse (ed.) *Curriculum research and development in action.* (Heinemann, 1980) pp.115–138.
AHSTS, Minutes of Council Meetings and Annual Conference reports.

74 ASE, *Bulletin* No. 6 (Sept. 1963) p.8.

75 Though acknowledged by the editor as a possibility for inclusion in the 1964 June issue of *SSR*, Harrison's paper does not seem to have been published. Details of his 'A' level physics projects were incorporated in Tapper's discussion paper, The Place of Technology in Schools, published in the *Bulletin* in Sept. 1964. An account of Harrison's work also appeared in *The Chartered Mechanical Engineer*, May 1964.
G.B. Harrison to E.W. Tapper, 15 June 1964.

76 ASE, *Bulletin* No. 10 (Sept. 1964) pp.24–8.

77 R. Walker, op.cit. p.118. D.R.O. Thomas of the British Steel Corporation, a representative of the FBI on the Development Committee, had secured promises of about £10,000 provided matching sums were forthcoming from government sources.

78 ASE, Minutes of Education Committee, 13 Feb. 1965.

79 ATES, Minutes of Council meeting 15 May 1965.

80 Schools Council. Coordinating Committee. Paper No. 39. May 1965.
Porter's background paper was Appendix A.
D.I.R. Porter's report, written during academic year 1964–5 as Senior Research Fellow at Manchester University, was later published as Schools Council Curriculum Bulletin No. 2, *A school approach to technology.* (London HMSO 1967)
A few days before the Schools Council conference on 6 May, Porter had attended the Cambridge conference of the ASE's Education Committee where he gave a talk on The School Approach to Technology, later published in the *Bulletin* No. 15 (Nov. 1965) pp.14–23.

81 The subject committee was previously titled 'Technical and Engineering Studies'.

82 Loughborough Training College was one of two major colleges in the handicraft field, the other being Shoreditch.

83 R. Walker, Project Technology. In: L. Stenhouse (ed.) *Curriculum research and development in action* (Heinemann 1980) pp.115–38.

84 E.W. Tapper to G.B. Harrison, 15 Feb. 1966.

85 I am grateful to Professor Harrison for allowing me access to correspondence and notes relating to this lecture, and to other related matters.

86 ASE, Minutes of Executive Committee, 28 Jan. 1967 and 22 July 1967.

87 J.A.G. Banks to D.W. Harlow, 21 July 1967.

88 D.W. Harlow to J.A.G. Banks, 25 July 1967.

89 In fact the morning session, from 10 00 a.m. until 12 30 p.m. included five speakers and a question and answer forum. Each speaker, Harrison included, was allotted 22 minutes for his contribution.

90 ASE, *Applied Science in Schools. A Two-Day Conference* (1967) p.7.

91 Ibid., p.19.

92 Ibid., p.21.
   The membership was: Mr L. Drucquer, Chairman of the Council of Engineering Institutions; Sir Stanley Brown, President of the Institution of Electrical Engineers; Dr C.G. Williams, member of the C.E.I.; Sir Frank Mason; Mr G.B.R. Fielden, Group Technical Director, Davy-Ashmore Ltd; Professor R. Nyholm, President, ASE; Mr. J.J. Bryant, Chairman, ASE; Mr. F.C. Brown, Chairman elect, ASE; Mr. D.W. Harlow, ASE; Mr. E.W. Tapper, General Secretary, ASE. The chairman of the Group was Lord Jackson of Burnley (formerly Sir Willis Jackson, an electrical engineer) and Miss F.W. Eastwood (ASE) was later co-opted.

93 Ibid., pp.27–8.

94 The Schools Council. Field Report No. 3 *Technology in Schools*. (London 1966) p.13.

95 C.B.I. Mss. 200/C/3/ETT/623/1. Memo to Education and Training Committee re. *Applied Science and Technology in Schools*.

96 Ibid., S. Moore-Coulson to J.A.G. Banks, 19 Oct. 1967. The decision was announced by Moore-Coulson at a meeting of the Consultative Committee of Project Technology on 30 Oct. 1967.

97 Ibid., Sir Harold Hartley to Hon. Montague Woodhouse, 25 April 1967. Hartley, like Sir Graham Savage, though severely physically handicapped at this stage, was a man of enormous energy. At the time of the November Conference on Applied Science in Schools he was aged 89.

98 Hartley's relationship with H.R.H. Prince Philip is so described in the account of his life in *Biographical Memoirs of Fellows of the Royal Society, 19* (The Royal Society, London 1973) p.364.

99 *Applied Science in Schools*, 1967, p.8 and p.19.

100 C.B.I. Mss. 200/C/3/ETT/623/1.
    C.G. Williams to J. Davis, 11 Nov. 1967.
    C.M. Woodhouse to S. Moore-Coulson, 13 Nov. 1967.
    C.M. Woodhouse to Dr Sharp, 30 Nov. 1967.
    In fact the appointment of Lord Jackson as chairman was intended to ensure that the C.E.I. did *not* 'take over' the Action Group.

101 William Luckin, Science apathy under fire. Doubts on relevance of technology project. *The Times Educational Supplement* (29 Dec. 1967) p.1454.

102 An account of the work of Project Technology was published a little later in *The Times Educational Supplement* by the same reporter.

W. Luckin, Brighter outlook for school technology, *The Times Educational Supplement* (19 Jan. 1968) p.168.

103 G.B. Harrison, *The Times Educational Supplement* (5 Jan. 1968) p.34.

104 Ibid.

105 E.W. Tapper, *The Times Educational Supplement* (12 Jan. 1968).

106 In this, and what follows, I am indebted to Professor Harrison for access to his records.

107 *Education in Science*, No. 26 (Feb. 1968) pp.11–12.

108 Dr C.G. Williams, School Science goes on show, *New Scientist* (11 July 1968) pp.86–8; and The Summer School, Sept. 24–7, 1968. Interim Report to the *Schools Science and Technology Committee*, 7 Oct. 1968.

109 See e.g. the ASE's own cooperation with Project Technology and Loughborough University of Technology, *Education in Science* No. 26 (Feb. 1968) p.22 and *Education in Science* No. 27 (April 1968) p.34.

110 *Education in Science*, No. 28 (June 1968) p.19.

111 R.H. Wakeley and J. Bausor, Engineering in the School Curriculum, *Education in Science*, No. 24 (Sept. 1967) pp.18–23.

112 Deryk T. Kelly, Some problems of project work, *Education Science*, No. 29 (Sept. 1968) pp.40–42.

113 ASE, Minutes of Executive Committee, 28 Jan. 1967.

114 F.S. Dainton, Presidential Address to the ASE Future Scientists: Who, Whence, Whither and Why? *SSR, 48*, No. 166 (June 1967) p.656.

115 A Policy Statement for the Seventies. *Education in Science*, No. 35 (Nov. 1969) p.13.

116 Ibid., p.14.

117 Science and General Education, 1971, *Education in Science*, No. 41 (Feb. 1971) p.32. Whilst the Policy Statement eschewed the use of the word 'technology' except in the Annex, it did recommend that 'science should be presented in ways which show how its applications influence the patterns of modern life and social organisation'. Ibid., p.31.

118 Science in the Curriculum for the 13–16 Year Age Group, *Education in Science*, No. 49 (Sept. 1972) p.17.

119 *Education in Science*, No. 53 (June 1973) pp.20–3, 29–31.

120 An Association view on school science and technology, *Education in Science*, No. 55 (Nov. 1973) p.19.

121 The Prime Minister's speech was published in *The Times Educational Supplement*, No. 3203 (22 Oct. 1976) pp.1 and 72.

122 For extracts from the unpublished 'Yellow Book', see *The Times Educational Supplement*, No. 3202 (15 Oct. 1976) pp.2–3.

123 *Education in Science*, No. 69 (Sept. 1976) p.23. *The Understanding British Industry* project was launched publicly on 12 April, 1976.
What Industry Wants, *The Times Educational Supplement*, No. 3204 (29 Oct. 1976).
See also: I. Jamieson and M. Lightfoot, *Schools and Industry*, (London, Methuen, 1982).

124 *Education in Science*, No. 71 (Jan. 1977) pp.15–17.

125 H.P. Ramage, Technology and School Science, *Education in Science*, No. 72 (April 1977) pp.31–2.

126 *Education in Science*, No. 73 (June 1977) pp.12–15.

127 *Education in Science*, No. 71 (Jan. 1977) p.13 and No. 74. (Sept. 1977) pp.10–11. The award winners received their cheques from the Duke of Edinburgh at a ceremony held at the Royal Society on 2 July 1977.

128 Report of the Education (Coordinating) Committee, *Education in Science*, No. 75 (Nov. 1977) p.15.

129 *Education in Science*, No. 74 (Sept. 1977) p.9.

130 See e.g. G.M. Kerr, Links with Industry, *Education in Science*, No. 77 (April 1978) p.20.
Young Engineer for Britain 1979 Competition, *Education in Science*, No. 81 (Jan. 1979) p.27.
Applications of Science and Mathematics in Industry, *Education in Science*, No. 82 (April 1979) p.11.
Schools/Industry Interface. *Education in Science*, No. 84 (Sept. 1979) pp.29–30.
How a professional institution can help schools, *Education in Science*, No. 91 (Jan. 1981) pp.21–2.
A useful review of various Schools/Industry Links was given in nine articles in *Trends in Education*, Summer 1979 issue. (HMSO).

131 *Education in Science*, No. 87 (April 1980) p.12.

132 *Aspects of Secondary Education in England* (HMSO 1979).

133 The Standing Conference on Schools' Science and Technology, *Report of the Autumn Conference 29 October 1980*, p.34.

134 Department of Education and Science, *Technology in Schools. Developments in craft, design and technology departments.* (London HMSO 1982)

135 Ibid., p.27.

136 The Engineering Council, *Policy Statement*, Sept. 1982, p.4. (para. 2.2).

137 *Education in Science*, No. 97 (April 1982) pp.12–13.

12   Facing the Future

1 ASE, Minutes of Council, Feb. 1980.

2 ASE, The Validation of In-Service Courses for Science Teachers. A report of the ASE Validation Working Party. Nov. 1980.

3 *Education in Science*, No. 95, Nov. 1981, p.16; No. 101, Jan. 1983, p.9. C.M. Wilson, The start of a new venture, *Education in Science*, No. 102, April 1983, pp.16–17.

4 *Education in Science*, No. 54, Sept. 1973, pp.36–7.

5 Yorkshire Region Committee, The Role of the Association for Science Education. Proposals for the Nottingham Conference, March 1974. B.R. Chapman, Some reflections on the future role of the ASE, and Postscript, March 1974.

6 *Education in Science*, No. 58, June 1974, pp.19–21.

7 Annual Reports for the period since 1977 have included references to the new relationships, especially the regular meetings with the Science Group of Her Majesty's Inspectorate. It was R.W. West's judgement that 'during 1976–77 we have seen the Association emerge as a major body that is being consulted more widely on key issues in science education', (*Education in Science*, No. 75, Nov. 1977, p.17).

8 Previous 'industrial Presidents' were:
1969 J.D. Rose FRS, Director for Research and Development for I.C.I. (see: *Education in Science*, No. 70, Nov. 1976, p.14).

1972 Mrs. M.K. McQuillan, Research Director, Imperial Metal Industries Ltd. Lord Stokes and Lord Robens were invited to serve as President for 1975 but each was unable to stand for election.

9 Branches Sub-Committee, Report to Council, Paragraph 5 (e), 18 March 1967.

10 Following interest shown at the Oxford Annual Meeting in the topic of 'Girls and Science Education' the Education (Coordinating) Committee established a new sub-committee early in 1976 to review evidence on the subject and to recommend appropriate action by the ASE. *Education in Science*, No. 70, Nov. 1976, p.17. A new sub-committee on Girls and Physical Sciences was convened in 1979 to be chaired by Dr Jan Harding. *Education in Science*, No. 85, Nov. 1979, p.16.

11 W.J. Kirkham, Notes from the Chairman to Autumn Council, 1976. Sept. 1976.

12 ASE, Minutes of Council, Oct. 1976; Jan. 1977; May 1977; Oct. 1977; Jan. 1978. Also: Working Party Report to Council, Council Structure and Function, August 1977.

13 J.L. Lewis to members of the Executive Committee, 16 May 1977, and response to the Elected Members Working Party.

14 The proposal came from a new Primary Schools Science Sub-Committee established in September 1982. Minutes of the first meeting of Primary Schools Science Sub-Committee, 5 March 1983.

15 *Education in Science*, No. 95, Nov. 1981, p.29. The writers state that the Association of Teachers of Geology was founded in 1976, but a representative of an association of the same name attended the inaugural meeting of the COSTA in Dec. 1971.
The correct date of the Foundation of the Association is 1967.

16 *Education in Science*, No. 104, Sept. 1983, p.16.

17 W.F. Archenhold, Looking ahead, Editorial in *SSR, 55*, No. 190, Sept. 1973, p.7.

18 Report of a meeting of representatives of subject associations held at the Association for Science Education, College Lane, Hatfield on Saturday, 4 Dec. 1971. COSTA, Minutes of meetings, 26 Feb. 1972; 8 July 1972; 24 Feb. 1973.

19 ASE, Policy Statement, *Education through Science*, 1981, p.26.

20 These and subsequent figures relating to expenditure and income are drawn from the published accounts, Treasurers' reports for the years in question and information supplied by the ASE General Secretary.

21 The description was quoted by B.G. Atwood, Chairman of the ASE in 1971, in opening the Education Conference at Nottingham, March 1971. *Education in Science*, No. 43, June 1971, p.17.

22 The words are those of Wilfred Llowarch in a letter to Frances Eastwood, 16 February 1978. Miss Eastwood kindly placed at my disposal a substantial amount of correspondence she had received from long-standing members of the Associations, in which they give their views on 'what your membership has meant to you'. Llowarch had taught physics at Oundle and Stowe before moving to the Institute of Education, University of London. He was a regular contributor to the Members's Exhibition at Annual Meetings. His testimony is typical of that from many others of his generation.

23 Frances M. Eastwood, in a document commenting on the proposal to write a history of the ASE, 1978.

24 At the Annual Meeting in Manchester, January 1983, a group of local industrialists was invited to 'see the ASE in action'. Mr John Barnes, Chief Education Officer for Salford, a member of this group, later described the ASE as 'an example to us all of teachers taking responsibility for their own professional development', *Education in Science*, No. 102, April 1983, p.20.

Acknowledgements

I am deeply grateful to those whose names are listed below for generous assistance in the preparation of the history of their Association.

Members of the History Sub-Committee established by the Council of the ASE: Professor E.H. Coulson (Chairman); A.A. Bishop; Miss F.M. Eastwood; Miss E.W. McCreath; T.C. Swinfen; E.W. Tapper (died August 1983).

B.G. Atwood, General Secretary, ASE
Mrs C.M. Wilson, Deputy General Secretary, ASE
K. Pinnock, Director, John Murray (Publishers) Ltd

Miss D.J. Alexander; H.G. Andrew; W.F. Archenhold; J.S. Arthur; Miss B.G. Ashton; M.J. Bailey; C.J. Ball; K.C. Barnes; Mrs. S. Bavage; Dr. P. Biggs; W.G. Bowden; E.G. Breeze; Dr C. Briske; Mrs. N. Broadbridge; W.R.B. Brooks; F.C. Brown; J.J. Bryant; Miss E.L. Buckley; R.N. Clarke; D.V. Clish; Dr L. Connell; J.K. Davies; Dr B.E. Dawson; E. Denne; W.H. Dowland; D.G. Evans; F. Fairbrother; G.W.E. Ghey; Miss C.M. Groves; D.W. Harlow; Professor G.B. Harrison; C. Holt; E.W. Jenkins; H. Jennings; I.G. Jones; C.W. Kearsey; Dr W.J. Kirkham; E.W. Lambert; Professor J. Lauwerys; Dr E.A. Lewis; J.L. Lewis; W. Llowarch; A.M. Love; Miss E.H.K. Matthews; Dr G. McCulloch; J.S.G. McGeachin; C.R. Marsham; J.G. Mitchell; Miss J.H. Mundie; Mrs E.A. Newman; B. Nicholl; G. Nunn; Dr G.W. Owen; Mrs. E. Preston; I.D.S. Robertson; N. Rowbotham; Sir Graham Savage; D.W. Scott; P.J. Scott; J.C. Siddons; G.E. Siddle; J.W. Stork; Miss M.W. Sutton; Miss P.M. Taylor; R. Thurlow; M. Todd; H. Tunley; Miss H. Ward; Dr R.W. West; Dr I.W. Williams; R.E. Williams; Miss M. Wilson.

Manuscript and other unpublished sources

1 *Official unpublished papers and committee minutes*
Association for Science Education, including Region records
Association of Assistant Mistresses
Association of Education Committees (University of Leeds Special Collections)
Association of Heads of Secondary Technical Schools
Association of Science Teachers
Association of Women Science Teachers
Conjoint Board of Scientific Societies (The Royal Society)
Federation of British Industries (Warwick University Modern Records Centre)
Institute of Physics
John Murray (Publishers) Ltd
Nuffield Foundation
Schools' Science and Technology Committee
Standing Conference for Schools' Science and Technology
Science Masters' Association
Technical Education Board, London County Records Office

2 *Private papers and correspondence*
Dr H.F. Boulind (by kind permission of Mrs Joan Boulind)
Professor G.B. Harrison
O.H. Latter (by kind permission of Mrs Mary G. Newnham)
Professor J.A. Lauwerys
J.L. Lewis
E. Semper
Professor A. Smithells (University of Leeds Special Collections)
R. Thurlow (by kind permission of Mrs C. Thurlow)

Name Index

Abbott Mrs C.A.   129, 165
Adlam G.H.J.   21, 47, 57, 58, 94, 95, 99, 144, 157–9, 161–2, 168, 206
Allanson J.T.   265
Allbutt Sir Clifford   27, 28, 29
Andrew H.G.   170
Archenhold W.F.   126, 282
Armstrong H.E.   16, 27, 28, 37, 134, 297, 298
Arthur J.S.   332
Ashford C.E.   8, 13, 14, 16, 17, 18, 19, 23, 24, 25, 26, 28, 296, 298
Ashhurst W.   96, 97, 224
Ashton Miss B.G.   120, 129, 241, 315
Atkinson E.J.   91
Atwood B.G.   127, 131, 133, 151, 282, 289
Ayres R.P.   98, 110
Ayrton Mrs. H.   43
Ayrton W.E.   43

Bailey Miss D.   69, 70, 71, 223
Baker H.B.   27, 28, 181, 182, 298
Baker T.J.   188, 206
Baker W.M.   14, 18
Bankes-Williams I.M.   96, 204, 206
Banks J.A.G.   269–71, 275
Barlow Miss F.L.R.   128
Barnes J.   344
Barrett W.H.   96
Bartle R.J.   150
Beament J.W.L.   247
Becher R.A.   243–6, 253
Beesley F.A.   157, 158
Bennett D.P.   132
Berridge D.P.   20, 21, 22, 24–5, 26, 177, 196, 297, 298
Bidder Mrs M.G.   45, 46, 49, 302
Biggs Miss E.   69
Birt Miss M.E.   54, 65, 69, 216
Bishop A.A.   126, 159, 163, 165, 166
Bispham C.   206–8
Blaikie L.   23

Bondi Sir Hermann   283
Bonsall E.N.   128
Booth N.   153, 283
Borchardt W.G.   18
Boulind H.F.   97, 98, 110, 126, 150, 222, 230–3, 236, 238, 240, 243–6, 249, 250, 253, 262, 263, 331, 334
Bourne G.   180, 181
Bowden Lord (Dr B.V.)   107, 310
Bowen Ursula   118
Bowker Miss H.M.   69
Brace W.S.   267
Bragg Sir Lawrence   147, 258, 337
Bragg Sir William   216
Breeze E.G.   114, 128, 150
Brierley J.   247
Briggs Lord   ix
Briske C.   128, 151
Broad H.F.   98, 105, 107, 112, 233, 250, 307
Broad S.T.   112
Broadbridge Mrs N.   128
Brock W.H.   9, 293, 295
Brown F.C.   98, 105, 107, 109, 110, 111, 120, 128, 272, 273, 274
Brown R.L.   129, 159, 165
Brown S.V.   94, 96, 213
Browning S.J.   131
Buckley Miss E.L.   69, 71, 104, 105, 120, 221
Budden Miss L.M.   223
Bull, Miss E.M.   69, 303
Burstall Miss S.   341
Buss Miss F.M.   43, 47
Bryant C.L.   25, 26, 58, 99, 157, 190, 208, 209, 211, 212, 213, 217, 222
Bryant J.J.   126, 131, 247, 251, 270, 274
Bryant Dr Sophie   35, 40, 43, 45, 47, 49
Bryant V.S.   21, 29, 96, 157, 178, 179, 183

Callaghan J.   276
Calvert W.J.R.   25, 96, 157

Subject Index